SIBERIAN ODYSSEY

A VOYAGE INTO THE RUSSIAN SOUL

ALSO BY FREDERICK KEMPE

Divorcing the Dictator

SIBERIAN ODYSSEY

A VOYAGE INTO THE RUSSIAN SOUL

FREDERICK KEMPE

G. P. PUTNAM'S SONS

New York

G. P. Putnam's Sons
Publishers Since 1838
200 Madison Avenue
New York, NY 10016

Library of Congress Cataloging-in-Publication Data

Kempe, Frederick.
Siberian odyssey : a voyage into the Russian soul /
Frederick Kempe.
p. cm.
ISBN 0-399-13755-6
1. Ob' River Region (R.S.F.S.R.)—Description and travel.
2. Kempe, Frederick—Journeys—Russian S.F.S.R.—Ob' River Region.
3. Siberia (R.S.F.S.R.)—Description and travel. I. Title.
DK771.02K46 1992
915.7'3—dc20   92-12468 CIP

Printed in the United States of America
1 2 3 4 5 6 7 8 9 10

This book is printed on acid-free paper.

∞

For my friends Vladimir Sukhatsky, Valentine Akishkin,
Viktor Kostukovsky, and Viktor Pelz—
and for the "White Birds" of Siberia,
in their fight against the weight of their own history

CONTENTS

ACKNOWLEDGMENTS

Without *The Wall Street Journal* and editors Lee Lescaze, Norman Pearlstine, and Paul Steiger, this book would not have been possible. The *Journal*'s support for book projects has made the American reading world far richer. More than two dozen books have been written by *Wall Street Journal* staffers during Norman Pearlstine's leadership at the paper, including James Stewart's *Den of Thieves,* Bryan Burrough's and John Helyar's *Barbarians at the Gate,* Alex Kotlowitz's *There Are No Children Here Anymore,* Thomas Petzinger's *Oil and Honor,* Alan Murray and Jeffrey Birnbaum's *Showdown at Gucci Gulch,* and Susan Faludi's *Backlash.* These books, among others, will be one of the lasting marks of Norman Pearlstine, who resigned in May 1992 to begin his own company.

In the case of *Siberian Odyssey,* the *Journal* played another role. For years, the *Journal* was derided (and derisively quoted) in Communist propaganda for its incisive reporting and editorializing on the Soviet bloc. For having been so right so early, so long, and so consistently, the newspaper enjoys great respect in Russia. I often only had to say the name of my paper to gain instant access. My newspaper and the free press more generally played an important role in bringing down a repressive system.

But there would have been no information for this book if not for Siberians themselves. Vladimir Sukhatsky, a journalist and entrepreneur, was the father of the expedition. Valentine Akishkin ("Dundee") edited and tried to write a few paragraphs of his own when he didn't like mine. Bear hugs to jazz pianist and journalist Viktor Kostukovsky—and to the editorial board and publishing house of his newspaper, *Izvestia*—who were consistently helpful in getting us access. Thank God that Viktor Pelz survived the Gulag so that we could work together. Elia Rikert also helped on a couple of key occasions.

I've seldom met a better reporter than Gerard Jacobs, a Dutch journalist of estimable talent and perception, who was the co-organizer of the expedition and my friend and adviser throughout. I received advice, guidance, notes, and helpful walks down memory lane with expedition members James Dorsey and Theo Uittenbogaard. Wytze van der Naald and Michael Hoffmann and their serious work almost (repeat, almost) made me forget my political differences with Greenpeace. Dutch photographer Paul Babliowsky brought the cameras and took most of the best shots.

And there were so many other Siberians who made the once impossible possible: police chief Vitaly Skhurat; prison warden Vladimir Lazik; Nikolai Krushinsky, in the Kuzbass; Sergei Sherbakov, in Mezdurachensk; Sergei Sergeyev, of Kemerovo's ecological laboratory; Stalina Ignatova, in Yurga; Evgeny Kucharenko, of the coal directorate; Wilhelm Fast and Tatiana Dmitrieva, in Tomsk; Yuri Perepletkin, throughout the Northwest; Agrivena Sopacheva, in Russkinskaya; Mary Golubchikova and Valery Troshin, in Vorkuta; Nikolai Dudnik, in Salekhard; and Nikolai Babin, with the reindeer nomads. They all reminded me that independent Siberians are the most likely of former Soviets to lead Russia into the twenty-first century.

Once I returned home, it was Kyle Gibson's thoughtful editing and warm encouragement that sharpened my thinking and helped shape every chapter. Peter Chase's incisive mind and keen organizational eye put me on course in the beginning, and he took time he didn't have to make sure I stayed there (thanks also to his daughter Nicole for briefings on Ninja Turtles). Sebastian Worel, of Lernidee Reisen in Berlin (now in business with the Siberians), Almut Schönfeld (the world's best assistant), and Gustav Beindorf were invaluable researchers. Deborah Seward, of Moscow's AP office, who introduced me to Russia, generously shared her expertise and linguistic talents. Alan Murray, author, *WSJ* Washington deputy bureau chief, and mediocre Monopoly player, gave of his scarce time to read and comment. Katie Hafner, coauthor of *Cyberpunk,* artfully helped hone the final manuscript when she should have been working on her own book. Thanks also to photographer-journalist Ed Serotta, to Gil Pimentel, and to Anja Grothe, Regine Noswitza, and Irene Bejenke for efficient, last-minute assistance.

I'm indebted to Rosa Berger of the Free University's Osteuropa Institute and to the John F. Kennedy Library, both in Berlin, for help in finding obscure information (and in keeping overdue books). Thanks to Gary Milhollin, of the Wisconsin Project, and Stan Norris, of the Natural Resources Defense Council, for help and understanding of the plutonium business.

I will never tire of working with Neil Nyren, my immensely gifted editor and part-time shrink (specializing in curing "Germanic mood swings") at G. P. Putnam's Sons, who provided guidance, encouragement, and good humor. He saw the potential of this project all along. Fred Sawyer led an efficient copy-editing operation. Thanks also, once again, to my lawyer/

agent Bob Barnett for his integrity, professionalism, and friendship—and for getting me started.

And *na zdroviye* to the crew of the *OM147* and to Captain Valery Ustinov, who provided smooth sailing, protection from pirates, and, quite literally, the shirt off his back.

"Just think what's going on all around us! And that you and I should be living at such a time. Such a thing happens only once in an eternity. Just think of it, the whole of Russia has had its roof torn off, and you and I and everyone else are out in the open! And there's nobody to spy on us. Freedom! Real freedom, not just talk about it, freedom, dropped out of the sky, freedom beyond our expectations, freedom by accident, through a misunderstanding.

"And how great everyone is, and completely at sea! Have you noticed? As if crushed by his own weight, by the discovery of his greatness.

"Last night I was watching the meeting in the square, an extraordinary sight! Mother Russia is on the move, she can't stand still, she's restless and she can't find rest, she's talking and she can't stop. And it isn't as if only people were talking. Stars and trees meet and converse, flowers talk philosophy at night, stone houses hold meetings. It makes you think of the Gospel, doesn't it? The days of the apostles. Remember St. Paul? You will speak with tongues and you will prophesy. Pray for the gift of understanding."

—*Dr. Zhivago,* BORIS PASTERNAK

SIBERIA

Novaya Zeml

Baidaratsky
Bay

Reindeer Nomad
Camp on
Kara River

Igarka

Vorkuta
Salekhard
Beloyarsk
Labytnangi
Nadim

Railway
Prison
Camp

Death's Road

Nadim River

Yenisei River

Ural Mountains

Vanzevat

Ob River

Torem Yogan
("The River of God")

"Two Tepee Lake"

Oktyabrskoye

Russkinskaya

Nizhnevartovsk

Khanty Mansiysk
Surgut

Aleksandrovskoye
Death Island

Narim
Kolpashevo

Ob River

Tomsk 7
Tomsk

Yurga
Kemerovo

Tom River

Mezhdurechensk

Ob Sea
Novokuznetsk

Chuvashka

Arctic Ocean   Arctic Ocean

SIBERIA

Ob River

• Moscow

MONGOLIA

CHINA

Pacific Ocean

Ob River

Altai Mountains

MONGOLIA

CHINA

0 100 200 300
Kilometers

Prologue:

THE BACK
OF THE WOODSHED

An' ef things is bad in Slobbovia—thass awful
—becuz, when things is good thar—it's frightful.

—Li'l Abner, 1947

Siberia has always been more a warning than a place.

I first heard of Siberia as a child, when my father, a German immigrant who came to America in 1928, jokingly threatened to send me there when I misbehaved. I didn't know where Siberia was then, but it was clear to me that no penalty could be crueler. Siberia was the ultimate back of the woodshed. Tsars and Communist rulers alike exiled their undesirables and enemy prisoners of war there. What place could be more punishing for them than this frigid landmass of some 5 million square miles, larger than China or the United States, but so cold and desolate as to seem unapproachable?

When I was about twelve, Siberia confronted me again in the Sunday morning comics, in a strip called *Li'l Abner.* On that day all the panels were frozen white in snow; pathetic characters dressed in rags stood up to their neck in drifts. That backwoods hick, Li'l Abner, had traveled, on Trans-Slobbovian Airlines, to a mythical, Siberian-looking place called Lower Slobbovia. It was cartoonist Al Capp's version of the most godforsaken place on earth, and it became his early and prophetic commentary on a system going seriously wrong.

No one wanted to live in Slobbovia, but no one could get a visa to leave. The most beautiful Slobbovian escaped by staying outside long enough to freeze blue and be exported to the West as art. The oldest Slobbovian, Clark Rasputingable, waited 127 years for a visa only to give it up to the ugliest woman in the world, Lena the Hyena. ("If I go—only I happy—if SHE go, EVERYBODY happy!") The Slobbovians were so poor that their favorite child, Little Noodnik, begged Senator Phogbound in poems for loans. They were so poor that they were even short on their own currency of Rasbucknicks (and it took 3 billion of those to make up $1.18).

But Slobbovians, like Siberians, were always a lovable lot. They knew their lot in life and regretted it, but they were fatalistic about it and didn't much expect it to change. Somehow they never perished.

From the days of my childhood forward, Siberia remained for me a distant and mythical place of untold hardship. When, as an adult, I read Solzhenitsyn's *Gulag Archipelago* on the cruelty of Siberian prison camps, or watched documentaries on the Soviets cutting oil wells through the ice, the modern images fit nicely with my childhood impressions.

I found it ironic that nature should have made Siberia so rich, as if bestowing Hell with gold mines—an additional temptation for the adventurer and fortune seeker. Throughout the 1980s Siberia produced three-fourths of all the Soviet Union's gas and oil and nearly half of its coal. The region was responsible for more than 80 percent of the country's hard-currency earnings. Without Siberia, the Soviet Union never could have afforded to be a military superpower. Only with Siberia did it have a chance to finance itself into the community of free-market economies.

However, as it is with mythical places, I never thought much about traveling there until I received a phone call in early 1991 at my home in Berlin from a longtime friend and reporting comrade, James Dorsey. He asked me to visit him in Amsterdam to discuss with a Dutch journalist the prospects of an "extraordinary expedition to Siberia." James and I had first crossed paths in the Mideast while covering Israel's invasion of Beirut in 1982. Six years later, during the American invasion of Panama, we rented a school bus near the Costa Rican border to carry us to the action. ("It's the first time I've gone to war in a schoolbus," James said.) He was a multinational, multilingual reporter whose instincts I trusted and whose company I valued. So I got on the next plane.

At an Amsterdam café, he introduced me to the Western instigator of the expedition, Gerard Jacobs, who was organizing the trip with a Siberian radio correspondent named Vladimir Sukhatsky. Jacobs was the sort of correspondent one met in the world's war zones and hellholes. His childhood had been tragic and his marriage disastrous (an occupational hazard). He had a weakness for small children, good books, strong drink, beautiful women, and romantic journeys. We hit it off immediately.

Gerard scribbled out maps of Siberia on napkins and across the back of a menu. I no longer recall what was decided then and what details were added later, but an expedition unfolded that was ambitious both in the territory we would cover and the answers we wanted to find.

The plan, we decided, would be to use the Ob River and its major tributary, the Tom, as the red thread that would tie together a series of stories aimed at exploring the Russian soul. It was an ambitious goal, but the setting was right for it. The Ob River was as long as the Mississippi, stretching from the Altai Mountains near the Mongolian border to the white nights of the north above the Arctic Circle.

The rich raw materials along its banks made it the land of Russia's grandest dreams, but its desolation had made it the pathway to Russia's darkest nightmares. Barges filled with prisoners and exiles had made their way north in the summer, and sledges and convoys headed up its frozen course during its long winters.

Yet the Ob was also the only pathway carrying civilization into the roadless Western Siberian wilderness. For centuries, the native peoples who lived along the River Ob in Siberia called the waterway "Grandmother." It provided for them and took them where they needed to go. One Russian author wrote that the Ob was the water that helped control the region's fire.

Some fire. Due to Siberia's extreme cold, the Ob is navigable for only 190 days a year on its upper reaches in the south and for 150 in the north, near Salekhard, where it empties into Ob Bay, which then feeds the Arctic Ocean. The freeze begins in mid-October, and the Ob system is totally free of ice only at the end of May or even the beginning of June.

We would take this unique road into areas where no American had been allowed before—and in some cases no Westerner. One stop would be Tomsk 7, a city ringed with barbed wire, where the weapons-grade plutonium was made for the missiles that assured the destruction of the United States in case of nuclear war. But we would also rent helicopters, sometimes for the price of a few bottles of vodka, to take us to the tepees of indigenous peoples who were slowly dying out.

Our Russian partners insisted that the expedition have a significant environmental aspect, so Gerard invited along two Greenpeace scientists who would carry out a pilot project investigating the significant environmental damage in the region. Their findings would also support our work.

I was happy to hear that we wouldn't be roughing it by paddling in a canoe or camping out on the river's banks. Our means of transportation for most of the trip would be a forty-two-meter-long boat with two decks, a cook, a shower, a sometimes-working sauna, and two small fishing boats. The ship had individual compartments for each of us. In the south, however, we would follow the course of the Tom River primarily by car and van—its waters were too shallow for our boat to navigate.

I sent a detailed proposal for the trip to my foreign editor, Lee Lescaze, himself a veteran overseas correspondent with time clocked, among other places, in Vietnam and Africa. No boss likes to let a reporter out of sight for five weeks, but Lescaze's response was that of a seasoned and thoughtful journalist who saw an unusual reporting opportunity. Within an hour of receiving my message, he had cabled back his response: BY ALL MEANS, PROCEED WITH SIBERIA.

Any reporter who knew the Soviet Union (and I had made twelve trips there) expected more disappointments than successes, so we overloaded our list of requests. Yet one approval came after another. One month before departure, I received a telex from Gerard Jacobs: EVERYTHING IS GOING WELL. I WONDER IF WE SHOULD WORRY.

Our luck was that Russia was opening up its most forbidden region and we would be among the first to take advantage. What we hadn't counted on was the timeliness of our visit. Our expedition would end three weeks before the August 1991 coup against Mikhail Gorbachev would fail, ushering out the Communist Party and the Soviet Union itself. Hence, the trip became a freeze frame of a country in historic ferment, and of its rich frontier simultaneously changing and resisting change.

Nothing illustrated the historic moment more than our stop at Kolpashevo, two weeks into the trip, where the spring waters of the river had cut into the sandy banks and emptied one of Stalin's mass graves. Seventy-four years of lies were crumbling like the riverbank, and truths were tumbling out like the bodies. For its symbolism, Kolpashevo is my first chapter, and it is the only one that appears out of chronological order.

Our voyage began in Kemerovo, where our flight from Moscow would land. It was a fitting place to launch my study. "Big Bill" Haywood, the most famous American radical labor leader of his day, had come to Kemerovo in the 1920s to found a Utopian workers' colony. He was from my hometown of Salt Lake City, the Mormon religion's capital, where naiveté is an honored virtue, so I felt a personal connection to the story of how his ideological dreams had run up on the Siberian rocks.

Before starting our 2,000-mile voyage north, we'd first drive south toward the source of the Tom, where we would begin our trip down the river at a village of the Shorish people, Turkic speakers known as the "Blacksmith Tatars" who wanted to reclaim hunting grounds on which were Russia's richest coal mines.

The next stop would be in the industrial Kuznetsk Basin, or Kuzbass, where coal-miner strikes in 1989 and 1990 had been the first important Russian worker uprising against Communism and Soviet rule. We would visit a maximum-security prison and talk to murderers, pick up drunks with police night patrols, and breathe air so polluted that birth defects were higher than anywhere in the country.

The Tom River would then lead us north into the long-forbidden territory of defense plants that had been relocated to Siberia during the Nazi invasion of World War II. We would stop in Yurga, where rocket launchers were made and where a German Lutheran minister interpreted my visit—

the first by any American—as a sign from God. At a top-secret nuclear-weapons facility downstream, a former employee would slip me secret documents.

At that point the Tom flowed into the Ob, which would take us through the vast wetlands of the Siberian Northwest. Here a helicopter would almost flatten me and armies of mosquitoes would gnaw at my flesh. We'd visit a place of cannibalism and Russia's richest oil fields, where pipe leaks were emptying lakes of oil into the swamps.

Our ship would then sail into the wild Siberian Northwest, where native peoples—among them the Khanty, Mansis, Komis, and Nenets—had lived for centuries. Natives would attack our boat in search of vodka and I'd launch a search for the Shaman, the natives' witch doctor who was said to hold the secrets of the ages.

We would emerge from the wetlands at the end of the river in Salekhard. There, we'd take helicopters to the tundra, where I'd ride with the reindeer nomads and then fly to an abandoned railway whose tracks were so bloodied they were known as "Death's Road."

The trip would end in Vorkuta, 100 miles above the Arctic Circle, a city literally built on the bones of the Gulag. I'd meet survivors of its camps, including one who insisted that she had tried to kill Stalin and another whose scars from the days of Stalin were indelible tattoos.

Indeed, the most intriguing tributaries on our route down the Ob River would be those into the lives of those who lived along the river's banks.

Aeroflot Flight 201 from Moscow to Kemerovo, where our expedition would begin, was like so many I had experienced in the Soviet Union. The flight attendants were surly and the rest rooms smelled of outhouse. Neatly cut squares of *Pravda* served as toilet paper. These had been slipped into slots that had markers above them showing a shoe and a brush. The designer had intended grooming instruments to be placed there, but Russia was down to basics.

Foreigners were still treated specially, with their own waiting lounges. They also boarded the plane last—a luxury whose importance was evident. The headrests were greasy and the seats, whose stuffing had spread to the sides, had a tendency to slide loose. Legroom was sparse. To fit into my seat, I stretched my left leg into the aisle and bent my right one so it pressed against the bag underneath my neighbor's seat (which was stuffed with vegetables and a plucked but not beheaded chicken).

My ample neighbor, a Siberian peasant, jabbed her pudgy elbow into my side every fifteen minutes or so to remind me that I was coming too close. But when I shifted my legs into the aisle, I came into conflict with the stewardess, who wheeled her badly aligned cart over my feet.

A bead of sweat dripped from my forehead onto Aeroflot's marketing blurb on my ticket: "You have made a good choice. Aeroflot offers you every condition for business and tourist trips. It guarantees comfort and hospitality." At least the price was right. At black-market rates, the flight from Moscow to Kemerovo, which was equivalent to the distance from Washington, D.C., to Los Angeles, cost three dollars.

Despite the discomfort, everyone on the overnight flight was asleep except for Vladimir Sukhatsky, the Russian father of the expedition, who had met us in Moscow. He was embarrassed that I appeared so uncomfortable. He regretted that Russians cared little about the sort of comfort or friendly service he had first experienced in the West a year earlier.

"You will meet many such situations here," he said. "They don't know better. I am thirty-five years old, and for thirty-three years I didn't hear the truth about my country or the world. Until earlier this year, I was a member of the Communist Party! I was! But now I am an idealist. I believe in friendship, in love. I believe in my wife and children. I don't want to deal with politics anymore."

He briefed me from across the aisle on the days ahead.

"You will find our region is the avant-garde of political life. People in Western Siberia live in the richest region but can't buy anything. There are many people trying to change things; they fight big odds. We don't know yet if they win or lose. We call these people 'White Birds.' I hope your work will help them."

For Vladimir, the White Birds were a distinct breed of individualists who were fighting for change against enormous odds. They were historians, journalists, politicians, coal miners, and native peoples—some of whom we would meet on our trip—who were struggling against the aftereffects of seven decades of repression and restricted freedoms.

I'd seen the first signs that Vladimir belonged to this breed when he received us in Moscow to take the southeasterly flight across four time zones to Kemerovo. We had a small party of three journalists, a photographer, and two Greenpeace scientists, but Sukhatsky had picked us up in a large tourist bus that would take us across town to Vnukovo Airport. "I welcome every man from the West," he said in his engagingly broken English. He walked down the aisle and shook each of our hands. He stood well over six feet tall and he walked with a powerful stride. He had looks that caused women along our route to swoon—a friend of mine would later describe him as a man with Mel Gibson's eyes and a young Jack Palance's rugged looks and bearing.

At the airport, he showed us for the first time his capacity to handle all problems and temperaments. Greenpeace's testing equipment made our luggage nearly 300 pounds overweight. Vladimir flashed a letter of support for the expedition from his province's governor with one hand and passed the baggage handler a couple of cigarette lighters, labeled "Welcome to Marlboro Country," with the other. The modest gift and the convincing air of importance got us through without paying a kopek.

Over the space of nearly a year, Vladimir Sukhatsky had wrestled with bureaucrats to gain travel permissions, had searched the region for sufficient supplies, had communicated with villages and towns that rarely dealt with outsiders, and had fended off criticism that he was becoming too enamored of the West. He even gained KGB clearance and a letter of safe passage for our travels.

"Thanks, White Bird," I said as we approached Kemerovo.

He beamed at the new nickname—which properly stuck thereafter. I regarded him as the Captain Ahab of our ship, taking on the Great White Whale of the Soviet Union.

Vladimir introduced us to the other Russian members of our expedition the following evening at a gala dinner to launch our voyage. For the purpose, he had reserved a banquet room of Kemerovo's best hotel, a fallen hostelry with cracked marble stairways, missing ceiling tiles, and faded, fake red velvet curtains that suggested a fallen bordello. He spoke over the disco music that was reverberating from the adjoining dance hall, where a wedding party was in full swing.

In one of the many toasts that would punctuate our trip, he related how the expedition had been born while he rode his single-speed Russian-made bicycle from his hometown of Kemerovo to Amsterdam. It was a trip of liberation after seven decades of restricted travel. During the four-month, 4,500-mile ride, he dreamt up a journalistic and ecological expedition whose members would be multipliers of knowledge and information about his region for the world. Together, his White Birds and their Western partners would then slay the evil spirits that remained from Soviet rule through a series of cooperative ventures.

The White Bird showed his talents again in his recruiting of interpreters. My own Russian was so limited that I feared that information much would escape me. Thanks to our interpreters, that handicap would turn out to be an advantage.

The first was Viktor Pelz, a sixty-eight-year-old survivor of the Gulag,* whose "scars" were a soft wisdom and iron will. At our initial dinner he didn't want to talk about the prison camps; he would only share the miraculous tale of how he survived later in our expedition, once I had won his confidence. Despite his age and hard life, he had the energy of a fifty-year-old. More important, the old people in whom the tragic history of Siberia was stored would more readily open up to a fellow *strafnik*.

The second interpreter was a forty-five-year-old school director, an intelligent and calm man who was leading the local fight for educational reform. His aim was to scrap the egalitarian ideology that held back his

---

*Gulag—The word, which has become the term used to describe Stalin's penal camps, is actually the acronym for the Soviet administration that ran the prison colonies.

people and to institute programs that would enable the talented to reach their potential. But what was most noticeable about him was his Australian accent. Valentine Akishkin had spent his childhood until age twelve in Australia. His father had been a prisoner of war in Germany and had emigrated "down under" after his release because Stalin was imprisoning POWs for treason. After Stalin's death, his father had brought the family back to Russia. Because of Valentine's accent and his irreverent outback humor, I called him "Dundee."

Both men were skilled enough in simultaneous translation that not a beat of conversation would be lost. More importantly, their easy and educated manner opened up those who might otherwise never have talked to foreigners speaking the most fluent of Russian.

But it was Vladimir Sukhatsky, the White Bird, who was the heart of the group. His grandfather, once a Polish officer in the Austro-Hungarian Army, had moved to the Ukraine when Russia had offered land for sale at inexpensive prices. But when the Red and White armies had begun to clash after the Revolution, Vladimir's grandfather had migrated west and become a coal miner and circus wrestler in Belgium. He'd bought passage to America, but the boat had left him while he was ashore buying food. He didn't have the fare for a second ticket. Homesick and broke, he took his family back to the Ukraine. Vladimir's father, a military officer, had been sent to Siberia as a prisoner in 1948 on charges of "spreading anti-Soviet propaganda." His son had been born shortly after his release in 1953.

These men—Viktor Pelz, Dundee, and the White Bird—were the perfect companions for a trip through Western Siberia. Few came to the region voluntarily, but Siberians' backgrounds as ex-convicts, fortune seekers, and adventurers and their geographical distance from Moscow's central planners made them more independent souls than other Russians.

In the spirit of the times, the White Bird had formed a company to manage the expedition and had taken on carefully selected partners who would also join us on our trip. One was Viktor Kostukovsky, a savvy local *Izvestia* correspondent who used his vast connections and his paper's weight to win us access and interviews. The other was People's Deputy Yuri Kaznin, a local ecologist whose influence opened doors.

The White Bird was a born entrepreneur, and he spoke proudly of his cunning means of purchasing food and supplies for our expedition. In a world of ration coupons, he deployed a letter of support from the local government to make purchases in chronically undersupplied shops. To avoid igniting a riot, shopkeepers asked that he come after hours and load groceries from the back door. Determined to serve spaghetti, he searched the entire province for tomato sauce before landing finally on two giant tins of tomato paste at a nearby factory's kitchen. But he had to sneak them past workers, whose lunch trays were growing lighter each day, by putting the tins in large boxes that made them look like paper supplies.

And then there was our "currency"—bottles of spirits brought along to help pay for our fish, helicopter trips, or any unforeseen expenses as we sailed north. Vladimir read off the inventory: "One hundred fifty bottles of vodka, sixty bottles of wine, twenty bottles of champagne and ten bottles of cognac." Some, of course, would be for our own consumption.

"Just don't anyone light a match," chuckled Gerard Jacobs at our opening dinner. The irreverent Dutch journalist would be traveling with me, as would James Dorsey, Dutch photographer Paul Babliowsky, and Dutch radio correspondent Theo Uittenbogaard. Because this book is about the Siberians and Russians, however, I have written little about this Western group—a collection of usually compatible free spirits who pursued their own interests each day and then compared and traded notes in the ship's galley at night.

The two Greenpeace scientists sat quietly as one Russian after another raised toasts at that first dinner in Kemerovo. Although we would travel together down the river, their paths of sample-taking and visiting laboratories rarely crossed our own.

Michael Hoffmann was a forty-year-old German ecologist with a gray-specked beard and academic demeanor. He had committed himself to cleaning up the former Soviet Union and was moving his home to Kiev, where he would study the aftereffects of the Chernobyl disaster. He viewed the polluting of the vast Siberian swamps to be as dangerous to the world climate as the disappearance of the Brazilian rain forests, which regenerated themselves far more quickly. Wytze van der Naald, a thirty-three-year-old Dutch chemist, had turned his energies to ecological work after seeing that most jobs in his field had more to do with poisoning the environment. He was hot-tempered, intensely curious, and fiercely committed to his work.

The only serious personality clashes would revolve around Yuri Kaznin, the potbellied Soviet parliament member who snarled behind his bushy mustache as Vladimir described his purchases of our "currency"— the vodka—and I scribbled this information in my notebook. "Why are you coming on this trip anyway?" he said. "You write only for rich people who only want to exploit Siberia [his description of *Wall Street Journal* readers]. For you, I suppose this is just a pleasure cruise."

Vladimir raised his glass again, trying to restore the proper collegial tone, repeating what he had said to me on the plane. "I want to raise a toast to ordinary, simple feelings," said Vladimir. "I was a Communist, but now I have a new religion—friendship."

And then the *Izvestia* correspondent raised his own toast. "Approach Siberia in a kind way," he said. "The Revolution of 1917 never really happened. It was nothing more than a revolt by a minority. But our region is playing a primary role in a new revolution. This is a battle of good against evil. The lines are drawn clearly."

The plane began to descend at about six A.M., local time, after an all-night flight from Moscow. I hadn't slept. I looked out the window and saw green, undulating hills and the wide, shallow Tom River.

"Ladies and gentlemen, we will be landing soon," said the flight attendant in Russian and then English, read slowly, each word mispronounced. "It is not allowed to take photographs or use video equipment over the territory of the Soviet Union or at its airports . . ."

I smiled as a handful of the passengers nevertheless pointed old cameras out the window and furiously snapped pictures. The prohibitions of seven decades of Soviet rule weren't respected anymore.

My insides churned with anticipation. I was landing in Siberia, the place my father had threatened to send me for punishment so many years before.

Chapter 1:

THE RIVER AND THE GRAVE

You can't hide anything from the river.

—VALERY USTINOV, *ship captain*

After decades of fearful silence, the chief lifeguard of Kolpashevo still spoke cautiously about the time, in May 1979, when the spring waters of the Ob River unearthed one of Stalin's mass graves.

At first, said Anatoly Patoykin, the bodies trickled out slowly, by ones and twos, knocked loose in frozen blocks of earth by giant ice floes from the thaw that crashed into the river's sharp bend. Then they fell in larger clumps, like rotten crumbs from an earthen layer cake of corpses; white-lime separated each batch of victims. The bodies had been among the more than half million "enemies of the people" that Stalin had executed in the late 1930s. Their secret resting place had been under the enclosed yard of what once had been the local prison.

The KGB, hoping to rid itself quickly of nature's intrusion into the Soviet past, sent two tugboats to the grave site. The crews tied the first boat to trees on the bank with fist-thick rope. The second tugboat held the first one in place as the captain gunned its engines. The backwash, which churned against the soft and sandy bank, had its intended effect. It set loose a cascade of earth and bodies into the river.

Patoykin inhaled the river air deeply into his barrel chest, still muscular despite his fifty years. He looked down the steep embankment over the site of the former grave and let out a heavy sigh. Below him on the beach, a fat woman sunbathed and three boys buried each other in the sand. The beach's only other feature was garbage. The sand was littered with rusted mattress springs, worn-out tires, scrap metal, and a tangle of tree stumps and branches. Riverside residents used the Ob as their garbage-removal service. They put refuse on the ice in the winter, and the river took it away during the spring thaw. The garbage often ran aground on the sharp bend where the grave had been.

Patoykin's forehead wrinkled with worry as he told a story he had kept to himself for years. His skin was leathery and red from a lifetime of exposure to the Siberian cold and wind. His icy blue eyes stared at mine. Then he turned to the river and spoke more to it than to me.

"I was standing here and saw what happened," he said. "I am certain of the facts because my friend was the KGB chief at the time and I helped him dispose of the bodies. Listen to me carefully, because I will explain what happened and you can explain it to others. After the first corpses appeared, the local Party and KGB asked Moscow: 'What should we do?' Moscow said, 'Get rid of them so no one sees them.' "

He pointed to imaginary places over the water where he said the KGB men had tied their tugboats to trees on the shore, which have long since been taken by the river. He said the ground on top had been still frozen, but underneath it was soft and sandy. The captains were surprised themselves by how quickly their boat's backwash worked. "It started an avalanche," he said. "An avalanche of bodies. The avalanche just didn't stop. And the bodies flowed into the water with the mud." Some bodies, he said, were cut into pieces by the propellers of the boat.

I had already been traveling down the river for two weeks when I reached Kolpashevo, but only then, while standing above the former site of Stalin's mass grave, did I understand what my trip was all about. The Ob river had unearthed not only a grave but also the lies upon which an entire system had been built. The collapse of its banks was perhaps a too-obvious metaphor for the crumbling of a state structure that could be held up only by the sort of repression that had created the grave in the first place.

I closed my eyes and imagined the scene, and then I looked again at the lifeguard as he continued talking. Patoykin's friend, the KGB boss at the time, told him that the orders had come from Yegor Ligachev, the Party secretary for the region. Ligachev would later become a Politburo member who led early opposition to Mikhail Gorbachev and his reforms. He and other Party bosses wanted to destroy the grave quickly. They wanted to contain this incident in Kolpashevo, at the southern extreme of the vast Northwest Siberian wetlands, where communication to the outside world was slow and unreliable and the only roads were the Ob and its vast array of tributaries.

"It would have been more humane to dig out these corpses and bury them somewhere else," said Patoykin, looking back to me. "But that's not what Ligachev wanted. He wanted the problem to disappear." Patoykin looked back to the river's wide bend and then down the steep embankment.

"The corpses were so well preserved after all those years in the frozen ground that those who had known the dead would have recognized their features. Their condition was remarkable—they hadn't decayed at all. And they were so light—like blotting paper. There was no unpleasant odor. Among them were women, also children . . . I saw that in every head there was a hole, a bullet hole. In some there were two holes. When they were shot, if someone wasn't completely dead, then I can only suppose they had to shoot a second time. The corpses were floating, floating away, like foam—they were so light. And the Party, the leadership, ordered my friend to get rid of them as quickly as possible. So the police and all those familiar to the police, those of us who had boats, were organized. I was also involved. For two nights and two days, my job was to sink as many of these bodies as possible. I would take a weight of iron that was tied to a wire, and then I'd wrap it around the body, twist the wire tightly closed, and then throw the body back into the water."

Patoykin repeated all the motions. I could hear the plop of each body in the water as he mimed throwing each corpse into the river.

"Just like that," said Patoykin.

Earlier that morning as we approached Kolpashevo, the sun's rays had streamed through the thin curtains of my tiny cabin. It was only six o'clock in the morning, but the sun had been out since four, after dipping over the horizon for but a couple of hours' rest.

The lodgings were simple, with cabins so small that I had to sleep in a slight curl. But we were hardly roughing it. This had been a pleasure cruiser for high Party officials, marked simply by its radio code letters, *OM-147*. Its length was 42 meters, its draw was 1.4 meters, and it displaced 170 tons. But it wasn't modern; it had been destined for the junkyard before the captain had had it repaired and restored in preparation for our trip.

Like the other twenty berths of the diesel-driven vessel, mine had been "remodeled" to increase comfort for its first Western passengers. That meant neat new reddish-orange curtains, refinished vinyl walls, and a refurbished bar and galley area in front, with carved wood paneling along the ceiling, where we would collect to compare notes and plan the next day.

But the other passengers were still asleep when I walked up a narrow and steep stairway to the captain's glassed-in wheelhouse. Captain Valery

Ustinov handed me his binoculars and pointed to the high riverbank. In forty-five minutes, he said, we would be in the town where the Ob had unearthed the mass grave.

"You can't hide anything from the river," said Captain Valery Nikolayevich Ustinov, who had spent most of his forty years working a waterway that had been his playground as a child. The light glinted off his even, unbroken row of golden teeth.

As we neared Kolpashevo, he pointed to a single-engine, propeller-driven Antonov 2 that was droning overhead. The locals called it a "cornfield plane," but there aren't any cornfields in the region. Only swamps and forests. The swamps produced the oil, and the forests the timber. In most parts of the northwestern wetlands of Western Siberia, where few towns are connected by roads, the Antonov 2, helicopters, and boats on the rivers provide the only transportation.

When we arrived in Kolpashevo, I spotted a small boy on a stretch of gravelly beach collecting night crawlers in a tin can. A Siberian Huckleberry Finn. "Which way is it to the site of the mass grave?" I asked. My question sounded ludicrous, but the boy responded as if I had asked him directions to the drugstore.

He nodded up the river. "It's that way, but you can't see it from here," he said. "Just ask anyone in town. At the shop on the hill—they'll know."

Kolpashevo was a seemingly insignificant dot on the map of Western Siberia, a town of 30,000 only a third of the distance along our way down the Ob. We had much farther to go before we reached the end of our trip at the Arctic Circle, yet we were already at the 57th parallel, on which Alaska also rested.

It was like many other towns we had passed along the river's banks. The paint was peeling off the warped boarding of its small wooden homes. Many of its dirt roads were impassable, deeply rutted from cars that drove through the thick mud, which then froze, dried, and hardened. Its raised wooden sidewalks kept pedestrians out of the muck. Steps allowed locals to walk over the sewage and water lines that ran above ground that was frozen much of the year. The wooden planks that covered the pipes were cracked and broken, and insulation escaped through the fractures like stuffing from an old sofa.

Yet this stop, like every other along the river, was a treasure hunt. Lack of easy communication made detailed pre-planning impossible. My great advantage was that few of those I would meet had ever run across an American before. Many spoke to me out of curiosity.

Before I went to the grave, however, I found Patoykin, who, townspeople said, was one of the few eyewitnesses who knew all the details and was willing to talk. At the shop the boy had directed us to, a saleswoman directed us to the lifeguard station, and at the lifeguard station an old man consented to walk me a mile down the beach to the lifeguard's simple wooden home.

Patoykin wasn't welcoming at first. He had told his story to the local newspaper and didn't want to repeat it. When I pleaded that I had come far to hear his tale, he reluctantly consented to drive me in his white Lada to the former grave site. The ride was over dirt roads with ruts so deep that my stomach jumped to my throat. But Patoykin was already thinking about the grave; what happened in 1979 reminded him of his grandfather's death in one of Stalin's camps. His grandfather, he said, had been the director of a grain-storage silo that had leaked. He had been imprisoned for economic sabotage after a rainstorm spoiled its stock. "He disappeared and we never saw him again," said Patoykin. "That was his fate."

"Fate"—the Russian word *Sudba*—was a term used more than any other in Siberia. *Sudba* was the Siberians' cruel companion, used to explain all the sadness, death, and cruelty that people had endured over the years. Why dwell too long upon tragedy, why fight repression, when it is inevitable anyway? Blaming *Sudba* took the sting out of the vicious turns in most Russians' lives.

Nothing seemed more revealing to me than the fact that Siberians had never seriously tried to alter the 3,500-mile course of the Ob. Except for a dam that had been built at Novosibirsk, the river generally took its natural course. Around the world, humanity has controlled its rivers, creating breakwaters and cement banks to guide the flow and stop erosion. But in Siberia, the Ob went more or less where Fate guided it. Each year, the river cut another large slice off its soft banks, growing wider and more shallow as it took trees, earth, and old houses with it. Villages have been moved, but the Ob hasn't been redirected.

Patoykin pulled up to the embankment and walked us to a place that had once been the corner of two main Kolpashevo roads, Lenin Street and Dzerzhinsky Street. The river had swallowed most of both of them. It had also exacted nature's justice by removing the ground that had held the former prison, the KGB station, and the grave—nearly a square mile of land, he said, had been swept away from the bend in the Ob over the previous dozen years.

What particularly angered Patoykin, a proud Siberian, was that the local Party newspaper had reported at the time that those executed were from a wave of Siberian deserters during World War II. "But we knew that wasn't true even then," said the lifeguard. "The fiercest divisions during the battle of Moscow were the Siberians—deserters were practically unknown among them."

The later KGB explanation of why the bodies were destroyed was that the authorities wanted to avoid an epidemic, but the lifeguard didn't buy that explanation either. "Anyone knows that when such a large number of corpses drop into the water that it can't be good for the ecology. That's when disease could have spread. Many people in those days drank their water directly from the river."

Yet Patoykin never considered turning down the KGB request that he help dispose of the bodies. "This was a time when you didn't say no when the KGB asked something. I also wanted to help my friend. We got so sick of the job that after two days we drove my boat to an island across the way and sat there with our heads in our hands." But by then most of the job had been finished.

He said, however, that many of the corpses slipped past him and other "body sinkers" and floated downstream. Local fishermen even brought some bodies to local hospitals, where pathologists did analyses, assuming the people had fallen in when drunk and drowned—not an infrequent occurrence in the early spring months when waters are high and cold.

Patoykin wished he could show me the awful scenes. He had had a movie camera in 1979 to record his newly born grandson—he was always a little ahead of others in acquiring such modern things. But he hadn't dared use the camera then. "I seriously thought about it. But we were still deathly afraid. I could have become one of those bodies. You couldn't help but think that way."

The only memorial that marked the grave site was a rusting metal cutout of a skeleton hammered into a thick birch tree. It looked like a Halloween project done in junior-high-school metal shop. Its legs dangled in a death dance, and two small pieces of towel were draped from its bony feet.

Local tradition dictated that mourners lower the coffin to its final resting place with the help of two long towels. The relatives tore their towels into small strips and gave pieces to all mourners for memory's sake. "Dundee," however, my Australian-accented Russian interpreter, said that Siberians now, being short on towels, instead used rope for this ritual. Such regular contributions to my understanding of Siberia had already made Dundee an invaluable fellow traveler.

Hammered into the tree below the skeleton was a thin metal plaque. Childlike lettering pounded into it had already begun to wear away in the wind and rain: BRIEMERBERG, PETER CHRISTOPHEROVICH, BORN 11-17-1888. SHOT BY THE NKVD. 22 APRIL 1939. THE CORPSE WAS SUBMERGED ON MAY 9, 1979 BY THE KGB. Two small pieces of human bone, found washed up on the banks of the river, rested at the base of the tree.

It was an inadequate monument, but it was the way most in the town wanted to remember the summer of 1979—not at all. A local muckraking journalist, Viktor Turbin, had mounted a frustrating campaign for a more fitting memorial. The local response had been tepid—he couldn't even get the townspeople to clean up the garbage that washed up on the shore.

In the summer of 1991, Turbin printed more than 1,400 names of those executed in Kolpashevo, with the dates of their deaths. A KGB source had provided them and said there were hundreds more. The revelations confirmed the townspeople's worst suspicions. Patoykin said he would drive me to the home of the daughter of the secret police chief who had ordered many of the killings.

As we drove away from the beach, a funeral procession crossed our path. A flatbed truck leading the crowd carried a group of mourners in their work clothes. It carried the coffin lid, some flowers, and several bottles of water to keep women from fainting and blooms from wilting. Old men marched behind, playing dirges on old trumpets and trombones.

A second flatbed truck carried the open casket. Family members sat flat with their legs outstretched, leaning their sides against the coffin and placing their elbows casually on its rim. They had baskets of food beside them, which they would eat as a last supper with the deceased at the grave site before the burial. Siberians, Patoykin explained, like to be close to their dead until the very end.

Nowhere did Turbin's newspaper cause more anguish than at the run-down home of Ina Stepanova, who for the first time could read about how much blood was on her father's hands. The documents showed that Stepan Stepanov had ordered the executions of "enemies of the people" at a pace of 150 a day during one week alone in early December 1937.

I found Ina Stepanova sitting with three friends around a card table on her cracked and uneven front sidewalk, playing games and chatting around the table—an after-work ritual in the neighborhood of single-level wooden homes built in the 1920s. Dundee introduced me, as usual, as a reporter from America's largest daily newspaper, *The Wall Street Journal,* on a Siberian expedition. It never stopped surprising me to see the magic the word "American" worked among a people who had never met one before. Doors opened, dinners were interrupted, and work stopped to satisfy my requests for interviews and conversations.

Ina Stepanova's friends watched enviously as she led us down a narrow dirt path to the rear door—the only entrance accessible in a yard overgrown with bushes and trees.

The hallway to the living room was booby-trapped with grandchildren's toys—a steel dump truck, some plastic dolls, various balls in different states of inflation, a broken jack-in-the-box, and a couple of stuffed animals. The trail continued to the living room, where she folded up the ironing board to make room for me to sit. Her bookcase was filled with worn volumes and a dusty television from the 1950s that she said had been broken for years.

Despite the obvious reason for my visit, she was welcoming. She had a Central European social grace, which she said came from her Hungarian roots, yet her appearance was Russian. She was hefty, her hands were calloused, and her bare feet had thick corns. Before I could pose a question, she began talking.

"You want to know if my father was a criminal." She said it was a question she thought about more each day. She was torn between her curiosity and her longing to protect her warm memories of a man she had loved all her life. "He was a very compassionate, upstanding, decent human being," she said. "He never hit a dog in his whole life. He never struck a child. He was a doctor, and he couldn't have killed. . . ."

Born Istvan Marton in Budapest, Ina Stepanova's father had been captured by Russian troops during World War I and sent to Siberia as a prisoner of war. Like many such Hungarians at the time, he never made the difficult trip back home. Even before the October Revolution, he converted to Communism and changed his name to Stepan Stepanov (from Istvan, which is the name for Stepan in Hungarian). Then he fought with the Communist partisans against the Western-backed "White" armies of Admiral Aleksandr Kolchak, who were trying to turn back Communism, starting in Siberia. At first he was a physician behind the lines, but his authority grew with time.

After the Red armies' victory, Stepanov's conspiratorial instincts and language abilities made him a natural recruit for Lenin's secret police. By the 1930s he was Kolpashevo's district leader of the NKVD, the Russian acronym for the People's Commissariat for Internal Affairs— Stalin's secret police and the forerunner of the KGB. That made him a capo of a Mafia that came to control Siberia and the Soviet Union through terror.

"He spoke French, English—several languages," remembered his daughter proudly. "But he never spoke Russian perfectly. He would have been a good doctor, but the history didn't allow it—he went to war and never stopped fighting."

However, as a purist from the early days of Communism, he was always skeptical of Stalin. When Ina brought home the standard schoolgirl's photograph of Stalin, he removed it from her bedroom wall. He never explained why. "He was a man of action and not words," said his daughter. "It was the way he was—strong, silent, and determined."

Until 1991 she had always believed that the executions had begun only after her father himself had been arrested and sent to the Gulag on Christmas Eve, 1937. His sin wasn't that he was untrustworthy, but rather that he was Hungarian. Stalin's mistrust focused particularly on his foreign-born lieutenants.

Her mother recognized the men who came from the Novosibirsk Troika—
a commission made up of Stepanov's NKVD superior from Novosibirsk,
the Party secretary and the regional prosecutor. It was a practical group-
ing—they could arrest, provide evidence, try, and sentence all at the same
time. Similar troikas were carrying out hundreds of thousands of such
arrests across the country.

But these three had been Stepanov's personal friends. They returned
December 30 to confiscate his things. The brightly wrapped presents were
laid on the floor, and Ina's mother was determined to go ahead with the
traditional New Year's Day opening of gifts—always assuming that the
mistake of arresting such a Communist hero would be reversed. But
Stepanov's former friends found enough evidence to incriminate him by
the low standards of the time: newspapers and letters in Hungarian and a
shortwave radio on which he listened to Hungarian broadcasts.

Ina said her mother often remembered in later years that her husband
had locked himself away in his study during those December days before
his arrest, when the executions were most numerous. He never came to
bed. Ina liked to imagine that her father's brooding came because the
killings were bothering his conscience.

But Ina Stepanova didn't doubt any longer that her father had ordered
the executions—and she didn't think he was forced. But she wouldn't
condemn her father. "There was a mood in the country," she said sadly.
"For seventy years, there were always enemies among us. He had a duty
and he had to carry out his duty. Our people also shot children in Afghanistan. It was all in the name of the Revolution."

Stepan Stepanov didn't stay in the camps long—only for three years
until 1940. Ina credits intercession by Lenin's wife, Nadezhda Krupskaya,
who knew of Stepanov's historical role and wrote letters on his behalf. It
was a time, however, when the guilty were more likely to survive than the
innocent. Her father thereafter worked in several penal colonies, usually
as an administrator—she couldn't know his history for sure because they
had lost touch. By 1943 he had abandoned his wife and daughter.

But Ina Stepanova wouldn't censure him for that either. She only
blamed the year 1937, when the world went mad in Russia with Stalin's
purges. "That year disrupted the life of our whole family—of millions of
families," she said. Indeed, in 1937–1938 some 7 million Soviets landed
in camps, where 2 million of them died. A further 1 million were executed.

Ina Stepanova looked at me, and again began to speak before I could
ask a question. "You shouldn't feel sorry for me," she said. "You must
wonder how it is possible that people live in the sorts of circumstances that
we endure. We always believed in the ideology that we were number one.
If things were bad, we still lived better than you did. We really believed it."

I hesitated to ask. But I wondered whether she thought her father ought to have been punished for his crimes. Why was it that Russians didn't seek revenge, justice? It was a question that increasingly puzzled me.

I recalled a passage that I had read that week from Solzhenitsyn's *The Gulag Archipelago,* in which he mused upon the thin line between the victims and the executioners. "Where did this wolf-tribe appear from among our people?" he asked. "Does it really stem from our own roots? Our own blood.

"It is our own. . . . If only there were evil people somewhere insidiously committing evil deeds, and it were necessary only to separate them from the rest of us and destroy them. But the line dividing good and evil cuts through the heart of every human being. And who is willing to destroy a piece of his own heart?"

Ina Stepanova wasn't surprised that the Russians had never demanded a sort of Nuremberg trials for Stalin's crimes. "You have to say clearly what a Russian is," she said. "If a Russian is beaten up for 364 days a year, and for one day a year he's stroked, then he forgives everything else. We constantly live in hope, waiting for something better."

She was certain that the time was now coming. After all the cruel turns of Russian history, I asked why this chapter should end happily. "What has changed is that I speak with you and have no fear," she said. "No one will come here with black boots in the middle of the night and take me away because I have spoken to an American."

She smiled that her only debriefers would be her neighbors, who were waiting outside around the card table for a full report. We had talked until far past dinnertime, but none of them had left. "I will have to tell them *everything.*" She winked, suggesting that much of our conversation would remain her secret.

The family of one of Stepanov's victims lived only a five-minute drive away from his executioner's home. In the front yard, an old steel boat, rusty and long unused, was turned upside down. A muddy path led past it to the backyard, where potatoes and tomatoes grew in neat rows behind a peeling, white picket fence. A small, squat old woman with tousled gray hair and a blue-green flower-print housedress appeared at the back steps, looking as if she had expected my unannounced visit. I mentioned the name of the man who had given me her address: Wilhelm Fast, the head of the Memorial Society in Tomsk that was investigating the Stalin years and looking after its victims. The name worked like a code word between co-conspirators.

Galina Nikiforova smiled a single-toothed smile and invited me in. We negotiated our way past children's shoes, their plastic buckets, and an old, hand-operated washer and wringer. Her cupboards were filled with Russian kitsch (cheap glasses, dolls, boxes). A stuffed owl stuck out from the wall on a highly varnished branch.

For Galina Nikiforova, however, only two features of the living room were worth mentioning—the large picture window looking out onto a birch tree at the side of the house, and the family photographs on the wall. She pointed first to the window, which was unusual in Siberia, where most windows are kept small to keep out the cold. But her father, who had been taken to his execution in September 1937, had preferred that his family have more light even if it must suffer more of the winter wind. "Siberia was never cold while my father was alive," she said.

Galina's grandfather had been exiled to Siberia as an officer who had been on the wrong side of the Revolution. Her father had been a school director, who had viewed his job as bringing a higher cultural level to the frontier. Galina pointed to an empty corner, where she said he would play music on the Harmonium, a small reed organ that was the centerpiece of family life. Her mother would sing arias from his favorite operas.

Galina then walked to the golden-framed photographs that showed members of a well-off family from the turn of the century. The men had intelligent eyes and stood with stiff, proud backs. They were doctors, scientists, and military officers. The women had high cheekbones and were dressed in white. Their hands were neatly folded on their laps. They had been educated, had spoken foreign languages, and had been musicians. Two of the women had been physicians. Galina looked lovingly at this lost heritage. Then she sat on her sagging couch covered with hairs of a dog that was nowhere in evidence.

She spoke of each of the characters on the wall in surprising detail: the headstrong female doctor, the uncle who had had a monument built to him for his work against cholera, and her grandfather, a handsome officer, who had come to Russia from Scandinavia to serve the Tsar. But she dwelt longest on the photograph of her father, a handsome man with a narrow face. She recalled what he had said to her when they had taken him away. She had been thirteen years old then.

"Don't forget that your father is innocent," she remembered him saying. "Fully innocent. You must continue your learning—just learn all the time. This is a misunderstanding, and your father will return soon."

At that point in our conversation, Galina's daughter walked in as if she had stepped out of one of the frames and from the white lace of her ancestors into a modern white sleeveless sundress. Nina Aleksandrovna Nikolayenko's skin was silken white and her eyes sad and deep brown. Her features were aristocratic, porcelain, and she sat erect on a kitchen chair with her hands neatly folded on her lap.

Like a Chekhov heroine, the young woman was holding desperately to her good breeding and grace against a decaying society that had broken her mother and family. Nina was an English teacher at the local school. She spoke Oxford English, although she had learned the language at a

Tashkent institute and had never traveled abroad. She was energetically teaching her three children English, hoping they might someday have the opportunity "to live normally somewhere else." She scoffed at my suggestion that Russia's new democracy must give her hope.

Certainly, she said, her children would never be able to live normally in Siberia or Russia during their lifetimes. In the meantime, Nina saw herself as carrying on in her grandfather's tradition of bringing culture to the Siberian wilderness. She taught at Secondary School Number Seven. She also played guitar and sang with a nightingale's voice. She hummed some bars from her favorite Woody Guthrie songs.

Nina was married to a policeman, a fact she didn't boast about. And she seemed a touch embarrassed about the owl on the wall that he had bagged and stuffed. Her husband was taking an extension course to be a lawyer, she said eagerly, but it was clear that he couldn't measure up to her father. "His type doesn't exist anymore here," she said. "He was a chemistry teacher who was well read, a musician, and he knew about physics and radioelectronics. He kept notebooks where he wrote down the details of all the operas he had heard in St. Petersburg, describing the sets and listing the names of the singers."

Nina's mother recalled that the men who had arrested her father had been obsessed with these notebooks. It was all they had taken as "evidence" against him. Galina Nikiforova said she would very much like to have them back someday. The old woman stifled a sob of the sort that often interrupted her reminiscences.

Like everyone in Kolpashevo, she remembered the winter of 1937–1938 as being a particularly cold one. After her father's arrest, her mother had wanted to take the family away, fearing she might also be imprisoned and her children sent to orphanages or for adoption. "But it was impossible to leave in such weather," Galina said. When nothing happened to the family that winter, Galina's mother decided to stay in hopes her husband would soon be released. They stayed and never left.

But the decline of the family was rapid. Galina's mother, the parlor singer, cleaned houses to feed the children. Galina still remembered the darkest day, when her mother sold the Harmonium to buy food for the family. The house had never been without music. Her mother never sang again, and the family lost its soul.

Galina as a young girl walked by the prison each day after school, defying her mother's orders to stay away from it. She hoped to catch a glimpse of the father she so loved. Rumors had spread through the town that prisoners were being killed. However, her family was convinced that Galina's father was alive because the guards continued to accept the clothing and the garlic that her mother had delivered to the jail by a friend. But the clothing, which was to keep him warm, and the garlic, considered medicinal and disease-fighting, never reached him.

After World War II, authorities told Galina's mother that her imprisoned father had died of cancer in 1943. But in 1954, Galina learned the truth. The director of the school at which she was teaching Russian language and literature interrupted her class one day to tell her that the KGB was there to see her. Although Stalin had died a year earlier, she was afraid. But the local KGB chief only wanted to correct the historical record—her father had been executed just nineteen days after his arrest, on September 22, 1937.

Bad fortune continued to plague Galina's life. Her husband had been an intelligent man, a highly gifted chemistry teacher. But he never fully recovered from a serious head injury and the loss of an eye at the front during World War II. He died in 1975. Four years later the Ob River began to unearth Kolpashevo's mass grave.

When a friend rushed to tell Galina what was happening, she hurriedly pulled on a sweater and ran stumbling through the night. She scratched with her fingers to find a loose paling in the wooden fence set up in haste to close off the site of the mass grave. A guard seized her, but he backed off when confronted by the stern determination of the woman. "I am entitled," Galina remembered having said in desperate tones. "I must be allowed to the grave of my father."

When she reached the embankment, she looked down into the brown swirling of the Ob. Some of the bodies caught in the waves were turning over and rolling in the waves. Pieces of the half-frozen bank kept caving in on the soft sand underneath, falling with great splashes. She started into the tumble of water and bodies, searching in vain for any sign of her father.

"I cried. I didn't move and I cried. Then I went to a friend and told her what I had seen. All she could say is that I shouldn't have gone— that it could cause problems for my children. But I wasn't worried. What more could they do to me? I had to go to the grave out of honor for my father."

Galina stood and limped to the cabinet, her old legs having stiffened during her long talk with me. She showed me a tiny, thumb-sized jewel box decorated with colored stone studs. Inside it was what she said was an infant's finger bone, yellow and brittle. Her grandson had found it on the beach of an island downstream from the grave. "People were finding bones all over the place for a while," she said. She had no remains of her father, so the small finger bone in its tiny coffin would have to do.

Galina returns to the embankment twice each year—on her father's birthday, July 17, and again on September 22, the day on which the KGB had said he was shot. On those days, she stands atop the eroding bank, some twenty-five feet above the river, and she throws flowers onto his watery grave.

*　*　*

Galina's daughter, Nina, would like her mother to leave the house, which has no internal plumbing. She was sad that her mother never quit Kolpashevo, a place that had caused her only pain. But without her memories, even the painful ones, Galina said she has nothing of value. "There is something spiritual about this house, about our family," said Nina. She turned to the photographs. "I have no money. I've got lots of problems. But I have my roots."

She spoke of the Russians as an uncultured race to which she felt only distantly related. She preferred to consider herself Scandinavian, like her grandfather. "Russians still like to think they are the happiest, strongest, bravest, and cleverest people in the world," she said. "But they don't have much life left in them. Something has happened to everyone. Millions of people from one of the culturally richest traditions of the world are thinking about bread—lining up for it, wondering from where the next loaf will come. What kind of people is it that thinks so much about bread?"

She paused, dramatically, and the monologue continued. "Russia is a country of fools. Those aren't my words. That's from Gogol. Not that much has changed." She described a Gogol story about a man who eternally studies how to break an egg, starving as he tries to discover how to do it. Russians, she concluded, are fools who can't break the egg.

"Look at my mother," she said. "Despite all she has lost, all they have done to her, she doesn't demand anything from the powers. She is she. Let them take it all, she thinks."

Yet Nina also won't push her mother to demand reparations. "This is our life," she said. "This is our fate." Again—*Sudba,* the long Russian shadow.

Nina looked at the photograph of her father. "I want this country to be full of such people. They were spiritually freer, they could learn languages and speak them among themselves. They weren't afraid of each other. It has become a tradition of *Soviet* people" (she emphasized "Soviet" sarcastically) "to be afraid of each other. Life is such that you must be careful—even now."

She nodded to her grandfather's photo. "My father's father was the director of a school district, just as Lenin's father had been. He had a two-story home, a big library, he played the piano and Russian folk instruments. He knew Latin perfectly—and Sanskrit. But we are thinking about bread, about how to get enough to eat and drink for the winter."

She saw that I had turned sad along with her. So she brightened, a theatrical change of mood to lift the spirits of a guest who was preparing to leave. "We went mushroom hunting recently," she said. "It was April twelfth. There were so many mushrooms—large, beautiful, and oh, so tasty. We brought back two bucketsful."

Dramatic pause.

"We could have brought home so many more if we had only had a car."

I thanked Galina and her daughter, Nina. I wanted to stay longer, but I had already delayed our boat's departure too often with my desire for another interview or an additional hour of conversation. I had opened emotional wounds in Kolpashevo, and I couldn't stay behind to attend to them. I saw Nina's mother holding back tears. I promised to return.

"Thank you for saying so," said Nina. "But we have a saying here: 'Good things don't happen twice.'"

Chapter 2:

TRAVELS WITH THE KGB

There will always be a political police.

—VALERY KOLOSSOVICH ZNIKIN, *KGB officer*

And so I found the symbol of our expedition in the sandy, high banks of a small town on the Ob. But our voyage had begun less dramatically more than two weeks before, in Kemerovo, in the offices of an official who reminded us that, despite a wave of democratization, change comes slowly along the river's banks.

Valery Kolossovich Znikin looked like a Siberian Al Capone in his blue three-piece suit (of the oily, double-knit variety), matching blue shirt, blue-striped tie, and navy-blue socks. He pumped up his inadequate height with two-inch platform shoes.

The KGB colonel's handshake was soggy and his eyes shifted nervously from mine. He was sweating. At age thirty-nine, and after a decade with the KGB, this was his first meeting with an American—or with any Westerner. He looked me over with the suspicious stare of a man who has at long last met the enemy.

Yet I had reason to be polite to the KGB man. He, as part of the KGB's effort to clean up its reputation, had given our expedition a letter of safe passage that would open up areas of Siberia that had never been shown to an American before. And that's why Znikin's office was our expedition's mandatory first stop. In a region where the KGB had been the de facto ruler for years, that letter was a required travel document. The price: to listen to Znikin's version of history and resist the temptation to ask questions that could be construed as unfriendly.

Znikin wasn't going to make that easy. He guided me toward the newly created KGB "museum" on the second floor of the gray, stone KGB building in central Kemerovo. The structure held down one side of the central Square of the Soviets. Huge pillars framed a simple wooden doorway, and barred windows on each side of the entrance were so thick with dirt that no one could look in or out.

No plaque of any sort identified the building, an act of secrecy which would turn out to be a convenient omission. A few weeks after my visit, the KGB would be disbanded. More accurately, it would be renamed for the fifth time in its seventy-four-year history. But it would be staffed by the same men, most of them former Communist Party officials, including Colonel Znikin.

On the landing of the black-and-white marble stairway was a white plaster bust of Feliks Edmundovich Dzerzhinsky, the founder of the country's original secret police—popularly known as the Cheka, after its acronym. It was Dzerzhinsky's men who had saved the Bolshevik armed coup of 1917 and destroyed the first representative government in Russian history. Golden lettering identified him here as "the founder of the Cheka and the Sword and the Shield of the Revolution."

No photographs would be allowed, Znikin said, not even of the local heroes of the KGB, whose pictures lined one wall of the hallway leading to the museum. Znikin had invited us on a Saturday so that we wouldn't accidentally see (or worse, photograph) the faces of undercover agents. He was troubled by our straying eyes, so he hurried us into his museum, which looked more like a large living room, with its high, molded ceilings, white oak paneling, and sofas so soft and deep my head sank below my knees when I sat.

"In every organization you have a piece of sacred soil, of history," he explained. The museum had been opened only a few months before our arrival and it was, said Valery Kolossovich, open to Ivan Q. Public—so long as he called in advance to make an appointment. So was the KGB listed in the phone book? I wondered.

Znikin conceded it wasn't, and perhaps the normal citizen would have trouble reaching him. "But all the journalists in town have my number," he said proudly. I wondered why they might need to call, but decided not to ask.

The two rooms had glass cases against the walls that were filled with photos, medals, documents, and even an old gun, used by one of the first agents in Siberia during the 1920s. It was a Colt revolver—American technology was valued even then, he said. There was no section in the museum for the role the secret police played during the darkest years of the Gulags.

I knew that so much of what I would be seeing might have disappeared when I next returned to Kemerovo, so I recorded every detail in my mind's eye. Znikin did me one better with the newest model of a Panasonic video recorder. Even before I sank into the couch, Znikin nodded to a young agent. A small red light flickered on and the agent began recording with a wide shot that would miss nothing. When I politely asked Znikin what use he might make of the tape, he pointed to my notebook and tape recorder and responded.

"You are recording me and I am recording you," he said. "That balances the sides. It is only fair play."

Znikin walked to an old phonograph and flipped a switch to play us a tune. It was a hymn that had been composed especially for the Kemerovo station in 1979. The words, Znikin said, had been written by the local KGB chief at that time, General Vasily Pchelintsev. "The music was written by an undercover worker in our department, whom I can't name," he said.

Znikin was proud to tell us that the singer was Josef Kobzon, whose patriotic bass had brought swooning women to tears during the Brezhnev era. If Moscow had had a Lawrence Welk show, Kobzon would have been its regular guest.

"The music will be played now, and it should make an impression upon you," said Znikin. "I think every man, every person, has a moment in his life when he thinks about his history. And there are things that you can only explain with music. When I listen to this hymn I feel something overwhelming inside of me. I feel pride for the workers of the Cheka— workers in the full meaning of the word."

The KGB camera recorded my bemused silence as I sat back and appreciated Valery Kolossovich.

The record was scratchy and the music sounded like it had been played under water, but that only added to its *gravitas*. Valery Kolossovich stood, and I assumed that so should I. The problem was that I stood six foot three, so I tried to slump beside the KGB man, who was standing at attention in his platform shoes. Valery Kolossovich looked square ahead, into the ages, as the music began.

> The Cheka man was forged in struggle,
> And he was hardened in fierce fights,
> Many years have passed since that
>   glorious time,
>
> And now his cap with a star
> And a worn leather jacket
> Are on display at the museum,
> But his job isn't yet done . . .

The music was heroically maudlin, just enough brass to make it martial, but plenty of violins for the heart. My host's face was pained—he looked near tears. He started to move his lips, and I feared he would break into song.

> *Our enemies are preparing fire and wars,*
> *Heavy clouds hang over the Earth,*
> *Let the Soviet homeland remain calm,*
> *But, comrades, it's too early for us to relax.*
>
> *It does not matter that our temples have grayed,*
> *And that we can't sleep all night*
> *   together with you, old friend,*
> *We are ready to retrace*
> *The path we have traveled.*
>
> *We honor the people's confidence in us,*
> *Our faith in our heroic motherland is strong . . .*

I looked at the camera—tempted to stick my tongue out at it. I wondered who would review this videotape later. I was already shifting nervously, trying to look disinterested should the tape ever land in CIA hands. ("We always had doubts about Kempe," I imagined some eager agent saying, "but who would have thought!") Then I remembered the travel permissions—the long trip ahead for which we needed the KGB. I felt compromised—and we had barely begun our trip.

And the music just kept playing.

> *No wonder we still carry the Cheka's proud name*
> *And have done so since December 1917.*
>
> *Again, we hear the order,*
> *The never-ending alarm,*
> *Accustomed to this call,*
> *Our women and wives wait*
> *With their usual faith.*
>
> *Dear Comrade, it's no coincidence*
> *That you and I are called, as before,*
> *Cheka . . .*

Valery Kolossovich was gulping back tears! He didn't look at us—but straight ahead, the perfect actor for the camera. No one could doubt his sincerity. But this indulgence was taking up the time I needed for asking questions. I was grateful for the onset of the closing verse.

> *You never read our names in the newspapers;*
> *Let the danger to the world pass,*
> *Those men, the majors and generals,*

With their gray hair,
Let them remain awake at their posts
until the light of day.

We bear the shield and sword of our motherland,
The enemies will never pass our trenches
Guarded by the eternal, ever-burning flame,
Dzerzhinsky's traditions are still alive . . .

After the music faded out, Valery Kolossovich said he wanted to show us around his museum. My temperamental Dutch colleague, Gerard Jacobs, who was not as willing as I was to quietly humor this KGB man, interrupted. He wanted to know more about how he viewed this region filled with angry coal miners, sensitive defense factories, polluting oil wells, threatened native peoples, and a history of forced exile, imprisonment, and execution. Wasn't his KGB co-responsible for 20 million deaths and 40 million "repressed" in prisons and camps, seventy years of oppression, and a failed secret war against the United States?*

"The KGB has a long and varied history," Znikin said, frowning. "I don't think the figure of twenty million is correct, though. I have heard it is closer to four million people. Yet it isn't very important which number is correct. It isn't right to count by figures. There should be only one approach to history!"

He left us guessing what approach that might be. Znikin enjoyed seeming mysterious; he liked to speak in riddles. He also like to write poetry, and local newspapers reluctantly printed his maudlin, badly rhyming work—who would dare turn it down? Poetry writing had become a craze among KGB agents in the region while Yuri Andropov, an amateur poet, had been their boss. The chief of the Kemerovo station—who had written the words to the hymn—dabbled in poetry as well. Many agents of his, like Znikin, also took up the hobby.

Znikin the wordsmith tried to help me understand the KGB through an analogy. "When you see a nice-looking girl walking down the street in an alluring outfit, you get nervous, don't you? She hasn't said a word, but you feel something tingling inside. Well, it is the same with the KGB and its effect on people."

Hmmm. I savored the momentary image of a long-legged KGB agent. I noticed that Znikin was starting to sweat again.

"Some people see only the bad side, the black colors. And others idealize, calling us the sword and shield of the Revolution. The truth is somewhere between. Our problem is that our profession is always in the shadows. Our happiness and tears aren't seen by the people. We don't

*The best detailed account of this terror, with calculations, is Robert Conquest's *The Great Terror: A Reassessment.* Oxford University Press, 1990.

think we are the most important profession, but we are certainly among the romantic and interesting professions . . . and no profession is older, except prostitution. But we are almost as old."

He held for a laugh, and he smiled at his own attempt at humor. I smiled, too, but more at the unintended suggestion that these two professions were close relatives. "It's hard to explain to you. If you were an FBI or a CIA agent, then I think you would understand better why I am proud of my profession."

He noted that the local KGB had already released information from historical documents to local newspapers and to the Memorial organization, which investigated past Soviet crimes and cared for the victims. He said that his organization would soon release two volumes listing names of those who had died at the hands of Stalin's secret police.

"Do I feel bad about the period before I was here?" he asked. "Should people be prosecuted? Well, how should we handle the journalists and the workers who were cheering hurrah to all those repressions as they were going on? Should we also bring before the court those people who sold Alaska to the Americans? That was also a crime. . . ."

"Alaska? What does that have to do—"

"Perhaps there were people who signed falsified confessions and used them to send people to their deaths. There can't be two minds about that. Of course I feel bad about that. But we also lost 20,000 workers of the Cheka who refused to carry out their orders. . . ."

The secret police as the victims? The approach was intriguing, but I asked whether he would have broken orders.

"I think *I* wouldn't have refused my orders," he answered. "It's easy for us to make judgments now, when it all seems clear as day to us from the documents. People clearly knew what they were doing. But I don't think that you can make a good analysis of that time looking from the point of view of today."

What I learned later, from another agent who passed on his views more informally, was that Valery Kolossovich was part of a battle for power unfolding at KGB stations across the country. That fight had begun on a low level in 1988, said the agent, but it had been accelerating ever since then.

The agent drew a picture of a KGB that had always been made up of two classes. The first group came into the KGB through the Communist Party. They were the KGB's leaders and fast risers. To the KGB rank-and-file, this group was known as the "White Bone"—*Belaya Kost*.

The second group, members of which were maneuvering to usurp power from the old Party types, was drawn from "the recruits." They were young men and women from any number of professions who were handpicked by KGB headhunters because of unusual talents demonstrated in any

number of professions. They considered themselves ambitious and patriotic. Their qualities ranged from linguistic and athletic ability to loyalty
and intelligence. They were trained metallurgical engineers, history professors, and even simple workers who showed talent and ambition. But they
had one aspect in common: they were closer to the public and more
sympathetic to rapid social change that so disturbed the White Bone.

The agent who passed his knowledge to me was clearly of this second
group. He explained that this group was the catalyst for change at the
KGB. He, for instance, had suggested to superiors that the KGB stop
looking after political enemies at home (something it was still doing) and
instead spend more time and energy on investigating economic crimes.
The KGB agents based overseas, he said, should spend their time checking
out the credentials of potential foreign business partners of local companies.

But those belonging to the White Bone, said the agent with a frown,
were winning the battle. He was likely to quit and open up his own private
detective agency. Many others in the second group were also giving up the
power struggle and looking for new jobs. The irony was that those of the
White Bone, and that included Znikin, were gaining a greater monopoly
on power in Western Siberia than they had ever had before, said the agent.

I wanted to know what Znikin had done in his career that had made him
most proud. For one thing, he said, he had "opened up the structure of
the CIA" while he had been an agent in the First Department, fighting
counterrevolution and sabotage. I wondered what that entailed—what
had he discovered?

"I'll show you my uniform, but I don't want to unbutton everything,"
he said. He toyed with the buttons on his suit.

He said the Kemerovo KGB looked after hijackings, kidnappings, ter-
rorism, and drugs. He also said that much of the KGB's time was taken
up fighting threats to the state of all stripes—subversive activities, sabotage, organized crime, and murders. "The most severe crimes—high treason as well," he said. He noted that three spies had recently been arrested
in Kemerovo.

That sounded interesting. What were their acts of espionage and their
names? "It's not necessary for you to know," said Znikin, using a phrase
he would repeat often. "Glasnost also has its limitations—its borders."

Znikin now insisted it was time to show me his museum. Valentine
Akishkin, our Australian-accented interpreter, pulled at my arm to stop
me before I could protest and ask for more answers. He whispered that the
KGB man would be highly offended if we continued to block him from
going forward with the agenda he had set for us. The Russian organizers
of the expedition would tell me later that it was at this meeting that the
KGB began to wonder if I was more than just a journalist. Before I had

arrived, someone had convinced them that I was an environmental reporter, thus increasing our access to forbidden regions. So Znikin and others noted with suspicion that I was asking too many questions about other matters.

Valery Kolossovich led us to the museum area of the large room and showed us a class photograph of local agents from 1930. One face was smeared out in the middle of the photograph—in the spot where the chief would have been sitting. A closer look showed two more faces rubbed out beyond recognition.

"I can't say why this was done," said Znikin. "Maybe the faces wore out over time because people looked at the photographs a lot."

Or maybe Stalin had the men killed?

He shrugged. "Maybe."

The other agent had been more forthcoming than Znikin about his organization's work. Much of its focus, since coal miners' strikes had first swept the Kuzbass province in the summer of 1989, had been to monitor the workers' leaders. Part of what angered "the recruits" of the KGB—those who hadn't been drawn out of Party organizations—was that they had been ordered to infiltrate strike groups and, where possible, compromise the leaders.

These local agents grew angrier yet when their chief, General Pchelintsev, humiliated them during a public speech he was giving. When one citizen stood to ask how much KGB agents earned, the general called upon those in the audience—who were under cover—to stand and respond. The humiliation was triple—they were engaged in a mission they didn't want, their cover was blown, and they had to reveal to fellow Kemerovans what they earned.

Valery Kolossovich conceded that the KGB viewed some in the workers' movement as a threat against whom society must be protected. "There are some such cases in my charge," he said, noting an item of law concerning social unrest. He said a spark would be enough to turn a crowd of miners into a violent riot, so agents maintained contacts with the miners and monitored some of them less obviously.

"We aren't fighting specific persons or leaders," he said. "We are merely concerned whether something is dangerous to state security."

"But does the KGB still tap miners' phones?"

Znikin paused for a moment. "Investigation work never stops—it goes on all the time."

Several months after I returned to the West from Siberia, I phoned my friends in Kemerovo to check on Znikin's whereabouts. Certainly, I thought, his kind had been purged after the August 1991 coup attempt had

failed. These were new times—and the Kemerovo KGB had been populated by old thinkers. But Znikin had appeared on a radio interview
program that very week, again as spokesman.

He was the front man for the renamed secret police, the Federal Security
Agency. Despite the new acronym and ownership (the Russian government), he said the organization would basically do the same work the
KGB had busied itself with previously. Asked for details, he noted there
was "some uncertainty in the higher ranks of government" about the new
agency's precise tasks. Znikin, however, had no doubts that it would
continue to be political.

"It is a fact that the KGB was the political brigade of the Party," he
said, almost with a note of pride. "The negative side of the KGB's work
shouldn't be forgotten, but no secret service exists without such problems.
Every sea has its foam. Those who think the political secret service will
cease to exist are just lying. The government, regardless of how democratic
it is, will force us to keep close watch on the political situation."

Before we left his museum that day, Znikin pinned onto each of our
lapels a tiny relief of Feliks Dzerzhinsky, the KGB hero who only two
months later would have his statue, wrapped in ropes, removed from
downtown Moscow. Znikin was pleased that I had accepted the small gift
so enthusiastically, not realizing that I considered this Communist kitsch
to be a collector's item—a relic of a fallen empire, very much like Colonel
Znikin himself.

Chapter 3:

AN AMERICAN IN SIBERIA

The Russian Revolution is the greatest event of our lives. It represents all that we have been dreaming of and fighting for all our lives. It's the dawn of freedom and industrial revolution. . . . If we can't trust Lenin, we can't trust anyone.

—"BIG BILL" HAYWOOD,
radical American union leader, 1920

With the KGB letter of safe passage in hand, we could now begin our trip, but first I wanted to stay a couple more days in Kemerovo to recover from jet lag and do some research. That night we had a long, liquid dinner to launch the expedition, and I retired to my room to charge my batteries for the grueling days ahead. I was happy we hadn't scheduled any morning appointments. Shortly after I dozed off, however, the knocking began.

The rap on the hotel door was solicitous, soft enough to be clandestine yet sufficiently repetitious to suggest urgency. I cautiously pressed the light switch to avoid electrocution. Some plan-fulfilling electrician had set it expeditiously between two sockets with exposed wires. I read my watch: two A.M.

The room smelled of stale sheets—washed in hard water without benefit of detergent. Groggily, I tried to pull a towel around me, but in a country where factories are unnecessarily large, the rough towel wasn't big enough to wrap around a leg.

My nocturnal visitor knocked again, this time louder and more insistently. I draped a sheet around me and opened the door a crack to see a shapely woman with dyed red hair. She was no older than twenty-five, but her Pharaonic eye makeup and crimson-painted lips conspired to make her appear older.

She wore a brown camelhair miniskirt that advertised her legs. Her black T-shirt, a size too small, was embroidered with rainbow lettering: G-U-C-C-I. A huge shipment of the shirts had arrived in Kemerovo that month from Italy (in a barter arrangement involving coal), and women all over town were wearing them.

When the woman with the crimson lips saw my bewildered look and heard my American voice, she glanced both ways down the hall and asked with unexpected innocence, "I make mistake?"

About then, a bolt of light illuminated the end of the dark hallway, where a door had swung open. A deep, hoarse voice barked for her. I opened my door wider to get a better view, and my sheet slipped off, leaving me fully exposed.

My nocturnal visitor giggled as I bent over to recover my toga. "You like me sometime?" she asked. By the time I stood back up, she had scurried quietly and quickly away.

Before I shut the door, I looked down the hallway in the opposite direction to see the ever-present "hall woman," a vestige of a Soviet past characterized by close monitoring of all foreign visitors. Her ample silhouette filled the hallway of the hotel floor that she ruled. She stayed in place long enough to let me register that I had been "caught" in a reportable transgression.

The door at the end of the hallway closed, but the young woman's heavy perfume lingered behind her, the scent of an ancient but now resurgent capitalism in a crumbling workers' paradise.

Unable to sleep, I returned to reading the autobiography of Big Bill Haywood. Haywood, the most renowned radical American labor leader of his time, had fled American justice and come to Kemerovo seventy years before me, hoping to create the workers' paradise that had eluded him in America.

One biography had described him as "tall, broad-shouldered and strong, with one dead eye and a black Stetson cowboy hat perched atop his scarred and scowling face." He had been "the very personification of proletarian rage, a capitalist's nightmare come to life."

With $300,000 of venture capital from Lenin, he and two other men—Herbert Calvert and Dutch-born Sebald Rutgers—had founded the Autonomous Industrial Colony (or AIK) in 1921. Lenin had leased them a steel plant, chemical factory, coal mines, and more than 20,000 acres of farmland in the Kuznetsk Basin, or Kuzbass, a coal-rich area the size of Indiana. In exchange they were to bring him 5,000 workers, mostly from America. Each would carry one hundred dollars' worth of tools and one hundred dollars in cash—a small enough down payment for paradise.

"It is a great experiment to create a big industry that will not feed a parasitic society, but will return to the worker the full product of his labor," Haywood wrote characteristically in his prospectus for the colony.

The AIK was a little-known chapter of American labor history—one that interested me all the more because Haywood had been a fellow Utahan, born in my own hometown of Salt Lake City in 1869, or about eighty-five years before me. The Mormons' promised land, nestled in a broad valley of the Rocky Mountains' Wasatch Range, had always been a place that bred belief in Utopias, even for its non-Mormons like the Haywoods. I had also been raised with a naive confidence that a better society was desirable and achievable. My idealism, however, had been tempered by more moderate times.

Haywood wrote in his biography of a Utah where violent conflicts were everyday matters, often involving disputes revolving around the polygamists who were his neighbors. Haywood admired the Mormons' early form of central planning—wide streets with orderly numbering, deep gutters where streams of mountain water irrigated rich gardens. But his autobiography contrasted this idyll with an enduring child's memory of a mob lynching a black man in a downtown stable.

"His face was ghastly, and although he was light-colored, it was turning blue, with the eyes and tongue sticking out horribly," he wrote. "I looked at the swinging figure and thought over and over, 'What have they done—what have they done—' It was as though a weight of cold lead settled in my stomach."

That childhood memory helped shape Haywood's self-image. He viewed himself as the campaigner for the little man against dark forces, for the worker against the capitalists, for that black against the hangman.

In the first decade of the twentieth century, Haywood gained national fame as the fire-breathing orator and organizer of the Industrial Workers of the World, whose members became known as Wobblies, which some histories say was due to a Chinese member's mispronunciation of the final two letters of the acronym IWW—Eye-Wobbly-Wobbly. At the union's founding in Chicago on June 27, 1905, Haywood laid the foundation for the most militant and romantic labor organization the U.S. had ever known. "This is the Continental Congress of the working class," said Haywood to 200 delegates representing 300,000 workers.

In the same year, a revolution was beginning in Russia. In 1905 Tsarist inefficiency, economic crisis, and the ripples from Russia's unexpected setback in its war with Japan fed a revolutionary movement throughout the country, including the first all-Siberian workers' strike. The Tsar crushed the uprising brutally, but that would provide only a brief respite.

In a communiqué to Odessa, the IWW Congress supported "our persecuted, struggling and suffering comrades in far-off Russia." Little did Haywood know then that these "suffering comrades" would be his last hope.

On September 28, 1916, a federal grand jury returned an indictment charging Haywood and more than one hundred other Wobblies with masterminding a "seditious conspiracy" against the U.S. war effort—Haywood would also later be charged with a conspiracy to overthrow the government. He was booked into the Cook County jail at age forty-eight, standing five foot eleven and weighing 226 pounds.

Only a month after his arrest, the prisoner Haywood heard of the Bolshevik Revolution, and he led his fellow Wobbly inmates in loud whoops and songs from their *Little Red Songbook*. Russia began to look even better after Haywood was convicted. His lawyers appealed to the Supreme Court, but they told their client they had little hope of success. So, while free on bail, Haywood decided to take up an earlier offer from a Russian agent to provide him a false passport and transportation to Russia to take up work as a consultant to Lenin.

Concealing his well-known appearance by wearing a giant black cloak and a monocle over his dead eye, blinded in a childhood whittling accident, Haywood boarded a ship for Europe, where he would then catch a train to Moscow. And when the boat passed the Statue of Liberty, he emerged on deck from his hideaway in steerage and said: "Saluting the old hag with her uplifted torch, I said: 'Good-bye, you've had your back turned on me too long. I am now going to the land of freedom.' "

The keeper of the Haywood flame in Kemerovo was Yevgenia Krivosheyeva, a small, plump historian who had fallen into her role almost by accident when she had arrived in Kemerovo in the 1950s. "I was working in the archives, merely doing my job, when I ran across these documents about the 1920s concerning the AIK. So I decided to do my thesis on the colony."

Professor Krivosheyeva kept to herself the most explosive information she discovered. The official version for the colony's fizzling out in the late 1920s had been that it had served its purpose, but instead, she found that Stalin had more likely disbanded it because of his suspicion of all things foreign. He'd also had many of the original colonists arrested and executed when his purges began.

"Nearly half of those colonists who hadn't already left the country were called spies and sent to prison camps, where many of them died," the professor said. "It was a great irony because many had remained here for fear of persecution back in America for their Communist views. But I couldn't publish that information anywhere."

The professor was involved in a project whose aim was to rebuild the forty-seven former colony buildings and log homes that still existed, but by 1991 not much had been done in a city that lacked syringes for its hospitals and milk for its people.

Still, the people of the Kuzbass, the most industrially developed part of Siberia, considered Kemerovo to be their garden spot. As I jogged through the city in the evening, I saw shaded, grass-covered courtyards clogged with children playing tag and old men playing chess. Teenagers and young couples took evening strolls, and coy young women in their best clothing flirted with suitors on the prowl. Many were wearing the T-shirts emblazoned G-U-C-C-I.

However, Haywood's paradise had turned sour long before I arrived. The noxious fumes from its coal-coking factory and chemical plants gave its citizens a far higher than average incidence of cancer and respiratory problems—and getting sick was a dangerous business in a city in which every hospital suffered shortages of the most basic drugs and equipment. One surgeon who lacked thread for suturing told me he was using strands from ribbons he had bought at a ladies' wear store.

But Professor Krivosheyeva saw none of the woeful present as we drove around town. She saw only the friendly ghosts of the past, the "roaring twenties" of Kemerovo that she considered her city's golden years. That was when Russian melancholy had been tempered by American square dances and celebratory feasts, she said.

"This is where they played American football," Professor Krivosheyeva said as we stopped beside a field overgrown with weeds where two cows were grazing. Rusted poles still delineated the old goals at each end of the turf. "They even had bleachers and everyone would come to watch. Jack Tuchelsky, a Polish-born electrician from Detroit, was the best player." The colonists wrote home about his prowess.

After the colony was shut down, Tuchelsky, who had worked at the steel smelter, landed a job in 1930 as the chief electrician at a new automobile factory in Gorky. But eight years later he was arrested and charged with industrial sabotage. His real crime was being a foreigner.

"At first he refused to confess," said Professor Krivosheyeva. "Then he agreed to the charges after long hours of interrogation. He died in the jail hospital in December 1938 of injuries he suffered while being tortured. You can imagine what they did to him. His daughter lives in Moscow now. She was very small when they took away her father to prison."

We climbed out of the van near a 250-foot bluff over the Tom River. The professor walked me to the best view of the Kemerovo Chemical Plant, which had been the colony's most important factory. It was still Kemerovo's most important employer. Several smaller plants surrounded it, all sending into the heavens a pipe-organ concert of pollution that turned the heavens an unnatural gray.

Yet colorful wildflowers covered the ground that led to the stone ruins of the amphitheater, cut into a recess of the hillside, where the colonists had watched theater performances, with the lazy Tom River as a backdrop. Stretching to the east was the taiga, the wild forest of Siberia. And, on a clear day, you could see low mountains on the horizon, a spur from the Altai Range near Mongolia.

The colony ran into problems early on. Haywood and the others never came close to their promise to Lenin of recruiting 5,000 workers; the colony never exceeded 500. The initial cold winter and inadequate housing prompted fifty of the first colonists to return home and complain bitterly enough to put off potential recruits. The housing shortage of the time, which has still not been solved in the seventy years since, had forced the firstcomers to spend their initial days in the boxcars of the freight trains that had brought them, before moving into the schoolhouses infested with cockroaches, fleas, lice and the ever-stubborn Siberian bedbug.

The next blow came when Haywood's IWW—along with the rest of America—turned against Soviet Communism. Haywood was in no position to sway his working brothers with his fabled oratory—they considered him a traitor for fleeing America while fellow Wobblies remained behind bars.

The colonists who did come had increasing problems with the Russians, who didn't look kindly on outsiders taking over their mines and factories and then telling them to work harder and more efficiently. The strains were fed by cultural differences.

The puritanical Americans couldn't grow accustomed to the Russians skinny-dipping in the Tom River, and the Russian men took it particularly badly that twelve Americans took Russian wives before the AIK was even a year old. "The colonists were taking their best women," said Professor Krivosheyeva. "These 'exotics' looked very good to the local women."

And Haywood criticized the Russians' lack of sanitary conditions. "Every kind of vermin invade the houses in abundance," he said. In the summer of 1922 the colonists built new, closed toilets, while digging up the open pits that preceded them and, with a certain righteous disgust, throwing lime on them.

Strains turned ugly in the early summer of 1923. Two Dutch engineers introduced a new, fast ferry, attached to an overhead cable and powered by the current of the river against the boat's rudder, but it capsized on its first day, and eighteen drowned—all but one of whom were Russian.

The colonists also began fighting among themselves. The American Communists and their Russian allies were at loggerheads with the Wobblies, who complained that they lacked industrial democracy and had become wage slaves of the Soviet State. At least once the dispute turned into a full-blown brawl, and most of the IWW workers left the colony before it shut down operations. The bulk of those who remained were hard-core pro-Soviet Communists.

The vicious cold, sparse housing, scarcity of food, and rampant disease among the early colonists had driven Haywood back to Moscow after only a few months. When he resigned his post as one of the colony's leaders in 1923, the *Chicago Tribune* said he "broke down and cried like a child." But the colony wasn't dead yet.

Despite their feuding, the colonists gained a significance out of proportion to their numbers, owing to their expertise and their can-do attitudes. Lenin advanced them an additional 2 million gold rubles (about a million dollars) in 1923, and he transferred to them the management of all local production facilities.

The year 1924 brought the high and low point for the colony. The powering-up of the chemical factory, dependent on huge coal cokers, set off celebrations including marching bands parading across the frozen river. Professor Krivosheyeva's eyes lit up at the idea of the spectacle. She said the project had required installation of a huge turbo-generator, which had provided electricity sufficient to light up surrounding villages.

AIK boss Sebald Rutgers had put on a show for some peasant women by taking wrinkles out of shirts with electric irons and cooking *blinis* on an electric grill. His only trouble came in convincing them to turn off the lights, for they feared that they would never come back on.

Many of the colonists were enthusiastic. Professor Krivosheyeva showed me an old copy of the *Kuzbass Bulletin,* the colony's newspaper, which reprinted an excited schoolgirl's letter written to a friend whose family was soon to join the colony: "In Summer it is warm and beautiful. We go swimming, fishing, boating, and hunting. In Winter we are sleighing, skating, etc. Bring your skates when you come. . . . Bring along some pigeons and a few parrots. And papa needs two steel fishing rods about 10 feet long and plenty of hooks, size 7."

But the death of Lenin, two months before the chemical plant began operating, burst the AIK dream. The colony would continue to operate for two more years, but Stalin was determined to shut it down. "The colony died with Lenin," said Professor Krivosheyeva. "It is a shame, because these were people of high qualifications, and they had great plans."

She believed Kemerovo would have been better off in the 1990s if it had kept the cultured and well-trained foreigners of the 1920s and their offspring. The professor frowned. She had caught herself in a nostalgic trance for a period she had never known, but the past, and its air of American optimism, was a welcoming port of escape. "We haven't come very far since then," she said. "If anything, we've gone backwards."

* * *

Ethel Grund had done her hair for my visit. It was blonde and curly. Her skin was neatly made up, enough rouge to complement her naturally rosy cheeks. I was late. She was nervously waiting, her table set with cakes and coffee made by her husband, whose orangish-red hair was the result of a botched dye job, and a bad match for his gray mustache.

She was the last survivor from the original colony's families who still lived in Kemerovo. She was an English teacher, but she talked to us in Russian because her father had never spoken the language at home except to call her his "little Pussy Cat." And she had called him "Mickey Mouse."

Ethel Grund was only forty-six years old, so she had learned second-hand about the colony from the long audio tapes and the handwritten autobiography that her father, Franz Grund, had left behind. "When I was a child, he never talked about it," she apologized. "The less the children knew, the less likely it was that they would blab out the wrong thing in school and land the entire family in trouble. He began to speak about the old days only when I was nineteen or twenty—old enough to understand."

Franz Grund's family had moved to the United States from Austria at the outbreak of World War I. As a teenager, he'd worked as a baker in New York. It was there, laboring from four A.M. until long after dark at slave wages, that he developed a hatred of the capitalist system.

"The world was such then that he stopped believing in God altogether, although he came from a devout Catholic family," his daughter said. "He joined the Industrial Workers of the World and the Communist Party. And like all young men who grew active in the movement, he knew of Bill Haywood and admired him."

So, when the AIK was being organized, he read about it with fascination in one of the IWW newspapers. At age nineteen he sailed to the Soviet Union, a place where he figured that a worker would be treated fairly.

Ethel Grund pulled out a thick, overflowing photo album and leafed through it lovingly. She fished out a small photo of a group of men on the deck of a huge ship. The photograph was worn, crumbled on the edges, a memento of the decisive moment in a young man's life. In it, Franz Grund held up a large handkerchief. He was smiling. "He was holding it up as a red flag as the ship set sail for Europe and he began to sing the 'Internationale,'" said his daughter.

Ethel Grund turned to a paper on which her father had written down the details for his residency permit in the Soviet Union.

Name: Franz Johann Anton Grund
Address: 413 W. 56th Street, New York
Nationality: Austrian

Profession: Baker
Birth date: March 21, 1902

"He collected everything," she said. "He was a very accurate man."

But he hadn't brought his U.S. identity papers. It was an intentional oversight that set apart the hard-core Communists who had committed themselves to Lenin from those who were only experimenting. However, not having papers also posed problems—he couldn't become a citizen of the Soviet Union without proof of who he was. The Communist Party, however, was more welcoming, and that membership was enough for him.

Franz Grund studied engineering upon his arrival, and within three years he had risen to become the deputy chief of one of the chemical plant's workshops. In 1936, however, as Stalin's culture of fear spread, the director of the plant took away Franz Grund's Party card and fired him. The Central Committee in Moscow had decreed that non-Soviet citizens couldn't be Party members. And the director knew his own life would be in danger if he had a suspicious foreigner on his staff.

Franz Grund began a lengthy process with the U.S. Embassy in Moscow to establish his identity—not an easy chore for a declared Communist. But he remained convinced that Communism was superior to the capitalist world he had abandoned. He didn't even change his mind when Stalin's men executed his brother-in-law, Isaak Goldfine. Goldfine was a Lithuanian-born Jew, an engineer who had emigrated to the United States only to return when given the chance to join the colony. He was arrested in 1937 on charges of participating in a Trotskyist plot against Stalin, and he was shot in 1938 in a village near Kemerovo.

Franz Grund knew he was taking a chance when he took in Goldfine's two small girls and his wife, who in 1937–38 regularly took deliveries of her husband's soiled clothing for washing. Once, after laundering some underwear, she noticed that a piece of paper had been stitched inside the material, but the water had washed off the writing, which had apparently been made in her husband's blood. "She couldn't forgive herself all her life for this," said Ethel Grund. "She always wondered what he had wanted to tell her."

A year after his brother-in-law's death, Franz Grund went to the local prosecutor and demanded that he be either arrested or allowed to work. The uncertainty was driving him crazy. The prosecutor ordered the manager to rehire Grund.

No one knew what divided the survivors from those who were executed in those times. Franz Grund often wondered why he lived and his brother-in-law hadn't. Ethel Grund guessed that her father made it through because he was so quiet and composed, not given to the verbal mistakes, idle jokes, or temper tantrums that so often resulted in arrest. "I remember that he would always tell us to be quiet, when it grew too loud among the children, because there were people downstairs."

Grund could never let go of the Communist dream that brought him to Russia. In 1961 he applied to the regional Party committee to restore to him his lost time of Party membership. In 1965 the Party reinstated thirty years of membership. "He saw the faults that emerged in Communism, but he always believed everything would be better," his daughter said. "He always told us that the bad times would pass by. Then he would sing the songs of his youth in America—revolutionary songs. He could sing 'The Red Banner' in English and in Italian."

Like Haywood, however, Franz Grund also could not abandon his attachment to America. The worse matters turned in Russia, the more nostalgic he would become. "He would watch any film that had anything to do with New York," his daughter said. "I wanted to learn about his relationship with the United States. I've tried to write to friends and relatives that I thought he had. They were in his old address book. But it wasn't a success. After 1936 my father never dared write to them anymore. I suppose they all moved since then. We don't move as often here as you do in America. When you get an apartment, you hold on to it. I still live in the home of my father."

By the time of my visit to Kemerovo, Haywood's only visible legacy was the pollution that spewed out of the smokestacks of the Kemerovo Coking and Chemical Plant, where Franz Grund had worked as an engineer until his retirement in 1973.

Just as many European cities were built around the steeples of cathedrals, the industrial cities of Siberia were constructed around factory smokestacks. Underneath its spires, the superstructure of huge twisting pipes and boilers looked like basement plumbing pulled out onto the surface and then magnified a hundred thousand times.

But the plant had long outlived its local welcome. The local council had voted to shut it down altogether because of its sulfurous pollution. What kept it alive was the city's economic distress—it remained Kemerovo's largest employer and taxpayer. The plant's director, a life-long Communist, had made a deal with the city that he would help the people with food and medical supplies if the council would stay the factory's execution.

"If you think too much about ecology, you won't have food to eat," said the plant's director, Leonid Shelyakin, who at age fifty-nine pledged to me that he wasn't about to change his Communist colors or the Lenin drawing that hung over his desk.

The council had opted to shut down a third of the plant's facilities until it cleaned up its production with new technologies, which would be required by 1994. The city fathers had faced an impossible choice between pollution and bankruptcy, so they had chosen dirty air for a few years more.

What the plant provided Kemerovo as an incentive was the purchase of a potato farm managed by Dutch partners, two dairy and meat-packing plants bought from Americans, technology for storing vegetables and fruits, buses for city transportation, and a factory to produce medical goods locally.

But the fumes of the factory were so noxious that the plant was forced to go a step further. It was relocating city dwellers who lived within a half kilometer of its factory walls, and it would likely extend the area to a full kilometer. Their life expectancy was said to be up to ten years less than that of those residing elsewhere in the city. None of them complained about their forcible relocation from some of Siberia's worst housing. Families around the plant had been crammed into two-room wooden-and-concrete barracks and shacks without indoor plumbing, homes left over from Haywood's days. Slag heaps reached nearly to their doors. Hot plates served for a stove, padding on the floor or a metal cot made up a bed, and an unheated communal outhouse provided toilets whose seats froze during the long winter. The plant's management had already moved 4,000 families, but thousands of Kemerovo's 600,000 residents still lived in such housing.

I asked why the plant wasn't moved instead of the people. "Even if our plant is torn down," he said, "behind us is another plant and behind that yet another. They are all in a row—I don't even have enough fingers to count them."

In the massive factory yard, under the hissing, whistling, and belching superstructure, workmen in white helmets frowned when asked about democratic reforms. "We met the initial changes with enthusiasm," said Pyotr Voitovich Semenovich, a plant repairman. Now he regarded the reforms, he said, as a man who must live in an old house during its reconstruction.

"You know you must be uncomfortable during the building," he said. "So you put up with it for a few weeks, then a few months, and then a few years. But the building is taking too long, so then you lose faith. A man's lifetime isn't forever. Our living standards were far higher under Brezhnev. The country is moving in the wrong direction."

At that moment of economic desperation, Kemerovo's hope rested in men like Anatoly Zaitsev, a fearless entrepreneur who had become highly popular among workers for his fairness and generosity. I wondered if Haywood might have felt differently about capitalism if he had foreseen that labor could reach an accommodation with capital that served both— something Karl Marx hadn't foreseen.

When I first met Zaitsev for a short courtesy meeting in his office, he balked at my proposal of an early-morning meeting the following day until I told him about the American concept of a power breakfast. Determined to live up to Western business practices, he immediately invited me to his home. He greeted me at eight o'clock, wearing green bedroom slippers, of Soviet manufacture, and a T-shirt marked MONTANA, a souvenir of a recent business trip to the United States.

A small American flag rose out of a crystal vase in his entryway, standing beside a green-striped can of Palmolive shaving cream and a brown bottle of Tabac cologne. They were reflected in the mirror behind them—a capitalist still-life. Most Russians have kitsch hanging from their walls, but his was different—a Japanese calendar and a decorative plate from a Danish life insurance company.

Anatoly Zaitsev also had a new Fisher VHS system and a large-screen Toshiba color television, but those were the only signs of his riches in the otherwise modest 180-square-feet apartment.

I had forgotten to tell Zaitsev that power breakfasts need not consist of much more than low-fat yogurt and fruit because it doesn't matter what's eaten, but what's said. His wife and daughter had filled the living-room table with a symphony of dishes that showed how little food shortages affected the well-connected—scrambled eggs with salmon, sausages, sautéed mushrooms, cold vegetable plates full of tomatoes and cucumbers, warm pastries, various cakes, and fresh brewed coffee. In his effort to be more American, he was one of the few Siberians who had given up smoking—but not cholesterol.

Zaitsev wasn't interested in talking to me about my favorite subject in Kemerovo, Bill Haywood. "He's not the sort of American we need here," he said.

"So which American would you most like to meet?" I asked.

"Ronald Reagan," he said without hesitation.

"But he called your country the Evil Empire," I said.

"Yes, I know it," he said. "And I think he was very right in saying it. We have had lots of evil here. And we still do. But it was Reagan's refusal to compromise with Moscow, and his Star Wars program, that helped bring Communism to an earlier death. He understood how to deal with the leadership. He made the Soviet Union have respect for the United States. And I think if the constitution would have allowed it, he would have been elected President for a third time. Isn't that right?"

I nodded. He was proud of this insight into American politics. I was surprised that the American dream had reached Western Siberia with such force.

The other American he would like to meet, he said, "is that Italian fellow who took that automobile company out of bankruptcy." He grew excited when I mentioned the name of Lee Iacocca. "Yes, that's him," he says. "His book is a best-seller. Americans wouldn't pay so much attention to a man if it weren't for something."

Zaitsev had a sparkle in his eyes that one rarely saw in a Siberia full of dull expressions and pale faces. When he had greeted me at his office for a short acquaintance session a day earlier, he had strode into the room with his chest forward, his body exuding dynamism and confidence. His face had a healthy glow of pink, running up over his bald head, which was framed by white hair curling out from his temples.

Zaitsev was Kemerovo's best-known entrepreneur, but he had been born poor in a village of the nearby Altai Mountains as the youngest of eleven children, of whom only four were still alive. Two of his brothers had died at the World War II front and a third had died of war injuries thereafter. His family had lost three of his siblings as infants, and one sister had already died of old age.

"Maybe you have less fear when you come from this sort of a background," he said. "You live your life your own way when you've gone through that. It forges your character."

Zaitsev had grown famous locally after he'd converted a coal company, whose unruly work force had earned it the nickname "the drunken mines," into a snappy diversified corporation. Through clever deals with Western distributors and a collection of joint ventures, he'd bartered for Western goods with which he then either paid his delighted workers or traded to other companies for materials he needed or products he could sell abroad.

He owned timber companies in Tomsk and Krasnoyarsk that had begun to supply the West, and he had another company that made plastic bags and other products from polyethylene, a derivative from his oil field. During a trip to the United States, he had acquired modern dairy equipment sufficient to launch a major milking and packaging operation. He had a joint venture with an Italian company to quarry a semiprecious stone they'd found in the region, of a sort that fit somewhere between marble and granite. "It's so unique that there isn't yet a name for the deposit," said Zaitsev.

Zaitsev had also launched a joint venture to produce goods from one of the richest raw materials of the vast Siberian swamplands, to the north. He couldn't think of the name of this "earth that burns," so he pulled out a hand-held computer dictionary, typed in the Russian letters TOPF, and out came the English equivalent—PEAT. Zaitsev treated this high-tech gear like a hacker who had worked on it all his life.

Zaitsev insisted that he cared less about the profits of joint ventures with Western partners than he did about the concept. After seventy years of bad management, he believed Russians could never crawl out of their mess alone. He was bitterly critical of the Germans, who had for so long continued to give Gorbachev loans that had artificially kept the Soviet Union alive. He saw joint ventures as the only way of committing the West to Russian success. "It's quite simple," he said. "The only way you really get the West to help is if its companies feel they will lose their investment if we fail." He argued that prices should be dirt cheap for such Westerners—the key was obligating them.

But Zaitsev had always been a sort of visionary. He had changed the system even before the system had changed itself. As early as 1982, when Brezhnev still ruled and he had only his "drunken mines," he was operating as a closet capitalist, trading outside of State channels the coal that he produced in excess of the State plan. "What I was doing was illegal—it was underground work," he said.

In 1984 the Party summoned him to Moscow for a dressing down. "You in the West will never understand how these things worked," he said. "They talked to you like a child, and you responded like a child, saying you wouldn't do it anymore. Then, when your parents weren't looking, you repeated what you had been punished for until you were caught again."

In 1988 he was among the first to take advantage of a new law that allowed him to withdraw his company legally from its ministry and then operate it independently after leasing the land from the government. His 11,000 workers, in their first democratic election, chose him as the company director. He, in turn, appointed himself as their social engineer.

He increased their salaries about 300 percent, but that did little to change their lives. "People can't buy anything with the money anyway," he said.

More important, he began a construction company that built them flats. Within two years, he said, all would have new homes. He had rewarded his best workers with Japanese color televisions and with videocassette recorders, and he had already sent more than 1,600 of them abroad on vacations so they could see what sort of life they should be striving for. He had supplied more than half his work force with automobiles, and 500 of them were driving Japanese cars. And all of this he had bought with his coal—while still making a profit.

"But why buy them cars?" I asked. It seemed a ludicrous extravagance in a country with more urgent needs.

"Why do you Americans need two cars?" he said with a sneer, as though I had somehow insulted the Russian people. "My workers need cars so they will feel braver and have their feet more firmly on the ground." What's more, he said, cars were a necessary part of the food chain. Families needed to drive from empty shop to empty shop in search of the most basic supplies, and almost every Russian had a small garden plot, usually outside the city, which was difficult to reach by public transport.

Only one problem: his workers had become the targets of a growing local Mafia. Thieves systematically collected their names and addresses and then robbed their flats, stole their cars, and in some cases demanded protection money.

So Zaitsev took it upon himself to strengthen the police force. He bought the Kemerovo police twenty patrol cars, including some Toyota and Nissan four-wheel-drives. Thanks to Zaitsev, the police could better pursue the criminals who were terrorizing his workers.

Zaitsev only regretted that he wasn't young enough to restart his life. With each trip abroad, he grew more determined to change things. "I saw real power in America," he said. His trips to Europe, Japan, and Australia had impressed him far less. "I had the impression that if you put the whole world against America that it could hold out. I saw Hollywood, Disneyland, and San Francisco. Can you believe it? The Golden Gate Bridge was built in 1930 [1937] and it will stand forever! I was impressed by Australia as well, but all the Australians could have used against Saddam Hussein would have been sheep. Hah, hah, hah!"

What had impressed him in particular was Nevada, a landscape far less blessed than Siberia with riches, yet abundant in wealth because it had cleverly found an attractive market niche. Someday, he said, he would bring gambling to Western Siberia. If it worked on the American frontier, it would certainly take hold in Siberia. "I would be pleased if we could re-create Reno, Nevada, in Siberia, but that is now a dream. First we must give people enough food, adequate services, and an infrastructure."

For now Zaitsev felt he still had to blend into the scenery and not stick out through any conspicuous consumption of his own, or flashy projects like casinos. Some local enemies were still combing his books to catch him in criminal offenses—Communism was gone but its bureaucrats remained in place and wanted to destroy him. He figured that it would take many years for attitudes to change, and in the meantime he kept a low profile.

"But I don't live badly." He shrugged. "I have a Volga, a dacha, two children, two grandchildren, and a wonderful wife. I am a rich man."

He thought that more Russians would be like him if only two historical Russian figures hadn't been cut off before their own social-engineering plans had taken root. They turned out to be the heroes of the anti-Communists all over Siberia.

One, Peter the Great, was a predictable choice, but the other, Prime Minister Peter Stolypin, surprised me. Both had been autocratic and figured that Russians had to be dragged and sometimes even threatened into a more modern world. Zaitsev liked to think he came out of their mold.

"Our people are children who never of their own accord would decide to learn," complained Peter the Great in 1723, just two years before his death. He had created the Russian Navy, taken measures to bring the nobility into check, and reduced the power of the clergy. Most revolutionary, he had forced Russians to cut off their beards. He was, in short, a warrior against the traditionally dark Russian superstitions and backwardness. The fact that he flogged opponents, and was said at least once to have roasted them over an open fire and allowed their corpses to be displayed publicly, was, of course, all in the interest of reform.

Yet Peter the Great's failure to bring his country into the West remained a cautionary tale for the 1990s—he had laid down a veneer of Western civilization, but that had merely heightened the tensions and differences. The masses resented the small, privileged aristocracy that he was creating, just as the masses were beginning to resent the Zaitsevs that made up a new elite. Still, insisted Zaitsev, "Russian attitudes would be different if Peter the Great had lived longer."

His second hero, Peter Stolypin, had been the Russian prime minister from 1906 to 1911. He had introduced an agricultural reform that had been engineered to avoid a revolution by winning the peasantry to the side of the Romanovs. In 1911 a double agent for the Socialist Revolutionary Party and the secret police had shot Stolypin dead at the Kiev Opera. If Stolypin had lived longer, Zaitsev insisted, the Tsars might have avoided the Revolution and continued to advance toward democracy, as was the trend throughout Europe at the time. Instead, the time after 1917 was lost years to Russian development. They sapped whatever spirit remained in the Russians. "What was absolutely shit was all this business about the struggle of the classes," he said. "It killed our best people, our bravest minds."

I wondered what Haywood would have made of his paradise lost. His own life's course in many ways mirrored the system in which he had stored so much faith—from the grandest dreams to the deepest destitution.

After Haywood had retreated from Siberia, he had lived lonely, vodka-filled days in his small apartment at the Hotel Lux, in a part of Moscow reserved for foreigners. A *Chicago Tribune* reporter wrote that he "sat alone and disconsolate in a small room . . . contemplating the ruin of his ideals, the frailty of human friendship, and the burst bubble of his Utopian dream."

Haywood never learned Russian, and he had no intimate friends in Moscow. In late 1926 he had married a thirty-seven-year-old Russian office worker, but they communicated only in sign language. So he suffered a double exile—from his native land and from Soviet society.

Perhaps Haywood might have felt better if he had known that half of his ashes would be buried in the Kremlin Wall (the other half, at his request, was buried in Chicago's Waldheim Cemetery with the victims of the legendary Haymarket workers riot). Yet, by the end of his life, his attachment to the Leninist dream had waned.

Early in 1928, shortly before he died, he asked a reporter in his last interview if the newly elected American president, Calvin Coolidge, might finally pardon him and allow him to return home.

"Boy, do you think I can ever get back? Do you think that guy Coolidge would pass me through? These people here have treated me fine. I'm all right—but this isn't Idaho or Colorado."

Chapter 4:

THE LAST OF THE SHORS

> Where are the blossoms of those summers!
> —fallen, one by one: so all of my family departed,
> each in his turn, for the land of the spirits. I am on
> the hilltop, and must go down into the valley; and
> when Uncas follows in my footsteps, there will no
> longer be any of the blood of the sagamores, for
> my boy is the last of the Mohicans.
>
> —JAMES FENIMORE COOPER, *The Last of the Mohicans*

"You must be here with the gravel," said the aboriginal fisherman. He weaved uncertainly toward me in green rubber boots that were a couple of sizes too large. His stale breath reeked of vodka, and the whites of his foggy eyes were blood red. Viktor Sergeyev was no more than forty years old, but he looked near death.

He had never met a white man who wasn't some sort of Soviet official, so it was natural that he should mistake me for one. The white men sometimes came to make sure that the children of his native Shorish tribe attended Russian schools. Less often they came to help modernize the village by grading a road or installing an electrical line. They never came out of curiosity, as I had.

"We asked for the gravel two years ago, so you are late—but we are still happy to have it," he said, trying not to sound too demanding. He spoke of the deeply rutted road that had been impassable for the lack of gravel. And now there was a new problem, he said. The river was cutting into its soft bank each year and working its way toward his vegetable garden and home. He wanted two truckloads of gravel dumped on the beach to stop the riverbank's erosion.

Viktor Sergeyev scratched the side of his face. Three long black hairs grew from his chin, extending from stubble that might have been a week old. His Shorish people had inhabited Southwest Siberia throughout its recorded history. But he, like other Shors, spoke a Turkic language that had been the gift of one of its many invaders. His broad, rough nose and lips looked strikingly American Indian, but the cheekbones and eyes were more Oriental, similar to those of the Mongolians who lived a few hundred miles away, across the Altai Mountains, which decorated the southern horizon.

"I will show you where the gravel goes," he said, beginning to walk toward the village of a dozen log homes across the street.

I apologized that I was merely an American journalist who had come to learn about his people. At that, the fisherman let out a silent whistle. He took his time to give me a second look, from my Gore-Tex boots to my Banana Republic work shirt. Even in his boots he stood only five feet tall, and he squinted as he looked up into my face, behind which was the bright morning sun. He put out his hand to shake mine.

"That's even better," he said. He figured the Americans had more gravel than the Russians anyway. And he began to walk toward the village again. "Follow me."

I protested with some bemusement that I hadn't any gravel. I said, however, that I'd love to talk to him—to ask him some questions about his life. He looked at me as if I were crazy. No one had ever come to ask him questions. He quickly excused himself, saying he had work to do and walked away. What good was a foreigner who couldn't solve his problems?

Our Shorish guide and interpreter, Aleksandr Chudoyakov, felt he needed to say the obvious. "He was drunk. I'm sorry."

Chudoyakov was embarrassed. We had picked him up at the government offices of the nearest city to this Shorish village, Mezhdurechensk, where he worked behind a desk as a city bureaucrat. At age thirty-five, his skin was smooth, not weathered like that of the fisherman, and his hands had no calluses. He had survived his culture's decline by adopting the ways of the Russians. He had been born in the village, but he found it disheartening to visit his roots.

Still, he readily consented to act as our guide. In the age of Glasnost he had become one of the Shorish campaigners for more national rights— language schools, cultural revival, and the right to recover lost lands.

"My people's feelings have been hurt by what has happened to their nation," he said. "They are trying to hide the pain behind a bottle of vodka."

"How much do they drink?" I asked.

"The problem," he said, "is that they don't drink in liters—but in days. If they start to drink, they will continue until all the vodka is gone. They have lost their culture and their friendliness."

We had spent one more evening in Kemerovo, after my day retracing Bill Haywood's tracks, and then the next day driven 200 miles south to the 400-year-old village of Chuvashka. From there we would begin our 2,000-mile northwesterly voyage that would end only after we were far above the Arctic Circle in the northern tundra.

When we had arrived at Chuvashka our only reception committee had been the fisherman and two scraggly cows that nibbled at the weeds growing out from under the headquarters of the local council. We had sat and waited for the arrival of the village elder, who was to tell us his people's history.

A wooden sign confirmed in faded letters that this single-story, two-room wooden structure was our meeting place—the home of the Executive Committee of the Chuvashka Soviet. Smaller lettering said it doubled as the region's medical clinic. Another wooden sign, nailed above the door, said in peeling red letters: SOVIET POWER IS THE POWER OF THE PEOPLE.

But no people were to be seen, and the building was locked. It looked like an abandoned frontier outpost. Behind it were the foothills of the Altai Mountains, green hills scarred by a single long and deep-brown gash—a strip mine that the Russians had cut into former Shorish territory.

We had come to Chuvashka in search of Siberia's roots. We wanted to come as close to the source of the Tom River as possible. That brought us to one of its tributaries, the Mrassa, a narrow and shallow stream that ran out of the low Altai Mountains. The waters were cold and clean at Chuvashka before they ran north into larger channels that passed polluted cities, oil fields, and the land of Stalin's prison camps that lay ahead of us.

But most of all I wanted to meet the Shorish people. The Shors were what Siberia had been before Ivan the Terrible's conquerors reached the region in the late sixteenth century. The Shors, like the American Indian, honored nature and lived compatibly with it. They had worshiped the Forest God for putting berries on bushes and nuts on the trees for them to pick and eat. And they had prayed to the River God and he had rewarded them each year with a bountiful supply of fish. When the frozen Mrassa thawed after the long Siberian winter, the Shors would thank the River God for the miracle that the fish were still alive.

In the golden days of the Shors, the Shaman was the witch doctor, wise man, and local oracle. He presided over all festivals and spiritually safeguarded his people. I wanted to visit one in Shorish territory, but was told that only frauds still existed. Only a handful had survived scientific socialism and Stalin's repressions.

With the Shaman had died most of the high celebrations. The highest of them all, for the Shors and their cousin tribes to the north, was held in honor of the soul of the slaughtered bear (from whom the natives believe humans are descended). The festivities lasted for five days for the males and four days for the females, the difference for reasons no one could explain to me. The rituals included wrestling, dancing, and odd pageants, often led by men wearing birch masks. One of the more bizarre rituals involved tying huge wooden phalluses to their waists and then pummeling other participants in a dance whose meaning seemed to have been lost over the years. These rituals occurred within view of the bear's head, for the Shors could not allow the bear to be bored.

And then the tribe would eat the meat—apologizing to the bear with each gulp. "I am sorry to be eating you," they would say to their spiritual antecedent.

I had read that Siberian aborigines had started scheduling the bear festival for outside visitors. But when I asked if one would occur during our expedition, our organizers reported that the locals would arrange anything for the right amount of vodka. Having heard the Shors were dying of drink, I decided not to pay the price.

A few of the old practices remained. For instance, the Shors who still hunted during the winters continued to sleep in pairs by the fire, so that the feet of one rested in the armpits of the other. Most other traditions, however, have disappeared, such as the burial practice of wrapping infants in birch bark and then putting them in a tree—apparently so that God had readier access to their souls.

The first detailed reports about the Shors came from Russian missionaries in the mid-nineteenth century, who were surprised to find that the Shors were already accomplished blacksmiths, using large deposits of iron ore and coal in the region. They had long provided the enemies of the Cossacks, the Mongol and Turkic warriors of the seventeenth and eighteenth centuries, with breastplates, helmets, and munitions.

For this, the Cossacks conquered them. But they also gave them the name "Kuznetsk Tatars"—the Blacksmith Tatars. The richest industrial basin of Siberia was named for them as well, the Kuznetsk Basin (or the Kuzbass). It was the Shors who discovered many of Russia's richest coal, iron, and gold mines—which they in turn gave over to the Russians in good faith that they would share in the profits.

Those Shors who didn't smith, hunted. Each small group had its own territory, and no family crossed into another's taiga without the threat of a clan-court prosecution and a sentence of thrashing. They hunted squirrel, caught sable with nets, set traps for ermine and Siberian marten, and bagged wild birds and goats.

Their realm began with undulating green hills in the north and led south to the mountainous taiga, forest land with a rich mixture of fir, aspen, and cedar. They also inhabited the high-grass marshes that stretched along the narrow river valleys of the Mrassa and Kondoma, and a dozen smaller streams, all of which feed the Tom, which then flows to the Ob and finally empties into the Kara Sea of the Arctic Ocean.

Unlike their cousins to the north—the reindeer nomads, whom we would also visit—each clan had defined territories that it considered its own. During most of their many centuries in the region, they moved only a few kilometers this way or that along the rivers, either after an important member of the family had died or the land stopped providing fur, fish, or berries.

The Shors, however, were only one piece of a complex mosaic that had always made Siberia difficult to rule. Siberia was made up of thirty-six different nationality groups, drawn together from hundreds of distinct clans. They were thought to have numbered more than 1.5 million at the beginning of the century, but by 1990 only 500,000 remained. The Shors themselves had declined from 28,000 in 1940 to 12,000 by the time of my visit, dying out from disease and drink—and from Shorish women's growing preference for marriage with Russian men.

After a half-hour's wait, the village elder arrived at Chuvashka's headquarters. He walked toward us uncertainly from his village home across the road, balancing his meager frame on a knotted cane. His blue-gray, pin-striped suit hung loosely over his bony frame. It was the only suit he owned, reserved for the monthly Communist Party meetings.

Fyodor Aponkin opened the door and guided us into a large office and then sat quietly behind its desk. He took off his straw hat and smiled. His small mouth then receded again into its natural pucker. His Oriental eyes were deep brown and filmy, like those of one of the aging roe deer that migrate to the Shorish southern regions during the long and snowy winters.

He didn't answer my first question, nor my second, and I wondered if I had somehow offended him—he only looked at me and our Shorish interpreter with his sad eyes. Through trial and error, we discovered he was hard of hearing, so our interpreter shouted: *"Tell us about your life!"*

"I've been living here since the day I was born," he said, looking over his shoulder and out the window toward the village. "I was born in 1914. I'm an aboriginal. My father, my grandfather, and I guess his father lived here as well. We've had a great many changes during my life. The Revolution was a positive thing for the Shorish people—at the beginning."

I could see that the old man was confused. For years he had known the Politically Correct thing to say to outsiders—who were either Soviet officials or their emissaries. And he had performed this role well, having survived when many of his people hadn't by becoming a Marxist and Party member.

Now he seemed torn between the slogans he had repeated throughout most of his life and the truths of what had happened to his people under Soviet rule. He recalled the dozen years during which Lenin had given his people their own semiautonomous region. Formed in 1925, it had been known as the Mountain Shor National *Rayon*. It had covered a land area greater than the size of Belgium, although more than 90 percent of it was mountainous taiga. Even in 1931, the first year that the railway made it to the region, the Shors still made up 38.8 percent of its population. The only partially independent rule nonetheless gave the people the feeling they were leading themselves.

But the rapid development that followed—and the shipping of tens of thousands of exiles, farmers, and workers to Siberia—reduced the Shors to just 13 percent of the local population by 1939. By 1990 twelve thousand Shors made up less than a fraction of one percent of the Kuzbass population.

Fyodor Aponkin remembered the years of his childhood—those immediately after the Revolution—as a time of optimism for his people. The Shors made their own clothing and constructed surprisingly warm boots out of the local reeds. He remembered playing games, which sounded similar to baseball, with a ball made out of wool from cow's hair.

Aponkin said his people's decline actually began in 1929, when the Russians forced the Shorish hunters and fisherman, and those who lived from berry-and-nut gathering, to work on collective farms. "The Shors no longer had any time to be what they were raised to be."

The Soviets put shovels into Shorish hands that had never tilled soil, and they put a people on shift work whose only rhythms had to do with the seasons and the rising and setting sun. Even the names of their months had reflected their work. May was the month of tilling the land and collecting adder's tongue (an edible fern). September was the month for hunting hoofed animals.

Opting out of the collectives was impossible. Shors who didn't join couldn't have property, animals, or buy goods from State stores (and there weren't any others). "No one was killed, but everyone was forced," said Fyodor Aponkin with a frown. He remembered how odd it was to visit his hunter father on a farm. During most of the year Fyodor Aponkin lived away from his family and studied at a Russian school.

"But the area didn't have enough sunshine on it and lacked sufficient fertile earth for the farms, so they changed the Shors' jobs," he said. "They put us into industrial cooperatives that made many small products. We made special oil from the sap of trees. We also made big rafts during the Great Patriotic War."

Stalin abolished the Shors' *Rayon* in 1939 and made the region a full part of Russia. But before he did so, he destroyed whatever small threat of resistance might have remained by arresting Shorish leaders and sending them to his proliferating prison camps.

"I have to be truthful," said Fyodor Aponkin. "During 1936 to 1938 Stalin's men took away very many leaders of our Shorish nation. In this village there were 200 people at the time of Stalin. He arrested maybe a fourth of them, and they didn't even know why. He called them nationalists, but actually there was no nationalism at the time. It was just invented. After that, our culture fell. We lost our leaders. The Shors became a depressed nation. We had no rights. The Russians called us names. When we spoke our language, they would say, 'Stop barking like dogs.' "

I asked whether he had been among those arrested in the Stalin period, when he was in his early twenties. "They collected us in groups and took us," he said. "For twelve days I was in custody myself. But they couldn't find anything on me. They let me go."

Yet everyone in town knew that they had very little on anyone. Fyodor Aponkin survived and thrived partly because he was willing to accept totally the Soviet religion—Communism. Even while he recounted to me the cruelties and humiliations inflicted on his people by the system, he defended the scientific socialism that had supplanted the nature worship of his ancestors.

He didn't know the names of his gods or the traditions of worship anymore—and he didn't see the point in studying them. "I don't believe in God or the Devil," he said. "I believe in a scientific approach to life. The Party committed lots of crimes and faults. I recognize that and we own up to it. But I still believe—I still believe in Communism."

And what did he think of the Russians? Were they evil? Did they destroy his people?

The old man looked confused as he struggled to decide the right approach. "We can't deny that the Russians have greatly influenced our lives."

He paused again, and then decided on the safe way out. "They positively influenced the people's lives in many respects by making us more cultured and bringing us more knowledge and more education."

I felt sorry for Fyodor Aponkin, who seemed to have sold his soul to a system and ideology that had failed. Now, at seventy-seven, all he had left was a native culture that was largely destroyed and which he no longer understood.

Fyodor Aponkin slowly led me across the street and down the rutted, muddy road—that was so in need of gravel—to his home. In a previous century, having the best lodgings in the village meant you were the best hunter or blacksmith. But Fyodor Apokin had been the best Communist, and he furnished his log home with bookcases filled with neatly printed— and mostly unread—volumes. Oriental rugs lay on the floor and hung as tapestries from the walls.

He pulled on an old jacket with a fruit salad of medals hanging from its chest. He had shrunk so much that it almost fell from his shoulders. He said he had become a Communist Party member during the war, in 1943. That was also the year he had been seriously injured on the front line at Smolensk, where Soviet troops had forced back Hitler's Germans from the gates of Moscow. "I was a platoon leader working the heavy artillery," he said. "I was wounded four times and finally hospitalized through the end of the war with a shrapnel piece lodged in my head."

The old man proudly introduced his son, Leonid, a fifty-two-year-old construction engineer. Leonid had been trained at an elite academy at Tomsk, the famous university city up the river, and he had made it in the Russians' world as a submanager on a construction site. He wore large round glasses with tinted plastic frames, and jeans—small emblems of urbanity in Siberia. He'd become a city dweller, and he could barely speak his Shorish language. But he also seldom chose to speak Russian, having learned that the safest way through life was silence. His quiet attentiveness gave him an intellectual and thoughtful bearing.

He said he had come back to the village only a week before I had arrived, owing to worries that his aging parents might not make it through the winter ahead without his help. "I worry that they can't any longer carry their own coal and tend to the vegetable garden," he said. "So I'll stay here—maybe for many months. Maybe I will settle here."

He recalled his youth, when many young couples and children were in the village. Now it was inhabited almost totally by the elderly. He remembered how the children would dash excitedly to the banks of the Mrassa to greet the special steamship that gave them rides. But now no children played in the streets, and no newlyweds built new log homes. And the river had fallen with Shor society.

The cause, said Leonid, was the Russian lumberjacks, who cut down the trees along the Mrassa's banks. They used the river to ship their trees downstream, but many of the trees sank to the bottom. The submerged trunks destroyed the breeding ground for the fish, and their sap poisoned the water, said Leonid.

What reduced the water level most, however, was the removal of the ground cover that held the moisture in the soil and slowly released it into the river. That caused the runoff water to come in a flood during the spring, but the river was low and impassable by late summer. "Now you can only take a canoe down the river," said Leonid. "It was once known as Fish River, but now there are practically no fish at all."

Yet Leonid said his own children, who were in their twenties, were considering moving to the village because there was so little food left in the city. But they didn't speak the Shor language at all, he said, and they knew nothing about the culture. Still, the simple fact that they were Shors had hurt them in the Russian world. Russians thought all the people of his race were drunken and lazy.

There was reason for the bad reputation, he said with a frown. His people weren't genetically equipped for the industrial world. "In the forest, a Shor wants to work like a horse from morning to evening because that is where he is from," he said. "But the Shors don't do as well in the

Russian schools because the language doesn't fit their genetic makeup. As well as they may learn it, it won't ever be natural for them to speak it or think in the language. There are borders the Shor just can't cross. Living in a culture that isn't your own is why we have drunkards and people who don't work at all. So we are a confused people. My blood is that of a hunter and fisherman, but my character was shaped by Soviet power."

As he spoke, I remembered the area around the Greyhound bus station in Salt Lake City, where I had grown up. Drunken Indians had often loitered with their bottles of cheap wine wrapped in paper bags. As small children, we had laughed at them. We had put our hands to our mouths and made the war whoop as we rode by in our parents' cars. They had been too beaten to show anger, and I had been too young to understand what had happened to their culture.

I asked Leonid what he knew about the American Indians. Did he feel at all related to them? Curiously, he said that he envied the Indians their reservations. He believed that the Indians had organized themselves better politically than the Shors—he had even read about a tribe in Canada that had gained a percentage of the profits from oil that had been found on its land. That was what the Shors now wanted from the coal miners that were on their territory, he said.

He was surprised when I told him that most Indians considered the reservations to have been the White Man's way of moving them to the side. The reservations had been the Indians' final defeat, I said. Leonid said their life was still far better than the life of the landless Shors, from whom the Russians had taken everything and given only Marx and Lenin.

He wanted to know more about how the American Indians lived, how they were educated, and how they organized themselves administratively. He was disappointed—and I was embarrassed—that I didn't have the answers. I had paid as little attention to the Indians as the Russians had to the Shors. "We really feel connected to these people," he said. "Like your Indians, we are out of nature and we care about nature. As nature has died, so have our people." He said they were like animals who had been taken from their natural habitat. How could such animals survive?

Leonid Aponkin said he had grown closer to the Indians through reading the books of Fenimore Cooper, most of which had been translated into Russian. Moscow had allowed such books to be translated because they taught Soviet children how imperialist Western society had abused its native peoples. But Leonid had seen a moral that was closer to home.

"The Last of the Mohicans influenced me greatly," he said. "I read it when I was young and I have reread it recently. I pitied the Indians their bloody struggles. Even as a child I thought I was reading about our people when I read Fenimore Cooper. Like the Mohicans, we too are on the border of extinction. Our ethnic group will disappear if we don't take measures now. It is almost too late already, and we soon could be lost to the world as a people."

We walked down the rutted road another time, preparing to leave the village, when the drunken fisherman who had greeted us upon our arrival came out onto the steps of his cottage and insisted we come inside. He had decided that he wanted to answer my questions.

Our urbane guide, Aleksandr Chudoyakov, tried to steer us away from the man—this wasn't the impression of his people he wanted to leave. It also wasn't the way he wanted to spend his limited time with us. But I insisted we at least look inside.

The fisherman's home was on the bad side of a small neighborhood—the logs didn't fit well together, the windows were filmy, and the steps leading to the door were mud-covered and strewn with dirty boots. The home had been built in 1925, and no one had yet taken the trouble to reinforce the mud that held it together with a more lasting cement.

Viktor Sergeyev was nonetheless proud to invite us in. While we stood in the kitchen, his wife and daughter, deriding the man of the house as drunk and crazy, screamed their complaints from the living room—the only other room in the house. The living room was spacious, but had little furniture except for mattresses that doubled as day sofas. The centerpiece was a large black-and-white television. The fisherman said the TV rarely worked because the electrical current, which had been brought to the village in the 1960s, usually wasn't sufficiently powerful to run it.

In deference to his wife we remained in the kitchen, which smelled of potatoes. He apologized that he was a little tipsy. He was still drunk from a wedding that his wife had organized for a niece at his home two days earlier. But he hadn't any vodka left to offer us—he had finished the last drops that morning. But, he said, reaching into a bucketful of yellow orbs, he did have plenty of onions.

He turned over another bucket to use as a stool, and I sat on a stepladder. Potatoes boiled on the coal-fired cast-iron stove which served as the oven and, in the winter, as the room heater. The family spent much of the winter in the kitchen because it was so much warmer.

"I've got potatoes. I've got cucumbers. I've got bread," he said. "What more do I need? They say Siberia is a hard place, but I have everything. Only the winter is a problem, but that's all right as long as we have enough coal to take and put in the fireplace."

He flipped open one of the hot plates atop the stove and then clanked it closed. "That is how we live in Siberia. If you've got potatoes, cucumbers, bread, and lots of coal for the fireplace, then you live well. So you see, you don't need to feel sorry for us."

* * *

If not for Glasnost and Gorbachev, the Shors might have died a quiet death. Instead they began to organize themselves when nationalistic furor overtook most of the Soviet republics. In March 1991 they joined six other nationalities that lived in the region to draw up a list of demands. Some of the delegates were old men who remembered the past, but most were young angry Shors of Aleksandr Chudoyakov's generation.

Their meetings were held in Russian—few of the young Shors could still speak their language. But their actions produced results—the University of Novokuznetsk opened a Shorish faculty. Its aim was to produce people who could speak the language so they could teach others. In 1991 the Shors had also published children's textbooks, through the fourth-grade level, and a rough dictionary—their first books since they had all been destroyed in 1936. "I've never studied the Shorish language myself," said Chudoyakov.

He said the books had abandoned the Shors' pre-war Latin lettering, however, instead using the Cyrillic that had become more familiar to young Shors. "We thought about using the Latin letters," said Chudoyakov, "but that would only make the learning doubly difficult for the Shors."

Then, in June 1991, the Shors and the other nationalities of the region had organized their first *"Pyram"* festival, a traditional gathering of villages that had given the people a sense of solidarity until the days of Stalin. That had brought even more activists to the national revival movement.

Aleksandr Chudoyakov, whose name means "Miraculous Jacob," was among the leaders. However, he never volunteered that fact, and he began to speak of his role only at the end of the day, as we drove back to Mezhdurechensk, the coal-mining city built on formerly Shorish land. He was disarmingly shy and quiet after years of learning that silence was the safest approach in Russian society.

I asked him why there had been no resistance, no Little Big Horn.

"The Shors at first greeted the Russians and thought they would bring them good," he said. The Russians had come with their advanced notions of making tens of thousands of people warm with the black rock in the ground. The Shors had shown the Russians where the coal, the ore, and the gold was. Many of the biggest iron mines are still named for the Shors who discovered them and then turned them over to the State without even a request for payment. They would get their fair share, they were sure. After all, this was Communism.

"Since then," said Chudoyakov, "the villages have been dying of drink. Shors were always known to be particularly kind. But we've lost our friendliness. Even in the villages, the Shors must now lock their doors. People don't trust each other anymore. We are losing our nation."

Chudoyakov and other young Shors had formed a new company, called Golden Shoria, whose aim was to win back the national soul—and make some profits. It had applied for exclusive land-rights use in vast former Shorish areas for hunting, fishing, and nut-and-berry picking. Its biggest profit-maker would be furs—sable, squirrel, and fox. It was a first step to gaining the sorts of rights American Indians possessed on their reservations. They would use the profits to help build schools and promote Shorish culture.

"The Shors have had so much taken away from them for so long—they now want their own hunting land—a sort of reservation where no one else can come," he said. The problem, Chudoyakov found, was locating Shors who wanted to lead the life of hunters and fishermen. "The problem is that the Shor doesn't know his own traditions, but there is a rebirth of national interests everywhere, and we are hoping that will help us, too. And hunting is in our blood, so it will come back if it is given the chance."

Other traditions, most of which could be found only in textbooks, would be more difficult to restore. Chudoyakov feared that the days of the Shaman and nature worship were gone. Chudoyakov admitted to being an atheist. "Maybe I am missing something," he said.

Yet the Shor council was thinking big. It had demanded that Russia return to it autonomy over the Mountain Shor *Rayon* that had belonged to it until 1939. That region had produced more than a quarter of Russia's coal output. Chudoyakov agreed that the demand probably reached too far—but it was a time in the former Soviet Union when each national group had to try for as much as it could get, to regain national confidence.

The Shors would settle for a percentage of the profits from the coal mines that were on its former territory, he said. That included some of the richest shafts in the country, including the largest mine in Russia— the Ratspatskaya. The Shorish council had already sent a proposal to the Russian government, offering it 27 percent of the profits against the Shors' 5 percent.

"The mine would work just as it did before," he said, "but with a share of the profits we could make some changes in our way of life."

Boris Yeltsin never responded to the powerless Shors. And the coal-mine companies were preoccupied with trying to find Western partners. They laughed the Shors out of their offices.

"We aren't surprised by the negative response," said Chudoyakov. "That is the way it is now. But we still have villages with no electricity. And there are no roads to reach many of them. How long can they go on treating us as if we were a people without worth?"

Chapter 5:

ASBESTOS JUNGLE

We should have killed that rat.

—ANATOLY MALIKHIN, *mine safety director*

My first mistake was telling our driver that we were in a hurry. I was late for an appointment to go underground with the morning shift of Russia's largest coal mine in Mezhdurechensk, a small coal-miners' city built on the former hunting grounds of the Shorish people I had visited the previous day.

In the calmest of times our chauffeur was given to rubber-burning starts and sudden stops. He was unfamiliar with the sensitive controls of our dark-blue Nissan van, rented from a local company, after years of imprisonment in sturdy but unresponsive Soviet cars. But that only encouraged him to experiment. For his enthusiasm, I had tagged him Nikita Lauda.

Given additional incentive that morning, Nikita careened around corners, flew over train tracks, and swerved past potholes. Mezhdurechensk's roads had an unrepaired character akin to the landscape around the city, which was scarred with gaping open-pit mines. When Nikita spotted a female road worker shoveling asphalt onto the road ahead of us, he screeched to a halt just inches from her rear end. She raised her shovel to bash in his already cracked window, but Nikita hit the gas and swerved past her toward our goal.

I screamed as he ran a final red light to turn left onto the straightaway to the mine. But I was too late. Nikita slammed on the brakes, locked the wheels, and slid into a small green Zaporozhets, a car so small and powerless that the Siberians call it "the soap dish."

Nikita jumped out of the van and onto the road to confront the other driver, a coal miner en route to the same morning shift we were to join. Our driver argued more enthusiastically than convincingly that both sides were at fault.

"Three hundred rubles and you are rid of me," countered the other driver.

Nikita protested that repairs could cost no more than fifty rubles for the fender-bender.

The coal miner said that such prices were available only at State repair shops, but they wouldn't finish the job "in my lifetime." So he'd hire a mechanic to do the work "unofficially"—and that would cost 300 rubles.

I was quickly learning how difficult it was to attach a price to anything in the Soviet Union. The average monthly salary could buy only ten packs of cigarettes. A bottle of vodka cost more than the monthly rent for an average apartment. An airline ticket from Moscow to Kemerovo cost less than a third of the price of the taxi ride to the airport. When I was in Siberia, $5,000 could buy a three-story downtown building—although you could never know for certain that the sale was legal.

To negotiate any price was a trick in a place where no one knew the value of things. But I needed a quick compromise, so I forked over the 300 rubles. Our driver was livid that I had paid too much. The victim was jubilant. I was only seven dollars poorer and had arrived on time at the Ratspatskaya mine.

After I arrived at the mine, I was escorted with Dundee to the newly carpeted and tile-walled changing room, where I slipped on the black-canvas work clothes, soiled white hard hat (with its lamp), and the black rubber boots that were a size too large even for my size 11 feet. What passed for socks were soft, large cloths that I wrapped with difficulty around my feet. The trick was to remove folds and lumps that could cause discomfort; I would pay for my failure to do that on the long trek to the coal face.

A cool wind carried the bitter, wet taste of coal dust up the blue shaft of the Ratspatskaya mine's fourth block as I slogged through the dark cavern with the morning shift over black puddles and decaying wooden rail ties, left over from a time when coal was removed by wagons instead of conveyer belts that were pulled up the slope by steel cables. The coal face was more than a mile away and more than 200 yards underground.

The Ratspatskaya mine was by far the most productive in the former Soviet Union, yielding some 7 million tons of coal a year. It was the black jewel of the Kuznetsk Basin, whose 15-million-ton output was 40 percent of the annual Soviet production. But the Kuzbass also produced 25 percent of the country's steel and some 10 percent of its chemicals.

A peasant named Volkov first found coal in the Kuznetsk Basin in 1721, and a local legend has it that he at first mistook it for black fertile earth known as *chernozem*. Volkov quickly realized the value of his discovery, however, and he is enough of a local hero to have a square named for him in Kemerovo, where a statue in his likeness stands hugging a large piece of coal. (This pose has given rise to such amusement that the local unemployed joke that they have finally found a job—holding the chunk of coal because Volkov wants to go on leave.)

It wasn't until the Trans-Siberian Railway was completed in 1905 that Tsar Nikolai II began development in earnest. He sent 2 million settlers to Siberia partly to help him regain control of a region that had begun to revolt shortly after his unexpected defeat at the hands of the Japanese (it is a war that many historians say began the downfall of Tsarism). This single-track line, running for nearly 5,000 miles, changed the face of Siberia. Despite the return of nearly half of the original settlers owing to the harsh conditions, Siberia by 1910 had become self-sufficient and a net exporter of goods.

But it was Soviet Communism that turned the Kuzbass into a region so industrialized that it became known as "Siberia's forge." It was once a wilderness region of only scattered population over an area of 95,500 square miles (about the size of Indiana or the three Baltic States taken together). By 1990 it had 3.2 million people and produced 300 times more than before the building of the railroad. Its reserves—easy to retrieve in some of the thickest veins on earth—could remain at the current output levels for half a century or more.

It was the Kuzbass miners who led the decisive strikes of 1989 and 1990, which had begun over a shortage of soap and escalated to demands for Mikhail Gorbachev's resignation. The miners hadn't gained all they sought, but the strikes had fed their pride and convinced them of their political strength. The miners' unrest had begun in Mezhdurechensk and then burned down the Tom River like a spark on a fuse, igniting worker unrest downstream in Novokuznetsk, Prokopyevsk, Belova, Leninsk, and Kemerovo.

"The workers were angry that one of the richest regions on earth produced one of its poorest peoples," said one of our two guides, Igor Lomakin, the deputy chief engineer. Lomakin, a small bear of a man, had the thick arms and muscular chest produced by twenty years underground. "So they took matters into their own hands."

By the time I reached the Kuzbass, those heady days were over. The system the workers opposed was collapsing, but Communism's fallout remained—resignation, low living standards, uncertain futures, polluted water and air—and, at the Ratspatskaya mine, unsafe conditions.

Our second guide, Anatoly Malikhin, said his primary concern as safety chief was Ratspatskaya's gas levels, which were so high that a complex ventilation system had been introduced to keep the 5,300 workers on the job. The faint sound of the system sucking in highly explosive air, and coal harvesters, operating in the distance, was all I heard other than my own footsteps in puddles as I walked down the damp, dark cavern. My black boots were too loose and my feet hurt. The cloth had already bunched up at my toes.

My hard hat crashed against a wooden beam of the low ceiling, and the light on it switched off. I fumbled to turn it back on just in time to spotlight a very fat rat running, or rather loping, across the rail tie by my too-large boot.

"We should have killed that rat," said Malikhin, a likable man who had been popularly elected by the men after their strikes to look after their safety. "It's not that the rats are dangerous. But they are considered a bad omen. Bad luck." They were the black cats of the mine, I thought, worrying about the consequences of one crossing my path.

Malikhin insisted that Ratspatskaya, one of the youngest mines, was also one of its safest. It had averaged only 3.5 deaths and twenty serious injuries per year—lost legs and such—since it had opened in 1973. The only major accident had come in 1981, when workers anxious to exceed the plan had put their coats over the gas-sensing equipment to silence alarms that required them to stop work and leave the shaft. "They didn't want to lose their bonuses," said Malikhin. "But what they got was a big explosion and twenty died."

So much for central planning.

White moss seemed to be growing from the mine's walls, ceiling, and floors. Malikhin said it was a highly effective fire retardant. He pointed to the same substance, in powder form, hanging in small cloth bags from rafters at intervals of about 300 meters. Should an explosion occur, the rushing air would burst open the bags, which would act as extinguishers.

"Whoosh!" said Malikhin.

So what did the wonder powder consist of? I asked, my helmet crashing against another beam, my boots almost falling off.

"Sand, concrete, and asbestos," he responded. "But it is asbestos that is the key."

I looked down the shaft. Asbestos for as far as the eye could see.

Malikhin was puzzled when I asked him whether it wasn't dangerous to miners to expose them to so much asbestos. He hadn't known about its cancerous side effects.

"Thank you for this information," he said. "The big danger for management is when workers learn how unsafe their mines are. If they knew international standards, they would never go down into the mines."

What Russian miners did not know about, he said, was black lung disease, which they suffered far more of than their Western counterparts because of recovery methods that didn't do enough to reduce the dust in the air. "In the U.S. you have ten milligrams per square meter compared to 130 milligrams here. When a Russian miner dies, his lungs are the color of coal."

After a thirty-minute walk down Shaft Four, we arrived at a dead end where the mine had collapsed only a few hours earlier. No one had been hurt, but Igor Lomakin apologized that we couldn't go forward until miners reopened the tunnel through to the coal conveyer that we had planned to ride out. My helmet again hit a beam, a wet piece of coal fell and I feared the tunnel ceiling would collapse on me.

Igor Lomakin took a gas reading. It showed the shaft to be far above the safe limit. He frowned. There was sufficient methane to blow us all up with even the slightest spark.

I held my breath and froze, fearing even the smallest movement might set off a blast.

But the deputy engineer only laughed. He was only joking, he chuckled. He had taken the gas measurement at the spot of a small leak from the huge rubber ventilating pipe near the ground that was sucking the methane out at a rate of 130 cubic centimeters a minute. The rest of the long tunnel was safe, he said. He took another reading to prove it to me.

Lomakin then pointed toward a small opening in the black landslide near the ground that had been dug out, just large enough for a human body, and he directed me and Dundee to crawl through it on our hands and knees. I emerged on the other side, covered by a layer of black dust that had worked its way up my nostrils and into my lungs.

Dundee came up cursing his chain-smoking, the mine, me, and the job as my interpreter that he had accepted, he said, "thinking we were off on a nice fishing trip down the river."

I was coughing and sweating when I saw a miner whose features could only be described as black. He was lifting a heavy steel pillar into place that would expand hydraulically and create a new support for the shaft. The Ratspatskaya was rich because the veins were thick, he said, but that also made the shafts more unstable than they were in thinner, less abundant deposits.

I wanted to ask the miner some questions, but Dundee protested. "Jesus, don't you ever stop? I can't even breathe." He then, as usual, played along.

At age thirty, Tony Buragin was a second-generation miner. His father had been sent into the mines as a prisoner. It was the high salary that had convinced Buragin to follow in his father's footsteps. His father had died young, however, and he figured that he would as well. "Age thirty is middle aged for a miner," he said. "Not many live much past their retirement age. If they are lucky enough to live until they are pensioned, they live a few more days and then they die."

The average age of the miners was forty-eight; their retirement age was fifty. The family of a miner who died on the job got his salary until his last son or daughter turned eighteen. But the death benefit was small at the time—only 1,000 rubles—not even enough to pay for a funeral. If the miner died during the winter, Buragin complained, the money wasn't even enough to hire a team to shovel through the frozen earth to dig a grave. The miners were fighting for a new law that would give families ten months' salary at the time of death. "But for now, miners live and die like dogs," he said.

The subject of death seemed a bit morbid so far underground, so near a partial mine collapse, so I asked about other benefits.

The miners' strikes had resulted in a tripling of salaries and of vacation time—from twenty-one to sixty-five days annually. The negotiators had written in provisions from Norwegian union agreements. Tony Buragin didn't know what he'd do with all the time ("Maybe I'll visit America if you invite me"), and he figured that it would be better to work a bit more and earn some more of the hard-currency goods that had been introduced as workers' bonuses.

The Ratspatskaya mine had struck a deal with a Japanese trading company, under which it had traded 50,000 tons of coal for two million dollars' worth of goods, primarily intended for the workers—refrigerators, TV sets, vacuum cleaners, VCR players, and washing machines. Under a complex scheme the workers received coupons that allowed them to buy the goods at token ruble prices from a special mine shop. If they so chose, they could sell them at a profit that sometimes exceeded their annual salary.

For instance, said Mr. Buragin, leaning against his pillar, a worker who bought a refrigerator for 400 rubles could resell it on the black market for 6,000 rubles (three times the top miner's salary at the time). A video system that cost 700 rubles fetched 20,000. And while the ruble in each paycheck was worth less with each day, the goods only increased in value. The deal with the Japanese had kept the Ratspatskaya miners relatively well off while the rest of society grew poorer.

The coupon system had been engineered to benefit the hardest workers and most productive miners. But the real winners had been the miners who had quit their jobs to act as the brokers who resold the goods for their fellow workers. "It isn't the best miners who are profiting," complained Lomakin. "It is the speculators."

After we walked a few hundred more yards, we reached the conveyor belt that was transporting coal out of the mine. It moved leisurely in the gaseous mine, at half its top speed, to avoid setting off an explosion with its heat or sparks. Lomakin stopped the belt so I could climb aboard, atop the thin layer of coal. When he restarted it, the small chunks of coal, the conveyor, and the steel rollers underneath provided a rough but oddly sensual massage. The air was cold against my sweaty face. Within minutes I was at the top of the shaft, taking the exit used by the miners every day.

Igor Lomakin was exultant at my enthusiasm as I breathed the fresh air outside. I squinted into the sun. I felt like a child with a new adventure under his belt. Dundee looked near death, not nearly as fit as his Australian namesake.

"You really feel like a man at the end of a day in the mine," said Lomakin. And I did. ("Jesus Christ," sneered Dundee.) Lomakin noted proudly, however, that his daughter was a computer programmer and his fifteen-year-old son planned to work as an excavator at one of the nearby open-pit mines.

"Cleaner work," said Lomakin. "The children know better than their father."

Our final stop was the miners' sauna. Once inside, I understood why the shortage of soap had helped start the miners' strike. The first wash used up half of the small, coarse bar, and still it had removed only the first layer of the thick black grime. The next layer, like a stubborn enamel, would be stripped by the heat of the scalding sauna, set several degrees higher than any I had ever experienced. I panted and my lungs burned with each tiny breath. Igor inhaled deeply. He used his thick arms, bulging with muscles from years underground, to whip me with a birch branch dipped in cold water.

He was merely warming up to his sales pitch.

Did I like the mine? he asked. (Whip, whip)

I admitted that I did. (Whip, whip)

Well, a big portion of the mine, he said, was for sale. The Ratspatskaya mine wanted to form a joint venture—using one-seventh of its total production—with a Western company. I, as the reporter for *The Wall Street Journal,* would be their conduit of the offer to the capitalist world.

He stuck the birch bough back into the cold water and slapped me a few more times, and then he whipped himself, rightly considering me not fit for the job. The new director of the mine, he said, would fill me in on the details after we showered and dried off.

The mine's new director, Gennady Poleshuk, could have passed for a California used-car salesman with his handsome gray hair, aging surfer's (actually coal miner's) body, and his canary-yellow, short-sleeved shirt.

He looked too small and shy for his expansive office, which he had moved into two weeks earlier after workers had elected him as their boss. A handful of men sat at a long table that could hold twenty. The wildly popular director had won his men's backing by leading their strike earlier that year, but now he would hold his job only if he made profits. And he needed the West to do that.

"I want you to make an advertisement in your newspaper," he said.

"You must say that this is a deal that the Western investor can't refuse. It will bring him profits far greater than he can have with your stock market—and the risk will be limited by local government guarantees on investment."

The buyer wouldn't even need to bring cash, he said. For just 2.5 million dollars' worth of mining equipment, he'd form a joint venture with any Western company. And the coal was some of the cleanest in the world, with only traces of sulfur. "Pure anthracite," said Poleshuk, picking up a piece on his desk that acted as a paperweight.

I recalled for him my time with the Shorish natives, who claimed that his mine was on their territory. I asked him whether he thought they had legitimate rights. Would he at least give them the 5-percent share of the profits that they sought?

He scoffed at the idea. The Shors couldn't help his business and they hadn't the power to enforce their demands—they were just 6,000 in all of the region, just 700 more than his total number of miners. "And they are all drunks," he said. Let the Shors have their language schools and museum, Poleshuk said. The partners he wanted were my newspaper's readers.

He said the joint venture had clearance from the provincial government, which was creating "a special economic zone" to sell all the production of its joint venture overseas. And the partner could take home his profits in dollars. The Western partner would get 30 percent of a company whose first year's profits would ensure a 300-percent return on investment.

Poleshuk thumped the table with the flat of his hand as if it were the hood of the perfect automobile. "Isn't that a good result? Where else can you match that?"

The problem, he conceded, was that the rest of the mine was still run according to old rules impervious to the bottom line. The mine could sell coal abroad for fifty dollars a ton, but the State continued to pay the equivalent of less than a dollar. And more than 70 percent of his coal was still sold to the State. Under any conditions, however, he said the deal for the West was a good one for a mine that he reckoned was worth 1.5 billion dollars.

And in rubles?

"It's difficult to make a calculation," he said. "So we don't anymore. We only talk in dollars."

In a world where central planning had broken down and the Russian government itself was in chaos, the dollar and Western partners had become the mine's only hope. Old contracts and obligations were void, and Russian partners could have the coal only in barter for goods that Poleshuk needed. He had recently traded 10,000 tons of coal for 400 tons of rails and rolled steel with a steel plant in Magnitogorsk. "We're back to the Middle Ages," he said.

Despite all the changes, a charcoal drawing of Lenin still kept watch over the mine director. In every office, the spot on the wall reserved for the Soviet Holy Father was known as "Lenin's place." Gennady Poleshuk acted embarrassed that I had noticed Lenin was still there. "I don't want to change things all at once, and I've only been in my job two weeks," he said.

Igor Lomakin, his face a healthy red from the sauna, glanced over his shoulder. "Let him hang," he said. "When we believe in God, we will hang him in Lenin's place. But this is a time for hesitating in one's beliefs."

I couldn't find the hero of the Kuzbass strikes at his mine, the oldest in the region and across town from Ratspatskaya. He didn't work there anymore, so I spent an entire evening trying to find his home among tens of carbon-copy gray apartment blocks for miners in Mezhdurechensk.

Even though it was almost midnight and I had come unannounced, Kokorin was delighted to invite me into his place of hibernation—a dingy fourth-floor apartment up a dark stairwell that he negotiated with the ease of a miner accustomed to black tunnels. I stumbled behind him, caught up on the cracked and uneven stairs. As uniform as all the four- and five-story prefab housing was in the Soviet Union, stairs rarely ended flush with their landings. Builders always seemed to add the steps as an afterthought, as if it hadn't occurred to them that humans would need to climb to the apartments.

Valery Kokorin was forty-six. He had a heavy chest, thick fingers, and a baritone's booming voice. Although he stood six feet tall, his manner made him appear much larger. Kokorin sat back on a wooden chair that he had pulled into the living room. His barefoot wife, in an ample, pink nylon nightgown, sat in the kitchen where she could listen in. She might just as well have gone to the apartment downstairs—Kokorin held court in a voice loud enough to rattle windowpanes.

It had been Kokorin's commanding presence in the mine that had rallied workers behind him in December 1988. They had turned to his angry courage as soap disappeared from the shower rooms and the ration of food put into their lunch pails grew gradually leaner. He'd collected 800 signatures on a letter that he had sent to Moscow's Central Committee of Unions; it had made some simple demands: more soap, an assured portion of meat each day, more food for sale in the mine stores (because miners didn't have time to queue in town), and payment, called *kopitniye,* or "hoof money," for the time it took miners to walk from the changing rooms to the work site.

The authorities hadn't responded. Some miners accused Kokorin of never having sent the letter. So he gathered more signatures for a second petition in the spring of 1989. He carried it to Moscow himself, threatening a strike if the workers' demands weren't satisfied. No one of any importance would meet with him. No one believed his threat.

So he returned to Mezhdurechensk and started to plan a work stoppage. The mine's Party secretary and director saw Kokorin couldn't be ignored, so they threatened him. "Be careful—you have children," Kokorin remembered the Party secretary as saying—referring to Kokorin's three daughters.

As the day of the threatened strike approached, the director ordered Kokorin to stay away from the mine, in terms he couldn't ignore. The director assumed nothing would happen without Kokorin to egg the workers on; he had underestimated the miners' outrage. The afternoon shift didn't turn in its lamps and identification tokens at the end of work—a sign that the strike was on. The miners collected the next morning and marched dramatically to Lenin Square, at the center of Mezhdurechensk, dressed in its black work clothes, wearing hard hats and carrying tools.

"We were all fed up," Kokorin said. "For twenty-six years we had worked and achieved nothing. We were incensed, and that is why we decided to do it. You aren't afraid of losing something when there is nothing to lose."

But three days passed and no other mines had joined in. Kokorin began to fear the strike would fail and he would be imprisoned. If his men remained isolated, they were certain the army would come to crush them. In the meantime the miners struggled to maintain order and to avoid giving authorities a pretext for a crackdown. They seized 500 bottles of vodka brought to demonstrations and strike centers, and they confiscated clubs, sticks, and anything else that could be used as weapons. They took over food stores to distribute goods fairly, and prohibited the sale of alcohol. The crime rate fell precipitously.

On the fourth day of the strike, word spread that mines throughout the Kuzbass were joining the work stoppage. Within a little more than a month authorities bowed to many, but not all, of the miners' demands, which by then included the removal of the mine director and a significant weakening of the Party organization in the mines.

What happened thereafter disappointed Kokorin. The miners had become a potent political tool that others wanted to exploit. Boris Yeltsin, who was then fighting for his political life, tapped the power of the Kuzbass miners. He flew to the region in August 1990, walked among the miners, slapped them on the back, and said he would defend their interests. They cheered mightily when he said, "I promise you freedom." They cheered louder still when he signed a treaty with the coal miners that agreed with all of their demands.

When Yeltsin's prospects worsened, the Kuzbass miners launched a strike in January 1991, calling for the resignation of Mikhail Gorbachev and of their own provincial governor. They demanded that the mines rule themselves (under leasing arrangements) and become Russian and not Soviet property.

What Kokorin had wanted was true Communism—workers' rule the way Marx had foreseen it. He thought the miners were being manipulated by political forces in Moscow, and they thought that he was wed to an ideology whose day had passed. He wanted Utopia; they wanted VCRs. "It was just like it had been in 1917," Kokorin frowned. "It all began well and ended badly. I only wanted that we could live under socialism, which we had never done."

Kokorin made his views known, in that booming voice, and his fellow workers—fed up with socialism—began to turn on him and favor other leaders.

Now no television teams shined their klieg lights on him to record his views on the new Russia. Workers didn't clamor for him to march them into a new era. Valery Kokorin had become an asterisk. The courageous worker who had started the first strikes in the Kuzbass, strikes that had helped change Russian history, was already forgotten.

Kokorin remained a member of the strike committee until a scandal removed the last vestiges of his power. Ironically, the Marxist was said to have taken advantage of his position by acquiring three video recorders and then reselling them at great profit. He denied this, but the Ratspatskaya mine withdrew its financial support from the committee until he resigned. Kokorin felt that he had been set up. His critics said he had been seduced by the perquisites of his new position.

It was no longer comfortable at the mine, so Kokorin took a job as a worker in a nearby factory. But he often sat at home and recalled the brief, heady period of workers' revolution. Before I left him, in the middle of the night, at the time when he would usually begin his shift, he wistfully told me how much he missed the taste of the coal dust on his lips and the camaraderie of the after-shift sauna.

Chapter 6:

INDUSTRIAL WASTELAND

Tiny dusty villages have turned into bustling
industrial cities with blast furnaces illuminating
the night for miles and miles in the once deserted
wasteland . . . cities are neat, immaculately clean,
spacious and well-planned and some of them, like
Novokuznetsk, can justly be called garden cities.

—GEORGE ST. GEORGE, *Siberia*, 1969

The doctors at Novokuznetsk's Hospital Number 7 know by the way the
wind is blowing whether they will have a busy day. If the air is calm and
humid, the poisons from two of the largest steel smelters in the world hang
in the air. The hospital's waiting room will then fill with patients complaining of bronchitis and cardiac troubles; parents will rush in with
children who can't breathe. Hospital emergency rooms across town will
register more heart attacks than usual.

When it rains, as it was doing on the day we arrived, the problems can
be worse. Storms bring the poisons to earthly levels in a sulfurous deluge.
"After a big storm," said Sergei Mineyev, the chief doctor of the hospital,
"the vegetable gardens turn yellow. The cucumbers die first. And if it rains
for a week's time, the tomatoes are finished. That's why you will see so
many gardens here where the plants are under polyurethane and in green-
houses. It's mostly to keep them away from our natural rain."

Unfortunately, Novokuznetsk can't provide its people with the same
protection. Dr. Mineyev, the quiet, thin, and calm doctor, ran the children's section of Hospital Number 7. He was a studious surgeon, in his
mid-thirties, who had made much of his life's work the saving of Novokuznetsk's children from the steel smelters' poisons. "The pollution hits
mothers and their children worst of all," he said.

For years Novokuznetsk natives suspected their health was worse than
that of most Russians, and Glasnost allowed health specialists to conduct

studies that confirmed their suspicions. In Novokuznetsk, there are four deaths to each three live births. The women of the city suffer an abnormally high level of menstrual difficulties and gynecological problems. Half of them have irregularities during pregnancy, ranging from miscarriages to premature births. And roughly half of all newborns come into the world with some sort of chronic illness or handicap.

As bad as the statistics are, the situation is even worse for the women who work at the Kuznetsk Metallurgical *Kombinat* (or KMK), the city's biggest polluter and the country's largest steel producer. Although he knew the results of a study on the KMK's female work force, Dr. Mineyev put me on the phone with the scientist who had conducted it, Larisa Aleksandrovna. The findings couldn't be empirical, because the factory wouldn't cooperate, so she had instead had to collect her data as the women came into the clinics and hospitals for treatment.

"We believe that all—I repeat, all—children born to women who work full time at the plant throughout their pregnancy have some sort of handicap," said Larisa Aleksandrovna. "They are often born premature, crippled, or they are stillborn." The study found that a large number of the children were born with open sores, which doctors linked to immune-system deficiencies. They also reported a rash of bone-marrow diseases and fifty mysterious cases of kidney problems of a type that they hadn't found registered anywhere else in the Soviet Union.

The problems were so severe that doctors in Novokuznetsk sought ways to remove pregnant mothers from the plant and put them into hospitals as soon as possible. "We try to get them away from the factory right away," said Dr. Mineyev. "But we are faced with a vicious circle. The women say if they quit working, they can't support the child. We tell them if they keep working, their child will be too handicapped to enjoy their support."

Dr. Mineyev had approached the factory's managers for help in organizing a more formal study, but they didn't want to cooperate in anything that might cause rebellion among their workers. Instead, the factory was opening its own hospital, where studies and treatment could be held more closely. "The plant managers have other concerns," says Dr. Mineyev. "But until they cooperate more fully, the city's doctors can only deal with the aftereffects," said Dr. Mineyev, whose nursery is often filled with premature babies on life-support devices.

My eyes watered as we drove through Novokuznetsk during a rainstorm. The city produced more steel than any other place in the Soviet Union. And it smelled it. The moist air reeked of rotten egg; I tasted metal with each intake of breath. Locals called Novokuznetsk the most polluted city in Siberia. No one had empirical evidence to prove the claim, but I had no reason to doubt it.

In the 1930s Stalin sent tens of thousands of forced laborers and Communist volunteers to turn the city into the industrial jewel of the Kuzbass. He turned a town that had no more than 20,000 residents before World War I into a city that had a 600,000 population by 1990. Stalin's dreams for Novokuznetsk were so heady, and personal, that he renamed the city after himself in 1931—Stalinsk. In 1961 the city fathers, with some embarrassment, restored the name Novokuznetsk—which means "new smithy."

Even during the 1960s and 1970s, many viewed the city's rapid development with wide-eyed wonder. In those days its wooden homes with hand-carved window frames gave it a charm that hadn't yet been overwhelmed by prefab low-rises and dirty air. "The city is built around an enormous park—a piece of virgin forest occupying 500 acres," wrote the historian George St. George in his 1969 book *Siberia*. "And were it not for factory chimneys and the open-hearth and blast furnaces illuminating the sky at night, one would think one was on a large university campus. It is the largest and busiest of the cities in the Kemerovo region, but it has an almost suburban charm."

Some suburbia.

It seemed the person best placed to tell me where this industrial Eden had gone wrong was the director of the plant upon which Novokuznetsk's hopes had rested, Vladimir Ilyich Kotykov. His parents had named him after Lenin, and the director of Novokuznetsk's oldest and dirtiest steel plant had been proud of the distinction throughout his life. He had remained a Communist Party member long after Boris Yeltsin had resigned and until the Party itself was banned.

Kotykov looked the part of a giant Soviet-enterprise chief who had risen through the ranks of workers and then Party members. His fists were large and his fingers thick and clenched. His neck was too thick to allow his top button to close, and he spoke with a commanding voice that none dared contradict.

He had tried to cancel our afternoon meeting, joining us reluctantly only after I had refused to leave without asking him about his pollution problem—a conversation he had agreed to during an earlier meeting that day which he had been forced to cut short. When he stormed angrily into the office, he announced, "Every minute of my day is planned, and I don't have much time. So make it quick."

Before we started, however, he left the long, glass-covered table in his office and barked some orders into a microphone that connected his desk with a control room down the hall. It was from there, a large hall that looked like a 1950s space control center, with flashing lights and dials, that he controlled his realm of 34,000 workers. In 1980 his plant had produced a tenth of the entire Soviet steel output (14 million tons) and all of its railway tracks. Although its output had fallen, it remained the largest steel producer in Russia.

After ten minutes of issuing orders, he sat at the end of our table and asked his vice-director to brief him before we could ask questions. Vladimir Kotykov looked restless and impatient. "They said they noticed lots of pollution," said his vice-director. "They said their eyes were watering and that they tasted metal on their tongues. I told them I didn't see or taste anything. I told them we didn't have statistics on pollution. I told them—"

The director cut off his babbling vice-director. He talked about the plant's difficulty in finding the capital to replace outmoded and dirty smelting and refining processes. "We are planning on doing a lot, but it is all in the future," he said. But he felt scientists and journalists were exaggerating the problem. "When you go outside the factory, the trees are still green, so it can't be so bad," he said. "And if the people in the city don't like the pollution, well, they can move to the village."

Business cards were the easiest gauge in a quickly changing Siberia of how forward-thinking a manager was. The most advanced managers had cards with Latin lettering and even Japanese characters. Kotykov had only Cyrillic cards. The two deputies who sat with us didn't have any cards at all. They consented to scribble down their names only after nervously drawing their director's nod of approval.

Kotykov knew he was expected to be a free-marketer, but he didn't like it. Everything about him—and his plant—had been forged by a system that was disappearing. He was born in 1939 and had never seen his father, who had died during the war. He had left school at age sixteen to earn money to raise the family, and had been working at the KMK plant ever since. He was a socialist success story, and he considered himself and his factory to be patriotic servants of a State that wasn't properly rewarding them.

Kotykov complained that reformers had stacked the cards against the plants like his that had literally built and then defended the motherland. "During the Great Patriotic War," he said, "the *Kombinat* made the steel for every second tank and every third bullet. Within weeks of Stalin's order in 1939, it shifted most of its production to that of war matériel." The KMK even had a T-34 tank resting on a pedestal outside the plant headquarters, beside a huge war memorial.

"Now they have told us: 'Dear Friends: Get out on the starting line with everyone else. We were not built for this sort of race. He who has a big wallet can run farther and he who has a smaller wallet may not even be able to start."

In order to earn the money the plant needed to modernize and cut down on pollution, Kotykov had begun to sell his goods to hard-currency customers in Japan, China, Germany, France, and Turkey—countries he had traveled to on sales missions that had once been carried out by the trade ministry. He didn't like the humiliation of begging for business; he still thought his first obligation should be to the motherland.

"We took a job of repairing a blast furnace in Mexico," he said. "When we arrived, we learned that we would be paid only a fraction of the price that Mexico would have given its own engineers to do the same job." He said with a sneer that he didn't like the idea of his former superpower providing the Third World with a cheap labor force.

And he didn't like Americans much more than Mexicans. He had tried to play on the plant's Chicago roots to sell a joint-venture idea to a group of American businessmen who had come to look at his operation. (The original engineers had been the Freyn Engineering Company of Chicago, in the early 1930s.)

So he had appealed to visiting Americans' sense of history. He had talked of the inaugural dinner that Mr. Freyn had hosted, an event that was still legendary in the town. Freyn had shaken up local leaders by throwing a bash in which he had violated Siberian traditions—he had invited women "to decorate the event" and had not served vodka. And instead of delivering the standard lengthy toast, he had instead said a few friendly words and then asked the band to strike up a tune for dancing.

"Today we have an old plant that our fathers—American and Russian—have built," Kotykov had told the Americans. "Being the sons of those fathers, we want to return to those traditions." But the Americans hadn't gone for the pitch.

"The conversation was pleasant enough," said Mr. Kotykov, "and they showed a lot of interest. They even told a number of jokes," he said, looking with disgust at a smile that crossed my face. I was about to ask him to repeat one of the jokes.

"You Americans are always smiling," he said, frowning. "But I never know what is behind the smile." He had never heard again from the Americans from Chicago who had visited him.

What Kotykov didn't discuss with those Americans, or with me, was the more unsavory side of his plant's history. Stalin had used mostly forced labor to build it: thousands of Kulaks, landowning farmers whom he had exiled to the region; prisoners from the many nearby penal colonies; local natives; and a sprinkling of "Communist volunteers." A housing shortage at the time had forced many who arrived to live in dugouts or tents that couldn't stand up to the cold. Many hundreds of them had died of hunger and exposure.

The Chicago designers and engineers had been appalled by their Russian partners' willingness to sacrifice so many lives for a steel smelter. They had been shocked to see workers taking off their coats and using their blankets to cover the cement so that it would be warm enough to dry in temperatures that were −40°F.

"It's mad," said a young American engineer at the time to the author

St. George. "They are building a tremendous metallurgical *Kombinat,* as they call it, with their bare hands, with nobody around but savage Mongolian nomads." (The Kuznetsk Basin was then part of Kazakhstan.) "And the workers . . . dispossessed rich peasants who hate the Soviets, local tribesmen who have never seen a screwdriver, and young 'enthusiasts,' as they call themselves, who have never held any tool in their hands. They are sleeping in old army tents and lean-tos in the bitter cold, which makes you gasp. It's a fantastic waste of time and labor. My colleagues and myself often felt like quitting and going home, pay or no pay, contract or no contract, just not to be a party to this horror."

The engineer falsely bet that the Russians would never be able to operate the plants on their own, "not in a hundred years." He wasn't the last to underestimate the willingness of Russians to endure cruelty and hardship. And no one then could imagine the lengths to which Soviet leaders, thinking they were bringing about their State's greatness, would go to complete even the least logical projects.

Novokuznetsk had been built literally around the KMK plant. By 1991 the plant was a small city—several kindergartens, eight collective farms, two museums, a dozen vacation homes, Young-Pioneer camps for the children, two theaters, several health clinics, and dozens of shops and canteens. It had a large gymnasium, a cultural palace for conventions, and its own hockey team, a perennial winner called, of course, the Steel Workers (Siberia's Pittsburgh Steelers).

At a time when he should have been adjusting to the free market and reducing his pollution, Kotykov complained that he instead had to find ways to feed his workers and their families. "Do you know what this steel-smelter director was doing this morning?" he asked. "I was determining where to find five kilos of sugar for each of our workers. You see, it's berry season and they need to make preserves. It sounds absurd, but that's the way my job is. A bootmaker should make boots and a steelmaker should make steel. But if I don't feed the workers, who will? First we have to find food for people, and only after that can we expect them to work as they should."

When Vladimir Ilyich Kotykov thought about what he could do to help his people, potatoes entered his mind first. Potatoes were filling, nutritious, could be used at every meal, would keep through a long and cold winter, were relatively easy to grow, and were cheap. Even vodka was made from potatoes! What food could be more perfect for a hungry people? Or more Russian?

The Russian word for potato, *kartofel,* was identical to the German word. The favorite of the Siberians was a tasty red-skinned version called *berlinka.* A Russian encyclopedia told me that Peter the Great had hired Dutch farmers to bring the potato to Russia. The peasants didn't take to it, however, condemning them as "the devil's apples," growing underground as they did. So Peter the Great had to force the peasants to grow them. Refusing to do so was punished with exile or imprisonment.

The potato became such a staple of the Siberian diet that my Siberian friends called it "the second bread"—*vtoroi khleb.* Local officials complained that Siberians, in fear of a hard winter ahead, were digging small potato cellars in the yards of apartment buildings and on strips of land along highways. The officials had given up trying to stop them.

For all this love of potatoes, Soviet central planners could never get the growing and distribution of them right. More than half the potential crop was lost each year because of bad harvesting, storage, and transport. So Kotykov called in Dutch farmers again, three centuries after Peter the Great.

At the KMK farm outside Novokuznetsk, the Dutch farmer Walter Sturm was doing his best to reteach Russians the art of potato production. His chiseled features and bronzed skin would have made him the perfect farming figure for a Dutch agriculture advertising campaign. He unhappily surveyed the KMK's vast farmland, where few people worked and equipment rotted.

Beside him workers played cards on a makeshift bench because their transport hadn't arrived to take them to the field. Another four took a cigarette break in a broken-down bus that sat on its axles. A half-dozen female field workers waited in an old van for more than forty-five minutes to be taken to their workplaces. Its loud motor was running the whole time, using up fuel. The scene violated Sturm's Dutch sense of order.

On an adjacent field, farm equipment lay rusting where it had been left outside throughout the long winter. Next to broken-down harvesters, tillers, and planting machines were stacks of spare parts rusting in their factory boxes. Manufacturers had sent the parts, according to plan, but the equipment they fit was no longer operating. However, the farm couldn't find parts to address the unplanned breakdown.

Another problem, said Sturm, was child labor. He pointed to an army of teenagers weeding an onion patch. Sturm said the Soviet practice of sending schoolchildren to work on collective farms during their vacations might have served socialist solidarity, but it resulted in holes dug too deep for planting, and weeding done so poorly that the roots were left behind.

"Just a very little properly applied chemical would replace those children," he said. "My hands are itching to change all of this."

But Sturm's job stopped at potatoes, and he was having enough trouble with that. He proudly took a pile of his soil into his hand and showed that it had a finer and thus more fertile grain than any other soil on the farm. His neat rows of potato plants also looked more orderly. But the problems confronted him even as he proudly told his story in Dutch to Amsterdam radio correspondent Theo Uittenbogaard, who then translated to me the story of an orderly man desperately trying to end the chaos of Soviet agriculture. First Sturm spotted a worker at the wheel of a weed-killing spray machine who had turned on the flow before the vehicle began to move. "If you stand there for three seconds, you ruin the soil and the vegetable!" he shouted.

He panicked again when one of the farm administrators drove his car under one of the sprayer's wings, nearly breaking off a nozzle. His workers were already in the practice of repairing such breakages with a cork, which caused the chemical to be applied in too great an amount in some areas and not at all in others.

"They don't pay attention to the machinery," he complained. "I brought in a tractor that cost 100,000 guilders. But on the first day, they ran it into a ditch. How they did it, I don't know—the road was six meters wide. But then seventy people looked at it lying there for two hours. None of them did anything. For me, that was 140 man hours lost. But they don't have a love for their work or for their machinery. They don't know the value of things."

In truth, they do know the value of *some* things. Toolboxes that Sturm shipped in from Holland disappear as soon as they arrive. And every piece of machinery sent from Holland came with enough spare parts to make up for calculated thefts along the way. Sturm rarely opened a delivery that didn't have hoses, pipes, and tools missing.

His biggest worry, however, was that he would lose most of his crop after it was harvested because of bad storage and transportation. He complained that the Russians stored the potatoes in tall bunkers, then released them down steep chutes into trucks and railways cars. "They bruise terribly," said Strum. "You can throw them away after that." Even if he could correct that problem, he feared the Russians would never get right the temperatures and ventilation of the storage areas.

To protect his crop, Sturm wanted to build a high-tech storeroom in Western Siberia that would be linked to a computer in Holland. The computer would read monitors and then control ventilation and temperature. That would take it safely out of Russian hands.

Only one problem. He would need reliable phone lines suitable for data transfer—and no one expected them to come for a decade or more.

Novokuznetsk isn't merely Western Siberia's pollution capital. It is also its jazz capital. A local jazz club organized a small concert at the local Writers' Club for members of our expedition. A band called Underground Jazz worked its way through "My Funny Valentine," "Sophisticated Lady," and "Satin Doll."

I was impressed by the soulful quality of the music. But my Russian colleagues were more impressed that the club had produced more than a dozen bottles of beer—a commodity they hadn't seen for months. It was reason enough for celebration, and we downed the rich, brown fluid from champagne glasses.

The pianist and leader of the band, Anatoly Berestov, remembered the days when his love of jazz had been considered daring. Now it almost had become trite, he conceded. Gorky had said that jazz was the music of the capitalists, and that made it interesting to a large segment of the young. The authorities, unable to stop the cultural pollution, had determined that jazz wasn't a decadent indulgence, but instead the music of oppressed black Americans that had its natural place in the Soviet music scene.

"But Siberian jazz was born in the prison camps," said Berestov, who was also the president of the jazz club. "Jazz is the music of freedom that is made in the condition of lack of freedom. Your blacks were looking for freedom in America expressed through jazz. The people in the camps found freedom through jazz, as well. People don't write beautiful poetry if they have a good life. They write poetry if they are miserable."

Berestov's father had played with the L'vov theater orchestra, and had come to Siberia just before the war on one of the many cultural tours arranged to help "civilize" the region. His father had fallen in love with a young Siberian pianist and stayed behind. In those days, just after the war, Siberia had seemed unusually cultured to him because of the intellectual level of the people who had been exiled and imprisoned there. Novokuznetsk had had more than a dozen theaters and concert halls.

Yet something had gone out of jazz since Perestroika, Berestov said. The Russians liked their jazz to be dark, mystical, and forbidden, a dangerous indulgence in a smoke-filled cellar. But jazz had instead become the hottest music in town. Novokuznetsk had thirteen jazz bands, and Berestov was organizing an annual jazz festival that he hoped would attract bands from around the world. "But this is the first time we've played for foreigners," he said. "We are very good here, but we don't know what our music would be worth in the West."

In a place where no one knew the value of things, their music was priceless. I luxuriated as I sipped the beer from the champagne glass and listed to the piano player play Duke Ellington's "Mood Indigo."

Chapter 7:

CRIME . . .

The more open society becomes, the more
crime we get.

—GENERAL VITALY SKHURAT, *Kuzbass police chief*

It had been a frozen Saturday in February, at just past two in the afternoon, when police chief Vitaly Skhurat had ordered his military-green
Mi-8 police helicopter to swoop low toward the weathered cement head-
stones and the low trees of the Tirgan cemetery outside the dreary mining
town of Prokopyevsk.

Below the chopper, the 200 chief figures of the Kuzbass region's two
major underworld organizations thought they had gathered secretly to
strike a *razborka,* a pact that was to settle a turf feud between them that
had already resulted in six murders. They had run in a panic for their cars,
which had been scattered along the road at the edge of the cemetery. The
pilot had taken the helicopter low, had dropped in fourteen paratroopers,
then had herded the gangsters toward the booby trap—thirteen special
agents who had been hidden in the brush around the cemetery and were
now blocking off roads.

Skhurat's plan had worked perfectly, and his cameraman had recorded
every detail of the raid from the helicopter, on Japanese video equipment.
The film would later be used as evidence against those arrested and to
identify any who had gotten away. But its frequent showings would also
feed Skhurat's growing local fame as a Siberian Serpico, the Kuzbass's
clean cop.

Skhurat took over the police force only in 1988, but his popularity had
grown quickly after he had sided with the local miners during their 1989

strikes and had disregarded his provincial governor's order to crack down in a way that he thought would incite violence. A little more than a month after I visited him, he would defy orders again and courageously cast his lot with Boris Yeltsin during the August 1991 coup attempt. Skhurat, never shying from a just fight, pronounced his support of Yeltsin in a dramatic television statement before anyone could know the coup would fail.

Skhurat had a sense of the theatrical. At age fifty-one, his flat nose and ruddy face made him look like a Bronx flatfoot, but his charm and warmth made him the sort of man to whom you wanted to confess crimes. Skhurat initially had wanted to raid the graveyard meeting with 400 to 600 of his own men, but the two local crime organizations had cleverly chosen a cemetery, located near the Tom River between Novokuznetsk and Kemerovo, that could be easily monitored. They had posted spotters on the only road that led to it, and General Skhurat knew they had also infiltrated his force.

So he had used only a small contingent of special forces and crack police from a new enforcement division that had been created to fight organized crime. The surprise had been perfect. Twenty-seven men had arrested 134 of the 200 gangsters, and not a single drop of blood had been shed. Skhurat found he couldn't charge most of his captives with any crime—they'd discarded their illegal weapons, and it wasn't a crime to meet friends in a cemetery—but he would show the video to witnesses of previous unsolved crimes and they would finger many of those who had been arrested. And, two weeks later, police would make surprise searches at the homes of those who had been freed. They found explosives, sawed-off shotguns, knives, foreign currency, and stolen jewelry and video machines. Their most lucrative crimes, however, were selling stolen vehicles and running protection rackets. The pilfered cars were often dismantled for parts that could be sold for perhaps as much as twenty times the price of an intact automobile. The black-market price for a windshield or spare wheel was half the State price for a new car.

This wasn't sophisticated organized crime—there were no Italian "crime families" or beheaded horses left under bloody sheets *à la The Godfather*. A like-minded group of unprincipled entrepreneurs was merely taking advantage of an economy of shortages, often doing little more than buying goods *en masse* from State stores by providing bribes, and then marking up the prices as much as ten times before reselling the goods through private-market salesmen whom they controlled. Most of the actual crime took place during the day, when burglars broke into homes that had doors that were easy to kick open. For many years nothing worth stealing had been inside. One of the hottest new businesses in Siberia was the sale and mounting of steel doors and the application of bars to windows. Siberians were increasingly considering these additions to be part of the cost of owning Western goods ranging from refrigerators to television sets.

Skhurat invited me to his operations center, where three men on radio-phones sat in front of a map of the region, with blinking lights indicating the location of calls. He complained that he didn't have the men, the know-how, or the laws to get at the new crime problems that had come with democracy and freer markets. "That's because our whole approach is wrong," said Skhurat. "We have to get into the business of concepts instead of criminals. To catch a criminal isn't the problem. We can do that easily. To break the organization is far more difficult. Our legislature needs to write new laws designed to go after racketeering. I can show you all the bosses and their connections—their whole structure. This wall wouldn't be enough to draw it all out. I know where they live and their positions—but I can't get to them."

Organized crime wasn't new, he conceded. There had always been high Communist officials willing to abuse their positions and stash away money in hidden accounts. But crime was now more widespread and lucrative. Moscow had set up a Sixth Department, aimed at organized crime, as part of the Ministry for Internal Affairs, in 1991. The department had con-cluded that there were 5,000 criminal groups in the country. But it didn't know how to destroy the groups that were often better armed and financed than the police.

What Skhurat said he needed was more men with economic expertise so that they could monitor the rash of new private companies that were being formed in Kemerovo. The gangs, he said, were using this new private sector to launder their ill-gotten income. And the more profit these crimi-nals made, said Skhurat, the more legitimate businesses they were coming to control and the more influence they were gaining. He feared they would soon be out of anyone's reach.

"It will end badly," he said. "We've only seen the tip of the iceberg. They are buying police, judges, attorneys—everyone."

General Skhurat paced. He often wondered out loud whether he was telling me too much. Then he would turn playfully silent, egging on more persistent questioning from my side. He relished the verbal sparring, which he always punctuated with a disarmingly sweet smile. He invited us into his spacious office.

Wearing a brown suit and tie, he sat down behind his highly varnished desk and hunched his shoulders forward like a panther about to pounce. His family had come to Siberia before the October Revolution, he said, when the Tsar was giving big plots of land to those foolish enough to think they could grow something on them. The general's father had died at the front while Vitaly was a young boy. Vitaly grew up quickly after that. First he worked as a truck driver for a factory, at a building site. But when he was twenty-five, the Party ordered him to become a policeman—the Supreme Soviet had begun a recruitment campaign in the mid-1960s.

Communism was supposed to have done away with crime, which was said to be a result of capitalist exploitation, but it hadn't worked out that way. Nowhere were crime problems greater than in the Kuzbass. The province had more criminals and ex-convicts per capita than any other region because of the large number of prisons that had always been there. Some 10 percent of the Kuzbass population of 3.2 million were ex-convicts, Skhurat said. By 1990 the region still had about 24,500 prisoners in thirty-six prison camps. After their release, most of them continued to stay in the Kuzbass, largely because other parts of the country would not give ex-convicts residency permits.

At first it seemed that Gorbachev's rule, led by his prohibition of the sale of alcohol in 1985, would reduce crime. But within a year lawbreaking had escalated as seldom before, bootlegging was rampant, and Gorbachev was backing off on his anti-alchohol campaign. His broad pardon of criminals in 1987, honoring the seventieth anniversary of the Revolution, had made matters worse. Some 34,000 convicts had been freed in Skhurat's region, and 90 percent of them remained in the Kuzbass, where they couldn't find jobs or housing and soon turned again to crime. Skhurat said that in 1988 every third crime was committed by that group.

"We had no work for them, no places for them to live," said Skhurat. "So they returned to their previous employment." Since then crime had been rising at a rate of 60 to 70 percent per year. Skhurat read off numbers in the emotionless way that Soviet factory managers once used to list production results. "I had 41,000 crimes last year—that's twice what I had in 1987. And at this rate I'll have 47,000 this year. And violent crime has increased ten times in the last three years." The police are so overburdened that less than half of all crimes are ever solved.

"I want to tell you a story that I probably shouldn't," said Skhurat, winking at me as he began recounting how he had broken the most successful bank-heist gang that Siberia had ever known.

Over a three-year period the overburdened Kuzbass police had built up a backlog of 230 unsolved bank robberies. The *modus operandi* had been similar enough for Skhurat to conclude that one group was responsible for them all. The getaway cars were always average vehicles without license plates, so there was never any way to trace them. The robbers also seemed to know where the watchmen were located and how to disarm alarm systems.

General Skhurat watched the robberies with grudging admiration, as the robbers got into the safes and out of the banks virtually without notice. "These were perfect crimes," he said. "We set aside a special team of agents to investigate. But they found nothing. No evidence, no fingerprints, no trails. This group knew all the ropes, so we figured it might have been an inside job. So we checked out all the bank personnel, but that didn't help either."

Finally, the bank robbers made a mistake; they killed a bank guard who tried to stop their getaway. They might have gotten away with that, too, but one of the robbers couldn't resist wearing the distinctive watch he had taken from the guard. One of the guard's relatives spotted it on his wrist, and he came to General Skhurat. "One of your police officers is wearing the watch of a man who was murdered," he said.

Skhurat began to tail the officer, and within a few weeks he called in five militiamen who turned out to be part of a gang of twenty-four involved in bank robberies that had netted them more than 1.5 million rubles—a tidy sum even in a devalued currency. "I learned that Lieutenant Ponamorev, of our force, was one of the leaders with his brother, a civilian," said General Skhurat. "He sat in front of me, in the chair where you are sitting, and he said that he had bought the watch at the private market. He denied everything at first. But we knew much more than he had anticipated. He and his brother were convicted to ten years in prison. But what hurt me was seeing that the poison penetrated my own police family."

General Skhurat arrested thirty-eight of his own officers in 1990, and he would arrest nearly a dozen more in 1991. "And I'm sure there are many more taking bribes who we haven't caught," he said. "I don't know how to stop this sickness."

While Skhurat fought underworld and corruption, the biggest enemy for the cop on the beat remained the bottle. More than half of all crimes were still committed by drunks. To get a closer look at the crime problems of the Kuzbass, I drove the graveyard shift with two cops named Aleksandr. It was easy to tell them apart. One was fat—the driver—and the other was lean. The fat one overflowed his uniform, stretching it at the seams. The smaller Aleksandr swam in his. They were a Siberian Laurel and Hardy.

Their mustard-yellow jeep had a small compartment in the back surrounded by steel netting, a holding pen for prisoners.

Both men carried long, solid, black-rubber nightsticks with rubber handles, and each had a concealed pistol. In Kemerovo, the police called the sticks *demokratizators* in honor of the age of Glasnost. The Aleksandrs thought this was quite funny.

Hardy was more talkative. Laurel was tentative, acting as if I were a blind date whose presence made him nervous. Neither had ever talked with a foreigner before.

As we cruised down one of the city's main drags, a drunken pedestrian zigzagged across the road in front of us, almost as if he were asking to be picked up. The Aleksandrs stopped and threw him in the back, a routine they seemed to know well. "You again?" said the larger Aleksandr, but the drunk was beyond recognizing familiar faces. He slumped in the pen.

The Aleksandrs told me that in the summer they picked up only the most violent or the most severely drunk. But in the winter, the cops were a lifesaving service. If they didn't respond quickly enough to a report of a passed-out drunk, they'd find him dead, frozen and pickled.

On this night, before they could take their prisoner into one of the five city "sobering-up centers," the radio crackled with an order from headquarters. A man attending a wedding party at a local restaurant was threatening guests with a butcher knife. The jeep raced to the scene. Or rather, it rolled at a somewhat less leisurely pace. Its engine was in bad shape, and its top speed was about forty miles per hour.

The woman waiting to sign the complaint had thick makeup, flaxen hair, and a dress too revealing for her ample figure. A drunken man, who appeared to be her boyfriend, had threatened her with a knife whose blade was long enough to have sliced off her neck with a single whack. The smaller Aleksandr neatly traced the blade on a sheet of butcher paper. The knife's magnitude would play some sort of a role in the sentencing.

The man in the white shirt protested mildly when the Aleksandrs put him into the pen. He protested more when the drunk beside him began to spit up. The stench was of vomit and vodka.

The radio crackled again. A woman had complained that one of her neighbors was allowing his German shepherd into the yard without its required muzzle. The Aleksandrs, who were driving past the address anyway, decided to stop in. It was a busy night, they said.

The middle-aged woman complained that the dog had already bitten two residents of her building, and she wanted action before it found a third victim. Other women gathered in the courtyard as well, insisting on police response. The Aleksandrs sighed—not the sort of dramatic stuff they wanted to show an American reporter. After climbing three flights of stairs, they pounded on the door of the dog owner. "This is the police—open up!" said the fat one, in the internationally standard manner.

A female voice shouted hysterically from behind the door. "We haven't done anything, so go away!" The police decided they would take her advice.

In the courtyard, the hysterical woman screamed in anger about their lack of action before calming down enough to sign a report. She protested as the Aleksandrs climbed back into the patrol car and prepared to drive off. "Bring Stalin back!" she shouted. "Then there was discipline—and cheaper vodka."

The drunk in the backseat had been conscious enough to hear. "Not that!" he shouted back in a slurred scream. "These bastards are bad enough."

The Aleksandrs looked at each other and exchanged a smile. All in an evening's work. They took their passengers to Siberia's version of a drunk tank.

When we pulled up to Medical Sobering-Up Place #5, one of Novokuznetsk's handful of drunk tanks, a police officer was dragging a half-naked man toward the door. The man's pants had dropped to his ankles, and his rear end was covered with mud. The officer bounced him across the stone pavement and then jerked his body through the doorway, where the pants temporarily stuck on a nail. The policeman pulled the man down the short staircase and then dumped him onto the cold cement floor, where he vomited.

One of the center's two medics, a hard-looking woman with an expression of numb boredom and hair pulled back severely into a knot, wiped his face with his trousers, which had fallen off by that point, and then covered his genitals with them. My Dutch friend Gerard, never shy of the embarrassing question, asked if he had been raped.

"I know all about that," said the woman with authority. "I worked for many years in a hospital where many of our patients were homosexuals." She pulled the drunk's legs apart and squinted at his buttocks through her thick glasses. "No, this one is okay," she said. "We look for a black circle around the anus. This one is normal."

On the wall above her head were two Lenins—a double dosage for a place so contaminated with the wayward proletariat. A sign hung between them, itemizing the penalties for public drunkenness and, in smaller letters, the rights of the individual. The cost for a night at the hostel, as the police called it, was a forty-five-ruble fine. The length of stay was twenty-four hours—or at least three hours beyond the time that the breath analysis instruments no longer registered alcohol content in the blood.

Major Vladimir Alassev, age thirty-four, was in charge of the "hostel." Except for its two grizzled doctors and some rudimentary analysis equipment, it looked very much like a prison. An old woman sat on a bench immediately in front of the half-naked man on the floor. Her head was in her hands and she was mumbling. A young man stood before the booking officer, swaying like a reed in the wind as he tried to remember when and where he had been born. From down the hall came the screams of men who had sobered up enough to recognize that they were in what looked very much like prison cells.

Major Alassev walked us upstairs to his small office, where we could talk in peace. The slogan over his desk had hung there for years: THE PARTY IS THE WISDOM AND THE HONOR OF OUR EPOCH. He saw no reason to remove it.

"Our first priority is to get all the drunkards off the street so that we have less crime," said the major. His head was perfectly round; his black hair closely cropped. He had worked for fourteen years at the hostel. He said cynically that it was his home away from home.

"A man changes in a certain way when he works here a long enough time," he said, applying a deeper tone to his voice. "The work disturbed me emotionally at first. I was aggressive when I would go home to my family. I wasn't easy to live with. But now I've recovered. And I don't drink anymore. I haven't had a drink in eight years." He said the job had caused vodka to lose its taste for him.

The hostel opened for business at about five in the afternoon, and it booked an average of seventeen drunks an evening—three or four of whom were usually women. On a bad weekend, however, that number could swell to fifty drunks, although the major had beds for only thirty-one. That left the riffraff sprawled out on the floors and benches, as they were on the evening I arrived. The total capacity at the city's five hostels was only 120. The major also had the right to turn repeat offenders over to a combined prison-hospital for "voluntary" treatment. If they refused, "then the treatment becomes obligatory," he said.

"Let me give you a tour of my facility," he offered.

As we walked back down the stone stairs into the "reception room," the half-naked man was gone. On the bench where the old lady had been sitting stood a muscular twenty-eight-year-old man who was stripped to his underwear. When he heard my English, he began shouting in my language. "Is this *democracy!?*" he shouted. "You tell people in West this Russian Glasnost. I am sitting in restaurant talking to my girl, and they take me here."

Dundee translated what he had said for Alassev, who was a bit embarrassed that this drunk seemed more educated than he was. "You are telling lies!" Alessav shouted, quite certain of this although he didn't know the man's story.

"Never!" the man in underwear shouted back, swaying some. "I'm normal man. I never committed a crime. Do you think I look like criminal? I've never been in a place like this. They get me for nothing! It is all shit! They humiliate me." Again Dundee translated.

Alassev nodded to underlings to take care of the man, and they grabbed him by the arms as the major continued his tour. We walked down the hall toward the cells from which I had heard screaming earlier. Major Alassev put on a determined look. He was walking onto his battleground. His small chest expanded and he held his fists clenched. He was playing the tough guy—he would show us that he was in charge.

In the first cell, three men were sitting lethargically on their metal cots without mattresses, and a fourth was sleeping. They all looked hung over. In a few more hours, Alassev said, they would be ready for release. When one began to stand, the major pushed him back down easily. Another began to speak, and Alassev told him to shut up. This group was beaten. The major slammed the door shut and moved to the next room.

The men behind this door were more recent arrivals. One old man stood up and began shouting incoherently. The major, who was far smaller than the man, pushed him against the wall, where he hit his head. The drunk then collapsed against one of the metal beds. As he tried to stand and fight back, the major easily pushed him back onto the floor. Alassev slammed the door behind us and strode to the third room.

When he opened the door, one of the prisoners lifted up his red T-shirt to show us a four-inch raw gash across his stomach, which was still bleeding. "I inflicted it myself to get out of here," he said proudly, describing how he had pulled a rusty nail from a wooden bench in the cell and stabbed himself with it. The regular prisoners knew the hospital was a better place than the hostel.

But the police officer who had brought him in, who was still loitering in the hallway, showed no sympathy. He said the hospital didn't have any guards for such troublemakers that evening, so the man would have to bleed and wait for qualified medical care until the morning. "Some people go to work as often as he commits a crime," sneered the officer. "We are waiting for him to do something serious so that we can put him away."

The next cell, the last one on our tour, held the problem cases. It was from this room that the shouts had come earlier. One young man came to the small, barred window of the steel door and pleaded sobriety at the top of his drunken lungs.

"Shouting isn't going to help you," Alassev said. "Drop dead."

The drunk then hit the steel door with his fists, and the sound echoed down the cement hallway. Alassev unlocked the cell and pushed him backwards. Three drunks fell to the ground like dominoes. As Alassev turned to explain something to us, one of the men, rising off the floor, grabbed him from behind. Again, Alassev pushed—this time harder. Again the dominoes fell. Alassev turned to leave, and another drunk leaped at him and tried to tackle him from behind. With a swift, practiced move, the major pinned his assailant to the floor by twisting his arm behind his back. Alassev released the drunk and then shrugged, and he quickly left the cell and locked the door behind him. The man resumed pounding his fists against the door as soon as it slammed shut.

As we walked toward the exit, we heard some shouting in English from a small cell with a steel door that Alassev hadn't included in his tour. I looked through a peephole at the muscular young man who had earlier stood screaming atop the bench. He was now strapped down with leather bindings to a heavy, metal device that looked like an electric chair without the wiring. This "special chair," said Major Alassev, was for those who couldn't be controlled through any other means.

Stripped to his underpants, the man tugged furiously at the straps, like a wild animal trying to break loose. Alassev opened the door so I could get a better view. The man was jerking his head so that it was flying against the metal backrest. "Is this democracy?" he repeated in English, over and over, clearly for my consumption.

It seemed a fair question, so I asked it of my host. "We introduced two of these chairs, based on an order we got from the ministry," he said. "When we put someone in a chair like that, it shouldn't be for longer than an hour."

What if the prisoner still isn't under control after that period of time?

"There are few situations where an hour isn't enough to calm a prisoner down," he said.

"Won't the prisoner hurt himself?" I asked, watching the young man straining and twisting.

"Don't worry, he is being watched by the medical staff," said Alassev.

It was time to leave Medical Sobering-Up Place #5, and I thanked Major Alassev for the tour. As I walked out the door, the twenty-eight-year-old man was still screaming for democracy and trying to break free from his leather chains. And the "medical staff" (the woman had been relieved by a male doctor with oily, pockmarked skin) was ignoring him and exchanging jokes with the booking officer. With the sound in my ears of their laughter, the prisoner's screams, and the pounding on the steel doors, I walked with relief into the cool Siberian night.

If this was a Siberian drunk tank, I was intrigued to find out what a penal colony would look like. I was scheduled to visit one the next day.

Chapter 8:

. . . AND PUNISHMENT

> Siberia. On the banks of a broad, deserted river
> stands a town, one of the administrative centers
> of Russia; in the town there is a fortress; in the
> fortress there is a prison. In the prison, Rodion
> Raskolnikov, convict of the second class, has
> been confined for nine months.
>
> —FYODOR DOSTOYEVSKY, *Crime and Punishment*

In the auditorium of Prison Colony #5, near the banks of the Tom River, the inmates' chorus had prepared a tune for its special visitors from the West—"The Volga Boatman." The singers' eyes were dull, their faces were hard, and their heads were shaved bald. But their voices were a voluptuous bass that made up in volume what they lacked in modulation.

> *Yo-heave-ho! Yo-heave-ho!*
> *All together, pull again,*
> *Yo-heave-ho! Yo-heave-ho!*
> *Strong arms bear the mighty strain . . .*

Each convict tried to sing more loudly than the other, assaulting the lyrics with the raw intensity of the criminal class. Among the dozen voices were prisoners convicted of murder and rape: just two of the banquet of crimes committed by the colony's 1,500 maximum security prisoners. As they sang "The Volga Boatman," I instead imagined charging Russian Cossacks.

> *All together till our task is done,*
> *Muscles gleaming in the blinding sun.*
> *Ai da da ai da. Ai da da ai da!*

Pull like giants, every one!
Yo-heave-ho! Yo-heave-ho!

During a break in their practicing, the singers talked about their lives. First there was Andrei, who was near the end of a ten-year term for killing his wife.

"She cheated on me," he said.

With another man?

"No, with a bottle of vodka."

The chorus, listening in from the background, chuckled.

The couple had been sitting in their small apartment, and he had left the kitchen table to relieve himself, he said. He really hadn't been gone that long, but when he returned he found that his wife had finished the entire bottle of vodka except for one small glass.

The choir laughed harder.

"So I got mad, and I killed her."

The choir was in stitches. Guffaws all around.

So, had he loved his wife? His sad eyes responded before the words had left his mouth.

"Yes," he said.

The choir fell silent.

Sergei, a fresh tenor just eighteen years of age, said he had killed his friend by striking him over the head with a piece of wood in a quarrel over a girl. They had been celebrating the anniversary of the October Revolution.

Were they drunk?

"Of course we were drunk," he said, treating the question as naive. What other reason was there to celebrate the anniversary of the Revolution?

Then there was Yuri, who at age nineteen seemed to have an extraordinarily long sentence of seven years for his crime, which he said had been the theft of a winter jacket. This required more investigation.

"Were you cold?"

"Yes."

"Was the jacket an expensive one?"

"It was."

"Were you drunk?"

"Yes."

"Did you use violence?"

"I had a knife."

"Did you use it?"

"I killed the man."

* * *

Prison Colony #5 wasn't the worst of the Siberian penal camps. If it had been, the authorities probably wouldn't have allowed our visit. But it had enough rapists, murderers, and perpetrators of other violent crimes to make the warden nervous and prompt General Skhurat, the regional police chief, to invite himself along to monitor our movements.

For safety's sake, Lieutenant Colonel Vladimir Lazik would only receive us on a Sunday, when he could reduce the danger that any of us would be taken hostage as part of an escape attempt. On weekdays, he said, when the inmates were working in the prison camp's two factories, they were in dangerously large groups and would have access to makeshift weapons.

In a briefing at his office just outside the prison walls, Colonel Lazik said that breakouts were a new problem, born with a freer society that was an easier and more worthwhile place of escape. There hadn't been much reason to break out in the days when the freedoms outside the camp's guard towers and stone walls hadn't been all that much greater than they were behind bars. The chances had also been much smaller then of escaping unnoticed into the tightly monitored Soviet Union.

The rise of organized-crime rings had also made Colonel Lazik's job more difficult. The crime bosses who had been incarcerated had quickly become the top dogs among the inmates. They had used the prison to recruit new manpower for the flourishing crime business outside, which the most resourceful of the inmates would join after their release. "We are more and more faced with prisoners who want to be General," said Colonel Lazik.

For weeks I had looked forward to these meetings with Russian criminals. I wanted to know what made a man turn to crime in Russia. I wanted to see how they lived. But shortly before we were to enter the camp, police chief Vitaly Skhurat delivered the bad news—he was prohibiting any meetings with the inmates. Colonel Lazik scratched his red mustache and smiled thinly and tightly, showing only a sliver of his silver teeth, as his superior, the General, undid all his promises of access that had prompted our visit in the first place.

Skhurat had been generous with his time and with information on crime in the region, but now he was drawing the line. "A penal colony is a penal colony," he said. "You should not wash your dirty laundry in public. It isn't necessary for you to talk to inmates."

I had come to learn that authorities no longer refused interview requests or access to information. Instead, they merely made the judgment that it wasn't "necessary" for the reporter. In this case it wasn't "necessary" because these two well-informed men would tell me whatever I needed to know about the prison. Skhurat couldn't imagine what worth there was in talking to prisoners.

I pleaded with him. I told him that any portrayal of the prison could only be more positive than the Gulag images of terror and starvation most Americans connected with Russian penal colonies. He smiled at my appeal, and nodded his approval to Colonel Lazik for our visit with prisoners. We then all walked together out the door of the concrete headquarters building, past the guard tower and then through the three layers of electronically controlled steel gates that separated us from the prisoners.

The doors clanged shut behind us, one after another, as we walked into the prison yard and came to the largest of a handful of four-story dormitories, situated opposite the headquarters building and the two small factories where prisoners made industrial fans and radio transistor panels.

Life was changing more slowly in prisons than in other parts of society. The Russian president had resigned from the Communist Party months earlier, on July 11, 1990, but the language of socialism was still painted red on the inner walls of the prison.

One banner said: WHO DOESN'T FULFILL SOVIET LAWS, WORKS AGAINST THE PEOPLE.

A large, permanent banner hung across the entire length of the main dormitory: THE PEOPLE OF THE USSR ARE EQUAL ACCORDING TO THE LAW, NO MATTER WHO THEY ARE OR HOW MUCH THEY EARN. It hung over a gray, five-story, cement Stalinist structure. Its entryway was oddly framed by trash cans in the shape of happy penguins. Their beaks were permanently open for garbage.

The inmates wore short-brimmed black caps and all-black uniforms— looking like bad guys in a Soviet Western. Some were playing volleyball in the yard to the left of the dormitory. Others loitered, smoking the filterless cigarettes that were part of their monthly ration of nine packages. Each prisoner was allowed to have as much tobacco as he wanted, however, if he rolled his own. The all-pervasive smoke was the camp's stale perfume.

Dundee, who by this time had become my almost constant companion, cursed to me under his breath that the convicts' ration was quadruple his own.

Eighty-two percent of the prisoners were under thirty years of age, Colonel Lazik said. He had twenty-eight convicted murderers, with sentences of ten to fifteen years, and some 400 rapists (seven to twelve years). But the atmosphere was oddly pastoral and controlled—a credit to the tough discipline that we had heard was enforced by handpicked prisoners who ruled over each barracks on behalf of the warden.

Soft Muzak of the sort I had heard so often in American supermarkets wafted out the windows of the prisoner barracks. It sounded like the 1,001 Strings playing the Beatles' greatest hits.

The walls of the dormitory hallway leading up to the prison library were decorated with rules that were so permanent that they were painted on.

They listed how many credits (going toward purchase of goods) would be given for good behavior, what payment would be given to each prisoner (depending on his productivity), and how often each prisoner would be allowed "conjugal" visits.

Inmates were allowed to meet wives or girlfriends at least twice a year, for three to five days each time, in the soulless quarters of a twenty-five-bedroom hostel set apart from the rest of the prison. The decor and sparse furnishings (a bed and a desk) were reminiscent of the cheapest Siberian hotels, and boarders cooked and ate in a common kitchen. But the warden said the prospect of these "sex vacations" helped him keep prisoners in order. Misbehavior would cost them the visiting rights. I walked up the stairs of the large dormitory building to the second floor with Colonel Lazik, to see a large, long room with two long rows of neatly made cots. The atmosphere was more military than penal. Fresh potted flowers were on windowsills, and men stood at attention by their beds. The scene was too perfect; Colonel Lazik had done some preparation for my visit. I wasn't likely to experience candid moments with the prisoners.

Colonel Lazik suggested that the best place to talk to prisoners might be the library. On such a sunny Sunday, I doubted that anyone would be there. But Colonel Lazik insisted, and in the library some Potemkin prisoners were waiting.

No interview occurred without the warden, the general, or guards listening in. I didn't complain—Colonel Lazik's concerns about hostage-taking made me welcome the watchful eyes. But the prisoners seemed oddly friendly, almost meek. Yet I would have little time to speak with them— Colonel Lazik continued to lurk in the background, not understanding why any prisoner needed to be asked more than a couple of cursory questions.

Colonel Lazik was proud to show me, on the front table with newly arrived books, a copy of Solzhenitsyn's *First Circle.* Only a half-dozen prisoners were in the library, and they sat a bit too silently over magazines and books. One prisoner held a children's magazine upside down. And when I sought interviews, all came to sit at the writing desks around me, according to drill. But even the handpicked had tales to tell.

Sergei Butilyn, prisoner number 6-66, was a thirty-five-year-old murderer. His laughing eyes and playful smile set him apart from the rest. He had used a carpenter's knife to kill a cousin who had sexually abused his mother. And he'd do it again—for his mother's honor. He had turned himself in at the police station, expecting the authorities to go easy on him, but had been upset when they had given him seven years.

When I asked about the tattoos on both his arms, he tried to hide what he called "mistakes." One on his right arm had a spider with a former girlfriend's name written on it. A second tattoo artist had blotted out the name.

He was finishing the last two years of the seven-year sentence, after which he'd go back to the coal mines. He'd already worked there for six years as an electrician, and after another four years he'd be eligible for a partial pension.

Nikolai Petrovsky had bigger plans for his after-prison life. He conceded it was his ambitious streak that had landed him in jail in the first place. He had been caught "stealing State property in large amounts." He said he had made off with 300 bottles of industrial spirits during Gorbachev's short prohibition period. He had wanted to make enough money from their sale to start up a bee farm. The term for prisoner 7-72: eight years.

Nikolai Petrovsky looked at me through glasses that were as thick as the bottom of a vodka bottle. They gave his gray eyes a house-of-mirrors distortion. His front teeth were all a brilliant gold. He was shocked when I asked whether the sentence wasn't a little bit extreme, particularly considering the shorter term for the murderer sitting beside him. They looked at each other.

"I've never really thought about it," he said. "You serve the term that you serve. We are each individually thinking about our own sentences, our own fates." There it was again—that irrepressible, unchangeable fate—*Sudba.*

Nikolai Petrovsky figured that he didn't have it so bad. For good behavior and horticultural interest, he had landed one of the prison's best jobs. He ran the vegetable farm.

The youngest of the "readers" in the library was a twenty-year-old who had been sentenced to three years for stealing ten rubles. He had robbed an old man in the stairwell of his own apartment block and been caught outside before he could get away. He hadn't even used a weapon. Using the black-market rate at that time, I calculated that he was serving a year for every dime that he had stolen.

"I don't know why they came down so hard on me—that's what they gave, and that is what I am spending," he said.

The penal system was inflexible. The laws had no provision for plea-bargaining. Probation and parole were unheard-of. Acquittals were rare and punishments were severe for the smallest of crimes. Behind this approach was a belief that the simple fact of the crime was more important than its degree or the worth of the goods that had been stolen. Even the most minor infractions could result in a year in prison. They were all dangerously anti-socialist behavior.

* * *

The saddest story of all was that of prisoner 6-62, Vladimir Novikov, who looked like someone's kind father. His handshake was soft and insecure, and he looked constantly embarrassed. He was fifty years old, and he was serving three years for attempted murder.

He had worked in a car-repair garage in a small Siberian village. His job had been to repair tires by vulcanizing them. In a country where new tires were almost impossible to come by, he had kept busy. He said that he had caught one of his fellow workers stealing gasoline and had tried to stop him.

"My fellow worker swore at me, he kicked me in the stomach, and he picked up a hammer to hit me on the head," said Vladimir Novikov. So the vulcanizer had picked up the knife that he used to cut the rubber and driven it into his attacker's stomach. He said the police wrote down his whole story—and they seemed to believe it—but the court still found him at fault.

"They said I had overused my legitimate right to self-defense," he said.

He'd been behind bars for more than a year, but he and his wife had managed to keep the news from his daughter, who worked in the Ukraine. He feared his incarceration could hurt her career. "I'm very embarrassed," he said. "I'm a very old fellow. I don't like her knowing about this. I've been very hurt by the whole thing. I think about it a lot—how I could have avoided it? I don't wish anyone to be in here—not friends or enemies."

The warden later said that the weak and the old were often mistreated by fellow inmates, who extorted their small monthly stipend and their cigarette rations and who, in the worst cases, raped them. "The people abuse me because I am older," said the tire repairman. "They are mostly young and they don't respect my age." When I asked what he meant by "abuse," he turned red and my half dozen guests all stared at their table tops with some embarrassment.

When we walked back outside, prisoners were lining up in shifts for their midday meal. They lined up in single file between blue-painted lines on the black asphalt. Inside the food hall, a gymnasium-sized space with a twenty-foot-high ceiling, several hundred men sat at long wooden tables, hunched over dented tin bowls. Other prisoners walked by them with huge caldrons of what passed for soup. It was a thin reddish fluid that tasted vaguely of tomato. A second course was a sour-tasting gruel whose only recommendation was that it quickly cut into any appetite.

The prisoners had a diet virtually free of fresh fruit or vegetables. The result was a long line of hollow faces and dull eyes, sitting in ghostly rows. They rarely spoke to one another. The only sound was of slurping soup and heavy spoons against the tin bowls. The inmates ripped off chunks from their hard, individual loaves of bread (no knives, of course, were allowed). They then submerged them in the lukewarm fluid, trying to soften the stale pieces some.

Against the wishes of General Skhurat, our Dutch photographer began to snap frames of the prisoners at point-blank range. Sensing unrest among his inmates, General Skhurat ordered us out of the hall, fearing that his blackbirds might take a Hitchcockian flight toward us. When the photographer protested that he only needed another few minutes, the general barked a firm *"Nyet."*

For the first time in three days, Skhurat was angry. This time he wouldn't compromise.

Colonel Lazik invited us back to headquarters, where a late lunch waited for us. We sat alone at a table at the center of the dining hall. The table groaned with food—raw fish, onions, tomatoes, cutlets, fresh vegetables, and sausage.

But before we began to eat, General Skhurat explained why he had been so uneasy about the prisoners in the dining hall.

A year earlier he had already dramatically resolved one breakout attempt at Prison Colony #5. A convicted murderer, who had added to his sentence by killing a fellow inmate, had been shipped to the prison from a higher-security colony for medical treatment at its hospital. Using a knife made in the metal shop, he had taken a nurse hostage and demanded that he be freed.

The first response of the prison authorities had been "to make a plan to shoot him dead," said Lazik. But General Skhurat, the local hero, had paced around the prison yard for about an hour, and devised an alternative plan. He had called for the prisoner's records, and they showed that he loved his parents and had a good relationship with them.

So he had pleaded with the prisoner through the door, reminding him that his hostage was a woman and mother. Having seen portions of letters written to the prisoner from his parents, the general had mentioned some facts from them. He'd said the parents wouldn't want their son to harm an innocent woman.

The general had offered to come in as a second hostage, which the prisoner had accepted, and then the woman was able to escape on a toilet break that the general had negotiated. "You know that no woman can be kept for so long without being given a chance to go to the toilet," the general had said to the inmate.

The final negotiations had become more like labor talks—the prisoner had even wanted to discuss the improvement of the nurses' working conditions and the increase of medical supplies for the hospital. The general in return had promised the inmate that he wouldn't spend a single day extra behind bars for the additional crime of hostage-taking and attempted escape. "And I have stayed by my word," said the general. Six hours after the crisis had begun, he had negotiated its peaceful end.

As the general told his story, Colonel Lazik poured the water glasses full of vodka, joking about the region's considerable pollution. "This is the best detergent for whatever contamination we have," he said, laughing. He raised his glass, took a giant gulp, and looked for me to do the same.

A non-drinker would have trouble working in Siberia. He wouldn't be trusted. A heavy drinker would have trouble ever remembering anything he had reported or reading the infirm scribbling in his notebook. So I tried to walk a line between the two, downing enough so as to appear manly and pacing myself sufficiently to remain conscious.

But this social demand had already begun to fog my mind, so I devised clever ways around it. The general lack of potted plants in Siberia removed one option. So I exploited the great advantage of vodka's lack of coloring and disposed of shots into partially empty water glasses. No one ever questioned why a visitor hadn't finished his mineral water.

The danger was in being caught, which would expose an even more cowardly nature than total abstinence would have. But I faced that embarrassment only once, when quite late one evening I poured a particularly large shot glass into a loathsome broth thick with gristle that I had early on decided not to finish.

When my local host's driver noticed that I was not eating the soup, he invited himself to a couple of large slurps before he looked up from the bowl at me suspiciously. He didn't complain, however, and repeatedly stuck his tablespoon in for more.

These means of reducing alcohol intake were only effective, however, because I was willing to drink a considerable amount at the outset to win my hosts' confidence.

So I looked Colonel Lazik in the eye and I took a manly gulp from the vodka-filled water glass. He smiled at me with approval. And he began to talk about the post-Communist changes at the prison, none of which pleased him much.

The first problem was economic. Like all prisons in the Soviet Union, Colony #5 was a going concern. Its two products—industrial fans and radio transistor panels—had an annual turnover of some 40 million rubles, "when the ruble meant a little something," said Lazik. Profits were nearly 20 percent of sales, and that money was used to provide most of the budget for the prison.

"But those days are over," said Lazik. The motors and metal for the fans came from Lithuania, Armenia, and Azerbaijan, and most suppliers weren't delivering anymore. During the fight for Lithuania's independence, a telegram from one supplier had read: INFLUENCE YOUR GOVERNMENT TO SUPPORT LITHUANIAN INDEPENDENCE AND WE WILL CONSIDER SENDING YOU THE MOTORS.

When Lazik could get parts and supplies, the prices had risen so high that any chance of a profit was lost. And Lazik still hadn't permission from the government to raise his own prices. So now he was thinking over ways to sell his production privately.

The second problem, he said, came with the shutting down of the Communist Party. Under orders from Moscow, the prison had shut down its Party organization about a month before we had arrived. That hadn't been a happy day for Colonel Lazik. More than a third of his 470-member staff regularly attended their Thursday-evening Party meetings. Their final session had been painful; no one quite knew what to say. "I didn't feel myself well at the meeting," he said. "We had a feeling of being betrayed. The good Communists were being punished because of those leaders who were bad. Why should we pay for their sins?"

The general tried to help his Western visitor understand. "It is like your game of baseball," he said. "I don't understand it, and I may never understand it, but it is in your blood. And it was in our blood from childhood that we wanted to be a Communist. It was a special atmosphere. First we were October members, then as youths were Young Pioneers and finally we were Komsomol [Communist Youth League] members. We were brought up with this ideology, and now we ask why we can't put our thoughts into reality. I remember when Stalin died, I cried, my mother cried, and my teachers cried. It was as if our father died. We broke up into pieces.

"Now we know who he was, and we are hurt by that. But we are Communists still. We just aren't as fanatic about it. The fundamental ideas were good, they were just spoiled." He said that if America had been as dogmatic about imposing a pure capitalism, it would have failed as well.

Colonel Lazik wished that he had something to replace the Party's social role at his prison. He said the order and discipline the Party brought to the workplace was far more important than any ideology. "I haven't any ideals anymore, no illusions," he said. "But the Party helped me solve disputes."

He again smiled that thin, tight smile. For example, he said, when a woman was upset that her husband was drinking too much or sleeping with another woman, she would come to the prison colony's Party cell to complain. "She would tell me, 'Throw him out, he is sleeping with another woman,' " said Colonel Lazik.

"And I would say, 'No. Where will he go if he leaves the Party?' I would tell her that the Party would give him a good strapping."

The colonel laughed when he explained that the "strapping" would often consist of publicly ridiculing the man for being caught and warning him that the next time he slept with another man's wife, he should make sure that his own wife didn't find out. "Who will play that role now that the Party is gone?" he said with remorse.

Chapter 9:

THE MIRACLE OF YURGA

This great visitation from Across the Water
is God's work.

—PASTOR LAMPE, *Lutheran minister*

The old woman, whom I stopped for directions, agreed to show me the way to the Lutherans' once-secret place of worship—through the overgrown field, over the small creek, and then up the steep hill. She said "the Germans" had met there, out of Communist earshot and eyesight, since Stalin had exiled them to Yurga in 1941.

I struggled to keep up with her as she balanced on logs, tiptoed through the mud, and obliviously pushed to the side tall stalks of marijuana plants that were growing wild everywhere. "They must not use this path anymore," she concluded. "It was the secret way of getting there."

A black dog barked angrily as we walked in the back gate of a log home, one among a row arranged neatly on the rise. It had been built fifty years earlier, but it looked new, with a fresh coat of white-and-green paint. The German construction was solid, showing none of the usual Soviet signs of decay; the vegetable patch had Teutonically straight rows of onions, tomatoes, potatoes, and cabbage. I could hear the faint sound of German voices lifted in song.

A young woman with a white scarf covering her head, alerted by the dog, peeked out from behind the door and waved us to hurry inside. "You are very late," she said, "but God bless you just the same."

The lay pastor abruptly stopped the service as I walked in. He asked, in German, that I introduce myself. I replied, also in German, that I was an

American, the son of German immigrants, and that I had come to acquaint myself with the way of life in Siberia. What I didn't say was that I was the first American who had ever been given permission to visit Yurga, a city whose advanced-weapons production had made it off-limits to foreigners since the day its construction had begun in 1939. Pastor Lampe seemed fully aware of the novelty of my visit.

He turned to the congregation, spread his arms, and declared a miracle. "This great visitation from Across the Water is God's work," he said, drawing a florid picture of a modern Moses parting the ideologically Red Sea. "This is a sign of God's mercy. Holy Father, my hands and feet are shaking."

And indeed they were.

His congregation of about forty was made up primarily of elderly women. It was also sprinkled with a handful of old men who sat ramrod straight and young women who looked coyly at me from behind their handkerchiefs. They were among some 400,000 Germans who had been exiled from their homes, primarily around the Volga River region, shortly after the Nazi invasion in 1941. The "Volga Deutschen" had come to Russia as colonists primarily during the reign of German-born Empress Catherine the Great. The Empress had lured them with land, tax-free status for up to thirty years, exemption from military service, and religious freedom. But Stalin dissolved the Volga German Autonomous Republic in September 1941 after the Nazi invasion. Then he shipped thousands of Germans to prison camps and exiled the rest, primarily to Siberia and Kazakhstan.

In Yurga, the task of the newly arriving Germans had been to build a city whose economy would revolve around an artillery plant that was being relocated from Leningrad to keep it out of Nazi reach. At the time, the only sign identifying the future location at a whistle-stop on the Trans-Siberian Railway read: STROIKA—meaning construction site.

Since then, most surprises in the lives of Yurga's Germans had been unhappy ones. So Pastor Lampe was working his Lutherans into a fervor about my arrival, and they riveted their eyes upon me as if I were human manna from heaven.

"Didn't the Lord God say that heaven and earth would pass, but not my Word?" said the minister. They all nodded in agreement. A handful of women began to sniffle. The morning light ricocheted off Pastor Lampe's brilliantly gold teeth (it looked as though he had buffed them before the service), and he wiped some perspiration from his brow with a well-worn blue-and-white handkerchief. "This visitation is a sign that we must continue our work. We will stand and sing."

After the hymn, the service should have ended, but Pastor Lampe declared an extension. He also extended God's forgiveness for my tardy arrival, a generous gesture, for even in Yurga, Germans are obsessed with punctuality. "No one is ever too late for You, O Lord," he said, looking heavenward. "The train hasn't yet left the station."

Behind him was a framed, handpainted drawing of a pastoral scene: white gates opening onto a fertile field of green. Under a perfectly blue sky stood a half-timbered Bavarian farmhouse. Below this very German portrayal of paradise was written in large, hand-drawn letters: FÜRCHTE-DICH NICHT, IN GOTTES HAUS IST IMMER LICHT—Fear Not, There Is Always Light in God's House.

The dreamy painting was in contrast to the reality of Yurga, a city of prefabricated five-to-nine-story buildings. It was the only dot of civilization for miles on the vast Siberian plain; its splendid desolation reminded me of instant cities I had visited on Israel's occupied West Bank. There was something Biblical about the place.

The morning light streamed through the window, but it was Pastor Lampe's words that provided the heat. "These visitors, who have traveled so far, they fear nothing," he said. "God brought them here. He led them to where they would find the Word. God protected them in their path. What should we fear when we are all bound together with Thee, great God?"

By this time most of those in the congregation, even the men, were sobbing, but no one was looking at me anymore. Pastor Lampe was the star attraction, and he had his flock mesmerized. The outpouring of emotion may have been a regular occurrence; the worshipers were all armed with handkerchiefs, into which they were weeping and sniffling. Pastor Lampe pulled out his handkerchief again, wiped his eyes with it, and then blew his nose as loud as Gideon's trumpet.

He then read from the Scriptures, I John, Chapter 2, about God's bountiful mercy. "He that saith, I know him, and keepeth not his commandments, is a liar and the truth is not in him. . . ." He spoke flowingly, but he read German haltingly, moving his finger slowly under each word. Like most of the Germans in town, he had never had the chance to study or read in his native tongue. Bibles had been smuggled in over the years, and their German songbooks had been handwritten from the memory of the older worshipers—many of the words misspelled.

After the lengthy reading he bade the congregation drop to its knees and pray. The combination of the mumbled prayers and the sobbing melded into a sad Gregorian chant. When the service ended, the entire congregation walked behind me as I left, an impromptu Sunday parade down a muddy road. The old women slipped me candies, and the pastor wished Godspeed to his visitor from Across the Water.

It seemed odd to me that it had taken so long for Yurga to host its first American. I wondered what sort of deep secret lay behind its arm's-length from the world. After all, it was forty-six years after the beginning of the

Cold War, five years since the start of Glasnost, and many months after Russian leaders had begun to open up their society to all comers. What could they be building in that defense plant?

"I can only tell you quite confidently that Yurga was closed to Americans until today," said Stalina Mikhailovna Ignatova, our guide in Yurga, whom I had met on the Saturday evening before my visit to Pastor Lampe's church. "We are happy to invite you as the first. But you will have to ask someone else about the plant and the production."

Stalina was an attractive, fashionably dressed woman in her mid-thirties. She had giant eyes, thick, rosy lips and a winning smile. She had a confident and intelligent manner, and was more urbane than most young women in Western Siberia. In fact, her only obvious blemish was that name. I had never met a woman who had been named after a mass murderer, so I sought an explanation.

"My mother wanted to name me Luda," said Stalina. "But when she came to the registrar in our village, it was the first anniversary of Stalin's death. On such an important day, he told my mother, she couldn't name me Luda but should name me Stalina. Stalin, you see, was still very popular in the villages of Siberia at that time—he still is."

When Khrushchev started changing the names of cities and towns that had been named after Stalin, it just so happened that Stalina was living in Stalinsk. And when Stalinsk was renamed Novokuznetsk in 1961, Stalina's mother thought it would be a good idea to change her little girl's name as well. "We inquired, but were told that according to our laws I could change my name only when I was eighteen years old," she said. "By that time I had graduated from high school and I didn't want to change my name anymore. I grew used to it—and there were two other girls on the honors board who also were named Stalina."

I had met Stalina in Yurga's only restaurant. I found it curious that it was empty except for our group. A waitress told me later that the mayor had ordered the restaurant, which was the local watering hole for Yurga's black-market dealers, to be closed to its usual clientele for the evening.

"You weren't supposed to come into contact with them," said the waitress. Out of the corner of my eye, however, I saw her go to the door on several occasions to slip bottles of vodka or champagne to well-dressed men with shapely, scantily clad women on their arms—their compensation for the evening's inconvenience.

Trying to shift my attention, Stalina briefed me on our program for the following morning, a Sunday. "You will get up in the morning before eight A.M., you will have breakfast at 8:30 A.M., you will then take a stroll through the old city at 9:30 A.M., after which you will meet the mayor at 10 A.M., then you will hold a press conference—"

I cut her off. I told her that I'd prefer wandering around on my own—although I did wonder what had become of our approved visit to the defense plant, euphemistically known as the Yurga Machine Factory. Would we visit there Monday before we headed downstream?

Stalina apologized. Our application to visit the plant had been denied—she didn't know why. She said we couldn't appeal the decision over the weekend because it was the director's forty-fifth birthday and she didn't want to disturb his celebration.

When I pressed, the parliament member in our delegation, People's Deputy Yuri Kaznin, began to speak in his politician's drone that was grating on all of us: "Old forces are still at work here," said Kaznin in his podium voice. He explained that even he, as a parliament candidate from Yurga, had been prevented from visiting certain plants during his campaign. "The Cold War isn't yet over in some places in Yurga. You can imagine how they view you, the first American, when you come into town and try to visit their factory. Nothing changes overnight."

I was visiting a world that was caught between past habits and new openness. My application to visit Yurga had been approved, but my efforts to discover why Yurga had been closed to outsiders in the first place were being rebuffed.

What we would learn only later—and not from Kaznin—was that the defense plant had sponsored his own candidacy for the Supreme Soviet. Stalina, it turned out, wasn't only our guide, but had also been the campaign chief for Kaznin and was also the personal assistant to the factory director. The director, in turn, was the *de facto* mayor of the city, who signed off on local budgets and provided many city services. With the Party in retreat, the factory had filled the vacuum. It seemed to run almost everything and everyone in Yurga—including Yuri Kaznin and Stalina Ignatova.

I altered Stalina's Sunday program and instead decided to attend church services and wander around Yurga to see how its people might respond to their first American visitor.

Stalina wasn't pleased that I had refused her invitation to go before the planned press conference for local reporters. Everywhere we went during the exhibition, local politicians wanted to use the expedition as an excuse either for a vodka-soaked party or for a press conference in which we could be paraded out as some sort of evidence of Western backing for their leadership. I politely told Stalina that I had such limited time in Yurga that I wanted to use it to collect information. I said, however, that I would be pleased to *interview* Yurga's local reporters.

More than a decade of reporting in the Soviet Union and Eastern Europe had taught me it was a waste of time to try to understand the machinations of the secret police. A Polish interpreter of mine during the early Solidarity strikes in 1980 had regularly discussed reports she had been forced to provide on me. I had sometimes edited them, and on occasion I even added a little spice. Writing such reports was the price interpreters had to pay for working with foreigners. She had asked that I schedule at least three official interviews a week so that she had something acceptable to report. I had done so.

But a decade later, Communism had crumbled and I felt less like compromising. While other members of the expedition fielded the local reporters' questions, I visited the Lutheran church and Pastor Lampe. After that, I drove across town to the newly built Russian Orthodox church, a small wooden building that looked like "the little chapel on the prairie." It was meant to be temporary. Beside it, workmen had laid the foundation for a more permanent stone structure (largely to be financed by the factory).

The church was decorated with cheap icons. As it was with most other goods in Siberia, the highest-quality icons were being sold in the West. Yet the people of Yurga didn't seem troubled by this, and they lined up behind the altar, where their priest was baptizing them in droves.

Father Vladimir Patchayev, with his chest-length gray beard and his golden robes, looked as if he had stepped out of the Middle Ages when he sat down on a wooden bench outside his church to talk. He said that he had worked at a track-switching station along the Trans-Siberian Railway until 1970, when he had been fired for expressing his religious beliefs too openly. After that, he had studied at a Moscow seminary and become a deacon and then a priest. In 1991, at age fifty-four, he had overseen the building of Yurga's first Orthodox church.

He said church attendance in the region had quintupled, and he was baptizing an average of 100 new members each week. Most of the baptisms were of children, but he would often sprinkle water on the heads of the whole family at the same time. "People without belief cannot live," he said. "They worshiped the false god of Communism for years, but now they are finding their way to the True Faith."

Father Patchayev's blue eyes were lodged deeply in his head, behind a long nose. Every few minutes he pulled one of two combs from his shirt pocket, each with several teeth missing, to groom his stringy charcoal hair.

He frowned that he had been forced to double the price of a baptism to ten rubles, but his own costs were going up and he needed to raise enough money to build his church. "With the devaluation of the ruble, it is just kopeks what the rubles mean today," he said. He also planned to build a small hotel to house visitors from surrounding villages who worked at state farms that had never had churches. These villagers were flocking to Yurga for baptisms and religious holidays.

"Our calling is to repair the degradation of the Russian soul," he said. "The system was killing man's personality. It has given us drunkards, swearing, men mistreating their women, and the destruction of mankind."

He planned to introduce marriages soon. It hurt him that so many newlyweds still laid bouquets of flowers at the city's Lenin statue. "It was recommended for wedding parties, and they got used to it," he said. "We must bring people back to their Russian traditions."

Down the street from the church, a long line was forming behind a different sort of altar. A brick wall was providing fresh drinking water for nearly half the city through three spouts. Because of the polluted river, the locals considered the quality of their tap water to be so bad that they were filling up bottles, buckets, and huge steel canisters with the well water.

"Many children here are born without fingers," Stalina had told me. "Children who are born here are often called yellow children because of their kidney problems." As so often on our trip, it was difficult to find statistics or empirical evidence to match the rumors. And the Greenpeace scientists with us said that sickness and water quality in Yurga didn't seem to be worse than at other stops we had made.

But in a country where the truth had been hidden for so many years, the people had grown willing to believe the worst about every aspect of their lives. And in a country where facts have never played a role, the two Greenpeace scientists who joined our expedition were growing frustrated by local officials and even ecologists who made broad generalizations without the benefit of factual support. The propaganda of gloom had replaced the propaganda of paradise.

That didn't mean that the pollution wasn't bad; it was. But the Greenpeace men, Wytze van der Naald and Michael Hoffman, often found problems in unexpected places. The quality of the drinking water in Kemerovo, for instance, was worse than that in Yurga. Yet the people drank it blithely.

The two Western scientists were surprised to find that errors in the purification process had made the Kemerovo drinking water even more poisonous than the water flowing down the Tom River.

The plants' chemists had apparently botched the process by adding chlorine too early. As best as I could understand it, the mix of the chlorine and the existing bacteria created additional toxins that made every sip a risk. "I wouldn't even shower in it," said Dr. Hoffmann, a German microbiologist not given to hyperbole. "And I certainly wouldn't drink it."

But the Kemerovo purification specialists weren't going to change the mix on the word of these Westerners. One of them even threatened to stop providing the Westerners data if they continued to criticize their work.

Greenpeace's second shock was that their fellow ecologist, Yuri Kaznin, had prevented them from taking samples at the site of industrial-discharge pipes. Wytze complained that Yuri wanted to avoid fingering individual polluters, but was merely seeking a general, Western-endorsed analysis that he could use on the political stump, particularly before his Yurga constituency.

Kaznin, a swaybacked Siberian with a thick black mustache and drooping eyes, had reason to lead the Greenpeace men away. Two of the factories were Defense Ministry–run chemical plants, the scientists learned later, and inspecting them too closely would be prying into national-security matters.

However, the mayor of Yurga, Yevgeny Cheprakov, was far less worried about his water than he was about 20,000 new citizens whom the central authorities were thrusting upon his city of 90,000. When Moscow had looked for places to put some of the 390,000 troops withdrawing from Germany, Yurga had seemed a good choice. It had plenty of room to build, sufficient food supplies, and a history of taking in new citizens.

·But the mayor, a relatively powerless man anyway in this company-run town, didn't know how he would provide for them. "Nobody asked us anything," he said. "They'll need drinking water, transport, electricity, schools and kindergartens." He was particularly worried about the effect on his city of the breakdown of army discipline; he feared soldiers might turn to crime—or at least dig up vegetables in the local gardens that grew near their new housing.

The area holding the half-finished buildings for the soldiers looked like the "green line" of Beirut well into Lebanon's civil war. Construction brigades were throwing up housing so quickly that the prefabricated cement slabs were fractured and lopsided. Huge chunks were missing. "I agree it doesn't look like much from the outside," said the mayor. "But it will be better on the inside."

Digging trenches nearby, a construction brigade cared little what the building looked like. They leaned on their shovels and squatted on the ground, their faces red from working long hours in the sun. Morale was low, and they gossiped about the many ways draftees use to escape service.

They chuckled about one draftee they knew who convinced the army doctor that he was mentally unbalanced by arriving with a bottle of vodka, taking a shot from it himself, and then offering the doctor one as well. The prospective soldier then checked his pocket for change and proposed that the doctor and he pool their resources and buy a second bottle together.

Once a soldier was in the army, escape was harder but not impossible, the soldiers said. "You can injure yourself, you can commit a small crime, and you can act like you're crazy," said a pimply-faced nineteen-year-old, counting the methods of avoiding service on his grimy fingers. He said some soldiers would regularly wet their beds until they were discharged. One took drugs so obviously that his superiors caught him.

They all spoke with respect for a comrade who had run away from their brigade a month earlier. "He had a wife who was about to give birth, and they wouldn't give him leave," said the nineteen-year-old. "He also had a bad heart problem that put him in the hospital, and his worries about his wife made it worse. But they caught him in Moscow, and now it will be even worse for him. They'll court-martial him and put him in a disciplinary battalion."

These young men had been in the military for only two months, but they already didn't like it. They asked me about America's volunteer army— something they thought Russia should introduce. All of them said, however, that they wouldn't sign up.

"We work night and day and we haven't any days off," said one, an eighteen-year-old, who balanced on his shovel while smoking a hand-rolled cigarette. He was a boy trying to act like a man. "We eat mostly porridge and tinned meat. We have a television but no electricity to run it. We don't understand why we have an army anymore at all. We don't have any enemies. But who will do the building and the dirty work if we don't?"

When I returned to my hotel, the Germans were waiting.

Word had spread through their community that an American who spoke their language was in town; they had organized a little get-together for me. A car brought me to a large hall, where local Communist Party leaders had once met. Lenin's banner still hung the podium.

But the music was the polka. The Germans were singing and spinning around on the dance floor. When I walked in, they stopped and then they applauded. This was a regular meeting of their *Wiedergeburt* group—the Rebirth Society—dedicated to reviving and nurturing German culture (and to regaining the German Volga Republic). I had become the main attraction of that week's meeting, along with my ethnic German interpreter, Viktor Pelz, a survivor himself of the Gulag. They set up a table where we could hold court.

Although I usually worked in English with Dundee as my interpreter, I chose Viktor Pelz for Yurga. He was an ethnic German who understood the city's history and people. Although I speak German, many of Yurga's Germans don't, so he would also translate from Russian when necessary.

The Germans of Yurga were a pleasant enough group. There were the Pepker sisters, twins who, at age seventy, still dressed in the same outfits (conservative and Quaker-like) and giggled in unison. They were Baptists (quite strict, they were proud to say), and they were relieved to hear that I didn't smoke—a sin that was too often committed among the Russian people. They were both moving to Germany at the end of that year.

There was Maria Bergmann, who had arrived with the first group of Germans in 1943. The heavy building had been done by prisoners of war then, she said, and the ethnic Germans worked in the defense factories. "But after five years they got rid of us all and gave us other jobs," she said. "I cleaned houses. The worst part of being shut out of the defense factory was that it was the warmest place to work—something you have to worry about in Siberia."

Friedeberg Leidewitz, born in 1937, said he as well would emigrate to Germany soon, "where everything is built well." He complained that his children spoke little German and his grandchildren didn't know the language at all. "They laugh when we speak German," he said. "Can you imagine? Having to apologize for speaking the greatest literary language that was ever invented?"

He remembered how, during his childhood in Yurga, the youth were divided between "Fritzes" and "Ivans." He would sometimes come home from school, crying, after children ridiculed him as a "Fritz." He wanted to stop being German then so that he would have fewer problems. "But now everyone wants to be German," he said—because Germans are being allowed to emigrate.

Lydia Hein was of the younger generation, in their thirties, who spoke German poorly if at all. She was surprised that I considered myself to be American, and not German, although my parents had both been born in Germany. I explained that immigrants in general were so proud to be American that they gladly gave up their previous nationality. I said that my German parents, who had come to America before World War II, were like so many other Germans who had lost pride in their origins after the Nazi years. To their shock, I said I had never considered myself to be German—only American.

This got a few of the Germans in the crowd worked up. "People aren't guilty for what their government did," said an older man.

"Our children were also sent to Afghanistan, and that wasn't their free choice," shouted a middle-aged woman.

"Stalin wasn't an angel either," the old man said again.

These Soviet-Germans were prouder of being Germans than the German Germans I knew. They openly argued that they were genetically superior to the Russians who had ruled them. This confidence had made some of the indignities of Russian life more bearable; they could assure themselves that their real roots were in Germany, a country that worked.

For them, being German was a badge of honor. They even noted that some 400 German words had entered the Russian language during the eighteenth and nineteenth centuries, often of the practical sort that their hosts didn't have in their own tongue—like *"Butterbrot"* (buttered bread), *"Stecker"* (electrical plug), *"Messer"* (knife), *"Glasur"* (enamel), and even *"Strafnik"* (prisoner, from the German word for punishment).

One retired gentleman, who had been a schoolteacher, expressed anger that I would not concede that I was more German than American. "You *look* so German," he said. "Surely, in your passport it is written that you *are* German." It was a natural conclusion in the Soviet Union, where nationalities—German, Ukrainian, or even Jewish—were listed in each Soviet passport.

When I explained to him that no other nationality was written in an American passport, he didn't believe me, so I had to show mine to him.

"But if your mother and father are German, then the child can't be a nigger," he said, upset that I would prefer being an American. "No, it is impossible. You are a German whether you want to admit it or not."

Lydia Hein raised her hand eagerly. She thought she had the explanation for why I viewed my German blood differently than did the ethnic Germans of Yurga.

"Your parents chose to be American," she said, "but we were forced to remember that we were German. If you had been punished for being a German, as we have, then you wouldn't feel so American."

Viktor Pelz, my German-speaking interpreter, saw that my sympathy for Yurga's Germans was restrained. I was sorry for them. But in a Russia where 20 million people had died because of the war—and perhaps another 10 million during Stalin's repressions—their plight didn't seem all that tragic by comparison.

He had quietly listened to the arguments in the hall, interpreting the intercessions of those young ethnic Germans who could speak only Russian. He occasionally explained to the Germans of Yurga how Germans live in the West, having visited Germany twice himself. But after the meeting, Viktor finally decided to tell me his life story, which he had kept to himself until then, so that I could better understand the history of *die Wolga Deutschen.*

He had been born on October 1, 1923, in a small farming village called Renavka, which was only twenty-five kilometers from the train tracks through the Volga region from Germany. His parents had moved there to purchase property in 1902, the year the village was founded. Viktor's was one of some forty families in Renavka, and he attended its one school with four classes.

Viktor's father had been the most educated man in the village, so he was its only schoolteacher. His grandfather had bought the largest house in town (it had been owned by a Russian who had sold most of the property of Renavka to arriving Germans after his farm went bankrupt).

Viktor remembered that in his home, like the others, the living room, stall, and barn were all under a single roof. But the German communities, he said, always had a higher living standard than the neighboring Russian villages. "Germans worked longer hours, from dawn to dark, and they introduced modern farm machinery earlier," he said. "And the Germans were always very frugal—my mother said she wore her first pair of new shoes at age seventeen."

Viktor recalled an idyllic childhood in a neat home that had a garden with fruit trees. "We didn't have much wood, so there was no fence at the front of the yard, but there were rows of roses there," he said. And his father and uncle worked 145 acres of rich farmland that had been given to their families.

"Everything was German—the language, the administration, and the people," he said. "We never saw any influence of the Tsar. He was only interested that we pay our taxes. But people kept their German citizenship and were proud of it. I remember that in 1933 Hitler invited all Germans to come back and be unified. Five or six families from our village returned to Germany. I was ten years old then, and I remember my father, because he was the most educated, helping the families fill out their applications."

The first problems in Renavka came with collectivization in 1929. But the village chairman saved Renavka from the mass exiles of well-off peasants that took place in neighboring towns by quietly and quickly collectivizing. No one held out and no one was exiled. But the individual farmers continued to live well.

More serious troubles came on January 11, 1938, when Stalin's men came and arrested eleven of the forty men in the village, during the purges that engulfed the whole country. The arrests seemed to have little to do with their Germanness. "They disappeared and no one knew why specifically these eleven men," said Viktor, who was then fifteen years old. But that was only the beginning.

On September 12, 1941, two strangers rode into town and told all the families to pack their bags. Within twenty-four hours they would be "relocated." No one could take more than 130 pounds of baggage. They were told to wear warm clothing.

The cows and sheep had to be left behind. On the morning the villagers left Renavka in cattle cars, recalled Viktor, the cows were crying. "Someone should have milked them. But what could we do? We left the apple and plum trees full with fruit. And we didn't know where we were going."

The villagers landed sixteen days later in an area near Tashkent, where they picked cotton until 1942, when the eighteen-year-old Viktor Pelz was called up into a "labor army." He was brought 1,000 miles north to Chelyabinsk in the middle of a Siberian winter. With three feet of snow on the ground, he and the others began to build a barbed-wire fence, guard towers, and trenches. "I thought we were building it for German prisoners of war," he said, "but we learned otherwise when we were nearly finished. I had built my own prison."

Once the "labor-army" soldiers realized this, many tried to escape. Most were shot while fleeing, but those captured alive were brought back to the prison, tried for desertion, and executed in front of the others, many of whom were already dying of disease and hunger. "In my camp there were 7,000 prisoners, and more than half of them died between March and May 1942."

Viktor Pelz had swollen up so badly from sickness that the doctor feared he would burst. No one could diagnose the problem or find a cure. One night, when orderlies monitored the patients and removed the dead and dying, they took Viktor's temperature and decided that he should be put in the isolation room for the incurably sick.

"I took a blanket and pillow with me and lay down in a spot on the floor beside two other men. It was dark. They were so restless and kept turning over so much that it disturbed me. Then I noticed that one was suddenly still. He had died. But his death didn't bother me; I cared only about my fever. I drew closer to his body because it was still warm. The man on the other side of me pressed against my back, also for warmth. But when I touched him a little while later, he didn't move; he had also died. I just waited quietly there, between the two dead men, until the orderlies returned in the morning. The orderlies were also Germans. They came in and hit the feet of the other two men. When their legs didn't move, they carried them off. One was already stiff. But when the orderly hit my feet, he was surprised when I raised my legs. I had been expected to die overnight. The doctor came in and was angry that the orderlies had put me with the others to die. But I didn't care. I couldn't have cared less about living."

Viktor nonetheless survived and was released in 1946, after which he became a schoolteacher. He knew that the punishment he had undergone was because he was German, but he thought that his story was one common to many—to all "Soviets." It was a story of people who had been so anesthetized by suffering and exhausted by hardships that they had lost much of the spirit they needed for the free market and democracy. "There isn't a family in Russia that didn't have a family member executed in 1937 or die at the front. You can only view it as fate when it happened in a whole country. Whether one was against it or sickened by it, that didn't help. The magnitude of the suffering and terror made people numb."

After much insistence, the elusive director of Yurga's defense factory consented to come to meet us the next morning—but not at his plant. He would come to the mayor's office.

Vladimir N. Yesaulov, forty-five, exuded confidence commensurate with his position. He was the real power of Yurga. He regarded politicians with the disdain of men who control them, and he was certain the Cold War never would have happened if industrialists in East and West had run things.

"Everything in this town was built by this plant," he said. "Some seventy percent of the flats were paid by us, eighty percent of the nurseries, and of the twelve schools, we built eight of them. We have our own college and technical school and health services, with a medical staff of fifteen hundred people. We have a resort. Even the guest house you are staying in belongs to us. Some fifty-five percent of all the workers of the city are employed by our plant. And if you include the teachers who instruct our children, then it comes to seventy percent."

Yesaulov was smoking as he spoke with us, but the mayor's office didn't have an ashtray for him. The maker of some of the most advanced military products in the country looked for a suitable substitute, but finally had to settle for a half sheet out of my notebook that he rolled into a cone. He knocked his ashes into it.

He wouldn't talk about the plant's current defense production, but he was happy to detail the history of the "Yurga Machine Factory." He said that it had begun producing 120-millimeter cannons in 1942. But in 1965 it had turned to far more advanced weaponry. Although I had been told by Western experts that the plant built mobile and stationary launchers for nuclear missiles, Mr. Yesaulov insisted that he built only launching systems "for the space program." He said production of such launchers still accounted for 47 percent of his sales. He conceded, however, that the plant belonged to the Defense Ministry.

Yesaulov had finished his cigarette, and it was burning down toward his finger. Still lacking an ashtray, he decided that he would spit on the burning tip. But his spit missed both the tip and the paper cone and landed on the table in front of him. A second attempt was more successful, but just as unsavory; the saliva hung from the doused stub before dripping into the paper cone.

Yesaulov conceded he had power, but he said that power also gave him great responsibility for the people of Yurga. If he fired anyone in this one-company town, no other jobs were available to them. So he was rapidly diversifying and adding new lines of business, knowing his defense orders would continue to fall off. He had bought dozens of sewing machines to get the women of the factory working in textiles, and he had signed a contract with a German company to make hydraulic cylinders.

One of the problems in attracting foreign buyers, he said, was the transport difficulty posed by the plant's location. Stalin's idea of building it far from the Western front had made sense only when the Nazis were invading.

Yesaulov, however, was already making plenty of products for export—cranes, two sorts of oilseed presses, forklift loaders, and excavators. He had begun to make campers to hook to the back of cars and small furnaces to heat flats. He also had plenty of agricultural goods from two large farms with 1,000 employees, 2,000 cows, and 4,000 pigs.

But he found that he was having trouble motivating his workers. "People worked before because they were afraid," he said. "Now no one is afraid, but we haven't found new motivations. The quality of work has fallen.

"People are different here. Russians aren't Germans. I couldn't stop being surprised by small incidents I experienced abroad. On a business trip in Germany, a small boy pedaled up to me on a bicycle. He offered to sell me a picture that he had drawn himself. They are businessmen from the time they are small boys. If our children need money, they turn only to the parents. When my workers need something—milk, shoes—then they go to the director. I am supposed to provide."

Yesaulov also complained it would be years before Russians could accept entrepreneurial success stories without jealousy. He had become co-director of a new joint venture with a Germany company, but he would have to be careful that his salary didn't appear too large to his workers.

"In the West, you say that if someone is rich, then you should try to become so rich, too," he said. "Here, if you see someone is rich, then you want to pull him down. We have been taught for seventy years that everyone should be equal. If my wife puts on a good hat, then the woman washing the floors wants the same hat. It will take at least ten years to change people, and we have to be careful in the meantime. You have to do it gradually or people will take an ax and who knows what will happen."

Yesaulov insisted he wasn't rich, but he acted with the well-heeled confidence of a character out of an episode of *Dallas;* the American serial's first airing in Russia coincided with my time in Yurga. I wondered if he had seen the show.

He and his wife were watching it every evening, he said, although it had caused something of a family dispute. "My wife said the life is something to wish for—and I suppose it's not bad," he said. "Myself, I didn't like it that JR would do business any way he could. Bobby was more respectable. It is hard to believe they are from the same mother."

Before it turned dark, I took a last stroll through Yurga. It was a cool summer evening, and a gentle breeze was coming off the river. Lovers were walking hand in hand, children were coming home from playgrounds, and men were sitting on the facing wooden benches that stood in front of the entrance to each of the prefab, ten-story apartment buildings.

Although no American had visited Yurga before, no one seemed surprised to meet one. David Livingstone, the Scottish explorer and missionary, had had the great advantage, as a traveler in Africa, that television hadn't preceded him with programs that would convince those he visited that they already knew all about his kind.

During the time I was in Yurga, Soviet television had been having a special American-program week. Every day, *Dallas* was shown twice— once at nine in the morning and once at nine in the evening. It was the most popular in a lineup that included *Little House on the Prairie* and *The Streets of San Francisco.* For the children, the programs included *The Muppet Show, The Jetsons,* and *The Flintstones.*

I joined five men sitting on benches in front of their apartment building, a meeting they said was a nightly ritual during Western Siberia's short summers. "I always thought that all Americans would look like Phillip Donahue," said Vladimir Golovanov, a thirty-year-old photographer, talking about the popular American talk-show host whose show appeared frequently on Soviet television. "Donahue has that easy confidence of Americans. He is an open man. I like the style."

He conceded that I looked a little more unwashed and rougher hewn than Donahue—but then this was Siberia. His friends agreed that they liked Donahue because he addressed problems that also affected them. I imagined some of Donahue's more unorthodox guests: transsexual couples and two lesbians who wanted to have a baby. I tried to imagine their commonality with the Siberians. Perhaps they had liked the show when Donahue himself had dressed in drag.

The boys on the bench seemed to have missed those episodes. "We haven't seen anything like that," said Golovanov. "Last week he had women on who were addicted to drugs," he said. "They talked about their lives—broken marriages, empty existences, miserable jobs. There are no differences between simple people."

His friends quickly disagreed. The difference, they insisted, was that simple people in America lived far better than they did. "When we see films on television, we are surprised how well people live—even the poor people have electric can openers and mixers," said Viktor Volchkov, a twenty-eight-year-old welder at the plant. Electric garage-door openers seemed to them to be the height of luxury in a place where no one had a garage.

They wanted to know the equivalent wages for their professions in America. They wouldn't accept my evasive argument that all education and health care was paid for in Russia, so one really couldn't compare. But I finally provided a conservative estimate.

They all sighed. That amount of money, translated on the black market, would have been two hundred times or more than what they earned. "Since Glasnost, we are only winning in that we have more knowledge, more information," said the welder. "And you can't eat information."

They pulled out their ration coupons to give their American visitor a taste of their lives—four packets of cigarettes monthly, a pair of socks each three months, 200 grams of flour each month, one kilogram of cereal, a bottle of vodka and one of wine each month. They showed ration slips for everything from macaroni (one-half kilo) and eggs (ten per month), to toilet soap (three bars), and sugar (one kilo a month except during the berry season, when three kilos were given to help those who wanted to make preserves).

The photographer began to burn one of his ration coupons with a cigarette lighter. "I can't get these goods even with the coupon because they don't exist," he said. "Even the paper is of bad quality."

One of the men's wives called from a window above us. It was time to call it a night. The men appealed for a little more time, shouting back that they were speaking to an American. Then they all laughed. Finally, they had an excuse to stay out later that even their wives couldn't resist.

"Have you seen *Rambo?*" asked the welder. He said that he particularly liked the one in which Rambo beats the hulking Russian giant to a pulp. "We weren't hurt by the movie," said the welder. "That wasn't a real Russian. His face didn't even look Russian. The fight was properly won by Rambo because he was right and the other man was wrong."

Did they ever believe the Americans were their enemies?

"Perhaps at one time," said Anatoly Maltsev, a repairmen on an oil rig. "We really thought the weapons we were building here were protecting us. But then we had Glasnost. It turned out they were only protecting the Communist parties in all those countries abroad. They were just putting spaghetti over our ears all these years."

About then, a local schoolteacher and her husband walked by on their way home from an evening stroll. I stopped them to get their opinion on Rambo, a character who was known by everyone in Yurga. Rambo, she said, had only caused her problems. "My students all act like Bruce Lee and Rambo, flying around and kicking things off tables—and kicking each other," she said. "Our students didn't know how to fight before, but now they are learning."

And had she seen *Dallas?*

She had, but she didn't know what such films brought Russians. If *Dallas* was progress, she didn't want it. "It seemed so artificial to me, the way they lived," she said. "I think the film is made for simple-minded people."

Her husband whispered in her ear, and she looked embarrassed. "I hope I have not insulted you," she said. "But that's the way I feel, so I thought I should say it."

I sat for a while longer with the men, and I put away my notebook. We chatted leisurely about cars, women, and politics. We exchanged jokes and addresses. And then I said good-bye and took a walk along the river with Dundee.

Gaining permission to enter the closed city of Yurga had been unexpected, but our next stop had been an even more absolute red zone for Americans. It was an entire city ringed by barbed wire and guard towers, and it produced much of the Soviet Union's nuclear-weapons material.

Chapter 10:

THE BOMB MAKERS

We're entering a closed area.

—VIKTOR PETRISHCHEV, *deputy director, Tomsk 7*

Six uniformed Interior Ministry soldiers carrying semiautomatic rifles greeted our bus at the iron gates of Tomsk 7, one of the world's most secret nuclear-weapons facilities. To our right, other troops searched a car's trunk, making sure would-be saboteurs didn't smuggle weapons or explosives into the city, which was ringed with two layers of barbed wire and electronically monitored fences.

To our left, soldiers checked papers of those leaving Tomsk 7. One guard slid a small mirror with a long handle underneath the chassis of a van. I imagined to myself he was trying to spot concealed nuclear materials or documents slipped through for sale abroad. Such fears had increased since the country had opened up and the economic future of nuclear scientists had grown uncertain. Libya and other Third World countries were trying to recruit some of the 2,000 to 3,000 Soviet scientists who could put together a bomb, some of whom worked at Tomsk 7. One Western intelligence-agency official had told me that the bulk of the plutonium for the Soviet weapons program had been produced at that site since 1978.

Tomsk 7, a city of 107,500, was a place of euphemisms. Its very name, a postal code of the larger and older city of Tomsk, fifteen miles up the river, was designed to deceive. Its prewar name had been Seversk, meaning "north." The nuclear facilities were known as the Siberian Chemical Combine, or *Sibkimkombinat*. Yet the "chemicals" were merely those used in the plutonium separation (or reprocessing) plant.

The gates creaked open slowly to allow our bus into a security space before a second set of gates. A soldier came on board to look over our passports. It mattered little to him that I would be the first American ever to be allowed inside the facility. Our escort was Viktor Petrishchev, the deputy director of the facility, so, after only a cursory examination, the sentry waved our bus through, including the two Greenpeace scientists and the two Russian journalists.

"We are entering a closed area," said Petrishchev, a small, mousy man with thick glasses and a monotonal voice. His dull bearing and bored demeanor reminded me of an accountant I once had. "I have only one request of you all," he said. "It is allowed to take photographs of any people or buildings that you want. But please don't take any photographs of the systems, guards, or the border line. All the rest is fine."

Petrishchev said we were passing through the biggest and most heavily traveled of the fifteen checkpoints that led in and out of the city. One could pass only with special identity cards given to each of the city's residents. Even immediate family members required special permission. Friends, cousins, aunts, and uncles weren't allowed at all. Tomsk 7 rested on the banks of the Tom River, just a few miles before it emptied into the Ob, and had a long stretch of sandy beach, but the only access to the water for city residents was through one of three guarded gates. However, democratization had loosened the regulations a bit; beachgoers needed only to show their ID on their way back into Tomsk 7 and not, as before, when leaving. "Permissions for family visits are also extended more quickly now and on a multiple-entry basis," said Petrishchev. "So you see democracy has also affected us here."

Since its construction in 1947, Tomsk 7 had been devoted to developing the means to destroy the United States and its allies with nuclear weapons. So I had viewed our application to visit the site as more of a dare than a serious possibility. When the approval had come, I gathered what little information was available on a site that had successfully guarded its secrets for more than forty years.

Tomsk 7 was one of the most important of the ten locations in the Soviet Union that designed and produced nuclear weapons. The U.S. had a mirror network at sites like Los Alamos, Livermore, and the Savannah River, which employed 100,000 people in thirteen states, but the American nuclear-weapons industry had never been as large or as secret as the Soviet program, which employed over 400,000 people. The Natural Resources Defense Council in Washington had calculated that when in full operation the facilities could produce 120 tons each year of military-grade pluto-nium, which could be turned into 20,000 nuclear weapons.

Tomsk 7's importance had grown in 1978, when the Soviet Union shifted another major reprocessing facility, Chelyabinsk 65, totally to civilian operations. That left Tomsk 7 producing most of the plutonium for nuclear weapons. Christopher Paine reported in the *New Scientist* that irradiated fuel elements thereafter were shifted from Chelyabinsk 40 along the tracks of the Trans-Siberian Railway to the Tomsk 7 complex, where five graphite-modulated, water-cooled reactors were operating.

Tomsk 7 was the site of the Siberian Atomic Power Station, a plutonium-extraction plant, an enrichment plant, and nuclear-waste-management facilities. In 1981 American interest in the facility increased after A. M. Petrosyants, then the chief of atomic-energy production, said Tomsk 7 produced plutonium as well as power. When two of its five reactors were shut down in 1990, the news agency Tass announced that the harmful effluents going into the Tom River would be halved. That naturally raised my own interest about what the full amount had been.

In July 1990 French scientists tested the waters of the Tom about a mile and a half downstream from the reactors, near the cooling-water discharge canal, and found that gamma-radiation levels were more than ten times higher than normal background levels in the region. And *Izvestia* reported that the radioactive-waste site is poorly fenced, and contaminated-water areas are open to elk, rabbits, duck, and fish. The French scientists reported that thirty-eight people had higher-than-permissible levels of radioactive substances in their bodies, and that seven were hospitalized. So I expected some political uproar locally, especially as the Ministry of Atomic Energy under one plan would store the bulk of plutonium removed from warheads under disarmament agreements on the seventy-five-square-mile territory of Tomsk 7.

When we visited the mayor of the neighboring city of Tomsk for a briefing on the day before our visit, he complained that he hadn't any administrative control over Tomsk 7 so he couldn't monitor its safety precautions. Tomsk 7, said Aleksandr Tscherkovsky, was a city run by the Defense Ministry. His city of Tomsk, founded in 1604, is one of Western Siberia's oldest and most important cities. It is a university city of 400,000, decorated with charming if dilapidated log houses with carved wooden door and window frames. Like Tomsk 7, it had been closed to almost all Westerners since World War II because of its concentration of defense industries, which came to the region during the first five months of World War II when Stalin relocated 322 large industrial and defense enterprises to Siberia.

But Tomsk 7, one-fourth the size of its sister city, was far more secret. It was as modern and high-tech as the Soviet Union got, and its population was young and well educated—scientists and specialists from every corner of the Soviet Union.

"The number of nuclear warheads produced by Tomsk 7 was enough to equip the whole army," said Tomsk's mayor, who insisted that not only plutonium but also warheads were made there. He was a Glasnost-era politician who complained that he had to rely on Tomsk 7 for half his city's heat, yet had no control over output. He couldn't tax Tomsk 7 or even visit it without a special permit. "Their main secret all these years is how the atomic-energy production has been utilized," he said. "Electricity and heat are only secondary products. The reprocessing and enrichment facilities use most of the electricity the reactors produce. The reactors aren't designed so the power can be transferred to us, so all we get is the heat from the reactors, which work as a sort of samovar giving off steam."

The mayor communicated little with the leadership of Tomsk 7; the radiation monitors that had been put outside his office after the Chernobyl disaster were the only way he would know about a meltdown. "But the biggest problem of Tomsk 7 for us is the reactor waste and how to bury it," he said. "They have radioactive substances that they've buried on the territory of Tomsk 7 that have a one-million-year half-life."

As we waited for our clearance to drive into the secret city, Petrishchev made small talk. He asked if I had seen the American film festival on Soviet television the previous week. "Of course you had the chance to see the films before," he said. "I envy you Americans your stable life. I think of you as a people who are very sure of themselves and whose world is steady. My favorite movie during the week was *Gone With the Wind.* I understood much more about the United States through this film—about your values and your prejudices. But I was also surprised by the quality—it looked like this film was made recently. It was so modern!"

The bus drove out of the checkpoint and toward Tomsk 7 down—what else?—Victory Street. We picked up a city official responsible for cultural and social life. He spoke through a microphone at the front of the bus.

His name was Valery Elsklaus, a forty-year-old Estonian. He said that before Tomsk 7 was built, the area had been inhabited by residents of a small pastoral village called Sosnovka, meaning pine forest. The village's old homes and many of the pines had been cleared. "We couldn't do anything else, because we didn't have enough territory for our city," he said. "But our city is growing more beautiful every day."

We drove down Victory Street past what remained of the forest and private vegetable gardens that were every resident's birthright. I saw raised areas of earth and I asked if they were shelters.

"Shelters for what?" asked the safety director innocently.

"In case of disaster," I said.

This was one of the many subjects that the officials of Tomsk 7 weren't willing to talk about. He said, however, that he didn't know of any shelters in Tomsk 7. The mounds were potato cellars, he said.

Our bus turned right from Victory Street onto Kommunist Prospekt. Three cloverleaf, seventeen-story buildings had recently been finished. Elsklaus was proud of them—they were the biggest and most architecturally interesting in a city of modern structures that were far better designed than any we had seen in Siberia.

Tomsk 7 was also more orderly and affluent than anywhere we had been. Multicolored signs advertised goods in children's shops and maternity and wedding stores that, surprisingly, were in stock. The average age in Tomsk 7 was less than thirty.

We passed a single large stone that marked the site where our guide said Tomsk 7's first church would be built. I asked whether the avenue would be renamed, from "Kommunist Prospekt" to something more Christian, but our guide didn't know—he hadn't thought about it.

We turned left off Kommunist Prospekt onto Theater Square, where I marveled at an enormous statue of Lenin, a massive black monument that stood like a revolutionary King Kong with his hand outstretched. From there, a right-hand turn led to Lenin Street, which ran parallel to a narrow park dotted with trees and joggers. Behind it were the fences and beyond that the beach. "We call that area *Beryozovo*—birch forest," said our Estonian guide, even mentioning the fence and barbed wire visible through the scattered trees.

Valery Elsklaus bragged that Tomsk 7 had more culture per capita than any city in Siberia. Along our route, he pointed out the musical theater, the children's theater, three cinemas, two music schools, an artists' institute, two technical universities, two public libraries, and forty additional libraries of various organizations. "In total, there are 200 different schools and institutes," he said, drunk with the numbers, the opiate of the central planner.

But something was missing from our tour. Where were the reactors and the enrichment plant that we were to visit?

"You won't be seeing such facilities," said Petrishchev. "It isn't necessary for you to visit them."

There was that phrase, "It isn't necessary," the Glasnost-era refusal. In a world where "it isn't allowed" was no longer *de rigueur,* "it isn't necessary" was its milder replacement.

"It was not considered to be of interest to you," he said.

But I wanted to speak to scientists and workers about their lives after the Cold War. "That's our business," said Petrishchev. And even if he wanted to show me such facilities, he said it would be impossible. Our detailed applications to visit, which included our biographies and passport numbers, had left out our birth dates and thus weren't complete. No one had mentioned this problem to us before. He said we were lucky the Defense Ministry hadn't rejected our visit to Tomsk 7 altogether.

The Greenpeace scientists whispered to me that they were probably at fault for the cancellation of our approved visit. A day earlier, local ecologists had grilled them on their organization's blanket opposition to nuclear energy, and the Greenpeace men figured authorities present then decided little good could come from our visit.

Could we at least drive by the enrichment plant? I asked Petrichchev.

Petrishchev consented and gave the bus driver instructions to leave our approved route. I figured we were close when we turned onto a side street called Kurchatov Avenue, named for the father of the Soviet bomb, the physicist Igor Kurchatov.

I saw a building site and began making mental photographs, certain that construction of some new secret facility was under way. I scribbled madly into my notebook, logging every detail, until our Estonian guide said, "This will be a sports complex with all the most modern amenities."

The bus turned off onto two smaller streets without any names at all. I looked everywhere, not knowing how I would recognize the guilty facility. Then we turned a corner and drove past a gray-and-mustard-yellow building complex set about 500 yards back from the road, behind red-and-white-striped barriers. A three-meter-high fence and a gate decorated with giant silver stars made it look martial.

"That was what you wanted to see," said Petrishchev after we had almost passed it.

So this was the nuclear soul of the Communist beast that had so threatened the free world. I was passing the epicenter of the Evil Empire, the radioactive core of the Red Threat, the well from which Soviet bombs were made. In my memory, however, it remains only a gray blur. Perhaps it was my imagination, but I felt that the bus driver, who had driven so slowly by the children's theater, had accelerated past the plant. I can describe the area in no important detail.

I wanted to ask the deputy director many questions. I had read that Tomsk 7's sister city in the Urals, Chelyabinsk 40, had turned the landscape around it into a disaster area. A report by American scientists Thomas Cochran and Robert Norris, of the Natural Resources Defense Council, said that thousands of workers had doses of radioactivity of up to 40 rems per year, sufficient to ensure that one of every four workers would die of cancer. For the first six years of its life, until 1953, Chelyabinsk 40 had dumped liquid, high-level radioactive waste into the river Techa and later into at least two different lakes with no drainage.

The Karatchai Lake, the largest of the waste dumps, had radioactive substances measured at a concentration of 120 million curies, almost two-and-one-half times that released by the Chernobyl reactor fire. The radiation on the banks was a deadly dose for anyone without protection. An explosion of a waste tank at the plant in 1957, called the Kyshtym disaster (after the nearest town on the map), had left a northeastern trail of contamination that scientists knew as the East Urals Radioactive Track.

Certainly, if Chelyabinsk 40 was so bad, Tomsk 7 couldn't be problem-free. I asked Petrishchev what impact the Chernobyl disaster had had on Tomsk 7.

He asked that I save my questions—we were about to arrive at a press conference planned for us, for which we had no forewarning. The meeting would take place in the plenary auditorium of Tomsk 7's city hall, in the shadow of the Lenin statue. Local television was waiting outside to film our arrival—proof of the new openness.

Inside the building, a crowd was already waiting in a large hall. The seats, nailed-down desks of the sort one finds in university lecture rooms, were filled with local press and plant officials and scientists. But two rows of raised seats on the dais, of the sort I had come to associate with the Politburo, were empty. Members of our expedition were to sit there—the star attractions of the press conference.

I protested. I was a journalist, and had come to ask questions, not to answer them. After some embarrassed discussion, city officials and plant managers who had come for this first-ever meeting with Western journalists shrugged and a half dozen of them took seats on the platform. We sat with the audience. What we learned wasn't surprising:

1. Tomsk 7 had never had a nuclear accident or mishap.

2. The health of Tomsk 7 residents was ten times better than the average in the Soviet Union (because workers were young and medical care was excellent).

3. The quality of the river water and on the territory around Tomsk 7 was no worse than any other city in the world.

4. Safety precautions were strict, and a Chernobyl-like disaster couldn't happen.

5. Scientists weren't leaving or taking offers from Third World countries.

After this warm-up I asked questions the half-dozen representatives wouldn't answer on the grounds that they weren't of an "environmental nature." They said they had received us only because they understood we were an ecological group. When I asked about a French contract to enrich uranium at Tomsk 7 for nuclear plants (part of new commercial efforts to keep the Soviet nuclear industry employed), I was told this was a commercial and not an ecological question.

Only after some insistence did one of the plant officials confirm published reports that the agreement called for 150 tons of uranium to be enriched. The contract was worth 50 million dollars the first year, but could be increased with time over a ten-year contract. "Our enrichment plant has some excess capacity now," said the official. "We have decided to use this opportunity."

The officials wouldn't discuss the transport of the French material or where the waste would be disposed. I asked about reactors that I heard had been shut down, and the officials judged this to be an operational and administrative question—again not in my brief. I pressed again. One of the plant officials agreed that the facility was old, having been built between 1955 and 1965, and that two of its first five reactors had been closed down already and the third would be shut down the following year. However, he thought new technologies would allow Tomsk 7 to keep its last two reactors—built in 1964 and 1965—operating for "probably another ten to fifteen years."

Having broken through, I asked what the military role of the plant would be in the post–Cold War world. The leader of their delegation went almost as ballistic as the missiles armed with his plutonium. "Yours is an *ecological* group, and these are not *ecological* questions," he protested.

I explained again that I was merely a journalist trying to collect information on Tomsk 7. I was not an environmental reporter. I asked if it wasn't true that Tomsk 7 was producing nuclear-weapons material.

"What material do you mean?" he demanded.

"Highly enriched plutonium that is used in the production of nuclear weapons," I said.

"The division plant makes only low-grade material for electricity," he replied.

Clearly, there seemed to be some difference between the "division plant" and the plutonium-extraction plant. Out of my depth, I tried to make the question as general as possible.

"Has any facility at Tomsk 7 produced weapons-grade material in the past?" I asked.

"We cannot add anything to what I have said. Our theme for the day is ecology," said the plant official.

One of the scientists then denied that Tomsk 7 had ever made weapons-grade material. "You supposedly know more about this place than we know behind the table," he said.

"You are saying that this is not a military plant?"

The scientist said it was not.

"This facility is not under the Ministry of Defense?" I asked. The group hesitated.

"This is a military plant and will remain a military plant," another scientist insisted.

The leader of the delegation then cleared his throat and said slowly and with pride: "This is a military plant, and we are working for the Ministry of Defense."

"So what you are telling me," I said, "is that this military-run reprocessing plant does not make materials that can be used in nuclear weapons?"

At that point I heard hissing in the audience. A member of the local press, holding his microphone out toward me, frothed. "You cannot ask such questions," he said. "Every society has aspects that aren't discussed."

"Aren't we entitled to state secrets?" said a second correspondent. The local press was turning on me.

I agreed that every state was entitled to secrets. My own country had many secrets that it quite successfully kept out of my hands. "But then say that these are secrets that can't be discussed for national-security reasons, and I will gladly stop asking about them," I said.

No one responded.

The press conference went on for a half hour longer, primarily about the details of nuclear-waste storage (it was done safely and there was no danger of leakage).

As I walked out of the hall, I was surrounded by local journalists. Some asked me unfriendly questions about the American nuclear-arms program; most just wanted to know my name. But as I came onto the steps, a man who identified himself only as a former engineer at the plant stuck two documents into my shoulder bag—they looked like letters. Each looked to be a dozen pages or so—typewritten on cheap gray paper that had small wood chips floating in it.

"You are a courageous man, and I saw that inside," he said. "I am a former employee of the plant. Please read these papers and print what is in them in your newspaper."

This was the moment I had long been trained to avoid—the planting of a document on a Western reporter who will thereafter be arrested as a spy. But the man was gone before I could turn the papers down. Yuri Kaznin, our Supreme Soviet member, eyed me suspiciously. My only choice was to play out the scene and see if any trouble followed.

The documents, perhaps, would be my test case of just how much Russia had changed. Would I be arrested? Or could these papers be the real thing—an informant trying to get an ugly truth out to the world? But before I returned to the boat with my new haul, I wanted to see a little more of Tomsk 7.

"I'd like to walk around and talk to people," I said to the plant's deputy director, who continued to be our guide.

He winced. "But it is now lunchtime," he said. "We must eat. And after that it will be necessary that you return to your boat."

"I can eat in America," I said.

"You aren't hungry?" he said ruefully.

I assured him I wasn't. I offered to allow him to join the others for lunch while I ventured out with Dundee. "You can't travel in this closed city without an escort," he said with a frown. "I will come with you."

He called a company van. "Where do you want to go?" he asked.

"Shopping," I said.

He looked bewildered and issued some orders to the driver. As we drove by shops, I looked desperately for food lines of the sort that one easily found in all other places in Siberia. They were the best places for conversation, where bored or agitated shoppers welcomed the time-killing distraction of a conversation. But in well-supplied Tomsk 7, I found only one relatively short line for coffee and chocolates outside a confectionery.

Dundee and I sidled up to two young mothers with tots in strollers. They looked cut out of the pages of *Vogue,* with stylish sundresses in that year's pastels, made after patterns they had seen in Western magazines. They had modern hair styles, just enough makeup, and children dressed in bright summer colors—also clothing they had made.

Svetlana Matveyeva, twenty-four, and Natalia Nazhina, nineteen, were excited and surprised to see an American in Tomsk 7, but they nevertheless hoped peace didn't go so far that the barriers around their city would be brought down. What concerned them wasn't terrorists but consumers.

"If we opened our borders, there would be nothing left in the shops," said Svetlana, whose high cheekbones, aquiline nose, and fair hair made her look something like Meryl Streep. "Our situation is better because no one can come from outside to take our food. My husband is a policeman. He is also happy about the fences because they help control crime." She said it was easy to catch lawbreakers because they hadn't anywhere to run.

Her only complaint was that the 25,000 employees of the SHK had far better access to goods than her husband did. Her friend Natalia, dark and lively, promised Svetlana that she would share access to such stores when her husband finished his studies at the local technical university and joined the Siberian Chemical Combine.

When I asked if there was anything they didn't like about Tomsk 7, the two women had to think long before coming up with something. "Weddings and graduations can be difficult because friends and relatives can't visit," she said.

By this time, Natalia's fifteen-month-old son, Ivan, had escaped his stroller, and his mother chased him around my legs, where he had taken refuge. Svetlana's toddler was on the loose as well. We continued talking as the two children turned my legs into their playground props.

Natalia whispered that frankly, except during a time of weddings or graduations, she was quite happy that Tomsk 7 protected her against unwanted relatives. "I can leave Tomsk 7 any time to see the people I really want to visit," she said.

I asked if the searches were extreme at the borders. What was it that the guards were seeking? Had any terrorists actually been captured?

The women giggled. The biggest border problem, they said, came just before Christmas, when Tomsk 7 residents tried to smuggle out small pine trees for friends and family. "There is a law against cutting the trees here, but people do it anyway," said Natalia.

Neither of the women worried much about the threat of a nuclear catastrophe. Everything else was so orderly and perfect in Tomsk 7—they couldn't imagine that safety measures at the plant weren't among the best in the world.

The plant's deputy director, Viktor Petrishchev, was loosening up. I bought him an ice cream cone—a sign of goodwill which he accepted. He consented to take me to one of the three gates that led onto Tomsk 7's sloping beachfront, which was rich with small trees and low brush.

As we approached, five soldiers armed with AK-47s and binoculars returned along a sandy path between two 3-meter-high fences. The sand between the fences was raked regularly so that intruders would leave footprints. But in past years, the fences' electronic sensors were most often set off not by spies but by a heavy wind or a stray beach ball.

It began to rain as we crossed through the gate, so we sought shelter underneath the roof of a closed snack bar on the beach side of the checkpoint. I chatted with a young couple and their parents, who were visiting from Tashkent. The young husband worked as a driver at "the plant," a job he had taken because of the good pay and the promise of a flat large enough for his family of four.

He had moved to Tomsk 7 at about the time of the Chernobyl disaster, but that didn't concern him. Petrishchev interjected that safety systems at Chernobyl had begun shutting down the reactor eighteen seconds after the alarm, while Tomsk 7's systems could shut down reactors within two seconds. "We are fighting for every fraction of a second," he said. "Our specialists here knew what the disaster meant. Many of them went to Chernobyl to help. But Chernobyl didn't prompt anyone to move from here—not one person."

When the young couple heard the plant official speak, they grew nervous about talking with me and walked away. Before Petrishchev could expand further on the safety situation, a dozen young boys, between ages eight and twelve, rushed under the roof for shelter, laughing and arguing about some game they had just finished on the beach. When they heard English, they began shouting at us.

"I want to go to New York," said one.

"There's a Big Ben there," said another.

"No, that's London," said a third. "New York has bandits. Doesn't it have bandits?"

In my most dramatic voice, I said New York had the most dangerous bandits in the world—plenty of them. The boys came closer to listen; they wanted to know what guns they carried and which crimes they committed. The boys wanted to visit this place of bandits.

They then asked other questions. How big are the skyscrapers? How many cars does every family have? What is the most famous company? One wanted to trade his chewed-on pencil for a fountain pen. Another wanted to see a dollar. "Does everyone learn karate and judo, like Bruce Lee?" asked one.

The questions came fast, with the hunger of children who thought they'd never again have a similar opportunity.

I asked what they knew about the United States.

"They have big shops there," said one.

"They sell chewing gum in America," said another, looking at me in hopes that I might have some.

"Pokyo is in America," shouted a third, a bit too confidently.

"No, Pokyo is in Japan," another corrected him. "America is where the Ninja Turtles live."

The Ninja Turtles? I asked. Had the Teenage Mutant Ninja Turtles, heroes to my nephews in Utah, reached Tomsk 7 before me? Who needed terrorists, when the youth could be subverted by cartoon turtles the size of humans, with names like Leonardo, Donatello, Raphael, and Michelangelo, who fought for right against the dreaded Shredder? I wondered if children could buy the Teenage Mutant Ninja Turtle toys that had been such a marketing rage in America.

No, the boy said. But he elaborately described how he had converted a toy rubber soldier into a Ninja Turtle like one he had seen on television. "I took some black tape, covered him up with it, and then burned part of his face away," he said proudly. The others agreed that the result was a convincing copy.

To these boys, America wasn't the threat that it had been to their fathers, some of whom had helped produce the nuclear weapons. It was the land of Ninja Turtles and New York bandits. The boys followed me and waved farewell at the checkpoint, where I passed under a sign that read: WHEN PASSING THE CONTROL AREA, OPEN UP YOUR IDENTIFICATION CARD TO THE SENTRY AND BE POLITE WHEN ANSWERING HIS QUESTIONS AND WAITING FOR PERMISSION TO PASS.

Petrishchev looked relieved when we decided to leave Tomsk 7. The van took us away from the beach, back down Victory Street, and then out the city gates and back through the forest toward Tomsk, where our boat was preparing to leave.

But before I boarded, the driver for a local businesswoman headed me off on the dock. He insisted I come with him. Vladimir had sent away the businesswoman a day earlier because he disliked her looks—fashionable, tight-fitting Western attire, blonde hair, and thick makeup. She wasn't the type of woman he wanted on the boat.

I told the driver that the boat was leaving in forty-five minutes, but I would come along if he would get me back before then. Surely I couldn't get into too much trouble in that time. And Dundee came along as my chaperone. The driver agreed to our schedule, and we sped off through the winding streets of Tomsk, past the eighteenth-century log homes and up a hill.

When we arrived at a run-down warehouse, the driver escorted me up a rickety stairway into offices that, in happy contrast to the building, were freshly painted and well furnished. Irina Undalova, the businesswoman, broke up a sales meeting. A half-dozen young men and women marched out.

In her late thirties, Irina Undalova was dressed more for Turin than Tomsk. Her black cotton business dress was tapered and feminine but serious. She didn't want an affair, as Vladimir had believed, but a joint venture.

She already had interests in timber, berries, herbs, and a local theater. In which one of these businesses would I like to form a partnership? she asked, rushing the sales pitch because of the lack of time.

I said I was merely a journalist and not a businessman. She decided that meant I would be most interested in the Tomsk's traveling theater. "The director is a man who speaks eight languages, and his actors can perform in any one of four languages," she said. "He can do Molière in French or Shakespeare in Russian."

Irina Undalova portrayed herself as one of the last surviving cultured women of Siberia, who was trying to bring back some of the life and grace that once made up the Russian elite. She was descended from an old royal family—Panius—that had been exiled to Siberia. Her features and bearing, whispered Dundee with admiration, were of the nobility. He was sorry that he had cooperated in banning her from the boat. "We got our royal name from the hands of Peter the Great through my mother's line," she said. "My grandfather was a priest in one of the Orthodox churches in 1937, and then he was sent into exile in Siberia. That is why I am here.

"I don't want to hurt your feelings, but you will never be as strong as I am," she said. "People in my country are only sleeping and crying, but I am doing neither. I am working. I cry only on the shoulder of the man I love." For the moment, she said, that man didn't exist, because she had abandoned her husband, the father of her nineteen-year-old child, who had never understood her ambitions.

I grew nervous about the time. I was keeping the boat waiting. Irina Undalova followed me out of her office, grabbing gifts out of her closet and shoving them into my bag—candies from a factory she represented and boxes carved intricately and beautifully by local natives. "I'm not afraid of anything in life except for my own soul," she said. "I'm sick and tired of having my old life. Give me some opportunity. Let's open a store for these products in Berlin, in Washington, wherever you want. . . . Just give me a chance."

When I returned to the boat, I turned my Tomsk 7 documents over to a smarmy fellow named Sergei whom Greenpeace had hired for translations. I hadn't spoken to him before, but he was the only spare hand on board who could work on the letters. He gave the papers a quick review. He said one had been written by a former Tomsk 7 employee who had resigned his Party position and retired. The employee wrote about inadequate safety precautions and haphazard weapons-grade plutonium coming up missing. A second letter, written by another employee, outlined the haphazard storing of nuclear materials that threatened to poison great stretches of local land.

Sergei looked worried, and he held the papers as if they were burning his fingers. If I had known beforehand what was in the documents, I might not have given them to Sergei. But he consented to translate them. I worried about letting the documents out of my hands, but we had no copy machine and I was certain they couldn't disappear on our small boat.

As it turned out, this was the beginning of the biggest crisis of the expedition. It would involve the *de facto* theft of the papers by a member of our expedition. But at the time, I was more concerned with a green ambulance that had pulled up to the harbor beside our boat. Was someone hurt? Vladimir jumped out of the passenger's door, smiling broadly. He had rented the ambulance, with a red cross in a white field on its side, to transport vast amounts of food and alcohol that we would need in the wild Siberian northwest ahead of us. There was spaghetti, rice, bags of potatoes, bread, boxes of apples, sacks of flour, and 160 bottles of vodka.

"Siberia lives on barter trade north of here," said Vladimir. "We will find it more difficult to find goods in the north. And after Tomsk, you often must pay your way with vodka." I learned that one bottle bought seven kilos of fish, five bottles bought a large sack of flour or a tree trunk, and fifteen bottles bought an engine for a canoe. "The land to the north is drunk," said Vladimir.

Once we had transferred our liquid currency into a locked storage area on the bottom deck, the boat left the dock and we sailed the final few miles of the Tom River before it flowed into Grandmother Ob, which in turn would lead us northwest into the largest wetlands in the world.

As the boat passed the fences and guard towers of Tomsk 7, Vladimir brought a silver tray onto the deck, with crystal shot glasses filled with ice-cold vodka. The Tomsk 7 harbor was filled with huge cranes hovering like prehistoric creatures over barges carrying huge military transport vehicles. He proposed a toast to the end of the Cold War, to the demise of Tomsk 7 and its barbed wire, to the river ahead of us. Vladimir then fired a flare high in the blue sky and vaguely in the direction of Tomsk 7, a modest act of defiance noticed only by ourselves.

Chapter 11:

WHERE STALIN
WAS KING

God made heaven, but the devil made Narym.

—A LOCAL SAYING

Our boat dropped anchor for the night in Narym, a sullen town a few hundred yards off the Ob River on a sleepy tributary called the Ket. The waves lapped against the side of the boat while the Russians, with some bewilderment, watched Vladimir's copy of *Hair* in English on the ship's video system. He had picked it up in Amsterdam. "It is my favorite," he said.

I retreated to the deck and felt the gentle, cool wind, which I imagined to be carrying Narym's ghosts. First I thought of the thirty-two-year-old Stalin, who had been exiled to Narym in 1912 by Nikolai II. Then I pictured barges full of Kulaks, the better-off peasants who had been exiled here from 1930 to 1934. Tens of thousands of them had died in the Narym region from exposure, disease, starvation, and executions.

When Stalin arrived in Narym on July 18, 1912, he knew he had to escape quickly. The previous April, police had opened fire on workers striking at the Lena gold field, killing 500. A wave of demonstrations and work stoppages were sweeping the country. Stalin had already risen to become one of the leading young Bolsheviks, but the Revolution was on the move without him. The ambitious son of Georgian peasants knew that if he didn't rejoin his comrades soon, history might leave him behind.

Stalin had been exiled to Siberia before, so he also knew he had to escape before winter or not at all. After that, the only flight was to frozen desolation.

Captain Valery Ustinov came out of his wheelhouse and sat beside me on deck. He pointed to the dark, abandoned banks, where I could see a handful of one-story wooden buildings and a boardwalk built to keep pedestrians out of the mud. He said the boardwalks sank into the swamps so often that the locals merely built one atop another.

"The villagers say that this was the harbor where a young village boy helped Stalin escape," the captain said. Just thirty-nine days after Stalin arrived in Narym, the impatient future Soviet leader had convinced a teenage boy to take him in a canoe to the Ob River, where he boarded a steamer that carried him away. Stalin had been living in the home of the boy's mother, and he had worked assiduously to win their affection.

"Who knows how history might have been different if the boy hadn't helped Stalin?" the captain said.

If only Stalin had died in Narym, like so many other political exiles, I would have had less misery to write about on my trip down the Ob. No man's signature had ever been so deeply etched on a river's history. But in Narym, there was a devilish twist. Stalin had turned his place of exile into a purgatory for his real and imagined enemies.

In order to collectivize agriculture, Stalin decided in 1929 to break the Kulaks (a term taken from the Russian word for fist), who made up 25 percent of the country's more than 100 million peasants. Lenin had tried to end private agriculture slowly, through tax laws and negative incentives, but Stalin was less patient. He saw farm production falling, and falsely blamed the only agricultural sector that could have helped him instead of the real cause—his own price-and-supply system. In December 1929 he instituted a policy of "liquidating the Kulaks as a class."

The forced collectivization brought 11 million households into collective farms within seven weeks. But it also met resistance. Rather than give up their animals to the State, many of the peasants slaughtered them. Between 1929 and 1934, slaughter and neglect reportedly wiped out 45 percent of the cattle, 54 percent of the horses, 66 percent of the sheep, and 55 percent of the hogs. In 1932 alone, 3 million peasants fled to the cities to join the expanding industrial labor force. But many didn't escape. Stalin's secret police deported 2 to 3 million Kulaks in the early 1930s, mostly from their farms in the western Soviet Union, to Siberia. According to an article that appeared in May 1991 in the Kolpashevo newspaper, the *Sovietsky Sever* (The Soviet North), quoting from KGB documents, one million of these were sent to the Narym region from 1930 to 1934, in barges during the summer and on sledges and walking in convoys up the frozen Ob River during the winter. The newspaper said some 800,000 of them survived long enough to reach the settlements. Less than half of those settlers survived through to the end of the 1930s.

The captain returned to his wheelhouse, but I stayed and listened to the Ket splashing against the boat and the banks. The sound reminded me of a passage I had read from Chekhov's little-known report on his travels through Siberia. In describing another tributary of the Ob, he had said it "neither booms nor roars but seems to knock on the lids of coffins down at the bottom. A dismal effect!"

Despite the grim history of the 1930s, the cottage where Stalin lived in Narym is still preserved as a historical site, and his memory is still honored. The large statue of him was removed in the 1960s, however, and the Stalin Museum exhibits in Narym, which once glorified his escape, his rule, and his World War II victory, was closed for rewriting and remodeling when I arrived. It would be reopened as a "Museum of Political Exile," cleansed of Stalin's memory to a degree that didn't much please its young director.

We found the director, a shy, twenty-seven-year-old history graduate from Tomsk University, at home. She readily agreed to show us around. This had been Galina Subereva's first job since graduation, and, like exiles before her, she hadn't volunteered to come here but had been assigned. She seemed out of place in this town of fishermen, lumberjacks, and sawmill workers, with her long brown hair, feminine manner, and fashionable mohair sweater. She, too, was in a sort of exile—from a romance gone sour in Tomsk. She had found new love in Narym, and a cause—to make sure Stalin didn't get a bum rap.

"Personally, I still refer to Stalin positively," she said. "He won a war and he saved us from the Fascists. Not only us but also the world. If not for him, what would have happened?"

Galina Subereva walked us to the entry hall to the museum, the only part of it that was open. She carried a translucent orange pointer, the tool of museum curators across Russia. She tapped it on a scale relief map of the town that depicted how it might have looked in 1596, when the Russians had created one of their first Siberian *ostrogi,* or forts. The word "Narym," she said, fittingly meant "swamp" in the language of the native Selkup people. She said the Selkups had sold sable and fox for salt and vodka to the Russian conquerors, whom they hadn't resisted.

She then wielded her pointer over another model of the town, which showed the beginning of the twentieth century, when it had been inhabited primarily by natives, and by Russian adventurers and Polish exiles and their descendants. The original Polish exiles had been sent to the region in the 1830s and 1860s for having revolted against Russia during a period when a large portion of Poland was controlled by the Tsars.

"That's when Narym began to be called a jail without bars," she said. "It was surrounded by swamps and rivers. Severe frosts reached sixty degrees below freezing [Celsius]. And if you did escape, where did you go to? There is a local saying here: God made heaven, but the devil made Narym."

There had been three churches at the turn of the century, she said, the most beautiful of which had been that of the Polish Catholics. The main road had been called Station of the Cross Street. But after the Revolution, the locals had torn down the churches and used the timber to fuel fires during the harsh winters. The only important building that remained from that period was a large two-story log structure with carved door and window frames that had been built for the richest Polish merchant in the 1840s. Station of the Cross Street, on which the Stalin Museum was located, was renamed Kuibyshev Street, after the first Soviet chief of heavy industry. He had been exiled to Narym after the Revolution of 1905–1907.

Nevertheless, Galina was fighting to restore the street's old name and gathering funds to rebuild the church. "I would like to make Narym a center of tourism," she said. She wanted to complete the work by 1996, for a gala 400th anniversary celebrating of the town's founding.

Galina scratched the bottom of her chin with her pointer. She said the small, two-room log cottage at the back of the museum, about fifty yards down a path of knee-deep grass, would continue to be Narym's biggest tourist draw. Nailed to one of the logs was a plaque: IN THIS HOUSE, THERE LIVED IN 1912, STAYING WHILE IN EXILE, JOSEF VISSARIONOVICH STALIN, A LEADER OF THE SOVIET GOVERNMENT. She used her large key to open a heavy padlock that kept the cottage closed and then let us in ahead of her.

"You are now in a typical peasant's house," she said. "Typical except for the fact that Stalin lived here. Local peasants would hire out rooms for to political convicts. This was good for them because it brought them more money and additional hands for labor."

We walked into a small room with a narrow iron bed, a samovar, a writing desk, and an icon on the wall. The icon didn't seem to fit. "Why not?" said Galina. "He was a seminarian and studied divinity." However, Galina wasn't certain an icon had been there at the time—and certainly not this icon. The only original items in the room, she said, were the wooden trunk that Stalin had brought with him and a thick brown blanket on the bed. "Stalin slept under that blanket," she said.

Dundee whispered as I looked at the blanket, "Go ahead and feel the bastard's blanket. Maybe you can still smell his sweat." The wool had the sandpaper-like coarse roughness of a horse blanket.

The Narym Place of Banishment, as the tsars had called it, had been the largest concentration of political exiles in Siberia at the time Stalin was there—some 300 people. By 1911 Bolsheviks there had created a secret organization, and by 1915 more than half of the exiles were members of the Bolshevik Party. The convicts had their own club, theater, and school. But Stalin didn't associate much with other prisoners during his periods of exile. Fellow exiles wrote that he would isolate himself from them, arrogantly holding himself aloof.

Yakov Sverdlov, one Bolshevik leader, wrote home to his wife about the time he spent with Stalin during the future leader's next Siberian exile in 1913. "We have come to know each other too well," wrote Sverdlov of Stalin. "The saddest thing is how under exile and prison conditions a man reveals himself in all his petty characteristics." In a later letter, he said Stalin "turned out to be impossible in personal relations. We had to stop seeing and speaking to each other."

Galina said that no personal chronicles detailed his time in Narym. "The name of Stalin isn't mentioned anywhere," she said. All that is known is that he was sentenced to three years of exile in Narym, that he arrived on July 18, that he escaped forty-four days later, on September 1, 1912, and that he thereafter slipped out of the country to plot with Lenin. "He was just walking around the place thinking about escape from the day he arrived," Galina said. "His life was full of such adventures."

I asked whether she thought, on balance, Stalin had been negative or positive for her country. "You are trying to provoke me," said the woman. "Everyone tries to provoke me here. Some seventy percent of our visitors to the museum are foreign, mostly Hungarians and Poles. They ask me these questions as well. I'll tell you what I tell them. I don't think you can blame Stalin for the deaths of the Kulaks. My personal opinion is that I doubt he knew much of what was going on. The problems happened locally."

And the local problems were great. The regional newspaper, *Sovietsky Sever,* reported from KGB documents that in 1932 alone 8,326 children died in the Narym region from famine and disease. Even pregnant women had to do hard labor by cutting timber, and that resulted in hundreds of miscarriages. The starvation was so great that the Kulaks began to steal from the collective farm. In 1932 such theft was made a capital crime, and 5,416 people were sentenced to execution. The numbers were so precise; I tried to imagine what sort of person would have kept such a close count of Stalin's victims.

Thousands arrived in the Narym region to find no homes and a desolate countryside without shelter. A long-secret report by the West Siberia Timber Production Department, dated February 22, 1932, said that 30 percent of the settlers were living in holes dug in the ground, and that the dugouts often collapsed and their inhabitants were buried. The luckier "special settlers," as the Kulaks were euphemistically known, lived in groups of more than a dozen (three or four families) to a single room. The cramped quarters were frozen in the winter and infested by bugs in the summer.

Severe epidemics broke out—smallpox, typhoid fever, scarlet fever, dysentery. Diseases killed one-fourth of all the special settlers in the Narym region in 1932. A special commission was sent to investigate, but,

Sovietsky Sever said, "the main scourge was typhoid fever. Authorities did nothing to try to check it, so it spread."

I asked this shy, attractive women, who folded her arms more tightly across her chest with each of my questions, if she really believed that Stalin—with all his access to secret-police information—didn't know what was going on.

"Everyone has to judge things in his own way," she said. "We are sort of mixed up. We have a lot of false information. But I still believe that if we had Stalin now, everything would be okay. I'm not a Stalinist, but if the leadership of the country would impose a little more order, we would all be better off." It was a surprisingly common point of view among simple Siberians.

Galina Subereva said it was indicative of the kind of generous man Stalin was that, once he became the Soviet leader, he looked after the family that had helped him escape from Narym. "He never forgot them," she said.

The daughter of the young boy who had helped Stalin escape still lived in Narym in one of a low row of small wooden houses, huddled together for warmth on one of the town's flat dirt roads. Inside the wooden front door, leading into a pitch-dark hallway, was a woolen flap to prevent the icy draft from making its way to the small living room behind it. There, seated on a bowed couch which rested beside a stack of overfilled cardboard boxes, sat Maria Dmitrovna Mishkina, age seventy-three.

She was small and gray, and complained of a hearing problem she had suffered since lightning had struck her house earlier in the year. "The doctor said my hearing would return in time," said the woman. She lived in the "new" part of town, built just after the war, and her wooden house looked orderly enough from the outside. But inside, it was stuffed to the brim with things: in the hallway, a sewing machine sat on a dusty table, small bottles rested on a soiled wooden floor, a chest was filled with medicine, and four or five hand-colored photographs of her children hung on the wall. The combined effect was one of chaos.

The living room was taken up with a broken, hand-operated washing machine, buckets, boxes, boots, drapes, cushions, furniture, and stacks of clothing. A padded cloth was laid out over the table where Maria Mishkina had been ironing. The only other room, the bedroom, had a high metal bed with three enormous cushions and a patchwork bedspread. Once again Chekhov sprang to mind. He wrote how Siberians lived hard but "like to sleep soft."

The living room wall was decorated with nothing but a crucifix. I was surprised that she had displayed no photograph of Stalin. She was embarrassed by this omission. "I would like to have one," she said. "But you cannot buy them anymore. I should have bought one when I had the chance. I feel sorry for what has become of the memory of Stalin. Perhaps he made mistakes. Everybody makes mistakes. I cried when Stalin died. I had heard about him since I was a small child from my father. I wondered how we would live on."

Her father, Yakov Agavanovich Aleyev, who died in 1967, would often talk about the night that he helped Stalin escape for just a small amount of money. He didn't know until years later that it was Stalin. "Stalin stayed with my grandmother, his mother," said the old woman. "My grandmother was a widow and had seven children. She was seventeen when she married, and her husband was forty. She rented rooms to exiles and lived off that. She cooked for them, did their laundry, and served them food.

"My father remembered that it stormed on the night he helped Stalin escape; there was lightning and rain. My father brought him to the harbor, and together they took the small boat to Shpalozavod [the nearby sawmill village], where a big passenger steamer was waiting. There wasn't a dock. The ship simply lowered a gangplank into the water. Of course it was risky; the police were keeping an eye on him. But nothing happened to my grandmother. I never heard that she was even questioned."

Her grandmother, Yefricinia Ivanova Aleyeva, never told the family very much about what Stalin was like. "She said he seemed a good man, but she did not talk much to him or to any of the prisoners. All she did was put food on the table. It was a long time after the escape that she learned it was Stalin. She only knew him by his original family name— Djugashvili. She didn't know until a group of men came from Moscow and said Stalin lived here. Many groups came from Moscow. They began to build the museum, they invested money, artists came from Tomsk, and they painted many pictures of Stalin. They were all in the museum.

"Of course my father was proud when he found out that he had helped Stalin escape. He was given a special payment of 500 rubles a month. He was a fisherman, and for him that was a great support. And the family received double rations. We could live well. It was a great honor. My father was very respected. He got whatever he asked for. He had only four years of school, but he was allowed to be a Party member. My father had nine children. It was very pleasant to be from the family of the man who helped Stalin escape."

Maria's gestures were the rough ones of a Russian peasant, and she sat on the sagging couch with her legs spread far apart. The first reward of her lineage, she said, was her first salaried job at age sixteen as a cleaning woman at the secret police offices. It meant year-round employment in a warm building with regular meals; few greater luxuries were available in Narym.

She worked there during the worst of Stalin's repressions, in 1937 and

A Russian cast of characters. Clockwise from upper left: organizer Vladimir Sukhatsky, the "White Bird"; interpreter Valentine Akishkin, "Dundee"; Yuri Kaznin, People's Deputy; Viktor Pelz, interpreter and Gulag survivor.
(All photos Wytze van der Naald)

Our forty-two-meter boat. Its only identification was its radio code letters, OM147. (*Gerard Jacobs*)

KGB colonel Valery Znikin casts a doubtful look our way.
(*Paul Babliowsky*)

Skeleton memorial
at Kolpashevo, where
the Ob River
unearthed one of
Stalin's mass graves.
(*Babliowsky*)

On the night shift in Novokuznetsk. (*Babliowsky*)

Shor elder
Fyodor Aponkin.
(*Babliowsky*)

Medical Sobering-Up Place #5:
a doctor ministers to a drunk.
(*Babliowsky*)

German women in the forbidden city of Yurga. (*Babliowsky*)

Soldiers at rest during construction of new housing: "We don't understand why we have an army anymore at all." (*Babliowsky*)

Prison Colony #5: the inmates' chorus sings "The Volga Boatman." (*Jacobs*)

Two Khanty tepees in the vast Siberian wetlands—"God's Unfinished Work." (*Babliowsky*)

Khanty nomad Aleksandra Davola: "The Russians came like grasshoppers." (*Babliowsky*)

The Khanty Shaman and his son at Vanzevat. (*Babliowsky*)

Two Nenets, the reindeer nomads. (*Babliowsky*)

Ruins of a former Gulag in Vorkuta. (*Gerard Jacobs)*

A Gulag cemetery. (*Jacobs*)

Julia, the "survivor." (*Jacobs*)

1938. It seemed odd to her that prisoners would sometimes be brought in and then taken away in their underwear, never to be seen again. "But I can't remember anything else unusual about that time," she said.

"Stalin knew nothing about it," she insisted, "but now he is being blamed for everything. Stalin did much good. He won the war. Two of my brothers and my first husband died in the war. My second husband was in the war, too, and he told me that things improved at the front after Stalin ordered the resignation of unreliable commanders and replaced them with braver officers.

"Everything would be better if Stalin were in charge. It didn't take long after the war before there was meat, smoked fish, butter—all kinds of food. Under Stalin there was discipline. Everyone was honest and worked well. During the war, soldiers shouted for Stalin as they went on the attack. Who would go to their deaths shouting for our leaders now? People are spoiled, lazy, and don't want to work. They shouldn't have started Glasnost and Perestroika until there was order. There is only one thing I can say: I was for Stalin in the past and I remain for Stalin."

To find another opinion, I rented a small motorboat at the same harbor that had served Stalin's escape, and I took it to the village where he had caught the steamer. The name of the village, "Shpalozavod," meant "Railway Tie Factory." The Kulaks' primary employment was as forced laborers cutting timber, then Siberia's richest natural resource. Most of the original settlers had died, but I had heard that a handful still lived in the village.

On the sawmill's wooden front gate was its original socialist symbol, a red star beside a circular saw. The gate, however, had a new-style slogan nailed to it: THE MAIN AIM OF PERESTROIKA IS TO CHANGE THE WAY YOU THINK.

I asked the director of the timber enterprise, Viktor Zuparev, how long the sign had been there. "I never noticed it," he said. "For me, it is only part of the fence." At its peak, the enterprise had produced 360,000 railway ties a year, but its output had fallen by two-thirds. "We just don't have the timber anymore," said Zuparev. "We have used our resources in a barbarous way. The chiefs of our industry thought they could take out the timber endlessly. Twenty years ago, logs came to this plant from forty rivers and tributaries in the region. But now they only come down nine because the other rivers no longer have sufficient timber for harvesting. Replanting never was a priority until now. There aren't any pine forests remaining of any importance."

He said strip harvesting had also reduced the water level of the river and its stock of fish. The most-often-used method of getting the timber to the sawmill, floating it down the ponderous Ob and its tributaries, caused many of the logs to sink and settle on the bottom. He said the small fish, drawn to the logs by insects that fed off them, were then poisoned by the saps and oils. He said sunken logs had also ruined the breeding grounds of the fish. Zuparev measured the decline of the Ob by the lack of fresh-water fish in local shops. "They are even shipping in frozen ocean fish to sell to us here," he said. "Can you imagine such a thing?"

Zuparev had grown up in Railway Tie Village during better times. His father had brought the family to the region after the war because of the high salaries and assured housing. His father had been a tailor, but he had given up that work after the war, when private employment was banned. "He thought working at the sawmill would allow him to feed his family better," said Zuparev. "But he had always been happier as a tailor. I wish I had learned his profession."

Despite the decline of the sawmill, men continued to come to him for jobs because they couldn't find apartments or sufficient food in the cities, but the lack of timber had forced him to cut back his work force from 500 to 350 men. Yet Zuparev had no intention of leaving Shpalozavod. He had raised his three children in town, and after living there for twenty-five years, he couldn't imagine being anywhere else. "I consider it no worse than any other place," he said. "But I also can't say it is any better."

Viktor Zuparev agreed to take me to the only Kulak couple whom he thought would be willing to talk to me.

We walked down the dirt roads of Railway Tie Village, paved with a layer of sawdust and wood chips. The homes were built of the timber yard's wood, and almost all were tidy and painted white. A small canal, which irrigated lush gardens, led up to the home of Fyodor Petrovich Poleshuk, who was sitting on the porch with his wife, Tatyana Ivanova.

She looked at me suspiciously through clear brown eyes set in a face deeply creased with wrinkles. She trembled some—no stranger had ever brought good news. Against her better instincts she opened the door to her home and invited us into her small and cozy living room. Oriental rugs, the black, red, and white sort produced in the Central Asian republics and sold everywhere in Russia, covered the walls and helped keep out the cold. Newspapers lined the cracks of windows to block drafts. The only photo-graph was a large, hand-colored black-and-white of their grandson, on a corner table. It showed him at age ten, but now he was twenty-four, said Tatyana Ivanova, and she was proud to say that he was manufacturing cassette tapes in the north of Siberia.

I sat beside Dundee on the giant, soft cushion that made up the couch ("Siberians live hard, but they sleep soft"). Fyodor sat on a chair in front of us and beside the sawmill manager, who would have to encourage them at several points in our conversation to continue talking. Tatyana Ivanova sat on a foot locker in the corner, a bit apart from us.

Fyodor Petrovich said that his father had been a Kulak with a relatively small landholding, three horses, two cows, and a dozen pigs. He had been exiled to Siberia in January 1930. Several months later, local Communist authorities told Fyodor he faced the same fate unless he would publicly denounce his father and work on the state farm that had taken over his family's land and animals. Fyodor wouldn't turn on his father. At a robust twenty-three, he found himself in a railway transport carriage to Siberia. Fyodor Poleshuk recalled the scene in the cattle car—men playing cards on the floor and women crying among themselves.

The secret police accompanying the train picked Fyodor as the "senior passenger," responsible for writing down names, distributing food, and preventing escape.

"You were guarding your own people?" I asked.

"In a way," he agreed. "My job was to see to it that no one opened the wagon when it was moving and that no one ran away."

How would he stop them from escaping?

"I told them the truth: if they left the car they would only end up in a far worse car—a prison on wheels," he said. "And I told them no one knew whether people put in those wagons would come out alive."

"And you stopped those who wanted to escape?"

"If they escaped"—he shrugged—"I would have been punished."

In search of a Kulak survivor, I feared I had found a collaborator. I looked at this old man who had outlived so many of his neighbors and fellow Kulaks. He still had a vibrant face, intense eyes, and strong frame. Even at age eighty-three, Fyodor Petrovich stood upright and tall, his face leathery brown from years in the Siberian sun and wind. He was buoyant, almost bouncy.

His wife looked older. She wore fear as obviously as the gray scarf she wrapped around her head. Yet she also had love in her eyes for the man with whom she had survived Narym. "Why are you writing down what Fyodor Petrovich is saying?" she complained. "They will take us to jail after you leave here." She stood up and begged her husband to stop talking to me.

Her husband implored her to sit back down. He told her "those days" were over.

"When were you born?" I asked, looking for a painless question.

"We were both born in 1908," he said.

"Within a month of each other," she said.

"She was born in February and I in March," he said.

"We were both born in 1908," she reinforced. "We are old and illiterate. That's how we are living. Nobody asks how we are."

"Nobody visits us," he said.

"No one cares how we are living," she said.

They were an inseparable pair—finishing each other's sentences and exchanging reassuring looks. Their love for each other revealed itself in every glance and gentle touch of an arm. An invisible link tied together their thoughts and even their speech patterns.

Fyodor Petrovich told how they had come to Narym.

"We took a twelve-day train ride from the Ukraine to Tomsk," he said. "Have you been there? We lived there. We stayed for three months. From Tomsk, we were taken by horses to the Narym region, on sledges up the Ob River. The whole trip took two months."

"The men walked," said Tatyana, "and the women and children sat in the sledges. It was forty degrees below [Celsius] outside. They were the sledges in which they would carry fish to Tomsk. They took the fish out, then they put the women and children inside. It still smelled of fish." She wrinkled her nose.

"Many of the old people didn't make it," he said.

Tatyana Ivanova again stood and reprimanded me for writing in my notebook. I had begun to scribble again because the old couple seemed to have grown more comfortable with me. I didn't want to risk forgetting any part of our conversation.

"No, do the woman a favor and put away the notebook," said Dundee, who had warmed to this couple. "You are torturing her." I hoped he would pay particular attention so that we could reconstruct the scene later.

"We shouldn't be afraid of anything," Tatyana apologized. "What can they do to us? We don't look so handsome, not very appetizing to look at."

Again, Fyodor asked Tatyana to sit down.

"I don't want the bench, I want the cemetery," she said, smiling at her own joke. "I am ready for it."

"When I was a young man, I was strong and good-looking," said Fyodor Petrovich. He remembered joining his father in the forest, cutting timber. His father died in 1933, only three years after arriving in Narym. When his father died, Fyodor Petrovich was 200 kilometers away, cutting timber. By the time he returned, his father was buried. He has never forgiven himself that. He never had a chance to say good-bye.

Fyodor Petrovich remembered that they had to register with local authorities every month. Any exiles who didn't have a monthly stamp on their identification cards were considered escapees—a crime punishable by death.

The couple talked about the hunger when they arrived in the small village of Alatoyava in the Narym region in January 1931. Tatyana Ivanova had a seven-month-old child whom she had to feed, along with herself and her husband. People died all around her but somehow she survived. "But we shouldn't say much about it, because they will take us to jail," she said quite seriously.

She frowned as her husband filled in more details. "Sometimes Tatyana Ivanova would go three or four days without putting a thing in her mouth. She was breast-feeding then, but there wasn't much for the child in that."

"Fyodor Petrovich had it better in the forest because he could find food—mushrooms and berries," she chimed in, in spite of herself. "But in the village we didn't know where our food would come from. But Fyodor Petrovich was a good worker, so we were lucky. He had to cut seven cubic meters of timber to receive a loaf of bread in a day, and he sometimes could do twice that—earning two kilograms of bread."

"I worked well," he said.

"He worked *very* well," his wife emphasized. "He was a Stakhanovite," she said, using the Communist term for a heroic worker that originated with Aleksei Stakhanov, whose 1935 feat of hewing 102 tons of coal in a six-hour shift had touched off a mass movement that bore his name. "They wondered how my husband could have such a high capacity for work," said Tatyana Ivanova.

The couple's breakthrough, said Fyodor, came in that year of 1935, when he had raised enough money to buy a cow. "Then we had no more fear of starvation," he said. "We had a potato patch and a cow and our monthly ration of flour. That was more than enough to live on."

I asked whether they were angry with Stalin. Did they blame him for their hard lives?

"What does he mean?" the woman asked her husband, genuinely bewildered that anyone should ask her opinion on such a matter.

"I don't know why Stalin did it," said the man, saying he hadn't given the question much thought. He didn't associate his hard times with Stalin, but only with *Sudba*—fate. Their lives turned out the way they had turned out—and that was that.

"How do we know why Stalin did it?" said the woman. "We are illiterate. We can't even speak Russian properly and we speak Ukrainian hardly at all. Neither of us can read."

The old man wanted me to know that he wasn't ever mistreated. That was important to him. "We worked twelve hours, but they always gave us the bread that we earned," he said. "We weren't cheated—except a couple of times in the beginning they would say that they paid us when they hadn't."

She laughed about a nickname that one of their friends, a clever Jewish exile in Narym, had given Fyodor Petrovich because of how hard he worked without asking enough in return.

"They called me a black bottle." He smiled. "They called me that because you couldn't see through me to figure out what was inside. I was illiterate but not stupid."

"Our story is simple," said the old man. "We lived through a hard life and now we are here. That was my life and I had to live it. What could I do about it?"

"We were special settlers who settled this region and we are living fine," nodded his wife. She said they had lived in their cozy home for sixteen years. They had two chickens, a pig, a potato patch, some cabbage rows, their pensions, and each other. As I wrote down these innocuous details, having once again slipped my notebook from my pocket, Tatyana Ivanova took exception again.

"You are laughing at us, thinking we are fools. We are only fools to be talking to you. Why is it necessary to write down all of this? I don't understand why it is important to you. We don't understand anything. We are just black bottles. We are dumb people. Maybe you want to take me to jail."

She paused and then she smiled. "Or maybe you want to take me to America." She brightened at that idea for a moment, and then frowned. "But I am too old to go to America. The cemetery will be my America."

Chapter 12:

DEATH ISLAND

Maybe the people were doomed by the Bible.

—BELINA FILOFILOVA, *age eighty*

When Bronislav Kraulitis runs his red tractor and its green reaper over the chest-deep hayfields of Death Island, he thinks now and again about what happened there sixty years earlier, when Stalin's exiles were said to have turned to cannibalism to survive.

"Sometimes I hear voices. And sometimes I do some thinking. Maybe I'm driving over their bones."

Kraulitis scratched his back with the bent wooden handle of his pitchfork, holding it by its prongs and twisting it around like a large toothpick. His red-white-and-blue hat, with English lettering spelling S-P-O-R-T-S, was dusty, and stained from perspiration. It held down a mat of red hair. Rivulets of sweat ran down his freckled chest and over his bronzed potbelly, which glistened in the sun.

Maps call the small patch of flat, sandy land in the middle of the Ob River "Rabbit Island." But the locals know the place, only about one and a half miles long and a mile wide, by another name: Death Island. Dundee said the Russian word combination, *Smert Ostrov*, had an odd sound to it. "It's unusual and it makes you kind of shiver when you hear it," he said.

We had anchored our boat at Nazina, a village across a narrow channel from Death Island on the right side of the Ob. The villagers say that the first "special settlers"—exiled Kulaks—arrived in the early spring of 1930, just after the Ob's thaw. It was early for the first steamboats, but villagers were happy to hear the familiar long blast of a ship's horn that heralded a delivery of supplies. Then they saw a small steamboat and a tugboat, which was pulling two barges, but the boats took a strange turn, not toward the village but in the direction of the abandoned island. They moored and then the hatches to the barges opened, releasing hundreds of people in peasant dress. Some were children.

The steamboat later brought military men carrying machine guns to the village. The commander walked down the gangplank and addressed a crowd of curious villagers who had gathered on shore. He said his men had orders to shoot anyone who tried to escape the island, and that villagers would be severely punished if they helped the exiles. Local legend had it that it rained that first cold spring night and much of the island was flooded. The next morning, when the island was hidden in a mist, two young boys took a canoe to see what had happened. They found many of the deportees dead, and twenty of them standing breast deep in the icy water in search of some escape route. The boys took a couple of women, who were holding infants, into their boats. When they all returned to the village, however, soldiers took the children away from their mothers. The soldiers then marched the women up to a hill just outside of town. The villagers heard gunshots and never saw the women again.

Until recently, only such legends made up the history of Death Island. But in September 1990, newspapers began to publish excerpts of secret reports of the 1930s that outlined some of the reasons the island had been given its name. *Sovietsky Sever* talked of barges in one case dropping off 6,000 "special settlers" on the island in May 1933. When they were withdrawn the following July, after authorities heard of mass starvation and even cannibalism, only 2,847 were still alive.

"These settlers were put on an island without food, clothing, or any other necessities," said the article. "They had no tools, no axes or knives. Forty to fifty percent were inadequately dressed. When taken on board the barges, they were badly treated. Guards threw stones and sticks at them. But that didn't seem to trouble the supervisor. The officials watched while the stronger settlers robbed the weaker ones. There were three reported cases of man-eating."

For me, Death Island was the Ob's Donner Pass, the Siberian equivalent of the survival story told to me during my childhood of a group of fortune seekers trapped by snow in the Sierra Nevadas during the California Gold Rush. Of the eighty-seven in the original Donner party, forty-seven survived, partly because of their recourse to cannibalism. What had happened on Death Island, however, wasn't as well documented, and I wanted to see if I could fill in some details.

Bronislav Kraulitis apologized that he couldn't help much. When he'd first started harvesting hay on the island twenty years earlier, he had seen the names and initials of some of the special settlers etched in the trunk of birch trees "with the sort of chemical pencils that you have to lick before you can write." But fires on the island had burned away that evidence. Other signs—the remains of dugouts, skulls, and shallow graves—had been washed away by the annual spring floods which cover the entire island.

"The villagers say Death Island was once twice its size," said the farmer. "I don't doubt that from what I've seen during my time here. A little more disappears every year."

Kraulitis had found human skulls in the region, but not on the island. He had discovered them about fifteen meters downstream when he had been hunting duck the previous autumn with his son. Hidden from the bank of the Ob by underbrush had been a series of mounds, each about three meters apart, the remains of dugouts in which exiles had lived. They stretched for about 100 yards. He also had found the ruins of what looked like barracks: raised areas of ground with the remains of a decaying wooden wall and empty spaces where doors and windows once were. And he found pits that appeared to be graves. In one, there were two skulls.

"I looked at them," he said. "I put them in my hands. One was round and the other was long. They were very dry. I set then down again, and I said a prayer. I said, 'Lie down with God and bless you." He shrugged. "What else could I say?"

Kraulitis frowned. He had been an exile himself. His mother had made the mistake after World War II of helping "the Forest Brothers" in Lithuania, a group of anti-Communist nationalists who were hiding in the Lithuanian woods. "Maybe some of the townspeople told authorities that we had helped them," said Kraulitis.

"I remember quite well when they came to take us," said the fifty-four-year-old Lithuanian farmer, using a haystack as his backrest. Dundee and I sat down across from him, cross-legged on our sweaters atop the moist ground. Kraulitis said he had been only eight years old when five men in uniforms, and bearing arms, told his mother and his brother, who was only two years old at the time, to pack what they could carry and to board a train for Siberia.

Two years later his mother died of tuberculosis. The farmer still remembered her spitting up blood in front of him. "I was ten years old then, and they took me and my brother to an orphanage," he said. Kraulitis absentmindedly swatted away fat horseflies that tried to settle on him. He had never known who his father was, he said, and his mother hadn't ever talked to her young son about him. "It wasn't necessary for me to know about it."

Bronislav's younger brother, lured by the Lithuanian independence movement, had returned to their birthplace in 1990, where he worked as a bricklayer. But Bronislav planned to stay in Nazina. "I've spent all my conscious life here," he said. "And my children are here—I'm Siberian, whatever that means."

Kraulitis excused himself. He had to return to work and relieve his son, who had been cutting the hay while we were talking. He was sorry he couldn't tell us more about the history of Death Island.

"But there's an old woman in town, a native Khanty woman," he said. "Her name is Belina Mikhailovna Filofilova. She saw it herself—with her own eyes. Anyone in town will show you where she lives."

Belina Filofilova was leaning against the white wooden picket fence in front of her small log home in Nazina, a relatively affluent farming village of neat gardens, flat dirt roads, and happy children playing games. The collective dairy farm had produced well over the years, and the people lived fairly well because of that. A young boy was spinning a bicycle rim along the road in front of him with a stick. At the school's playground across the street from Belina's home, two girls were climbing on giant carved wooden bears and reindeer, happy figures that held up shining slippery slides.

Belina Filofilova greeted us as if she had been expecting our visit, and she opened her door and guided us into her living room. She looked like an old Indian woman with wide, high cheekbones and long, narrow eyes that almost disappeared in her deep, dark wrinkles. Her hair was like steel wool in its texture and color. She wore thick, knitted woolen socks. I thought she would have appeared more natural in colorful folkloric garb than in the ordinary, mass-produced flower-print Russian housedress she was wearing.

The old woman didn't know her age. On her passport was printed 1917, but she suspected that she was older than that. The children of the village gathered around her like goslings to a Mother Goose, but the stories that lured them were hardly fairy tales. They skittered into the doorway and sat on the floor, and she began to tell us about Death Island in a simple, peasant's Russian.

"In those years, we lived in a village up the Ob River called Ambari [meaning storehouses]. It used to be called Chigasino, for a native who lived there. Chigaskia was his name. When Soviet power came, they built government storehouses there—for food, bread, sugar, and things. That's why they changed the name. I remember when the barges with the settlers first came in the spring of 1930. They were loaded off barges onto the island like cattle. It was raining. Later it turned to snow. It was a cold year. Most were young; they looked like students. I can see them now when I close my eyes.

"Sometimes one would escape the island and come to the village look- ing for food—they wanted to know how to reach the railway line. I was working at a small dairy plant. When I came home from work one day, my mother told me there were four boys that she had put in the *banya* [washhouse]. It was a small room built in the backyard of our hut. When you wanted to wash your whole body, you would pour water onto hot stones that you would put in there and steam would come up. Mother had reported the escapees to the local authorities, who said we had to keep them with us there until someone came for them."

Belina said that the authorities warned the family against helping the boys in any way. They even posted guards in front of the washroom door. She said the guards weren't soldiers, however, but "activists," members of the Communist Youth League. But her grandmother nevertheless would sneak the boys small bits of food that she hid under her apron. The boys said they had been arrested and deported for not having proper passports. They had fled the villages for the cities during the rounding up of Kulaks, but then they had fallen victim to new passport requirements designed to stop the internal emigration.

"Once, when the guard was gone, my grandmother opened the door, and I saw the boys—they must have been about eighteen years old. My grandmother fed one and he felt better. The second one approached me. He had a scarf around his neck. Their coats were black. City coats. One was wearing long boots. He said, 'We're all from Moscow. I was merely going to my aunt's house and I didn't reach there. I was taken away because I didn't have a passport.' That was his only crime."

"And then they were removed. To where, God only knows. You never asked such questions. The people were all very afraid. We lived our life in fear. . . ."

Without pausing, she began to talk about another exile who had reached her village. "He was swollen by hunger," she said. "I don't know how old he was. Probably thirty. But he looked like an old man. A swollen old man. I was afraid to let him in. But I couldn't turn him away—he was a living man. He wouldn't come in because he said we would be punished if we allowed it. So we put him in a small shed that belonged to the river navigator, the man who would guide the boats through this part of the Ob. They only kept the buoys there. Later, that man we helped slaughtered the navigator's cow. They say he ate the meat raw. Then he disappeared. Where he disappeared to, nobody knows. Terrible, terrible, just terrible."

She shook her head. Her steel-wool hair was streaked with gray strands. The children were silent and waiting for more.

"Then, in the winter, one woman came. She was with a convoy of people traveling on sledges up the river. It stopped in our village for the night. She asked me to give her something to put on her feet. 'You see my calves,' she said. 'They have frozen badly.' "

Belina Filofilova remembered that the woman told of how the exiles had walked behind the horses up the frozen river but hadn't anything warm to put on her feet. So Belina gave her some thick stockings, and the woman took off some thin wrapping draped around her sticklike legs. "Her legs had signs of frostbite—brown, swollen patches of rotten meat," said Belina. "And she had slices of her calves gone, carved off by others after she had fallen down and started dying."

"Why did they cut her calves?" I asked.

"To eat them," said the old woman. "Just to eat. They ate each other. They fried the meat on the fires. People later found heads on Death Island—but they found no bodies."

The old woman sobbed a little. The children looked sad.

"Once when I was a teenage girl, I was with one of our fishermen who had blocked off a part of a small river a long way from here so that he could more easily catch fish. He was calling his dog. The dog didn't come, but we heard a cry. The place was desolate, in the taiga. He called the dog again. And we heard another cry. It sounded to him like a woman's voice. He went to the spot where he had blocked the stream and there she was standing. We asked her how she got there. She was young—no more than eighteen or nineteen. She said, 'There were three of us—two young boys and I. One of the boys sat down on the stump of a tree to rest and he died there. Just before I reached here, the second boy died.' "

Belina said they brought the girl to her aunt, who gave her some clothes to wear. The girl explained they had escaped from the island by tying together small logs to build a raft held together with strips from their underwear—the only expendable clothing they had. "They were looking for the railroad to escape, but there was no railroad near where we lived," she said.

Out of fear, the locals would routinely turn in these escapees to the authorities, who then sent them off to another exile area. "Later, a commission came to investigate all the deaths," she said. "It was led by a military man; I think he was an officer. He was looking for his own wife, who was with one of the groups. He discovered that she went crazy and then was shot by the others. They said that her breasts then were cut off to be eaten. It was terrible what was going on. Just terrible. We were afraid of what was happening on the island. . . .

"Maybe that was the course of life. Our life, they say, is led by the Bible. Maybe the people were doomed by the Bible. Maybe we had to go through this—to go through Stalin. Who knows? What can you do about it when it is your fate? What can you do?"

And there it was again, fate, *Sudba,* following me down the river—and hanging over Siberia—like a shadow.

"Now we have to make a new life. What is past is past. Still, people like you seem interested in the old. Seems to me that to make a new life, you have got to know the old life so that you don't do it again.

"Ambari doesn't exist anymore. Now we live here. They destroyed the old village and brought us together in this collective. We were sad. The forest there was so thick that you had to walk sideways through it. They've taken all those trees now, cut them down. We used to plant fine fields—we grew oats, rye, and potatoes, too. You could have lived off those fields forever. And what gardens we had! We were crying when we were taken away, but they wanted us all together here. So much of it just didn't make sense. It still doesn't make sense to me why things happened the way that they happened."

Chapter 13:

GOD'S UNFINISHED WORK

You can hear the blood in your ears in a
place like this.

—MICHAEL HOFFMANN, *Greenpeace scientist*

I was sprawled out on my stomach across our helicopter's vibrating steel belly to get a better view of the great swamplands of the Siberian Northwest through an open trapdoor. The mayor of Aleksandrovskoye, the timber-and-oil town where we had begun our flight at dawn, anchored me by sitting on my feet. The chances of slipping through were remote, so I considered his gesture a ridiculous precaution, but the inviting scenery did seem to draw me toward it.

The gray shadow of our helicopter passed over what appeared to be a Japanese garden of epic dimensions—slow, bloated brooks and ponderous, wide streams; stretches of twisted dwarf birches of prehistoric appearance and mossy turf and bogs in endlessly different shades of greens, yellows, and browns.

Michael Hoffmann explained that we were flying over a landscape formed by glacier movements during the ice age. The receding ice masses had left detritus—fragments of rock and sand—that was more than 120 feet deep. Water collected in depressions that were sealed by clay and silt, which formed a number of ancient lakes. "The swamps can be compared to a gigantic sponge," he said. "Even between the bodies of water the ground is mostly wet." Hoffmann was a soft-spoken "limnologist," someone who specializes in just about everything concerning aquatic systems and all creatures in and around them.

He looked through one of the round side windows, down at the land-

scape, with uncharacteristic excitement. Below us were the largest connected swamplands in the world, stretching over an area three times the
size of Texas—2 million square kilometers (772,000 square miles). They
ran from a line to the south that runs through Krasnoyarsk–Tomsk–
Novosibirsk–Omsk–Sverdlovsk and to the Ob Bay and the Arctic Circle
in the north. The bog, Hoffmann said, held back water equal to the
two-year volume of the entire Ob system's flow. The stringy peat, which
had slowly grown atop itself since the ice age, was six to twelve meters
thick.

Scientists know this unique piece of earth as the West Siberian geological platform. The locals, however, call it "God's Unfinished Work"—
Bozhiya Nyedodelka—where God forgot to separate the land from
the water, something He should have done on day three of His ambitious
work week.

"Everything is endless in Siberia," Mayor Aleksei Vasilyevich Selever-
stov had told me on the ground before we had taken off. He, like so many
Siberians, said it was Jack London's story "The White Silence" that had
inspired him as a young man to venture into the Siberian wilderness. He
had worked in the wilderness as an oil geologist before turning to politics.
"Behind you," he paraphrased London, "in front of you, and all around
you is endless silence."

This was not a "swamp" of the sort I had always envisioned—the tall
grasses of the Florida Everglades or some brooding, tepid, slimy waters
through which man-eating reptiles slithered. Instead, the Siberian
swamps, as seen from above, seemed an inviting wonderland.

When I spotted an elk standing in the middle of one of the shallow
lakes, the mayor directed the pilot to swoop low for a better view. The
elk stood alone, his giant antlers twitching at the sound of our chopper.
The mayor said the elk remained far from the banks to stay clear of
mosquitoes so large and hungry that Russians called the worst of them
"flying piranhas."

However, standing like that in the open, trapped in the water, was
perilous for the elk, the mayor said. Despite poaching prohibitions, helicopter pilots carried hunters over the swamps for a price (usually no more
than a bottle or two of vodka). The elk didn't have a hope against their
airborne enemies. I stood up and then sat back on one of the benches
running along both sides of the helicopter. I looked out of one of the
round windows for other signs of life but could see none. Only an elk,
standing alone.

This helicopter trip had been scheduled for the two Greenpeace men,
who were investigating one of the world's natural wonders and determining just how much damage the oilmen had done to it. A local journalist-
turned-entrepreneur, Aleksandr Kalashnik, had come along with the
mayor to act with him as our guide. The journalist was a kind man who

later wrote and recited sappy poetry for us about Russia's democratization.

"There once were sables, mink, and other fur animals, and their pelts were worth gold," he said. "But Siberia has been overhunted. There is a fine of 1,500 rubles for poaching, but it's not enough, because hunters can earn more than that with every sable skin. You can often fly for miles and miles without seeing a living thing."

Kalashnik looked out the window with me. "All you see is water. There are deep lakes and shallow lakes, small and large lakes. Some date back to the ice age and others are created each year. Some have fish, but the shallow ones don't. During the winter a one-meter layer of snow builds up on the swamp, and underneath ground freezes up to two meters deep. Any lakes less than five meters deep freeze solidly."

The swampland lies primarily between 50 degrees and 75 degrees latitude. Its most southerly point coincides roughly with the U.S.-Canadian border and reaches northward to a point equivalent to the most frigid regions of Alaska. The tsars considered the region good for little more than the banishing of political enemies and the extortion of valuable furs from naive natives, but then geologists discovered that underneath the swamps lay huge reservoirs of oil and natural gas. The first gusher in the region came on June 22, 1960, near the desolate village of Shaim. For the next three decades the Soviets battled the elements to get at the hidden riches, which in the end financed the country's efforts to become a military superpower. Oil deposits in Western Siberia provided 60 percent of the Soviet Union's annual output and some 80 percent of its foreign-currency earnings.

The major oil fields, however, were still to the north of where we were flying. The Aleksandrovskoye region had for years been more important as a provider of timber from its taiga: forests of pine, fir, birch, and larch that had inspired Russian poetry for centuries. "I was told that the taiga is without sound or fragrance," wrote Chekhov in a short piece called "Journey Through Siberia." "But during my entire journey through these woods, birds were singing at the top of their lungs, insects were buzzing, the needles, heated by the sun, filled the air with a heavy odor of resin, clearings in the forest and the borders of the road were covered with pale-blue, pink, and yellow flowers that caressed more than the eye. . . . The fascination of the taiga lies not in giant trees or in silence, but in the fact that perhaps only the migratory birds know where it ends. The first day you pay no attention, the second and third day you are astonished, the fourth and fifth you begin to feel that you will never escape from this monster of a forest."

Half the territory of the Aleksandrovskoye area was swamp and the other half was taiga, and the two were engaged in a battle for predominance. The forests had been slowly expanding their edges until the Russians arrived, but mankind's building of roads and careless propensity to start forest fires had tipped the balance to the swamps. "The original taiga is vanishing step by step," Michael Hoffmann told me.

He said the yearly loss of forest all over Western Siberia amounted to more than 15,000 square miles. Western ecologists are only now starting to recognize, he said, that the loss of the taiga—combined with the disfiguration of the swamps from peat and oil extraction—could have as negative an effect on the world climate as the loss of the Brazilian rain forests, in which the total biomass is less and regeneration is faster. He said that carbon dioxide is the most important greenhouse gas and is bound in the swamps in greater amounts than in any other land ecosystem.

Soon our chopper carried us to one of the biggest problems. As we flew farther from the river, the swamp had turned to taiga and then the taiga had turned to scorched earth. Forest fires of 1989 had burned the ground into a brown-and-black blanket. Tree trunks were scattered chaotically like blackened toothpicks across a dead landscape. "One-fifth of the taiga was burned off," said the mayor. "The problem is that we hadn't any effective way to fight the fires—we still don't. The fire burned for two months and we didn't have a single plane of our own to drop retardant. People came with bulldozers, shovels, and axes. There were some specially trained parachutists, but not many. The union and regional government left it up to local officials, and the local officials didn't have the means or the know-how."

Such fires were virtually unknown before the oilmen came in the 1960s. By laying dirt roads to drilling areas without adequate drainage, they created dams that flooded one side of the road and dried up the other. The problem was in part the result of abandoned campfires, but the mayor said the more frequent cause of fires was vodka bottles, discarded by oilmen in the snow during the winter. When summer came, the bottles acted as a magnifying glass for the sun's rays.

"But we were losing the forest even before the fires," said the mayor. "The Forestry Ministry only took and never returned. Until June 1991 the timber companies had no requirement to replant. Everyone wants to take from Siberia but no one wants to give. Under Communism, Siberia has belonged to everyone, so it has belonged to no one."

But the journalist-entrepreneur, Aleksandr Kalashnik, saw business opportunities in this burnt forest. He instructed the pilot to land in an opening in the taiga, where some harvesting of the damaged trees had already begun. "I want an American company to come and take this wood before it goes bad and is filled with insects," said Kalashnik.

We landed and he jumped out of the helicopter onto the meadow and instructed me and Viktor Pelz, who would be my interpreter for this trip, to follow. Our dreamy flight over nature had become a fire sale. Kalashnik walked over to a stack of freshly cut tree trunks. They had remained standing after the fire, but their roots had been destroyed, so they needed to be harvested. "Just look at this wood," he said. "Nothing is wrong with it."

He sunk a hatchet into one of the trunks to prove that the product was only charbroiled; the meat inside was yellow and healthy. "I've got thirty-six million cubic meters of very good timber," he said. That was enough to build a ten-yard-wide boardwalk from New York to Cape Town. "Even in twenty years this wood will still be good enough for chipboard." He said those who would do business with him could operate tax-free, sell 70 percent of the wood for hard currency abroad, and have their pick of local labor. "Be the first to come to Siberia and we'll treat you right," he said.

The helicopter pilot, who had kept his motor running and blades turning, waved for us to come back. He was running short on gas. The helicopter began to lift off before my trailing leg was fully inside. Kalashnik grabbed me by my vest before I could fall back onto the scorched taiga.

About fifteen minutes later we descended toward Point 93, an oil-drilling station that was a brown scar interrupting the swamp's greens and yellows. It looked like a giant sandbox, made from tons of dirt dumped into the swamp, and a rusty oil rig stood in the middle. Not far from it were wooden shacks that housed the drill operators and geologists. This, the mayor said, was one of the most promising new drilling sites in the region.

The pilot landed the helicopter on a pad built of pine logs. The chief geologist and the drilling foreman for the station came to greet us. They walked us down a boardwalk, past men playing chess in the noonday sun, toward their "offices."

The geologist, Viktor Sedonov, was Point 93's intellectual, with his glasses and thin face. He was the only man on the site wearing a shirt with its buttons closed.

Aleksandr Lindt, the drilling foreman, looked more like a good ol' boy off a Texas rig. His bare chest was dark brown, and beads of sweat dripped from his neck down to a small puddle that rested on the ledge over his belly. "Our living conditions are dreadful," he said, inviting us inside to see.

Their combined office and home filled two rooms of one shack. There was nothing personal in the shack—no centerfold on the wall, not even a calendar. The bookshelves, made of birch stems, had only a couple of cheap, dog-eared novels. The radio, produced in the 1950s, was covered with dust and crackled so that the news couldn't be understood. A condensed-milk can, with its top cut off, served as an ashtray. It overflowed, and the shack smelled of stale smoke. A geological map rested on one of two beds.

An adjacent shack, where most of the workers slept, had seven cots crowded together. It had no closet or even pegs on which to hang clothing, so the workers' garments rested over a log on the floor. A couple of wild dogs slept there as well, drawn inside to escape mosquitoes.

The fact that the crew was likely to strike oil soon raised little excitement, said Sedonov. The men had low salaries, bad food, and deplorable housing, and the free market hadn't yet brought the bonuses for oil strikes that were routine in the West. The drillers stayed on site for a week or so before returning home for a week's rest. The geologists would remain for fourteen days or longer at a stretch, but their off-periods were also longer.

Sedonov complained that the oil rig they used, a leftover from the 1960s, leaked a barrel of oil into the swamps for every barrel that it drew. He was less bothered that he, as chief geologist, earned only half the salary of his drilling foreman.

"Right now it is still better to be a worker," he said. "But none of us are satisfied. The equipment is bad, the pay is bad, and the food is bad. What have we accomplished in life? We have damaged nature and our own health. Nothing more. We understand now that this life isn't worthy of mankind."

While the oilmen continued to complain, I excused myself so I could join the Greenpeace scientists, who were at a nearby lake taking earth and water samples.

The businessman, Kalashnik, guided me toward them over narrow wooden boards laid over spongy earth. The boards ended about fifty yards from the banks of the lake, and a local scout led us from there. He used a staff to probe the bog for spots too soft to walk on. Where the bog was dark green, he said, it would usually hold a body, but the sections that were even a little yellow were quicksand.

Paul Babliowsky, the Dutch photographer in our group, hadn't heard the scout's warnings and stepped off the path to snap a photograph. He sank up to his chest before our scout rescued him with his pole.

At the lake, Michael Hoffmann probed the water and the stringy moss with various instruments. "It's just as we thought," said the Dutch chemist, Wytze van der Naald. Wytze was an athletic-looking scientist from Amsterdam, who carried a backpack, wore a tank-top T-shirt, and sported a small earring. He had a ready laugh, but was deadly serious and intense in his work, having dedicated his life to fighting man's destruction of nature.

He scowled as he read gauges showing the low oxygen level in the water;

its high acidity and the lack of conductivity meant that regeneration would be extremely slow. "Every bit of ecological harm done here will either be irreversible or will take decades to repair," he said.

"In such situations," said Hoffmann, "minute pollution and changes of atmosphere can have large consequences. The swamplands have little ability to absorb abuse. They are much more sensitive ecologically than almost anything we know—much more so than the rain forests, which are in constant and very rapid growth. The vegetation grows slowly here, and recuperation is difficult."

Viktor Pelz, our sixty-eight-year-old interpreter, frowned. "We have a saying in Russian. You can't shave a second coat of wool from a golden sheep."

The two scientists regarded the vast swampland with the concern of doctors standing by the bed of a difficult patient. We began to walk from the larger lake to a dozen tiny ponds on a pastoral bog meadow to take more samples. "The only place where I have felt so overwhelmed was in the Sahara," said Hoffmann, scratching his charcoal beard and swatting away a mosquito. "You feel so small. You see the history of the land here. And there is such an enormous silence, just as in the Sahara. You can hear the blood in your ears in a place like this."

The businessman returned from some low brush beside the lake with an assortment of wild berries for my sampling. The best were *moroshka,* sweet yellow cloudberries that melted in the mouth. Then came *klukva,* blue, sour wild cranberries that would be terrific on breakfast cereal. He had other samples as well, whortleberries and crowberries, each with a distinct and refreshing taste.

I dropped the berries in horror as I heard a roar overhead and then a scream. The roar was of our helicopter, whose belly was directly over my head and descending fast. The scream was my own. I thought the pilot had gone mad and decided to flatten me. I jumped from the path that the scout had carefully chosen and thus sank to my knees in the yellow muck before Viktor Pelz pulled me out and than pushed me toward the helicopter, which had altered its course at the last moment and was hovering above the bog just a few feet from us. I followed Viktor on board and the Greenpeace scientists followed me.

I was cursing and shaking with anger and fear when the helicopter lifted off. I looked for someone to hit or at least blame. Viktor tried to calm me down. "The pilot was only doing us a favor," he said. "It is very difficult to walk in the bog, so they tried to come as close to our position as possible to pick us up. They flew directly over us, because to do otherwise would create a huge wind that could have blown you off the path into the lake."

My heart was still racing as we flew off. I wanted to remain angry, but the Russians were laughing so hard at my soaked pants and frightened face that I began to laugh as well. They told the story again and again as we flew over the swamps and taiga; their deep waves of laughter competed with the roar of the helicopter as we flew over "God's Unfinished Work" to Aleksandrovskoye, where we would reboard our boat for an all-night sail to Nizhnevartovsk and Russia's richest oil country.

Chapter 14:

Broken Dreams

Without purpose, individuality doesn't exist.

—VALENTIN RASPUTIN, *Siberian author*

When I woke up and looked out my cabin window, the view was surprisingly urban: the skyline of gray and dingy pastel apartment blocks made it seem as if we had magically returned to Moscow overnight. The impression was misleading. This was Nizhnevartovsk, the center of the rich West Siberian oil fields, and the buildings had risen in a hurry during the boom days of the 1970s and 1980s, when a fishing village had been transformed into a dusty city of 220,000.

On deck, I could taste dust and oil in the morning air, and the river was coated with a thin film of grease that stretched for hundreds of yards. A bus waited for us on shore, with two oil-field veterans who would be our guides. Nikolai Ivanov, a production manager, was a slight, quiet man with pale skin from inside work. His friend, Yevgeny Balshagin, had chiseled features and leathery skin roughened by the elements. He was a trouble-shooter, a specialist in recovery technology and in laying and repairing pipelines. His V-neck, red T-shirt fitted tightly over his muscular chest. He resembled Charlton Heston.

After about a twenty-minute drive outside of town, we reached the edge of Samotlor Lake. In the summer heat, the sandy plain that ran up to the vast, shallow lake resembled the terrain around the Great Salt Lake in Utah. Yet underneath Samotlor was the largest single oil find in Russia, if not the world. The reservoir of crude was even larger and deeper than the lake itself, which was eleven kilometers long and eight kilometers wide. On its horizon were the black outlines of oil rigs, but that didn't dissuade locals from using large portions of the lake as a recreation area.

Two five-ton trucks were parked in waters so shallow they reached only halfway up their huge tires. Their drivers had already dived into the water for their morning bath. Despite its width, the lake was only six feet down at its deepest point. While the truck drivers laughed and lathered, two small girls ran from the beach into the water with gleeful splashing and laughter. A woman who appeared to be their mother used the time to beat the dust out of a large rug that hung over her car.

We didn't need to drive far from where the children were swimming to find areas blackened by oil. No one washed or played there. One part of the lake was desolate except for a refinery and some drilling rigs, built on islands of sand. Through the murky water, I saw old and rusty pipelines, held to the bottom of the lake by cement blocks, many of which had broken loose, leaving large gray fragments scattered near the pipes.

At one point on our tour, Nikolai Ivanov suddenly stopped the bus on a street corner that was as ugly as any other in the oil fields. An old rig, painted a shiny silver, stood in back of a chain link fence. He instructed us to leave the bus to visit this "monument to the oil workers." By that point we had learned to resist the propensity of Soviet hosts to overload agendas with visits to monuments and museums, so we protested, not knowing that we were personally insulting our guides. Both of their names were on a plaque listing the original pioneers who had worked at the site of the first gusher in the region.

When we learned this, we consented with some embarrassment to a brief visit. In those days, Ivanov remembered, wild Western Siberia had been a place of black gold, open spaces, rich nature, and boundless opportunity. "We believed the contribution we were making would improve society, allow it to live better. This *was* a land of romance," he said, "a land of nature. This is where . . ."

He hesitated for a moment. Finishing the sentence seemed to hurt him.

". . . this is where all my dreams were. In those days it *meant* something to be a Siberian."

Everywhere on our expedition, we found that Russians, Ukrainians, Lithuanians, and Estonians—the same people who refused to be tagged as "Soviets"—were proud to call themselves Siberians. And they also seemed to me to be the people most likely to grasp the ideas of the free market, often expressed with an individualism that was lacking in most Russians that I knew.

Some experts in Washington even predicted that Siberians, in time, would try to break off their rich and desolate region from Russia, as they had done after the Revolution, when Kolchak, with Allied support, conquered much of the region and began moving west, before Red armies turned him back and defeated him in 1920. Independence was still in many of their souls.

In his book *Siberia on Fire,* the Siberian author Valentin Rasputin wrote that this individualism evolved because "Siberia was settled by a desperate people, by those who had reason to seek refuge in a bleak and distant land, who hoped to live here amid the freedom and justice denied them in their previous homeland, who . . . relying only on themselves, went off to remote parts to live in solitude. In all cases this required an indomitable spirit."

So what happened to that spirit during the seventy-four years of Soviet rule? "Without purpose," Rasputin wrote, "individuality does not exist."

Yet Ivanov and Balshagin, like most Russians who had moved to Siberia, still considered themselves to be the moral descendants of the Russian Cossacks who had first conquered the region in the late sixteenth century. The modern Russians came in search of oil, but the Cossacks were after furs, which they demanded as a tribute, or *yasak,* from the natives.

Before the 1500s, Russia and what later became known as Siberia had merely been khanates of a larger, Tatar-ruled empire that had been at its height during the thirteenth century under Genghis Khan. When it had fallen apart in the mid-sixteenth century, the ruling Siberian khan, Ediger, turned to Russia's first tsar, Ivan the Terrible, for help in hanging on to his crown. He offered Ivan a sable skin for each male inhabitant of his region, in exchange for Russia's protection.

But Ediger was overthrown by a distant relative, Kuchum, who had other ideas. Kuchum refused to pay the tax, and in 1571 the Russian ambassador to the khanate was murdered. Ivan, who set the standard for cruelty that Russian rulers would follow for years to come, wasn't about to take this insurrection lying down. He summoned a famous and rich merchant family, the Stroganovs, and offered them a deed to vast portions of Western Siberia, adjacent to their own interests in the Urals, if they would agree to conquer it at their own expense. They had resources the Russian government did not.

The Stroganovs called upon Yermak Timofeyevich, a Cossack, to form an expeditionary force. He brought 540 men and the Stroganovs added 300 of their own. With guns and armor, the Cossacks easily conquered Kuchum's capital in 1582, which was known both as Kashlyk and Sib-ir ("the sleeping land"). And that is how Yermak became the conqueror of a region that became known as Siberia.

Kuchum had his revenge in 1584, a year after the new "Siberian land" had been incorporated into the Russian State. He ambushed Yermak on the banks of the Irtysh River, the Ob's largest tributary. Yermak, in trying to swim to safety while still wearing his armor, drowned. But the setback was short-lived, and the Cossacks quickly regained the upper hand and rode eastward.

Despite the lore about Yermak, the Russians actually took Siberia with surprising ease. The natives rarely put up a fight. In the beginning of the eighteenth century, the 300,000 Russians in Siberia were double the number of natives. The conquering of Siberia, wrote Rasputin, "was something supernatural; those people were somehow different, somehow special, for they felt an unusual urge and knew a wonderful passion . . . the annexation of Siberia required a different sort of skill, one that nobody displayed to a greater extent or employed with greater talent than the Russian, with his exceedingly patient body and spirit—it required the skill of the pioneer."

Ivanov and Balshagin, the two pioneers of Nizhnevartovsk, were cut from this cloth in only one respect: they too had shown exceeding patience. Their patience, however, was for a system that had greedily taken their oil but never rewarded their work. They invited us back to their administration headquarters, a small white wooden building, to explain to us where the dream had gone wrong.

The desert heat had built up a thirst in me, but I still couldn't stomach the mineral water put in front of us. The lukewarm fluid was unpleasantly flavored with metallic-tasting bits that floated in the discolored bottles.

Ivanov looked emaciated and beaten; he wore a permanent scowl and he hunched over the table. Balshagin had a glimmer of laughter left in his eyes. He was fifty-three, one year away from his planned retirement, and he complained that he didn't have the money to buy a pension home—one of the few goals he had set for himself.

He said he earned 1,800 rubles a month, which was a lot of salary at that time. "But you can only buy ten packets of cigarettes with that," he said. "Or you can feed yourself—but don't try to feed a family."

He had seen *Dallas* that month, but he insisted he wouldn't want that amount of money, the sort of wealth he was certain came only through exploiting others. "It would also be a problem to find something to do with so much earnings," he said unconvincingly. "Such an amount of money can only cause headaches." He was happy not to have exploited his society like oilmen elsewhere had exploited theirs.

But hadn't the Soviet system exploited *him?*

"We were willing to give up our own well-being because we were dividing everything for the whole country," he said. Balshagin and Ivanov were both lifelong Communists. They disapproved of Boris Yeltsin, Russia's president, who had quit the Party that had made him what he was. They still considered Communist principles to be ones worth fighting for.

"I consider the Saudis to be far more exploited than the Russians," he said. "Lots of countries in the world exploited the natural resources of Saudi Arabia. But we worked only in the interest of the State, our State. With the State having the oil in its hands, it could improve conditions uniformly."

Playing devil's advocate, I argued that his Soviet system hadn't improved conditions, but had instead spent profligately on armaments it never needed. His sacrifices, I suggested, hadn't helped society, but had only allowed Moscow to build missiles it never needed against a threat that never really existed.

Neither of them disagreed, but Yevgeny's friend, Nikolai, intervened. "We still feel a sense of responsibility for our society," he said. "Everything we've tried to build isn't lost. There have been bad Communists, but Communist principles are good. Perhaps we are not growing rich, but it is our responsibility that keeps us working here. If it is not me doing the job, who will do it?"

Yevgeny, sweating a little through his red T-shirt, sighed. "Maybe I didn't work enough for myself," he said. "And I've certainly done plenty for the State. But it is uncomfortable for me to think of working only for myself. Isn't there more to life than that?"

Nikolai, knowing that there were Greenpeace scientists among us, tried to change the subject. "What we feel worst about is what we have done to the environment," he said. "The main thing they wanted from us was capacity, and we gave them that. But nature paid."

"Tons, tons, tons," agreed Yevgeny. "We never counted money or nature. We only counted kilometers of pipeline and tons of oil."

A pattern had developed in my conversations with intelligent Siberians who had long believed in their political system. At first, they held on to comfortable rhetoric, only to hear for themselves how foolish their words sounded. Then the barriers came down. A silent rage, formed over years, oozed out slowly, as if from a long-festering wound.

"Maybe I have been cheated," said Yevgeny. "I don't know for sure because I haven't seen other lives. I do know that our ecology is destroyed. That's true. And ten years won't be enough to repair it. Even if we shut down every oil field, we'd never get the nature back. We've spent a lot of labor in this region, and I suppose we don't have so much to show for it. We have lost our youth here—and maybe our lives."

He said nothing had so scarred the Siberian landscape as a decision made at the beginning of the development of the oil fields to send the oil, water, and gas together in transport pipes from the fields to the shipment points and refineries. Almost everywhere else in the world, those elements are separated at the source. The result in the Soviet Union was that a highly sulfurous compound had been created that eroded pipes prematurely.

"Pipes that should have had a minimum life here of a dozen years lasted only half that long or shorter," said Nikolai Ivanov. At first the Siberian oilmen had suspected Western sabotage when they had seen slices through the bottom of the pipes that looked like knife cuts.

"We thought that our German suppliers had purposely given us bad pipes, so we had them analyzed," said Ivanov. Although the problem was discovered in 1976, it took four more years before the oilmen determined that their practice of transporting all the elements together was to blame. But by that time they had laid a network of 11,000 kilometers of pipes, more than enough to cross the entire United States, across a territory larger than Holland, that was more than two-thirds swampland.

The two men revealed statistics that would have been secret only a few years earlier—they lost 6 to 7 percent of production to shutdowns, breakages, and leakages. Breakages alone cost them 500 tons of oil a month, and that figure was growing with every month of age on the pipes. With each year the pipeline bursts increased, from 343 in 1985 to more than 2,000 by 1990. Ivanov said part of the problem was their lack of contact with Western experts, whose advice might have allowed them to avoid many of their difficulties.

"To be honest," said Yevgeny Balshagin, "we've got more breakdowns than you do anywhere in the United States—we've probably got more than anywhere in the world."

Then there was the problem of repair. The rapid thaw of spring multiplied the breakages, but reaching the affected areas first required helicopters to dump tons of sand, and then a road or platform of logs had to be built for heavy machinery that was flown in. In the interest of expediency, the oilmen often made shoddy but fast repairs to avoid falling below the production plan, but their quick fixes would routinely fail again a year or two later.

The two men tried to make me understand the pressure they had been under from central planners who had not understood the problems in the field. They complained about the fines the technical inspector had imposed for breakdowns that hadn't anything to do with human error. "It was a humiliation for the whole team," said Yevgeny. "Every year the breakdowns increased, and the fines—one hundred or fifty rubles for each individual—were of a size that meant something. Sometimes a whole team of one hundred people would have to pay. Until the breakdown was finished, no one left the work site. That's why we are gray-haired now."

Nikolai said the oilmen unwittingly increased the speed of the pipe corrosion even more by pumping in river water for use in drilling work. "The water had lots of microorganisms and seaweed, and that was transported into the line. At the temperatures we were using, these microorganisms created more bacteria that again increased the corrosion," he said.

The oilmen had added chemicals to the oil-water mix to help cure the problem, but that had only slowed the corrosion. "Just as we haven't found a medicine that makes a man young, we also haven't found compounds that can solve this problem," said Ivanov. He also feared that the compounds he was using to retard the corrosion might have other dangerous side effects. The oil-production company simply had not had adequate time to test the process before instituting it.

Just as the Russian oilmen had waited for orders from central planners in the past, now they were yearning for foreign advice and joint ventures to reverse a steady decline in production levels. "We have no alternative, because we don't know how to handle our problems," said Ivanov.

At Samotlor, the oilmen had already hired a French company to build a plant near the oil fields that would put a special anticorrosive lining in all of their pipes. The cost, however, would be enormous, and it would take years to redo the entire network. "It would be far better if we would just take everything apart and start from scratch," said Ivanov.

To clean up what was already in the swamps, they were negotiating with an Italian company that could use the waste from oil spills to make various petroleum products. No one in Siberia had ever taken measures either to clean up the mess or to make use of it, said Balshagin. It wasn't part of the plan. Usually, they only dumped sand on the worst areas to hide the black blemish.

Before the year was out, oil companies from all over the world were traveling to Nizhnevartovsk and concluding deals. Although Russia remained the world's largest producer of oil (it was pumping 10.5 million barrels a day in 1991, compared to Saudi Arabia's 8.4 million barrels), the equipment and recovery methods were so outmoded that the fields suffered an annual reduction in output despite vast remaining unexploited reserves. Production had fallen to a sixteen-year low, and exports had declined to two million barrels a day, less than half of what they had been even two years earlier. On the current downward curve, the Soviet Union would need to import oil by 1994.

The Western Siberian fields reached a peak output of 389 million tons in 1987, but it had been all downhill since then. Output was 310 million tons in 1991 and was expected to fall even further to 266 million tons in 1992. Part of the problem was that the oil was being depleted, but the greater woes were the pipeline problems and the lack of technology to recover oil more efficiently and from more difficult-to-reach reserves.

The pioneers of Siberia struck me as a sad ilk. Once-proud Soviets, the Siberians of legend and descendants of Yermak were waiting for foreign deliverance and hoping to hang on to their jobs. Again I thought of Rasputin, who wrote of how Russians had grown so accustomed to preserving their place in society that they really didn't care much whether that position took them anywhere. In one short story, he wrote of a bus pulling

into the station, and of Russians piling in with their goods and plans, only
to have the driver disappear and not return:

> We sat there for ten minutes, then fifteen, inhaling the smell of the sacks
> of potatoes piled on the backseat; we were a silent lot, feeling sluggish
> at the end of the day, and no one let out a murmur of complaint. We
> sat mutely, content simply to be sitting in our places. How little, I've
> noticed on more than one occasion, our people need; scare them by
> saying there won't be a bus until morning and a furious outcry will
> erupt, until everyone is in a complete stupor, but rush the same bus in,
> load it up, and let it stand there until morning—and they'll remain
> satisfied and believe they've gotten their way. Here the principle of one's
> rightful place is apparently at work; your place can be occupied by no
> one else and given to no one else but you, and whether this place takes
> you anywhere or not isn't really that important.

What is supposed to change in Russia, in Siberia, is that work should
take Russians somewhere. Space on the bus isn't enough anymore—now
Russian reformers want the bus to have a destination. Yet that was still
an alien concept for most Siberians.

Ivanov and Balshagin were relieved when I asked them about their first
years in Siberia. The stories came more easily than talk of the present.

Yevgeny recalled how during the first winters, it had been 60 degrees
below ($-80°$F), and even inside it had been 20 below ($-5°$F). "To know
when to close the schools, teachers hammered nails only partly into the
floors, one for each board, across the floor of the room," he said. "When
the eighth nail into the room had frost on it, they would close the school
for the day."

Nikolai recalled the days when there was only a single exploratory rig
retrieving the first oil. The oilmen earned only 270 rubles a month, but
they didn't really care. They built log roads to get to distant drilling sites,
spending weeks in the wilds, and they stopped along the way to feast off
the berries. Nikolai remembered the occasional ship arrival with another
delivery of fortune hunters and adventure seekers. The boat would depart
with an equal number of passengers who had given up their fight against
the elements, usually after only a few weeks or months. But Ivanov and
Balshagin never even thought of retreating.

"Remember the problem you had with the sign you were painting?"
laughed Nikolai.

"Yes, Nikolai, I do," said Yevgeny, smiling.

"Will you tell them, Yevgeny?" asked Nikolai.

"You tell it better, Nikolai," replied Yevgeny.

So Nikolai spoke of the spring when Yevgeny, with a couple of other workers, had been painting a big sign extolling the virtues of Marxism-Leninism or some such. He had left for lunch and returned a couple of hours later to see that one of his workers, in a fur coat, had fallen asleep atop one of the freshly painted giant letters. When Yevgeny got closer to wake the worker, however, he saw the fur coat was a bearskin, worn by a live bear. When the bear stirred, Yevgeny ran back to the camp along the only path over the swamps—a narrow pipeline. He laughed that he had no idea how he had balanced on the pipe at the speed he was running.

When he returned a little later, with his friend Nikolai and a rifle, the bear was gone. Only his footprints remained, in Communist red across the sign. "So we put it up that way," roared Nikolai, slapping Yevgeny on the back.

Before we sailed farther north, into a land that was the center of the Khanty and Mansi native peoples, our Russian organizers consented to host a press conference for a dozen members of the local press in the ship's dining area. I had by that time made it clear that I had come to Siberia to learn and not to pontificate, so I sat to the side while others held court.

The self-appointed star and spokesman of our expedition was Yuri Kaznin, who explained to the Nizhnevartovsk press, dressed in its Sunday best, that we were an ecological mission that would measure the water quality of the Ob. He spoke of the Greenpeace men, who would leave behind equipment for an international laboratory he was establishing in Kemerovo. Then he rattled off statistics for which he had no empirical evidence, illustrating the problems of the region.

As Kaznin talked, the journalists slowly quit taking notes and began to look bored. When he finished, Gerald Jacobs took the stage, setting the record straight and explaining that this was a journalistic expedition which he had organized with Vladimir, and that they had invited ecologists along, including Kaznin and the two Greenpeace scientists. He said that environmental questions were just one portion of our research, which was dedicated to investigating various aspects of the Siberian and Russian character. He spoke then of mass graves, former prison camps, and current social problems, all of which were being investigated by the expedition. The journalists listened intently and took notes, not missing Gerard's indirect confrontation with a Supreme Soviet member.

Then the Dutch chemist, Wytze van der Naald, tried an old Greenpeace tactic to work up local opposition to the oil-field polluters. He pulled out a bottle of "water" that he had extracted from one of their lakes where a pipeline had burst. It was black with oil. "This may be getting into what you drink," he said. He held it up for any photographers who might want to snap shots, but there were no takers.

The German biologist, Michael Hoffmann, said in his calm voice, "If the current trends continue, you have to assume that the forest and the swamps themselves are endangered. They will not remain as they are and in time they could disappear."

But the powerful moment was lost on this audience, which had other concerns. I interrupted the press conference to ask the local reporters why they seemed to have so little interest in these ecological matters. A female radio correspondent replied: "We have three priorities: bread, milk, and then bread again. Ecological problems are in another world for us." Every time I heard such comments, showing how far out of step Western concerns were from those of Siberians, I thought of the line from Brecht's *Three Penny Opera: "Erst kommt das Essen und dann kommt die Moral"*— first the grub and then the morals.

A few hours later we set sail up the Ob. I wanted to take the opportunity to sit down with Sergei, the student translator, to see what progress he had made on the "secret" documents from Tomsk 7 concerning the disappearance of plutonium. But I learned that Sergei had been fired for incompetence. He'd left the boat in Nizhnevartovsk to catch a commuter boat back to Kemerovo. He had turned over all the documents he was translating for Greenpeace to Yuri Kaznin. So I assumed Kaznin also had my Tomsk 7 papers.

The parliament member, smarting from Gerard Jacobs's slight during the press conference, denied that Sergei had given him anything belonging to me. When I asked if I could look for myself, because I would recognize the Tomsk 7 documents, he refused. He took my description of the papers and said he would search for them. "But I very much doubt they are there," he said. "Sergei never mentioned them to me."

I was kicking myself for ever letting the papers out of my sight. I should have waited for their translation until I returned home.

One of the Russian members of the expedition took me to the side to give me a warning. He said that Sergei had told Kaznin about what I had given him for translation, and that Kaznin had told him not to return the papers to me. Yuri was complaining loudly to the other Russians that I was pursuing "black information" without concern for the people or the region. My Russian friend told me not to forget where I was. "Remember that even now every such trip involving foreigners has someone on board who must inform for the KGB," he said.

It was past one A.M. when I went to the top deck as we sailed through oil country. An occasional gas flame provided a distant orange light. But as we sailed farther north, on the beach we saw the smaller flames of Khanty native fishermen in their small camps along the shore. The only other dull flame was on the deck below me, where my Dutch friends were lighting up their "Yurga gold," the wild-growing marijuana that they had picked in the fields of Yurga, the defense-production city upstream. The wind carried the sweet smell of their smoke up to me as I looked at the black and silken river.

Chapter 15:

TWO TEPEES

The Russians came like grasshoppers. And like
grasshoppers, they didn't do as much good
as harm.

—ALEKSANDRA DAVOLA, *indigenous Siberian*

The reindeer scattered. The smoke from the fire beside the herd, built to keep the mosquitoes and deerflies at bay, swirled wildly. Water from one of the Siberian swampland's thousands of lakes rippled and sprayed the campground. Two dogs, caught in the storm, barked furiously as our orange Mi-8 helicopter descended.

A dark-skinned woman in colorful native dress looking much like that of the Navajos I learned about as a child scooped up a little boy and girl and ran for the only cover available, a tepee, one of two huddled together on a small piece of moist turf between two lakes. Their canvas coverings buckled in the wind of our chopper.

Our pilot didn't dare set down on the spongy turf, so I jumped the final two feet to the ground. Behind me was a native historian, a diminutive woman in a blue polka-dot dress, who would act as our interpreter. Behind her was our scout, a native fisherman who had been the navigator for the pilot. While the helicopter disappeared over the horizon, the historian walked toward the tepee to calm the woman. Visiting helicopters, after all, had seldom brought good news—only oilmen who took the land and hunters who killed the squirrel and sable.

And she recognized this one, which belonged to the dreaded oilmen. We had rented it from the geologists for a mixture of rubles and vodka.

Like most Khanty, Aleksandra Davola lived far north of where she had been born. Unlike her ancestors, who had moved with the seasons, her clan moved to keep one step ahead of the oilmen. With each move, the weather grew colder and the animal and fish life less bountiful. Aleksandra Davola now lived within a day's trip of the top of the River Torem Yogan—God's River—at whose source the tribe's most important god was said to reside.

Aleksandra Davola's young boy, Sergei, ran out of the tepee to round up the last of the stampeded reindeer, which were slowly returning to their protective fire. After exchanging pleasantries with Agrivena Sopachova, the historian, the native woman restarted her doused campfire and hung a blackened teakettle over it. Her four-year-old niece followed her and peeked at us from behind her aunt's skirt.

Across the small lake in front of her tepee was an open hut, with a roof made of bark and narrow tree trunks, where she stored the food that would keep—flour, cereals, and sugar. She had dug a deep hole, which she called her refrigerator, in the ground near the lake to keep her fish and other perishables.

"I am sorry the men are not here," she said, referring to her brother-in-law and his twenty-one-year-old son, who had left for the village two days earlier in search of ammunition. "They are better talkers than I am." She stuttered nervously in Khanty, a Finno-Ugric language distantly related to Hungarian, Estonian, and Finnish.

Her two eldest daughters, she said, had taken the two dugout boats that morning to visit the neighbors. The nearest neighbor, she said, was "after three lakes and then on the fourth lake"—a half day's trip away. To get there, the daughters rowed through the lakes, picked up the lightweight canoes to carry them over the narrow strips of land, and then rowed again.

Aleksandra was one of 28,000 Khanty and Mansi natives who populated the vast Siberian Northwest. They were two of thirty-six indigenous Siberian peoples that included the distantly related Shors, whom we visited at the beginning of our expedition. In 1911, just six years before the October Revolution, the native people had accounted for nearly an eighth of Siberia's 8,100,000 inhabitants (1,060,000). But Stalin's mass exiles and centrally planned economic development had increased the influx of non-native population, while the Siberian aboriginal peoples had been hit by a blight of alcoholism and desperation. By 1990 the natives were only 500,000 of the Siberian population of more than 25 million. They didn't even have a common ethnic or geographical name, like "Africans" or "American Indians." Ironically, the newcomers, the Russians, categorized the natives as "inorodny"—aliens.

None of the Siberian aborigines' lives were altered more by development than those of the Khanty and the Mansi who lived in the broad Ob Basin of the northwest. The area possesses Russia's richest oil and gas deposits. We had begun our flight to Aleksandra Davola's tepee in Surgut, an oil workers' city 100 miles south of her that appeared out of nowhere in the 1960s.

"The Russians came like grasshoppers," she said. "And like grasshoppers, they didn't do as much good as harm." Wherever the Russian swarm moved, she said, it left the land barren. The Russians shot the Khantys' game from their low-flying helicopters and snowmobiles, often simply leaving the carcasses behind because they were too much trouble to pick up. Aleksandra winced and shook as she mimicked the sound of the snowmobiles: "BRRRRRRR!"

She frowned as she pointed to her reindeer, a sickly-looking lot. She said the reindeer had been much healthier when she was a girl. She thought that was because the broad-leafed grass that they ate, called *yagel,* was sick as well. Often after rainstorms, the grass was stained with a thin black film from the oilmen's pollution.

Aleksandra Davola was a woman of deep sadness and few words. For every sentence she spoke, I had to ask several questions and then wait patiently as she stuttered out an answer. Agrivena Sopachova, the historian, would often take over when she saw the burden was too great for the shy woman.

"We feel 'the people who came' [the description natives use for the Russians and other nonindigenous residents of Siberia] have put a big mountain in our path and we can't pass it," the historian said. "It is the same as chopping a man's head off. They have taken away our way of living. If they would leave us alone on our land, we could provide for ourselves—without the industry, without the builders, without the geologists, and without the oilmen."

She said the Russians had also depleted all the important lakes of fish. There once had been enough fish in each lake to feed several families for many years. "But now there are only the names left. We have a pond called Fish Lake that has no fish. There is Pike Lake, but it has no pike in it. There is Perch Lake, but you can't find perch there." Aleksandra had moved so far north that the lakes weren't even named yet. When I asked her what the lake in front of her tepee was called, she noted sadly that it had none. She had never lived on a lake without a name. She and her family had left the last settlement because the geologists had begun to explore for oil there. The geologists always had been the most friendly to the natives, but now the Khanty knew the oilmen and their wells would follow them.

"We just came here this year, after the thaw," she said. "Life has been more difficult since the children's father died. It is the seventh year since he died. Sergei was only four years old then. Now he is eleven. We had thirty reindeer then. Now we have only ten. I am not able to care for more than that." (Agrivena whispered that no Khant would tell me the exact number of his reindeer—to do so had been considered bad luck ever since the forced collectivization.)

It was painful for Aleksandra to talk about her husband's death. I sat on a log she had provided as my bench, and she stood in front of me—looking only at the turf, digging into it nervously with the toe of her green rubber boot. It was her summer footwear—in the winter she would wear warm moccasins made of reindeer skin. "The children's father had an attack of tuberculosis during the winter," she said. "I couldn't get him to the village because I had children who were too young to be left alone. And that's how the children's father died."

How could a man of nature contract tuberculosis? I wondered.

Aleksandra said that her husband had been forced in the 1960s to work for a *sovkhoz,* a collective state farm, which was gathering together all of the natives' reindeer. They then slaughtered hundreds of them for meat. "He helped to collect the reindeer in the cold rain and bad weather," she said.

"My husband was always sick after that," said Aleksandra Davola. "But the man who was the chief of the *sovkhoz* got a special award."

"Was he Russian?" I asked.

"I don't know what nationality he had," said the woman. "I only knew he wasn't a Khant. He was one of 'those who came.' "

Aleksandra Davola turned silent again, and the historian again began to talk. Aleksandra moved to the side and made a stool for herself, placing a flat wooden plank atop a small, sawed-off tree stump. The four-year-old girl mimicked her movements, using a smaller board and smaller stump nearby. After a few minutes, Aleksandra began to prepare a lunch for us, placing bread on a low table built from the wood from the dwarf pines that grew in the swamps. The girl mimed her steps. The woman took a piece of bread in her mouth to taste it. The girl took a sugar cube in her mouth.

The Dutch photographer, Paul Babliowsky, snapped a Polaroid of the eleven-year-old boy and handed it to him. The boy watched it turn from white to familiar images. He looked behind him to see the log fence and tepee and match them to images in the picture. Then he pointed to himself with great pleasure.

"We have a saying," said the historian, who had observed both scenes with me. "If you want to understand, you only need watch. A Khant never asks questions when he goes to the village and sees something new. He observes it. Then he reaches his conclusion. He will ask a question only if he can make no sense of something through observation."

I noted to the historian that the Khanty nomads lived in tepees almost identical to those of the American Indian. "In all parts of the world, history has some inherent rules," said the historian. She said tepees could be built quickly, could be moved from place to place easily, and had architectural qualities that kept natives warm in the winter and cool in the summer.

She said you could determine how wealthy a Khant was by the quality of his tepee. It wasn't like the old days, when tepees were lined with animal skins in the winter and boiled birch in the summer. Then you could tell wealth by the nature of the furs. Now affluence was revealed by the quality of the canvas. Rich Khanty had a thick woolen canvas for the winter and a lighter-weight one for the summer. Aleksandra was poor—she had only lightweight canvas and covered it with woolen blankets during the winter.

A long-legged bug of a sort I had never seen before—it looked something like a praying mantis—climbed onto my green sweater. As I reached up to knock it off, the petite historian quickly grabbed my wrist. She gently picked the insect off my sweater and threw it behind me, where it escaped unharmed. "We believe that insect carries the soul of the reindeer which feeds us," she said. "So we will never kill it, although it can hurt you when it bites."

She said it had been my fault that the insect lighted on me. I had grown uncomfortable on the log provided for me and had sat on the ground—the insect's habitat. "You were no longer in your proper place," said the historian.

Agrivena Sopachova wore the city clothes of a Russian woman, but she was leading a campaign to keep alive the Khanty culture. She was small and stubborn, and she wore the look of contained anger noticeable among many of the educated native peoples.

"When I was in school," she said, "they didn't allow me to speak my native language. But I did anyway, and I wore the native dress. Later I saw that this unrealized consciousness was something very important. I saw the riches of our society that were being lost."

So she began to collect the folk tales of the natives on a tape recorder. She transcribed them into a language whose written form had all but disappeared since its books had been banned in the late 1930s by Stalin. Before then, under Lenin, the Khanty had printed their first alphabet and books ever, in an effort to spread literacy among the natives. Because of a lack of linguists, however, the job had gone slowly and few books had been printed.

I asked her to tell me her favorite story. But she turned to our scout, Sergei Kechimov, who was said to be the best storyteller in the region. He had remained silent until then, but he sat up proud and erect as he began to tell his favorite.

"Torem [the Khanty word for God] sent people to live on earth," he said. "But he didn't tell the people how they should live. And the people didn't care much for the land they lived upon. They made a lot of waste.

They did harmful things to the water and air. It became so bad that they couldn't live on the land anymore, so they wanted to return to Torem. To reach him, they constructed a high house. They kept building higher and higher to climb to Torem. They built and they built. Torem looked down upon them. He said: 'The people are running back to Torem, but Torem will not have them.' He blew down the tall house and it fell to pieces. The people scattered in all different directions. They found that they all spoke different languages and couldn't understand each other anymore. So they couldn't speak to each other to do evil. They had to do good because there was no other way of survival. So now we have come back to the beginning of the story."

Before he could tell a second story, we saw the helicopter approaching. Aleksandra Davola thanked us for coming. She said she had decided upon a name for her lake. "I will call it Two Tepee Lake," she said.

The name satisfied everyone. Aleksandra Davola looked quietly pleased. We ran to where the chopper was hovering and jumped up to the outstretched arms of the copilot, who pulled us back inside. Our next stop was the refueling and equipment station that stood on a hairpin curve farther down God's River.

The geologists had begun exploring for oil at Fox Mountain, near the top of the holy river, where the Khantys' highest god is said to reside, during the February before our summer expedition. The oilmen had never come that far north before, and the natives feared they would sully their holiest place. So an old hunter with a shotgun took eight of them hostage and then escorted them overland back to Surgut, where he delivered them to their bosses with a letter. No more exploration should take place on Khanty lands, it said, without the approval of the native people's elected councils.

This being the age of Glasnost, local ecologists from the Surgut area joined forces with the natives for the first time. Within weeks the regional council of Surgut voted that exploration in the region would be temporarily halted until the oilmen could reach an agreement with the natives.

News of the old man's courage spread quickly through the region. The Khanty considered it one of the few bright points in their history since Yermak the Conqueror had first led his Cossacks through the West Siberian plain.

The view from the helicopter as we approached a refueling and equipment station at a lower point on God's River was of four giant fuel tanks and a half dozen smaller ones, a pile of scrap and a dozen wooden shacks in which the oilmen lived. Television had recently reached the settlement, and all the shacks had antennae rising from them, appearing for a moment like the crucifixes of the electronic age on the holy river's bank.

After we landed, we located the middle-aged shift leader of the eighteen-man work force, Valentin Shadokhin. When he learned where we had flown in from, he ridiculed the Khanty for trying to hold up the inevitable march of Russian progress. They ought to join the modern world, he said. They ought to realize that there was plenty of wetland in Siberia but only so much oil—and the world needed all of it.

I asked the shift leader if he knew the name of the river in front of him. He scratched his deeply tanned potbelly and pulled up his jogging pants, a chocolate-brown synthetic material that quickly slipped back to its original precarious position far below his beltline.

"Something like Tromgan," he said, coming respectably close to Torem Yogan, the name of the Khanty God.

I asked if he knew what the name meant.

"I don't know," he said. "Probably something Khanty."

I told him it was the holiest river of the indigenous people—God's River.

"We have all been atheists in the Soviet Union," he said with a chuckle. He said he had read parts of the Bible for the first time only two years earlier. He liked the business about honoring parents and not committing adultery. He thought that made sense.

"I can believe this part of religion," he said. "But I am not yet ripe to accept that there is a God." And he certainly wasn't about to believe in the Khanty God, he said, if he couldn't even decide about his own.

I argued that wasn't the point. The people who lived on the land believed in the god, and they felt the oilmen were about to invade a sacred place. Couldn't he respect their feelings and look for oil elsewhere (or at least give them a cut of the profits)?

"We have tried to educate them, to build homes for them, to help them come into the modern world," he said. "But it all comes to nothing. What we give them, they drink away. And if we gave them money from what is earned from the oil, they wouldn't know what to do with it. It is hard for them to understand what money is."

Perhaps out of spite I decided to tell him an aspect of long unpracticed Khanty clan law that I had been told about earlier that day. I said that the Shaman, the natives' priest, condemned those of his people to death who killed animals in excess of their needs, who cut too much timber, or who urinated in a river that provided their fish. The Shaman's order was executed secretly, and the executioner usually killed the violator in the middle of the night by stabbing him or slitting his throat. "The Shaman's rulings were always carried out," I said.

The man with the potbelly laughed. "I've heard about their Shaman," he said, taking a gulp from a big ladle of water out of a bucket by his side. "They are either charlatans or drunks. I am not afraid of them unless they are coming after my bottle."

The helicopter had started up and was ready to take us back to Surgut, where our boat was docked. The water from God's River flowed through rusty pipes beside the chopper and sprinkled the dust on the takeoff pad. As we lifted off, the shift leader waved and smiled from below, satisfied that he had set me straight about the natives who were trying to hold back progress in Siberia.

Chapter 16:

In Search
of The Shaman

It is good luck for our voyage that it is raining.

—ANDREI KIPRIANOV, *son of the Shaman*

When Yegor Kelmin was young, his parents taught him about their gods —for water, for fire, for fishing, and for hunting, two additional gods for protection (one for men and one for women), and the chief God, who ruled over all from the source of the rivers at the Continental Divide. Through the rivers, they said, He flowed through the ground to His people.

Yegor Kelmin was born in a village called Oughut, which meant "top village" in his native Khanty. His parents gave him the name Yok, which was taken from their word for "God." They knew he would be a special son. But like many intelligent young men his age, he left his father's world for Russian society, where he could get ahead.

He first went to work as a bricklayer, earning well and helping to build the Kamaz automobile factory on the distant Kama River. The Russian construction workers called him by the worldly name of Yegor, unable to pronounce the name Yok, and they gave him the family name Kelmin— from the Russian word for a bricklayer's trowel: *kelma.* Yegor was an ambitious soul, however. After a time, he continued his studies and graduated in philology from the university in Surgut. It was his education and Glasnost that had brought him back to his roots; he came to believe deeply in the ancient religion of his father.

When Kelmin saw that the fish and animals weren't surviving the Russians, he could only conclude that the old faith was, well, closer to God.

"It made more sense to me than the religion of oil recovery and strip timber cutting that had forced my people from their land," he said. So in 1989, when the Khanty and Mansi native peoples of the Siberian Northwest started an organization to represent their interests, Yegor Kelmin became its president for the oil-rich Tyumen region. We met aboard our boat in Surgut, a city of 100,000 on the banks of the Ob that had been built for oil recovery.

His first step had been to draw up a list of native people living in the surrounding area, something that had never been done before. They numbered 348 families in Surgut and 2,500 in tens of settlements with names like Utyabol, Lantorsky, and Tugelny. Few Khanty lived in the places where they had been raised—almost all of them had run away from the oilmen. Kelmin himself was the last of a dozen survivors from the Tribe of the Reincarnation of the Snake, which in the 1930s had numbered some 500 families with 30,000 reindeer, and had inhabited land graced with clear streams brimming with fish and taiga rich with bear, sable, blue fox, and wolverine.

Kelmin insisted that to this day no snake would attack him or anyone traveling with him. A Russian ecologist, who accompanied him to our boat, swore that he had been witness to this amazing power. "I know it is strange," said Kelmin, "but you cannot deny what is true."

In the old days, said Kelmin, the Shamans were the enforcers of tribal rules regarding sins against nature. The rough English translation of the word Shaman is "witch doctor," but the Shamans had always been much more than that to the native peoples of Siberia. Almost all aboriginal Siberians followed the ancestral and animistic religions also common among American Indians and such Central Asian peoples as the Mongolians and Kirghiz. For them, the Shamans were physicians, priests, and prophets. They cured ills with homemade remedies, led the high celebrations and prayers, and communicated with the spirit world in a state of trance that was induced by dancing, chanting, and beating a drum.

The diverse nationalities of Siberia shared a common clan structure that was held together by the Shamans, who presided over the occasional councils and seasonal rituals that brought together scattered bands of related nomads. The aboriginal Siberians had a religious belief in the guardian spirits of nature, and the Shamans ruled over the blood sacrifice of animals that propitiated these spirits.

In the nineteenth century, Russian missionaries at first tried to destroy the Shamans and impose their Orthodoxy. But the Shamans and the natives adjusted; they made their religion an odd mix of both faiths, using icons and nature worship side-by-side. The second wave of "missionaries," the enthusiasts from the Communist Youth League, Komsomol, caused more damage. Their antireligious campaigns brought the prohibition of Shamanism and the confiscation of ritual costumes and medicine bags. Stalin killed the most rebellious Shamans or sent them to the Gulag. Many others were undone among their own people by Soviet propaganda that mocked them as being nothing more than cunning charlatans out to exploit ordinary natives.

Yet, even in the 1990s, a few Shamans were said to be still around and operating. I wanted to meet one so that he could teach me about the past and predict for me the future of his people. "You will not find them," said Kelmin. "They will not reveal themselves to you." To do so, he said, was a sin that no true Shaman would commit.

I wasn't ready to give up however, so I visited the ethnographical museum in Khanty Mansiysk, more than 200 miles downriver from Surgut and just a couple of miles off the Ob on its major tributary, the Irtysh. It was the capital of the Khanty and Mansi National *Okrug,* a district the size of France over which the local population had limited autonomy. The museum seemed the most likely place to find my next lead.

The museum was housed in a restored Khanty hut, and the sloping grounds around it were preserved as well. The hut had a slightly tilted, two-sided roof covered with strips of birch bark sewn into large panels over the wooden planks. On top of the birch bark was a row of thin poles—the joists. The front of the roof projected slightly and rested on the log columns, forming a porch. A small, high door led into the hut, where a fire was burning—not because it was cold, but to keep away mosquitoes. On the walls hung Khanty wooden tools, some old weapons, and handicrafts: purses, needlework, and beads.

A half-dozen women sat on two low benches in front of the fireplace and sang Khanty songs in a nasal drone. The songs sounded remarkably similar to American Indian music I had heard in southern Utah, with their pounding rhythms and monotonic chanting. The dances, as well, had the same stooped, rough quality.

After the performance I sat on a wooden table outside with three of the women. The oldest, Yevdokia Nyumosova, had recently become the director of a teacher's college at which she was preparing natives to pass on their language and culture to further generations. She was only fifty-five, but her face was heavily creased with wrinkles. She had the high, broad cheekbones of the American Indian.

The two younger women, both in their thirties, had finer, more Oriental looks. Rionarda Olzina at age thirty-six had provided much of the impetus behind the museum. She was divorced from her Russian husband and talked with the religious fervor of the born-again. Tamara Gliminova had a more intellectual approach. She knew many of the traditions couldn't be maintained in the modern world. But, at age thirty-one, she hoped to preserve their memory for posterity so that her half-Russian children would become familiar with their roots.

I revealed my quest to find a Shaman carefully and, at first, indirectly. Why was it was that no men had been involved in their performance for our group? I asked.

They looked at each other and then related to me the sad history of the Khanty men.

"The men began to let us down in 1582 when they failed to resist the first Russian conqueror, Yermak, who also occupied this village," said Rionarda Olzina.

Yevdokia, the older woman, defended the Khanty men by saying that in the beginning they hadn't known any better than to trust the Russians. "The Khanty were not a warmaking people, and the men had never prepared to fight before," she said. "They thought they would always have land—because God provided it in bountiful and unending supply. They didn't think fighting was necessary."

But the younger woman countered with disgust. She said the failure to stop Yermak had been only the beginning. Then came the tax collectors for the Russian provincial governors, the *voyevody,* who by the middle of the seventeenth century demanded ten sable pelts from each married man and five from each single man. That made the *voyevody* rich, because they passed only a small portion of the furs to the tsars.

The Russian emphasis on fur hunting caused the men to pay less attention to the traditional fishing, reindeer-breeding, and hunting that was needed to feed their families. The Khanty revolted in the early seventeenth century, and again in 1841, when the taxes grew too oppressive and the Russians seized their land. But the uprisings were put down quickly and brutally. After these setbacks, the Russians tightened the grasp further by seizing the best hunting grounds and fencing off rivers—taking the fish before they reached the Khanty population farther downstream.

The men, said Rionarda, also did nothing to stop the imposition of Christianity in the eighteenth century. The missionaries carried out baptisms so rapidly that the process was almost complete by 1750. After the Revolution, she said, the men again didn't fight the forced collectivization. The best resistance the herdsmen could muster was the slaughter of their livestock before the collectives could take them. Historians say herds of cattle and horses fell by more than half between 1928 and 1931. Among the reindeer herders of the north, the loss of herds was more than one-fourth from 1931 to 1934. But leather-jerkined Bolsheviks with their pistols were enough to tame the natives easily.

The men's final failure, Rionarda said, was alcoholism. Vodka rendered the Khanty men helpless to withstand the mass migration of Russian workers in the 1960s, when oil and gas were discovered in the Khanty Mansiysk region.

The other young woman, Tamara, added her venom to that of Rionarda. "It began with Yermak, but the men failed us again against the oilmen," she said. "This time it had nothing to do with not knowing about the Russians. This time they were drinking when they should have been defending us."

The older woman again inserted a tone of understanding. "Civilization was coming so fast that the men couldn't grow accustomed to it. They weren't strong enough to resist this force. They also couldn't find their place in the civilization."

She spoke of ten village boys who had recently attended a nearby technical school to learn tractor driving. But when they had returned to the village, there was only one tractor. "One or two of them busied themselves driving it," she said. "And the rest drank. No Khanty girl will marry a Khanty boy, because he can't show that he will be able to provide for her and her family. Without a family, he drinks even more." And those who have wives, she said, frowning, give them children born with defects because of the alcoholism.

"And how many of the men among the Khanty have a drinking problem?" I asked.

"Rarely can you find a person who doesn't drink," Yevdokia said.

Both of the young women had married Russians. "No Khanty men were worth marrying," said Rionarda. "The women have been far better at adjusting to the changing life conditions of the modern world. We have been braver and more flexible. They have lost their courage."

Rionarda conceded that she had once deeply believed in Communism, but now she had reconverted to her people's ancestral beliefs. She hated the fact that modern life forced her to sin every day. By living in the low-rises built by the Soviets, she said that she was forced to suffer the sin of having an impure woman walk over her head—and over the "holy corner" that she said must be observed in each Khanty house.

The holy corner was a place to take presents for God. The gifts could be clothing, food, or whatever new was brought into the house, a bottle of milk or even a video recorder. "The gift should be placed in the holy corner for a short period of time—sometimes no longer than ten minutes," she said.

I asked what she meant by an "impure" woman.

She said it was any woman during menstruation.

I asked if she still believed that definition of "impure" after her Soviet education. "It seems normal to us that a woman should occupy her right place," she said. "It didn't bother our mothers and grandmothers. Our main job should be our children."

Rionarda had created an impossible life for herself. On the one hand she was convinced that she could not marry a Khant, because they had all turned drunk and hopeless. Yet she had divorced her Russian husband and now wanted to live the traditional life of the Khanty woman. How did she reconcile this? I asked as politely as I could.

Her friend Tamara tried to help. Her Russian husband and two children didn't speak a word of the language, and she didn't expect to change them much. "I'm living the life we have now—the modern life," she said. "These traditions that Rionarda speaks of are of the older generation. We should remember them and pass them on as history. But we cannot live this way."

The older woman said she would be happy if only the Khant could hold his head high again. She took the white scarf from her head and showed her charcoal hair. "The name Khant has been a curse," she said. "They use it only to abuse us: they call us drunkards, people who eat raw meat—all the worst. They call our children names. The children used to come home from school crying. For me, as a teacher, this was a most difficult and painful problem."

Yevdokia looked directly into my eyes. "Now we don't know what culture we are living. Is it Soviet? Is it Russian? Or is it our own? I fear it is nothing at all. And that is why so many get drunk, why some kill themselves, and why some merely retreat into themselves."

None of the three women gave the Khanty people much chance of surviving as a people. Soon, said Rionarda, all that will remain will be her museum and some die-hards singing songs and dancing dances. "We ourselves will still be alive twenty or fifty years from now," she said. "But in one hundred years the Khanty will exist only on photos."

Tamara agreed with her friend. "When they spit into your soul for this long, there is little left," she said. "We never understood the Communism that was forced upon us, just as we didn't really understand the Christianity that came before that."

Yevdokia was doing more than any of them to keep the nation alive. She had helped with the printing of the first Khanty textbooks since their banning under Stalin. She had also traveled to Canada, at the invitation of the government, to learn about the lives of native peoples there.

"We perhaps are doing more in the way of printing books and preserving our language," she said. "But we are far weaker politically than some North American tribes and are less likely to survive as a people. The Russians consider us fools, but let them come into our society and adjust, being forced to speak our language and live our ways. No wonder our people are disoriented. Our people are dying out even before they are dead. Little will be left after another generation. Those who have ambitions and ideas rarely marry their own kind. I have two children. God didn't give me any more. My daughter married a Ukrainian and my son married a Russian. My generation is coming to an end and there isn't a generation to replace it. That is what we are standing before."

So what had become of the men who should have saved their society from this fate? What had happened to the Shamans? Did the women know where I could find one?

They said the mayor of the small district around Oktyabrskoye, a seventy-mile sail downstream from Khanty Mansiysk, was the son of a famous Shaman who had died not long ago. He would know to whom his father had passed the medicine bag. But the women warned me—the mayor made his career in the Communist Party and had turned his back on his people.

Rionarda also warned me about the fate that faces Khanty who guide foreigners to the Shaman or the holy places where he carries out his rituals. "My friend took Russian scientists to the holy places," she said. "Her husband didn't die his own death [meaning he killed himself or was murdered], the mother killed herself, the son died while serving in the army. Another son has been ill all his life, and my friend is not well, either. My friend said that God damned them all."

Nevertheless, we sailed the next morning to the village run by the Shaman's son. He looked almost identical to a savvy South Korean politician I had met several years earlier while covering national elections in Seoul. Like the politician, Andrei Kirillovich Kiprianov had dark, shrewd eyes and neatly combed, wavy black hair. His walk was confident, between a strut and a swagger. Unlike most of the men of his nationality whom I had met, his teeth were white and perfect.

Kiprianov would have preferred sitting and talking politics. But, looking somewhat bemused, he consented to take me to the local Shaman—who had taken over after his father had died of sarcoma. It began to rain as we boarded our boat and began the thirty-mile trip downstream to the village where the Shaman lived, which was called Shakhaly (meaning "backwater").

"It is good luck for our voyage that it is raining," said Kiprianov as we sat at a table in the dining area beside two bottles of mineral water. I noted that he didn't drink.

"Is that a Khanty belief regarding rain?" I asked, always looking for more material.

He looked at me as if I were crazy and shrugged. "I always thought it was a Christian superstition."

Kiprianov said that his family's home village was across the Ob River from Shakhaly. It was called Lokhtotkurt, which meant "city on the bay." Russian conquerors had seized it in the late sixteenth century and forcibly baptized its residents. Then they had given his family its name, Kiprianov, taken from that of famous Russian Orthodox Metropolitans of the fifteenth century. "We were given the name because of our family's strength and power," he said. The second family in the village was called Angachupov. No one knew why anymore.

Russian missionaries then and in the years thereafter built churches at every small village we passed along the Ob. They were usually on a small rise above the river, small wooden buildings whose crucifixes had disappeared with the October Revolution. Most were now used for other purposes; in Oktyabrskoye, for instance, the church had become a telephone switching station.

Andrei Kiprianov said he had been born in a log cabin "like Abraham Lincoln." But, instead of reading the Bible or any Khanty equivalent before the fireplace, he had been raised on *Das Kapital.* "I had a clever father," he said. "He was a Shaman and a Communist at the same time. He led a sort of double life."

His father carried out the sacred rituals of the Shaman in secrecy because the Communist Party to which he belonged wouldn't countenance such heresy. For that, he received gifts from local villagers. But he never missed his Party meetings. For that, he received other perquisites—housing and goods.

Andrei said his father couldn't read or write, but as the most intelligent man in the region he understood the value of literacy. So he urged his favorite son, Andrei, to leave the berries and fish behind and turn to books. Andrei Kiprianov credited his father for his own survival at a time when so many other Khanty men had turned alcoholic or destitute. "Although I was the second-born of four sons, he thought I was the most clever," said Andrei.

The mayor insisted to me that he was no longer a Communist ("the word is a red rag to a bull in our country"), but he wanted to explain the downfall of his people—and nations more generally—"with the help of Marxist economic theory."

He said collectivization had destroyed the Khanty because they were a people "who thrived by separating themselves one from the other." They lived in two- or three-family clusters in small settlements. Each settlement was self-sufficient, with its own piece of territory to hunt, but none provided for a larger whole. "When collectivization came, the Khanty weren't prepared to combine their talents and survive and modernize, so they died," he said.

He looked at me, pleased with this philosophical perspective. He talked about his people as if they were a foreign race to which he didn't belong. "The Khanty were not personally as developed as 'those who came.' They hadn't learned interrelations. They were still living in a feudal way."

Andrei Kiprianov breathed deeply and slowly, taking long periods of time between sentences. As he talked, we sailed slowly down the Ob, past vegetation that was lower than it had been in the south. The river was so broad that I could barely see across it. On the left bank, the sandy beach had been cut into neat layers by the different stages of the spring thaw. Stretches of the right bank had been scraped by ice floes into long, flat beaches. Now and then our boat would pass small temporary fishing settlements, there just for the summer, which looked welcoming, with their fires and one or two wigwams or small huts.

Kiprianov sat hunched forward on the edge of his chair. He shifted his head nervously back and forth, never looking me in the eye, as he talked. He sipped and swallowed from his mineral water methodically. "Many Khanty do not realize why their development is so far behind," he said. He said his people were simply "genetically flawed" for the modern world, "both intellectually and physically."

This saddened me. A man who could have helped his people seemed to have abandoned them. "I respect my people," he insisted, "and it isn't their fault that they can't handle the situation. But in order to defend the clan, they shouldn't focus on the folk songs and the hunting and fishing. They should focus on intellectual and physical development."

Just as I was about to write Andrei off as a bloodless opportunist, he opened a small window into his own soul. "I wish my brothers had listened more to my father," he said. "But they are all dead now. All three of them."

How had they died? I asked.

"The usual way," he said.

One had been beaten to death. As it was with most such fights, it had begun with vodka and name-calling and ended with bloody hands and hangovers. "That was five years ago," he said.

More recently, his youngest brother had been run over by a boat while swimming in the Ob. His older brother, a ship captain, had drowned a couple of years earlier when he had fallen off his boat. "The conditions were unclear," Andrei said. "Everyone on the boat said that no one saw him go overboard."

I asked if drinking or foul play had been involved.

Andrei's head shifted from side to side more rapidly. "The only thing I can say is that my grandfather lived to be sixty years of age, so it was possible for our people. The generation of my father had an average age of just forty. In my generation, most men don't live past thirty."

From a tribe of Kiprianovs and Angachupovs that once numbered several hundred, there were now just three men other than himself (ages thirty, fifteen, and eight) and about twenty women. All of the women, including his four sisters, had married men of non-native nationalities. Andrei himself had married a Russian woman whom he had met while studying Marxist economics in Novosibirsk. In the area he ruled as mayor, there had been 14,500 people of whom 4,500 were natives in 1960. Thirty years later, the population had grown to 35,000 but the number of natives had fallen by two-thirds, to just 1,500.

* * *

I asked about his father. What was it like to be the son of a Shaman?

He recalled vividly when his grandfather, whose health had turned bad, had transferred the Shaman job to his father. Andrei had come along. As part of the ritual, they canoed and rowed between three sacred places on the borders of the two families' territories. In the middle of the area was the holiest place, a patch of land next to a big lake called Sora. They had brought a sacrificial goat, which they slaughtered. Andrei also remembered that they had crossed themselves in the Christian way, and that there were icons in the holy places in addition to the animal heads that they also worshiped. The mixture of Russian Orthodox symbols and Shamanism, he said, was frequent among the "converted" natives.

Andrei's hands began to shake a little. "I was so afraid," he said, repeating that phrase several times.

"Of what?" I asked.

"Of everything."

He was afraid of the songs and afraid even to touch one of the trees or plants in the holy place. "I was afraid something unusual might happen. I was afraid of death. I always had inside of me this great feeling of life, and something there frightened me."

Perhaps, I ventured, that fear was what had made him choose not to follow his father's steps as a Shaman and instead become a Marxist economist and Communist Party member. There was nothing like the fearsome mystical to scare one into scientific socialism, I said.

He gave me a befuddled gaze. Dundee insisted he had translated my comment perfectly, but "he just doesn't get it." So Andrei continued his story.

Although he wasn't recognized by his people as a Shaman, he said, he had inherited his father's talents. Shamans were self-selected, he noted, and usually set themselves apart with their natural gifts of healing and prophecy.

Andrei said that on two occasions he had foreseen the results of his final examinations at the Novosibirsk Institute before they had been announced. In May 1990 he had known the precise tally of the local vote in his favor even before the balloting had taken place.

More troubling, Andrei said he had foreseen the death of his brothers. He knew one brother would be murdered, after a dream in which he had seen his brother lying in a coffin on the river. Two weeks later his brother was dead, beaten to death by Russians following a drunken brawl.

Shortly before the drowning death of his second brother, Andrei had remained at home while his brothers went hunting. Andrei said that a sense of foreboding had overtaken him. "I felt loneliness of a depth I had never experienced before," he said. "I knew something fateful would happen. My brother drowned shortly thereafter."

On the third occasion, the motor to his boat stopped cold over the spot in the river where his brother would be run over by a boat and then drown a few days later. "I drifted for a while," he said, "taken away by the current, before I could start the motor again. I knew where it would happen before it happened. It was just about here," he said, nodding his head out the window, as we turned toward Shakhaly Harbor.

A steep embankment separated the harbor from the town of neatly painted, well-constructed wooden houses, with their vegetable gardens and picket fences. I followed Andrei as he walked up a long wooden stairway toward the village and the home of the Shaman. He had grown uneasy about introducing us to him. He explained that this man lacked the special talents of his family. His father had turned the job over to him because there simply wasn't anyone else to do it. "Let me apologize in advance if he is a little drunk," Andrei said.

We walked past a large cabbage patch and turned left on the main street, which was a muddy stretch of deep ruts and stagnant rain puddles. We then walked past the boarding school where Andrei had studied. It was painted fresh green, and beside it was a soccer field, where two cows slept in front of the goal. A few villagers walked up to Andrei, whom they recognized, and complained to him about the condition of the roads. He explained he had no money nor equipment to help them.

When we arrived at the Shaman's house, the front door was sealed shut with a large iron padlock. The neighbors hadn't seen him since the previous day. They said he might be out gathering berries (it was the season), fishing, or perhaps he was merely drunk. So he might be stumbling through town.

We walked through Shakhaly, first passing the offices of the collective. Boards that had once listed the annual and monthly production figures were blank. The discipline of central planning was fading, but not yet replaced by a free market. And there was no Shaman.

We stopped at the local museum, dedicated to a backward people's transition into socialist workers. The woman who could tell us about the history of the village had the day off. And no one knew where the Shaman could be found.

We passed the Cultural Palace, which before the October Revolution had been the Russian Orthodox Church of the Resurrection. The local Party meetings had taken place there. It had also doubled as a movie theater. Two frames for signs hung outside the building. Above one was written: TODAY'S SHOW. Above the other was written: COMING SOON. Both were blank. Nothing today in Shakhaly; nothing coming soon. And still no Shaman.

So we gave up and walked back to the beach. Andrei bid us farewell and began to walk along the sand, to catch a commuter boat that would take him back to Oktyabrskoye. He began to walk off arm-in-arm with a drunken fisherman who had recognized him. But before he did, I asked him how he had avoided the plague of drinking that had decimated his people.

He corrected me. He drank vodka and was quite proud of his capacity to hold his booze. I smiled. I had romanticized about Andrei, thinking his survival had come because of some rare discipline. But his success in the world of the Russians had come partly because he could hold his liquor. "I can down a bottle of vodka at a sitting and still keep control of myself," he bragged.

The captain had fired up the engine when I came back on board. The White Bird had put on the evening's music, Ray Charles singing "Yesterday." He also had stew ready, with fresh fish from the Oktyabrskoye fishery. As we sailed downriver, I went to sleep in my cabin, knowing I had only one more chance to find a Shaman before we left the homeland of the Khanty and Mansi people.

When I woke up, however, and looked out my porthole at the fishing settlement of Vanpan (meaning "broad beach"), I gave up hope. Vanpan was nothing more than a collection of eight wooden fishing boats standing on a beach in front of four weathered wooden huts. Certainly no Shaman lived there.

I walked inside one hut, disturbing a breakfast of heavily salted raw fish. The room was infested with mosquitoes, flies, and bedbugs. Siberians even had local jokes about the irrepressible insects. One had it that a Siberian laughed hilariously as he saw his home burning to the ground. When a neighbor asked him what was so funny, he replied, "I was just thinking about the bedbugs."

Hanging from the roofs, over the entrances to the huts, were rows of dried fish fluttering in the cool morning wind. The silent local answer to chimes. "This fish is what got us through the war," said Boris Rusmilenko, who had been born in 1936 but looked much older. "We didn't have any bread, but we had plenty of fish."

At age fifty-five, he was the oldest man in the settlement. His skull-like face had only a thin layer of skin stretched tight over his bones. His eyes were as red as the caviar he sometimes found in the *osyotr* fish in the Ob River beside his camp. His face had a permanent bristle.

Vanpan was a summer fishing settlement, occupied from May 20 to October 20, roughly the time during which the Ob remained unfrozen at this extreme northerly point. Two small families occupied Vanpan—about thirty natives in all. They were managed by a Russian from a nearby collective, who spent his summers fishing and his winters playing cards in Novosibirsk.

Having shown us his dried fish, Boris now wanted to show off the area where the wild berries grew, down the path from his hut. My Dutch-made Jungle Oil was failing to repel the stubborn Siberian mosquitoes. It was their high season, which Chekhov called "the Siberian equivalent of the Egyptian plague." They so persistently chomped into my flesh that I began to retreat to the boat.

Before doing so, I offhandedly asked Boris if his clan had a Shaman. He jerked his head to the side and looked into my eyes. His son, in his thirties, a heavier, oafish version of his father, did the same. "What do you know about the Shaman?" the father asked suspiciously.

I summed up my knowledge and reviewed for him my quest for the holy man. Boris Rusmilenko whispered that the ancient knowledge of the Shaman rested within him. Boris was a Shaman. He was slowly passing that wisdom, he said, on to his son. The son nodded his head stupidly and excitedly.

"Do you want to see our holy place?" Boris whispered.

I nodded that I did.

Boris looked deeply into my eyes. Suddenly I felt like a child who had heard too many stories about the haunted house before being invited in. I was actually afraid to follow this Shaman—in retrospect a laughable reaction, because there was a catch.

"We can't go empty-handed to the holy place," Boris said. "We must bring an offering."

"What kind?" I asked.

"Vodka would be best," he suggested.

"Does God drink?"

"God doesn't drink," he responded. "We drink for God."

Until that moment I hadn't done anything to contribute to the Khanty blight of alcoholism, a plague as deadly as any other. But this, after all, would be an offering, not a payoff. My curiosity had grown so great that I was an easy touch.

Wanting moral support, I invited along Gerard Jacobs, James Dorsey, and Dundee. They retrieved a bottle of vodka from our well-stocked ship. Boris inspected it, nodded his approval, and we were off. We climbed into his wooden fishing boat, which leaked slowly through its pine planks. Boris struggled with the outboard motor, wrapping the short rope around the starter with some difficulty. He pulled and fell backwards into my lap. Then he stood and pulled again. The shot of gas propelled the vessel from the shore into an oncoming boat. It stalled. No one was hurt, but we all laughed nervously. Boris repeated the process and we were soon on our way across the bay to his holy place. His eyes had turned serious and determined—but were still red.

It was morning, and fishermen were pulling in their nets, left overnight on the bottom of the 150-feet-deep waters. They worked the area with difficulty because of the logs at the bottom that caught their nets and in which the fish could hide. Still, these were some of the most fertile waters on the Ob, full of pike and even the large *osyotr,* the most valuable fish in the Ob save the Siberian white salmon.

After a slow, ten-minute ride, Boris banked into the sandy, overgrown beach. He stepped ashore and sank to his calves in the soft earth. Boris led us up a ten-foot embankment, using some hanging shrubbery to pull himself up. The roots gave way and he fell back onto us. A second effort succeeded, and we followed.

We walked about 100 yards onto the island, down an overgrown path, and into a small group of birch trees. An army of God's mosquitoes resisted our advance. Boris apologized that he hadn't been to the holy place since the thaw—so the path had become overgrown.

I knew we were there when I saw two empty vodka bottles hanging from thin tree branches stuck into their throats along the path to the larger birch tree that was at the center of the holy place. That tree also had a bottle dangling from a branch. At the tree's base lay a large jar in which homemade brew was made, turned upside down. Previous offerings. Up the trunk at chest level (Boris' eye level), where the tree began its natural split, hung two cloths containing a large number of coins. Boris lifted the bottle at the base. Underneath it, he dug up more coins that had been buried.

"The coins up high are dedicated to God," he said. "Those in the ground are dedicated to those who have died."

Boris said that altars had once been nailed to such trees. They had held golden figures. The problem of theft and the lack of gold had ended that practice. Sometimes, he said, the natives would bring wooden totems and put them on an altar.

I asked how he knew the rules of worship at the holy place. "God told us that we should do it this way," he said. "It is obligatory that an adult male come here each year. But no one is allowed to come more than two times. It is particularly necessary to come if the fishing is bad."

He showed us hatchet marks on the lower part of the trunk, beneath the hanging coins. "Each man who comes here makes two cuts. If they meet cleanly in a *V,* then he has much time to live. If the cut is bad, you die within the year."

He showed his own cut, a very clean one. He showed a sloppy cut, and said the man who had made it drowned six months after he had visited the holy place. Drowning, I had learned, was a frequent cause of death among fishermen who drank a lot and seldom learned to swim.

Boris didn't want to stay long. Gerard handed him our bottle and Boris set it down by the base of the tree, above the buried coins. He turned to walk away, and we followed him.

After venturing ten yards from the tree to a clearing, Boris stopped. "Why are you leaving the bottle behind?"

Gerard noted that he had left it for God.

"That is not how we do it," said Boris. He walked back to the tree, picked up the bottle, unscrewed the cap with his teeth, sprinkled the ground around the tree with a generous swig, and then returned to us in the clearing. He instructed each of us to take a swig with him and thereafter rotate around once "in the direction the sun turns." He demonstrated and we each followed.

Boris brought the rest of the bottle back to the boat—a little less than half remained. He took another shot for the road and then focused his gaze on James's new hip-high fishing boots, asking for them as a sort of payment for our unique experience. When James refused, he pouted angrily.

His wife was waiting for us at the shore as we putted in. Boris sideswiped one of the parked boats and glided onto the beach. His wife wanted to know how the trip had gone. "Did you leave behind coins for God?" she asked.

Gerard answered that he hadn't known that was required. We then explained that we had instead left an offering of vodka, which Boris had poured out around the tree. She looked disappointed.

Gerard asked Boris whether he had committed a sin by showing nonbelievers the holy place. Boris shook his head of alcoholic cobwebs and then turned to us sadly, disappointed in himself that he had forgotten this ancient law (and surprised that we had known of it). "It was one of my mistakes," he said sadly. "And you may have trouble getting down the river now."

His wife said we would be all right as long as her husband was alive. She was more concerned with another part of the story. "Maybe you should have left some coins behind, but you shouldn't have poured out any vodka. That isn't part of what God expects."

Chapter 17:

DODGE CITY

They were just testing you.

—ALEKSEI SYBIN, *local official*

The roar of the ship's engines signaled that the captain had put on the brakes and we were pulling into a new port. The villages had grown smaller and the mornings cooler as we traveled north. I looked out my porthole at a Siberian riverside version of a scene familiar to me from a childhood of watching Westerns on television.

The Khanty men who made up most of the town's population were suspiciously eyeing the strangers who had sailed into town. Some of them loitered on shore and others floated near our forty-two-meter boat in their small wooden fishing boats powered by tiny outboards. Our large vessel was of the type that usually just sailed by the small fishing town of Vanzevat. It was shortly after seven in the morning, and they didn't look welcoming.

But I wasn't worried. I was more concerned about the coat of dirt that encrusted me. So, with the approval of the captain, I jumped overboard in my bathing trunks, a plastic bottle of grapefruit shampoo in my right hand. My Russian friends followed with a soccer ball. The ball and the shampoo flew from one person to another until everyone was lathered and laughing. It was a rich luxury on a crisp Siberian morning.

The citizens of Vanzevat, a village of 450 fishermen and dairy farmers, regarded us with looks that alternated between curiosity and loathing. Near our swimming area, a farm woman dumped out some milk waste. It spread in a white slick toward us. She wasn't about to change her habits for a few intruders swimming in her river. I returned to the boat and the others followed.

In a goodwill gesture (and to replenish supplies), the captain that morning had traded a bottle of vodka to one of the fishermen for three river pike. It had been a critical error. The villagers now knew we had white gold aboard. And the price the captain had paid, far above the going rate, suggested we were a soft touch.

At high noon (give or take an hour), the fishermen attacked. They came in boats from three sides. Leading the assault party was a grisly character in a soiled orange T-shirt. He had a gauze patch hanging precariously over his left eye—the adhesive tape had come loose over half of it. A leather bandoleer was slung over his shoulder. I couldn't tell whether he was drunk or just hung over, but he looked awfully thirsty. The one-eyed bandit demanded our vodka—or any other drinkable spirits aboard—including men's cologne.

When the captain refused, the pirate leader pulled himself up from his fishing boat onto the starboard side of our ship. Just as he was about to board, the captain's mate pushed him firmly in the chest and he tumbled ignominiously back into his boat.

He recovered, then picked up his rifle and aimed it at our ship. "I have bullets—and not just ordinary ones," he announced. "They are dum-dums." The captain explained later that these bullets rotated differently, and were made of extra-soft lead so as to cause more damage. "Either you give us vodka or we'll start shooting."

The captain maintained his calm and refused. At that point Viktor Kostukovsky, the *Izvestia* correspondent, pulled out his flare pistol and aimed it at the fishing boat. "You are drunk, so you might miss," he said. "But I can set you on fire with this—and my aim is much better."

Two of the one-eyed pirate's friends wrestled the rifle out of his hands and convinced him that their initial assault on the *OM-147* had failed. "We'll be back after sundown," shouted the leader, shaking his fist. He pointed to the fuel tank and said he would put a bullet into it and blow up the ship if we didn't turn over the "warm water" by sundown. At this northerly point of the Ob River, that would mean about two A.M.

The captain, fearing for our well-being, wanted to sail out of town immediately. But two of the Russians who ran the town came aboard to assure us that the natives wouldn't strike again.

"They were just testing you," said Aleksei Sybin, the deputy chief of the local state farm and fishing enterprise. "That's normal for this village. They are just curious about your ship. Once you stand up to them, they back down—most of the time."

He invited me to join his family at their home—thus keeping me a safe distance from the Khanty. The captain gave his okay—but he wanted everyone back on board by nine P.M. so that we could leave this Siberian Dodge City by dark.

Aleksei's home was the largest and best furnished in town—three large rooms with a full kitchen, a bedroom, and a living room furnished with rich bookshelves and a color television that had the clearest picture I had seen in the north of Siberia. They never turned it off, and their teenage daughter was glued to a youth gymnastics competition when I walked in. Their large garden, including a greenhouse, was well tended. The yard in front was demarcated with a neat picket fence.

Aleksei and Irina Sybin were a handsome couple in their mid-thirties who considered their family to be an island of culture in the Wild West. She was blonde and lively, a teacher of English, German, and history for the forty children of Vanzevat's only school.

Aleksei was tanned and muscular, the healthiest-looking person I'd met in Siberia. He wore a gray tank-top T-shirt that advertised VEKTRA—THE WORLD'S BEST CLOTHING PROTECTOR FOR SELF-APPLICATION. He didn't know what the English writing said, but was happy to have a T-shirt with so many words on it that he could resell for ten times what he had paid for it a year earlier. He was due to take over soon from the state farm's retiring director, but he was already acting as the village sheriff, mayor, administrator, and employer.

Irina considered herself to be the moral descendant of the Decembrists—the revolutionary aristocrats who had risen against Tsarism in 1825 and had been banished to Siberia. The wives of those who had been arrested came with their men voluntarily, and their plans to bring culture to the wilderness became legendary through the celebrated poem by Aleksandr Nekrasov, "The Russian Women."

Aleksei said the draw was high salary and adventure. In the Sybins' hometown of Astrakhan, on the Caspian Sea, he never could have earned so much, nor had so much responsibility at such a young age. "I'm the police, the judge, the tax collector, the mayor, the law," he said. "I've got to do everything."

As sheriff, his problems had redoubled since Perestroika. Before then he had simply thrown errant natives into the cellar under his office until they cooled down or sobered up. "We've had to stop that now," he said. Now the closest police were a 150-kilometer helicopter ride away, so he called on them only for the worst cases. Still, Vanzevat wasn't as dangerous as it seemed to me, he said. In the last three years the town had had only three murders and five drownings (all alcohol-related). There was also the drunken fisherman who had accidentally burned himself to death. "Other than that, it's been quiet," he said.

And the Sybins' daughter, Natasha, was the perfect daughter for the model family. At age thirteen, she was already beautiful enough for her parents to be planning a life for her as an international model. "That is why I study English," said Natasha, taking a break from the television. She would begin fashion-model training courses as soon as she grew two more centimeters and reached the required 1.7 meters (about five feet seven inches).

She was already tall for her age, slender and blonde. She walked erectly. She could even parade gracefully with a book resting on her head, a skill she demonstrated for me. She had decorated the kitchen and her bedroom with calendars and photographs showing scantily clad and nude models from Japanese and Western fashion magazines. The walls of the outhouse at the side of the garden, down a neatly graded path, were similarly decorated. When I visited it later, Marilyn Monroe's face, on a yellowed newspaper clipping, looked directly at me from the back of the door.

Irina wouldn't let her prize daughter study in Vanzevat. She was merely home on vacation. She was getting a better education in Astrakhan, where she lived with her grandmother. "They have trouble getting along; my mother doesn't understand a girl her age, but it is better for her future," said the ambitious mother.

And the perfect family's perfect daughter also had the perfect friend. She was one of the Khanty children, and her name was also Natasha. At age fourteen, she was one of the best students at the school and was so pretty that every young boy was after her—but she knew she was too good for them. Irina proudly said the two girls were the stars at the nightly disco at the House of Culture.

The two Natashas blushed. They begged me to escort them to the disco that night. I said I would if the captain would let us extend our stay. The disco didn't even open until 11 P.M. and went on until 2 A.M., after which it turned dark in Vanzevat for only about an hour or two before morning.

Irina bubbled with questions about the West. She told Natasha to bring out their favorite "book," a two-inch-thick German mail-order catalogue from the Neckermann company. Aleksei had picked it up on a business trip to the "Big Earth," as Siberians called the area west of the Urals. He had bought it for sixty rubles—nearly a fifth of the average monthly salary at the time. But the price had been worth it. The catalogue was dog-eared from use.

"Can you really purchase all these things," asked Irina, "or do they just appear on paper?"

When I said all the items in the catalogue were generally available for sale, she sighed. She turned each page lovingly, as if for the first time. The two girls sat to each side of her as though she were reading them a bedtime fairy tale. They touched the photographs as though stroking the cotton, lace, and silk. The section that intrigued Irina and Aleksei most were the thirty-two pages of lingerie.

At about that time, Igor Vasilyevich, the state farm's chief, walked in the back door, having heard an American visitor was there. He picked up

the book to see what everyone was so excited about. He let out a whistle
of approval. "We can make a business," he said. "You send me the ladies'
underwear and I will send you fox to go around women's necks. Or an
occasional bear skin, if you prefer." He was certain that he could sell the
underwear far more quickly, and at better profit, than I would be able to
unload the fox.

The two teenagers left us for a swim in a small stream that fed the Ob
so that the adults would be alone to talk. The Sybins set the table with the
perquisites of their station—Armenian brandy, chocolate, sausage,
cheese, raw *muksun* whitefish, and self-smoked Siberian white salmon,
called *nelma*. The chief of the state farm raised a toast.

He spoke of his grandfather, who had been one of the first officers to
share a hard drink with American soldiers as they met on the banks of the
Elbe at the end of World War II. "Now I am drinking a shot with an
American for the first time in my life—so here's to Russia and America!"

He had met Americans once, when he had been fishing in the Indian
Ocean in 1968. They had played volleyball together. The Russians had
won. "Here's to Russia and America again!" said Igor. "We should divide
world power between us and get along."

He cut off a hunk of the white salmon. It looked like a thick slab of
bacon and tasted deliciously greasy, smoked, raw, and rich. This was
Siberian filet mignon, the most valuable cut of fish available. No fish cut
the effect of vodka better. No fish could be served that honored a guest
more.

The Sybins said they had wanted to come to Siberia for only three years,
after which they had planned to return with their earnings to Astrakhan
and its sun, watermelons, and storks. But eleven years later they hadn't
any plans to leave. They liked the money, the power, and even the cold,
said Aleksei.

He pointed to the moose antlers on the wall and showed photographs
from hunting trips for fox, goose, grouse, and duck. "In Siberia you feel
freer, more like a man," he said. "When it gets forty to forty-five degrees
below [Celsius], that's when I love it most. The snow crunches under your
feet. Your breath condenses as soon as you've let it out. It is so silent that
you can even hear your breath as it comes out of your mouth. The wind
burns you just with a little breeze."

Irina brought out a cat that had strayed outside during one of the
coldest days. The top half of each of its ears had literally frozen off. "The
worst problem in the winter is drunks," said Aleksei. "If they pass out,
they may never come to again. Fire is less dangerous than the cold because
you feel it burn."

I asked Irina if she liked Siberia as much as Aleksei did. Aleksei answered. "Maybe it is hard on my wife, but I told her this is what we must do and that is what we are doing."

Irina swooned. "Many Russian men aren't so decisive," she said. "I like the way he is."

Socialist slave masters, white and Russian, have ruled the natives who have been the primary inhabitants of this town ever since it was created in 1936 by forced collectivization, carried out primarily by withholding supplies and deliveries of foodstuffs to areas that hadn't consented to join the collective.

Discipline had been a problem from that time on. The drinking grew so bad in the 1960s—after the oil and gas men came to the region with their vodka—that Vanzevat imposed a ban on the sale of alcohol in 1968. The prohibition was still in force when I arrived. Vodka was sold locally only on holidays. So I wondered how it was that the fishermen stayed drunk. When I later walked through the village, it seemed half of its men were in a stupor. "They spend all their money on gas to drive the boats to neighboring villages that have vodka," Aleksei complained. He said his fishermen also traded their catch to passing ships, such as ours, for vodka.

I felt even worse about the captain's trade that morning.

"I lose at least fifty percent of my catch or more to drinking. Either they don't catch it because they are drunk or they sell it off to get more drunk."

Aleksei poured us out a fifth shot of brandy. He said he would like to fire workers for drinking, but then they would have nowhere to go, and he'd have no one to replace them. "They would stay here even if I fired them, and would continue to fish with their families," he said. "So we punish them by withholding pay."

But Aleksei was tired of talking about the Khanty. Instead, he said with a laugh, he wanted to talk about the Hunts. He pulled out a volume as dog-eared as the Neckermann catalogue, with plenty of underlined sections. In Russian, the book was called *Texas Riches,* and it was the story of the Hunt oil-and-silver dynasty. He said one of the Hunts had been making lots of news in Siberia, traveling through the oil regions, hunting and talking about investment opportunities.

"Hunt earned all his money with his own hands and the sweat off his back," said Aleksei. "I want to do that, too. I want to earn what I am worth. Why do I have to share what money I earn with those who work less? I'll never be as rich as Hunt, but I would like to have more than I have got."

What would he do if he were a millionaire? I asked.

"First, I'd travel the whole world with my wife," he said. "Then I'd settle in a place where the sun shines all the time. I would buy a two-story villa there with an indoor toilet. I'd have a yacht and three cars—a BMW for myself, a Volvo for my wife, and a Jaguar for my daughter."

Why those cars?

"I like BMWs. My wife needs a solid and safe car, but it shouldn't draw attention to her. But my daughter is so beautiful. People should notice my daughter in the world. She could wear the car like a beautiful dress."

Aleksei conceded that these were curious ambitions for someone who at the time of my visit was still a Communist Party member—and he would remain a member until the Party was banned. "Without being a Party member you didn't get anywhere," he said. "We didn't believe in Communism. We believed in our careers."

He said he had stopped paying his dues after Yeltsin resigned from the Party, but the local Party chiefs had visited him and made it clear that his job could be in peril if he didn't pay up. So he did.

I told a couple of my favorite jokes about the Party and its leaders. They laughed politely. I asked if they knew jokes. They hesitated a long time. One of the chief reasons for being arrested during Stalin's days was for telling jokes, said the collective chief. He said they were comfortable telling jokes among themselves—but uneasy telling them to foreigners. Still, the *sovkhoz* chief consented to tell his favorite. "And it involves Nancy Reagan," he said proudly.

"Gorbachev visits the United States," he said. "Nancy Reagan gives Raisa a gift of a Cadillac that is worth $100,000.

" 'I can't take it,' " protests Raisa. " 'What would the Russian people say about me?'

"So Nancy Reagan says that Raisa can buy it—that way it won't be a gift. But the Reagans will charge only one dollar.

"Raisa agrees to the arrangement. But she only has a five-dollar bill, and Nancy Reagan doesn't have change.

" 'That's all right,' says Raisa. 'I'll take five Cadillacs.' "

The two teenagers returned from their swim. I excused myself, saying I had work to do on the boat. What I really wanted to avoid was more drinking. It was early in the day, and I was already having trouble scribbling in my notebook.

The two girls begged me again to come to the discotheque that night. What could make them a bigger hit than showing up with the first American ever to set foot on Vanzevat soil? The Russian Natasha wanted me to meet her new friend, a nice boy with handsome, dark, wavy hair and a terrific sense of humor. Perhaps bringing me would enhance her in his eyes. Her affection for the boy was only twenty-four hours old, but she was almost giddy. "It is hard to find a boy who likes to talk, and we had such a nice conversation," she said.

I asked Irina if she wasn't a little worried about letting her daughter go out so late at night in this drunken village. "There is a deterrent factor your captain cannot understand," she said. "We all know each other. If anyone does anything, everyone else knows about it and you have to live with it the rest of your life. And in the summer bad things seldom happen, because it never grows dark. You never do anything too evil during the White Nights."

I convinced the captain to stay a few hours longer, allowing me to attend the Vanzevat disco. But in the early evening a second group of about a dozen natives stormed the boat. This time the pirates were all under age fourteen.

I and the Greenpeace interpreter, Ella Rikert, headed them off on the gangplank leading off the bow and plied them with questions, after which I promised there would be a reward.

"What do you know about America?" I asked. She repeated my questions in Russian with a kind, motherly voice.

The dozen boys fell silent. They all looked at each other and then shyly back at me.

"Who lives there?" I asked.

"Capitalists live there," said one.

"George Bush lives there," said another, proudly.

"How are Americans different from you?"

"They are capitalist," said one.

"They are millionaires," said another.

"Do you want to be a capitalist?" I asked.

They all answered "no" simultaneously.

"I want to be a Communist," said one.

"A Communist is an honest and brave man," said another. "He is not a rich man."

I wondered what these native children knew about their people's alcohol problem.

"What do you know about hard drink?" I asked.

"Do you mean vodka, Bio-cream, or hair tonic?" said a boy with a hoarse voice, whom the other children called Kolya. He was the smallest of them, but, I would learn, he was also the oldest, fourteen years old. He had a smear of dirt across his face, and his hair was blond over Khanty features—the product of a Russian father. He was the toughest and most outspoken of them. "The men drink hair tonic sometimes and the women get poisoned from it."

I asked whether any of the children drank.

Silence.

I assured them that they wouldn't be punished. They should tell the truth, and I would do nothing to hurt them. I only wanted to learn the truth. I reminded them of the reward.

"I drank once or twice," said one voice meekly.

"I drank once, too, champagne," said another.

"I drank Grandpa's vodka," said another.

"I drank *brazhka!*" said Kolya, again speaking the loudest, about his consumption of home-brewed beer. They all laughed when he talked. He was the class cutup. He pulled a package of cigarettes out of his pocket and lit up.

I asked how old they had been when they first drank. The voices sounded one after another, shouting ages ranging from six to ten. Then they began accusing each other of lying and concealing information that the others knew to be true. But those feuds quickly evolved into fond, shared recollections of the drunken times they had had with each other, like good ol' boys recalling past adventures.

"I was eleven when I first had *brazhka,*" said Kolya. "I had half a glass. A full glass is 200 grams. So I had 100 grams. Is that clear? That was my first drink."

They all laughed.

I asked Kolya if he could tell me how *brazhka* was made.

"You have to add some yeast, you have to have sugar, then you bring the water to a boil. Then you put the sugar in, then the yeast, then some more sugar. Then you seal the top with a piece of plastic tablecloth, then tie the top of it tight. You put it near a warm place—somewhere near the stove. It ferments then and becomes strong."

For what it was worth, I gave the boys a short lecture on the perils of drinking, which seemed a bit hypocritical considering my morning. They acted attentive but unconvinced. I thanked them for being so honest with me. My reward for them seemed terribly tame by then—a couple of wrapped chocolates and a package of Juicy Fruit gum for each, which I'd brought along from the West, expecting to meet more innocent youth.

For my reward, they sang a favorite school song, about a crocodile who was happy that it was raining on his birthday.

> *The magician will come in a blue helicopter,*
> *And he'll show us films free of charge,*
> *Birthday greetings he'll give us,*
> *And probably a share of ice cream for all.*

At ten P.M. a small delegation from our ship made the short walk to the House of Culture for the disco. Like the other buildings in town, it was single-story and wooden. Beside it were empty glass-enclosed display boards where the socialist slogans and pictures of Communist heroes had once hung. Two wooden benches with peeling paint sat on a decaying wooden porch. Mosquitoes filled the damp evening air.

My teenage "dates" hadn't yet arrived. Irina Sybin arrived ahead of them and said they were still primping at home, so I walked inside to the deafening sounds of the nondescript disco music one hears from Bangkok to Berlin.

The DJ sat alone on the stage of the small theater, from which the tinny sound system blasted the music. The dance floor was a small cement area in front of the stage, and some ten rows of hard wooden theater seats—about six across on each side—filled the rest of the large room. Lights at the bottom of the stage flashed as unrhythmically as the youth of Vanzevat danced.

The crowd was young, between ages eight and sixteen, except for the Russian physical-education teacher, who gyrated in the middle, and an older woman who slithered in her tight T-shirt in one of the corners. Kolya, the teenage *brazhka* expert, sat on Gerard's lap and told us that the woman was the town slut. The other dancers stood mostly in one place and moved their bodies to some internal drummer who didn't hear what was playing. The girls danced together in a group, and each of the boys danced by himself.

To escape the high decibels, I retreated outside to the front stairs of the single-story wooden building. The entry hall had a plaque with the names of villagers who had died in World War II. At the door, some of the older boys, ages fourteen to sixteen, hung out on the wooden steps, smoking and looking for a fight. One told me that a brawl broke out every other week or so. "It usually isn't over a girl," said one of them. "It's usually over a bottle. It's harder to find a bottle than a girl."

Within minutes a swarm of mosquitoes drove me back inside. But the music forced me back out. I shuttled back and forth until the teenage girls arrived with Irina. The Khant, Natasha, wore a black-and-white print dress with a large bow tied around her waist that looked as though she had picked it for the prom. The would-be model was all in white. They looked oddly normal and healthy—and out of place—at the disco.

After a few awkward dances, I bade them farewell. But before I left, the Khanty girl asked me if she could just look at an American dollar—she had never seen one before. It seemed important to her, so I gave her one as a good-luck charm, telling her never to spend it. She asked me to sign it. It seemed an odd request but she was immensely pleased when I consented. She promised she would never spend it.

The girls and Irina walked me to the boat at one A.M. While we had been gone, some townspeople who had heard of the threat to our vessel had brought goodwill gifts—fresh milk from their cows, several large jars of wild berries, and another thick slice of Siberian white salmon.

As I walked toward my cabin, I saw the two chiefs of the collective in the galley drinking with the Russian members of our expedition. I retreated to my cabin, but the ship didn't sail for another three hours because the local VIPs weren't ready to leave the boat. I later learned that the White Bird had to coax them off, but only after they had already put a significant dent in our vodka supply. The Russian bosses had consumed what their Khanty workers had been unable to pilfer.

Chapter 18:

NUCLEAR SECRETS

I am a patriot and you are a journalist who is after
"black information" that could harm my country.

—YURI KAZNIN, *People's Deputy*

Vladimir announced that we had begun our longest uninterrupted stretch of sailing down the Ob, for nearly two days before reaching the end of the river. So I took my laptop computer up the steep stairway to the deck and used the time to commit notes to a computer diskette. I had made a daily ritual of storing impressions and notes, a high-tech indulgence that so intrigued the captain and his mate that they gladly rigged an outlet running off the ship's power so I could work without using batteries.

As I looked at the river from my rooftop vantage point, it seemed misleading that I had been describing Grandmother Ob as a river. She was a landscape. A look at my relief map showed the Ob system to be a wild collection of blue lines ranging from hairline thin to finger thick, running through dark and lighter green areas marked with clumps of grass, denoting swampy lowlands. The Ob had 1,400 tributaries, and even the main stream now was dividing itself into two, then three and four parts, before it would come back together and empty into the Ob Bay at a rate of 400 cubic kilometers (250 cubic miles) of water every year. That was enough to provide the Arctic Ocean with about 12 percent of its total intake through drainage.

Every spring, the Ob covered its vast floodplain in the north with waters that could spread from fifteen to fifty miles in width and remain for as much as a month. The river seemed to be trying desperately to drain the swampland with all its floods and tributaries, but it would never succeed.

As we sailed upriver, a number of boats passed us, and native fishermen worked from camps on the beach. It seemed that everyone was in a hurry to get maximum use out of the Ob before it closed for business in late October, when its 190-day annual freeze began. Yet the settlements grew smaller and farther apart as the river took a sharp right-hand turn just below the Arctic Circle.

While I worked on the deck, Yuri Kaznin toiled below on the bow, in the space between the two small fishing boats that we carried on board. He was cleaning and salting fish and then packing them to take back to Kemerovo, where they would be a delicacy. The Soviet parliamentarian had several missions on the expedition: ecological (saving the Ob), political (promoting himself), and economic (making a profit). As a partner in Vladimir's company, Yuri would receive a healthy share of the money we had paid for the expedition.

The Ob acted as a sedative, and after a couple of hours' work I left the deck to retreat to my cabin for a nap. En route I stopped in my tracks in the gangway that passed in front of Yuri's room; his door was open and documents were scattered across his bed. From the hallway I could see the two letters that had been given to me at Tomsk 7, documents that reported the disappearance of nuclear-weapons material. Yuri had repeatedly denied having these papers, which disappeared when a translator left our expedition. The translator had left most of the material he had been working on with Kaznin, but the People's Deputy had always denied having my papers, which I now saw on his bed. Beside the documents was a sheaf of other letters and newspaper clippings on Tomsk 7 to which I also would have liked access.

I walked farther down the hall to my room and flopped on the bed to work out a scheme. Should I "steal" what was rightfully mine? Or should I confront Yuri with the fact that I knew he had the letters in the hopes that he would then surrender them to me? Perhaps the conspiratorial nature of Russians was infectious. I came up with a plan that would not only retrieve the information but would also test Yuri. I decided first to photograph the letters and, only thereafter, to ask Yuri to return my documents. But I hadn't microfilm or the rapid-firing cameras of *Mission Impossible,* so I drafted photographer Paul Babliowsky, an adventurous soul who eagerly joined my subterfuge.

He brought his tripod and camera to my room, where we would lay the letters on my bed, page-by-page, and use my sheets as the backdrop. But then I needed to work out a plan of transferring the documents from Yuri's cabin to my own without being discovered.

I opted to make several trips to his room, taking only two or three pages each time. That risked discovery because I would be walking into his cabin more frequently. However, if Yuri returned while Paul was photographing, he would be less likely to notice missing pages. Then, when he left his cabin, we could continue our work. I took the additional precaution of drafting my friend James Dorsey as a lookout, whose job was to monitor Yuri's movements.

So I tiptoed between my room and Yuri's once, twice, three, and four times without problem, always carrying two or three pages, which I then returned to their place on his bed before taking more. Paul calmly snapped each sheet. As I opened my door for the final shuttle, with three pages of the letter in my hand, Yuri walked heavily in his natural hunch down the hallway toward my door, just behind James Dorsey, who was sounding the alarm. I was saved by his reluctance at this point in the trip even to acknowledge me. He didn't look up but simply walked past me toward the toilets.

I raced to his room, quickly replaced the three pages, took the final two sheets, and after Paul snapped them I returned them to their spot on Yuri's bed only minutes before he returned to his cabin and shut the door. Paul, who hadn't noticed this close call while concentrating on his work, said the light had been perfect, and the writing on the pages would come out clearly.

To sneak into the cabin of a People's Deputy and photograph documents in his possession was enough to be arrested even in a more democratic Russia. Yuri could easily have labeled me an American spy. Who else would take this risk to get information on one of the Soviet Union's most secret facilities? I am still not certain why I became so obsessed with the Tomsk 7 documents. In part it was my suspicion that Yuri's lying could only mean that some explosive secret lay in the papers. But what motivated me as much was the certainty that the letters were my rightful property.

Even before my photographic larceny, however, the tensions between Yuri and me had become the major subplot of our voyage. Yuri's friends pleaded that I be more deferential to the parliamentarian, for they sensed he was hurt that he hadn't become the center of the expedition's attention. They thought all the problems, even involving the apparent pilfering of my documents, revolved around the fact that we hadn't acknowledged Yuri as our leader.

"Just a little bit more attention would help," said one of his friends. "He's a little bit of a child that way. But if you give too much attention, then he will be suspicious."

I had tried to follow this advice, having no interest in a confrontation with a man of Kaznin's stature. (A friend of his, however, pointed out that the Soviet Union had 2,600 People's Deputies, so that Yuri was in a club that wasn't all that exclusive.) But when I asked him easy questions about the environment, his information was shallow and unreliable. When I asked him more difficult questions regarding Tomsk 7 and the defense plant that sponsored his candidacy, he refused to answer. When James

Dorsey had asked him a couple of days earlier why he wasn't helping us with information on the nuclear-energy facility, he replied, "I'll tell you why I am not helping," he said. "I am a patriot and you are journalists who are after *chernukha* [black information] that will hurt my country." He said that he, as a scientist, understood better than irresponsible journalists what information was reliable and what was not. So, he seemed to be arguing, he was right to monopolize control over the data.

That evening after dinner the negatives of the documents safely packed away, I put the second part of my plan into action. As we all sat in the dining area working on our various projects, I confronted Yuri. I told him that I had, by chance, seen some documents on his bed that resembled those I had been given at Tomsk 7. Yuri said he was sure that wasn't the case, but he would have another look. I described again to him exactly what I was looking for.

Yuri walked to his room, with everyone watching, and he returned with newspaper clippings and documents, but not one of those that had been given me in Tomsk 7. He invited me to return to his cabin and look for myself. So we walked there together, but the bed had been cleared and the documents put away. I asked Yuri if I could take a look in a fanfold file I saw beside the bed where I saw one of the letters poking out. I claimed it as my property, and he gave it to me without protest, acting surprised that it was there and treating it as unimportant. The second letter, which I didn't see, was on film, so I retreated. Yuri's friends lurked in the hallway and heard much of the exchange, and one came to me afterward in some embarrassment and apologized.

"I always knew Yuri had problems," he said, "but I didn't think he would ever go this far. But you could tell by the tone of his voice that he was lying to you. Sometimes he gets a little bit crazy." He then recounted all the good Yuri had done Kemerovo so that I wouldn't think all badly of him. "He even took in his sick grandmother," the friend said.

The heading on the letter given to me by Yuri, written by a former Tomsk 7 engineer named Nikolai Nikolayevich Guriyev, was entitled "The Reasons Why I Have Resigned from the Party." He described a nuclear-waste disposal system that had poisoned the earth and air from the 1950s on. The allegations couldn't be confirmed with a second source, but the local Tomsk 7 newspapers had considered his views important enough to have printed portions of the letter. The fact that many parts of the letter had been published made me wonder all the more why Yuri had gone to such lengths to keep the information from us.

Guriyev wrote that for years poisonous fluoride gases had been released by the plant between midnight and three A.M. so that residents wouldn't see the radioactive materials, "but any expert can see the improvement has been only partial. Most of the cleaning equipment to prevent the contamination of the atmosphere doesn't work properly."

The engineer said that for years the plant bosses had been able to deny there were any radiation-related sicknesses among the workers, and been able to present a clean bill of health for the plant because of "the lack of reliable and fast-working equipment to monitor the buildup of radioactive materials in the body."

The letter was also damning regarding the disposal of nuclear waste. Materials that should have been kept separate, it said, were mixed during disposal, and there were insufficient safeguards to prevent the waste from getting into the groundwater. The writer alleged that officials concealed evidence of contamination. "Thousands of hectares have been poisoned by radioactive waste," he wrote. "These areas will be unusable for more than a quarter of a millennium. And the worst case, which no one can rule out, is that radioactive release in the upper levels will get into the groundwater. The insufficiently purified waste water goes from purification plants through the rivers Tom and Ob into the Arctic Ocean."

Shortly after I returned to Berlin, I received the negatives in the mail from Paul Babliowsky with the contents of the second letter. It was often vague and left many questions open. But its content made clear why Yuri didn't want it to fall into my hands.

A. V. Straishyt, a former employee of the "plutonium factory," as he called the reprocessing facility, outlined in some detail lax accounting methods that allowed ninety kilograms of plutonium oxide to disappear from the books and apparently also from the plant over a ten-month period in 1967. By falsifying the amounts of nuclear-weapons-grade material that was produced through extraction procedures, plant officials concealed the loss, which would have been enough to produce several bombs.

Straishyt didn't know what became of the material, and he didn't venture any theories, but several months after I left Siberia articles appeared in many Western newspapers that Russians were trying to sell stolen Soviet nuclear-weapons material in Italy and Germany. It was unlikely to have been the same lost Tomsk 7 material, but the articles demonstrated that such missing weapons-grade plutonium was a real problem.

The lost plutonium was only part of a pattern of corruption and mismanagement that Straishyt outlined in the letter. He wrote of building projects in which plant bosses used accounting calling for the payment of dozens more workers than were actually involved. Someone apparently had pocketed the extra money, and he named those involved. He also said that officials had concealed from higher authorities the problem of drinking and discipline among their staff, which not only hurt the plant's efficiency but also increased the risk of nuclear accidents.

"Misleading reports and falsification became the means of evaluating production and productivity," he wrote. He offered files and documents that he said could prove his points and appealed for an investigation that "could allow the improvement of our moral condition."

Straishyt wrote that after he had blown the whistle, he had been transferred to less sensitive employment at Tomsk 7 in 1973, but even then he had seen more corruption. The state farm of Tomsk 7 worked with 10 or 20 percent the number of workers for which it was receiving government payment, he said, suggesting someone was pocketing money designated for employees who didn't exist. Near the end of the letter he concluded, "This is the history of the adventures of the plutonium factory and of the atomic-energy authorities . . . what's important about the enumerated facts aren't the traces of lies or my own desire to criticize or do harm. Rather this is a question of wanting to show, and to make known to the public, the sorts of violations against State interests that have brought the country to the edge of catastrophe . . . our country has grown impoverished materially, morally, and ethically, and atomic-energy officials . . . haven't played a small role. For many years the leaders of the plutonium factory . . . cheated the people and the State. . . ."

As I read all this I thought of Yuri again, and the lengths to which he had gone to hide this information from me. Yuri was making his political reputation as an environmentalist who was trying to undo the sins of the past, when such information had been routinely hidden from the public. His son was also studying to be a journalist. Shouldn't that have made him more willing to reveal details like these? His friends had speculated, however, that the expedition was getting out of his control and he feared that his own report would lack drama compared to ours. And there was speculation that he had several masters to please.

All I knew, as our boat closed in on the Arctic Circle, was that my conflict with this parliamentarian had begun to concern other expedition members. My Russian friends feared that Yuri's embarrassment and anger might be turned on the expedition in some way.

On the morning after we arrived in Salekhard, Yuri disappeared, attired in a clean, pressed shirt and dress pants. He was off to meet someone important. Rumors circulated throughout the boat that his appointment was with the KGB, but no one really knew that for sure. The speculation heightened the atmosphere of intrigue.

I also left the boat that morning, for Salekhard, a small city of 25,000 dedicated to fish-packing, boat repair, and sawmills. Its wooden homes were built on stilts atop the permafrost. In the Nentsy language, the city's name meant "town on the cape." Our first stop was at the sad monument at the north of town that marked where the Arctic Circle runs through Salekhard. It looked like an aluminum-and-cement version of McDonald's arches. Its cement base was crumbling and the weedy dirt around it was littered with cans of air freshener that local youths inhaled for getting high.

In the early afternoon, while I was in town, a local KGB officer had come on board the ship, unannounced, to ask questions about me. I later learned he had climbed directly to the bridge to interrogate the captain, who knew little about his human cargo. So the captian summoned Vladimir.

The KGB man, said Vladimir, was "the young, sleepy, red-cheeked type of the sort popular with village girls." He wore Montana-brand blue jeans, which were the rage among the Siberian young. The KGB man flashed his red identification card past Vladimir's face so quickly that all that was legible was the rank: KGB major.

The KGB man particularly wanted to know about "the American, Frederick Kempe, from *The World Street Journal* [sic]," who was busy collecting *chernukha*—black information.

Vladimir took the KGB major out to the deck and tried to calm him down, but the major planted himself behind a table there, leaning forward on his elbows and speaking from what sounded like a prepared script. Although foreigners had an "outwardly friendly" appearance, he said, "in reality they are deceitful people."

"They are collecting information, later to be used against us," he said. "They use words of democracy to cause us economic losses."

The KGB man cited the problems posed by a French ecological group that had recently passed through. After they had filmed local natives complaining of oil and gas exploration, he said a French company had pulled out of negotiations for a 200-million-dollar contract. "Therefore, not all should be shown to the foreigners," he said.

Vladimir was surprised the KGB man already knew of our intention to rent a helicopter for two trips, one to visit the reindeer nomads and the second to fly over abandoned tracks built by prisoners from Stalin's camps leading east to Igarka. Vladimir had only just begun writing the formal requests for the helicopter-rental from the local airport when the KGB man came to the ship, so only expedition members knew of our plans.

Vladimir was too generous a soul to say that Yuri had informed someone, but that was his suggestion. I also recognized much of Yuri's rhetoric in the KGB man's accusations—the wording was often identical.

Vladimir quoted the KGB man as saying, "The foreigners will fly to the tundra. They will say that the Khanty and Nentsy don't want oil rigs and gas fields. This will be published in their yellow press. The capitalists are not fools. They'll learn that it's not stable here and they will not invest money."

Then the KGB man wanted to show off his knowledge, so he complained that Americans mistreated their Indians far more than Russians abuse their natives. "They even make the Indians live in reservoirs," he said, using the Russian term for any one of various sorts of receptacles for fluids instead of the word for reservation. Vladimir stifled some laughter but didn't correct him.

Then came a final warning. "Give them the facts about our nationality problems and they will use them against us," he said, before repeating a phrase expedition members had already heard from Yuri Kaznin. "Just offer this American journalist your finger and he'll bite off your arm."

Vladimir delighted in telling the story later. But in the collapsing Soviet Union, where democracy was slowly gaining in force and influence, no one at the time quite knew how much to worry about the KGB's attention.

One part of the KGB had made our entire expedition possible, but now another was trying to intimidate and restrict our movements. Old ways were dying hard, and new ones emerged only very slowly and uncertainly.

"Don't worry," laughed Dundee. "Your time in jail will make a nice newspaper article."

Yet the Russians were concerned enough to advise me to make duplicates of my computer disks and then give them to Dutch members of our expedition with my most important notes. The Dutch didn't seem to interest the KGB.

Despite the KGB warning, Vladimir went ahead with our plans to visit the frozen land of the reindeer nomads, and he successfully gained permission to fly us there in a helicopter over areas that had long been shut off to foreigners, to a settlement 100 miles above the Arctic Circle.

Chapter 19:

THE REINDEER NOMADS

For the Nentsy people this is home, but we call this
region . . . "the Edge of the World."

—NIKOLAI BABIN, *state farm boss*

Our pilot peered with concern through the misty windshield of his helicopter and over the vast green carpet of the Siberian north. He had lost his bearings in the thick fog that had been slowly descending on the tundra like a heavy gray curtain. Our guide, Nikolai Babin, wrestled with a large relief map that showed him where to find his workers, reindeer nomads, whom we were to visit. His Baidaratsky State Farm, named for the bay around which it was located, operated over a territory on the Yamal Peninsula the size of the Netherlands.

The fog forced the pilot to bring his chopper down to what would have been treetop level if the tundra had had any trees. The locals call it "the cold desert" for its low fertility, meager precipitation, and immense flatness. No vegetation sinks its roots through the soil more than six inches, where the permafrost begins. So none of the many plants that flourish during the two-month summer grow more than knee-high: moss, lichens, dwarf shrubbery, grasses, sedges, and herbs that bear tiny but colorful blossoms. Before the fog had come in, the extreme northerly location, 100 miles above the Arctic Circle, and the flat expanse had created the impression that the world suddenly ended on a frozen ledge at the tundra's periphery.

"For the Nentsy people, this is home," said Babin, who tried to look unworried as the helicopter flew in a snake pattern in search of a reindeer herd. "But we call this region *Krai Zemly*—the Edge of the World."

With fuel running low, Babin directed the pilot to retrace our route back down a narrow stream, toward a camp we had passed twenty minutes earlier, which had not been our destination. The stream's water was clear. Although it was late July, scattered patches of snow decorated its banks.

We had brought along an interpreter and adviser, Ramon Salinger, who had been born to a nomadic family of Nentsy reindeer herders. Salinger, a city official in Salekhard, was studying law to help protect his people. He knew the tundra better than any of us. "The mist comes suddenly in the autumn and then it remains a long time," he said. "It is the way nature tells the nomads to move south and prepare for the winter."

As I looked through the fog with Babin and Salinger, a mystical sight materialized before us. Poking gently through the fog were three tepees, arranged in a tight triangle on a slight rise beside the stream. A half-dozen reindeer loitered in the campground beside wooden sleds. Puffs of smoke escaped from the top of each tepee to mingle with the mist.

The sound of our chopper brought Aleksei Vokuyev, the local brigade leader, out of the center tepee. He looked Russian or even Nordic, with a ruddy complexion and red hair—not uncommon features of his Komi people, but they made him appear very unlike other natives I had visited in Siberia. Two young women, both in brightly colored native dress, stood behind him and studied us. Little heads poked out of the other two tepees, and several Nentsy children, looking a cross between Eskimos and American Indians, scampered excitedly, holding their hands over their ears. The chopper roared off to refuel. Babin worried that the weather might prevent the pilot from retrieving us that evening.

Aleksei invited our entire group—three ecologists, three journalists, and Salinger—into his spacious tepee, where the two women, Sasha and Nina, had put a pot of tea on the fire. The tundra's only wood, scrub birch and scrub alder, burned with little smoke, although the branches were wet and their leaves green. It was one of God's efficiencies.

Aleksei, at age twenty-nine, was in charge of the six herdsmen and four women workers at the camp. The women cooked and were responsible for setting up and dismantling the tepees and then moving the clan's belongings from site to site. Because it was summer, the camp was also filled with children who were sent to Russian boarding schools during the winter.

"We have been camped at this bend in the stream for two days," said Aleksei. "We were last at a camp by a lake that was full of fish, but it is growing cold and it is time to move south." He said the herd would remain only two more days at its current location, after which the reindeer would need the fresh grass of a new spot. His 5,000 head of reindeer, he said, were currently grazing about two miles away, but they would return in the evening.

Each year the herd traveled more than 250 miles, from its northern grazing area to its winter camp in the warmer and tree-protected taiga in the south. The tundra during the winter, he said, is swept by winds called *purga* that are so strong they knock the reindeer off their feet and topple the tepees. The winds reach seventy to ninety miles per hour, creating wild clouds of snow and sweeping the tundra down to its icy surface.

Aleksei spoke shyly, unaccustomed to talking with outsiders. He looked nervously to his boss, Babin, when I asked my questions, seeking nods of approval. Sasha, the twenty-three-year-old woman who seemed to be looking after Aleksei, hung on his every word. Like Aleksei, she was Komi. She had pale skin and reddish-brown hair and, like Aleksei, looked unlike the other natives in the camp.

Sixty percent of Babin's 650 employees were from the 29,500 Nentsy people, an Oriental-looking nationality. They spoke Samoyedic, a guttural and agglutinative language vaguely related to Turkish. "Nentsy" in their language means "man." Somewhere they must have crossed paths with the North American Eskimo. The Eskimo word for seal, *nesak,* is similar to the Nentsy word, *neyak.* Other words for Arctic phenomena are also quite similar.

But Aleksei and Sasha were Komis, a generally more developed and educated nationality numbering more than 400,000 that spoke a Finno-Ugric language. Pre-Revolutionary history books called the Komis "Permians," taken from the cousin Vepsian language's term *pera maa,* "the land beyond." The Komis began interbreeding with Russians as early as the twelfth century, which was when they first began paying the Russians tribute. Most Komis had left the tundra for villages and cities, such as Syktyvkar, the capital of the nearby Komi Autonomous Republic.

Aleksei and Sasha exchanged intimate glances, and I took them for young marrieds. I asked how they had met each other. Looking embarrassed, neither one responded. Sasha blushed that they were only cousins. Both were single and beyond the age that native peoples usually married. They didn't volunteer any information about their relationship, but the subject seemed a matter of discomfort for others in the camp.

Their tepee was well appointed, almost cozy. It had wooden planks covering the dirt floor, and atop them were mats filled with dry grass. Across the mats was an almost wall-to-wall carpet of reindeer skins. In a pinch the tepee could sleep fifteen. It was even equipped with cloth curtains that pulled out at night to separate the tepee into rooms that offered a degree of privacy. But Aleksei's tepee was the good neighborhood in a very small town.

I saw later that his poorer neighbors to either side had neither the wooden plank floors nor the plush carpeting of skins. Aleksei's tepee also differed from theirs in that it had an altar at the rear, opposite the entrance. A long red silken sheet hung down from the red-painted wooden mantel, on which rested some eight icons and other religious paraphernalia. The cloth also acted as a screen to fence off a storage area for household goods and food.

Aleksei said the icons, two of which looked very old and valuable, had been passed down through generations. He had displayed them even during the most atheistic days of Communism. Even though the herders had practiced a sort of Orthodoxy, some continued to believe in the Nentsy god, called Num, who was thought to have created the earth and all living things. His son, Mga, was the evil spirit who brought illness and death. The women also had a god, Ya-nebya, or "Mother Earth," who looked after them during childbirth. After giving birth in the tepee, the women would purify the dwelling by sprinkling it with marsh tea and then thanking Ya-nebya. But such births were increasingly infrequent since Babin had opened the village hospital at the headquarters of the state farm.

Traditional burial practices were elaborate and complex, partly owing to the difficulty of digging graves in the permafrost. One practice called for bodies to be buried in a log structure raised on poles about a half a meter off the ground. In other cases bodies were literally mummified in reindeer skin and then buried under a sled whose runners had been broken (so that it wouldn't slide off in the wind). Before the state took ownership of the Nentsy herds, the natives would leave several slaughtered reindeer by the grave to feed the soul of the dead man, which remained on earth for some time. The Nentsy believed that the soul could cause harm to the living if it wasn't treated well, so once a year relatives would visit the grave, ring a bell suspended above it, and say, "I have come to see you," thus demonstrating that the dead man's soul had not been forgotten.

Yet their ancient religion had been so confused with Russian Orthodoxy that most of the herders didn't know where one ended and the other began. For instance, one of the icons on Aleksei's mantel was of St. Nicholas, who seemed to me an appropriate figure among reindeer and so close to the North Pole. (My attempt to explain St. Nick and Rudolph the Red-Nosed Reindeer to Aleksei fell flat.) The Russians of the north had always revered St. Nicholas, and the Nentsy had adopted this custom after they had been converted in the early nineteenth century—methodically baptized family by family. The reindeer nomads had even gone so far as to make sacrifices to St. Nicholas and then smear reindeer blood and fat on the icons. Aleksei's icons had telltale discolorations.

We all—Dutch, American, Russian, the Nentsy city official, and the Komi herder—sat cross-legged along the two sides of a low, narrow wooden table which the women were loading with food. There was reindeer sausage, to be eaten with wild berries or mustard. There were chocolates, raw fish, and dry bread. (The nomads received a large bag of bread each month, delivered with mail and newspapers. They sliced the bread and then dried it over the fire to make it last.) There were also moist rolls to dip in deer fat, a popular dish with tea in the morning and evening.

The main course was venison, served as it had been for centuries, boiled in its own rich brown gravy. The pot was suspended on a hook from one of two narrow beams that ran across the tepee. The beams also acted as a place to hang wet clothing to dry.

Outside the tepee, the bloody, bug-eyed skull of the skinned and quartered reindeer was perched on a wooden tripod, a grisly obeisance to the animal who was, to the nomads, the region's most valuable natural resource. Never had I dined so close to the natural habitat of my main course.

A Russian anthropologist had determined that reindeer composed 85 percent of the Nentsy diet, usually boiled or smoked, but also eaten raw. But meat was only part of the story. "Reindeer have given the people all they need to live," said Ramon Salinger, the Nentsy city official. He said the deer also provided lard and blood for the diet, and brain for baby food. Their fat had long been used in lamps that were molded from deer gut; the skins provided boots, clothing, and covering for tents. Reindeer leather was made into shoelaces, lassos, and harnesses, and tendons served as thread and weaving string. Tellingly, the Nennish word for the wild reindeer was *ilbets*—"means of subsistence." A herd of 70 to 100 reindeer provided a family of ten with everything it needed to survive for a year, and each of the six herders in our camp had 200 reindeer set aside from the herd as his private property.

Aleksei stood up. He had heard something. A few moments later I heard it, too. A low roar, like distant thunder, was rolling toward us through the ground. "The herd is returning," he said.

When I walked out of the tepee, I saw a sea of antlers on the horizon, bobbing up and down like small brown waves. The reindeer were so close together that their bodies constantly bumped against one other. The muted drum roll of their hooves against the ground mixed with the dry cracking of antlers colliding. Two herdsmen rode toward us on their birch sleds, known as *khans*, pulled by four reindeer. They were all-weather vehicles, with upward-bent runners that slipped across the snow in the winter and slid easily across the tundra's slick summer grasses and moss in the summer.

The reindeer in the front row on the left was the specially trained leader, whom the other animals followed. The herdsman controlled him with a rein attached to his antlers. He encouraged the other animals with a thin wooden stick called a *tyur*, which looked like a long, flexible pool cue with a tiny round knob on the end that snapped against the reindeers' necks. The six herdsmen worked in pairs, each taking a twelve-hour shift, then resting twenty-four hours before starting again.

One of the returning herdsmen offered me a spin around the camp area before he retired to his tepee for an after-shift tea. I held tightly to his coat, a *malitsa* made of deerskin with the fur inside, as he forced the winded animals into a sprint. The Arctic wind blew frozen moisture against my face as we raced around the camp in a ride so entertaining that I was giddy when we returned to camp.

The old man of the brigade, Nikolai Vasilyevich Okoteto (see the jacket of this book), then took me for a stroll into the middle of the herd. Nikolai Okoteto didn't know exactly how old he was, probably about sixty, but he did know that he had spent his entire life with the reindeer. He looked on approvingly as teenage boys, who hadn't yet achieved the status of herders, whipped lassos over their heads as they chased individual reindeer that raced away from them. They were trying to rope the bulls that would lead the sleds of the next shift of herders. Pulling a sled was so strenuous for the reindeer that the same bulls were never used for two consecutive shifts.

I worried about the smallest of these Nordic gauchos, a five-year-old boy, who had gone to the middle of the herd with his miniature lasso and was mimicking his older brothers. I feared he would be trampled as he ran up to bulls and then threw his lasso at their flanks, but he wasn't discouraged by his assured failure, and he chased one bull after another. The animals never hurt him although they galloped away within inches of the boy. "There are more dangers in the city," said the old man. "Many things happen there. People die unnatural deaths in the city. But not here."

The reindeer that weren't running from the young men were pawing the ground with their front hooves, a habit learned in the winter to break through the snow and ice to reach the grass and foliage underneath. As harsh as winter was, however, Nikolai Okoteto said that his animals preferred it to the mosquito-infested summers. Although the old man had never heard of the concept of global warming, he said summers had turned longer and hotter, creating a greater problem of mosquitoes for the animals.

It began to rain, so I retreated to the lunch table inside the tepee, where the others sat over tea. Ramon Salinger talked about the days before the Nentsy had started their own breeding and herding, when their nomadic life had consisted of following wild reindeer. They had used decoys, he said, usually one of their own tame animals, on whose antlers they would tie leather loops. When the decoy was sent into a herd of wild reindeer, fights began and the wild animals would entangle their horns in the loops. That made them an easy target for hunters.

Salinger was one of the more educated of the Nentsy, and he had been a delegate at a convention on July 7, 1989, which had issued demands to expand the national territory and protect the rights of the nomads. The laws that had resulted from that meeting, giving new preferences to national groups, had resulted in an increase of their officially registered numbers from 29,500 to 34,500. Many people of mixed blood had for the first time seen profit in claiming their Nentsy nationality.

Even in his blue suit and green turtleneck, Salinger looked at ease sitting cross-legged in the tepee, and he didn't see himself as being any more "civilized" than the herder. "Russians think that civilization is the suit that I'm wearing," he said. "I consider civilization to be the unity of man and nature. By that measurement, the nomads are more civilized than the Russians." He said that the Soviets, who had greedily pursued the oil and gas on his people's territory without worrying about nature, were now bankrupt. "Our people have a saying: A man who is greedy will in the end pay twice as much."

He said his people also had another saying, which seemed to explain why the Soviets inflicted so much pain and suffering on each other and their neighbors. "If a man isn't happy, then all those around him are in danger," he said.

After he had graduated from a nearby college, Salinger had become a sports teacher, which he had seen as the best means to promote his nationality through regional and then countrywide competitions in traditional Nentsy sports. These included a contest that involved jumping back and forth over a sled as often as possible over a given period of time, and broad-jumping as many sleds as possible. Salinger was the 1979 Russian lasso-throwing champion.

Sports had been the most likely place for Salinger to express his national consciousness during the Brezhnev years, but the Gorbachev era had opened possibilities that prompted him to enter politics and begin extension courses to become a lawyer. He was now fighting for more sovereignty for the resource-rich region and the right to keep more of the growing natural-gas revenue at home. But most of all, he wanted to make his people proud to be Nentsy. "I fear we were becoming a gray mass—not Russian and not Nentsy," he said.

I heard another low roar. This time it wasn't the herd, but the snoring of Yuri Kaznin. The People's Deputy, wrapped in a herder's coat, was curled in the corner, apparently having been bored by the discussion and by the native people.

Perhaps his long nap was for the better, however, because during lunch he had told a joke that had made our hosts shift uneasily. "Why do Nentsy carry two sticks when they go out to the tundra?" he said. When no one knew the answer, he gladly replied, "It is for when they take a shit—they use one to beat off the wolves and the other to break off the shit that freezes when it comes out." The natives squirmed while the Russians roared.

Gerard laughed at the snoring politician, and he asked Aleksei if he had ever met a Soviet parliamentarian before. Aleksei smiled and said that he hadn't.

"Is he as you thought he would be?" Gerard asked.

Aleksei and Sasha both looked embarrassed for Yuri.

"He is a man like any other," said Aleksei.

Sasha and her elder sister, Nina, never spoke to us, yet they were educated, having both attended local schools, and I sensed they wanted to join the conversation. So I asked them whether they were worried by the gas exploration in the region. Were they concerned for their children's future?

Sasha looked at Aleksei for encouragement before she responded. He looked toward his boss, Babin, and Babin's nod of approval was passed back down the chain of command to Sasha.

"We are afraid," Sasha said. "We are afraid for the reindeer. The animals eat only clean grass and food, so they could starve if the oilmen pollute it. My grandmother and grandfather told us that in their days the reindeer were healthier. The skins were thicker and the fur was richer. My grandparents say the reindeer then were stronger and could pull a sled more easily."

The state farm director interrupted. "The condition of the reindeer has nothing to do with pollution," Babin said. "It is because we now have herds of 3,000 and 5,000 instead of the 1,000 or less at the time of her grandparents. That has been our chief mistake. This affects the grass they eat and it also attracts more insects to them."

The natives, however, were also afraid because of reports in local newspapers about underground atomic testing that had taken place to the north of the Yamal Peninsula. Russian newspapers had recently reported that nuclear waste had been dumped in the bays of Novaya Zemlya, a large, crescent-shaped island to the north, where some Nentsy had been sent in the eighteenth century to establish Russia's claim to the island in a dispute with Norway. Soviet newspapers have reported that from 1964 to 1986, no fewer than 11,000 containers of waste were sunk in the shallow waters of the Kara Sea between the island and the Yamal Peninsula. They reported that in some cases, when the containers wouldn't sink, those responsible for them had shot them full of holes with their machine guns.

I asked Sasha if this worried her.

She looked at the director.

"Say your opinion," said Nikolai Babin. "Speak, child, and tell what you feel."

"Yes, I am afraid," she said. Nina nodded that she was frightened as well.

The director belittled them. "They don't know what it means and they have no reason to fear," he said. "They are living in undamaged nature. Nothing disturbs them here."

Sasha retreated behind the silken altar and busied herself with pots and pans.

The women didn't eat or drink with us. They weren't allowed to dine with company. For several hours they had only looked after the men's needs. So now it was time for us to take a walk on the tundra, to leave the tepee, so that the women could make dinner for themselves.

After a short stroll I visited the "bad side of town," one of the two poorer and smaller Nentsy tepees. Strips of reindeer meat were drying into a jerky over poles that stretched across the middle of the tent. Three children in reindeer-skin overalls played at one side. Their grandmother sat across from them, sewing together reindeer-skin boots for the winter. Her husband, the old man who had taken me into the herd, happily invited me for tea.

When I asked him how the reindeer nomad's life had changed during his lifetime, he shrugged. "We work the way we always have," he said. "But it's much harder than before. Now we are told we need to save our money for ammunition, for leather goods, for canvas. I need canvas for the tepee, but what can I trade for it? I don't have enough reindeer. I will also need to trade ten reindeer to the collective for a motor for a fishing boat." He thought his reindeer should be worth more than that.

Babin, uneasy about leaving me alone with his workers for too long, walked into the tepee and interrupted our conversation. He insisted that the free market would improve life for all of his workers. Babin was famous in the region for having turned his state farm into an economic success story.

In the village of Byelozhersk, the headquarters for the *sovkhoz,* he had overseen the building of enough homes for all of his 650 workers and their families in the space of five years. The village was the center of all his activities, which ranged from fox hunting and fishing to reindeer-breeding and the production of shoes and coats from the furs. With the *sovkhoz*'s profits, he had built a hospital, introduced central heating and running water, and built a boarding school so that children weren't sent too far from their parents.

Like many Siberians who were thriving in an economically freer Russia, Babin's formative years had come during the relative freedom of Nikita Khrushchev's rule. From 1959 to 1967, he had been the leader of a Communist Youth League chapter in Tobolsk, where he had studied to be a veterinarian. He said people of his age group, in their mid-forties and early fifties, were leading free-market forces, and the barriers were posed by the older Stalinists and the younger members of the "stagnation generation" of the Brezhnev years.

Babin saw the future of his farm in foreign sales. He had formed a joint venture with a Swedish company which bought him equipment to make reindeer sausage. But the biggest money-maker came from an elixir made from deer antlers. The "concentrate," as he called it, promoted longevity, corrected lethargy, and promoted potency. It was said to be an aphrodisiac. He sold it, through a San Francisco partner, primarily to Koreans and Taiwanese. California and Amsterdam were also good markets.

So Siberian reindeer nomads were helping to supply sex shops around the world. I asked Babin if his elixir was effective. "Why do you think there are so many children in this tepee?" he asked. The old man laughed, and his two sons smiled. In the autumn, Babin said, when the reindeer are slaughtered, the men would often take out the marrow from the antlers, warm it up, and then eat it. "Then their women have to watch out. The antlers have biologically active materials that have remarkable consequences."

The director said it hadn't been easy to convince the natives to saw off the antlers from living reindeer, which was necessary because young and soft antlers were by far the most valuable. For the Nentsy, it was like chopping off their children's arms on the promise that it would bring wealth. Some refused altogether. Women cried in their tents. Others merely shook their heads and wondered why generations of Nentsy had never found it necessary to cut off the antlers.

They feared it would cause the reindeer to die. "It didn't seem natural," said the old man. "We learned that the reindeer can grow sick if we cut off the antlers in the moist weather [when the chances of infection are greater], so we try to do the sawing when the days are dry and the wound heals more quickly."

I asked Babin how the potion was produced.

He explained in some detail the entire process, which involved putting bits of the horn in seventy-proof alcohol and then letting it sit there for forty-five days. That, he said, created a medicinal concentrate that people took by the drop. "If that doesn't work for your potency," said the director, laughing, "you can tie one of the horns to your penis and that will make it stand up straight."

The old man and his sons laughed again. So did the old lady.

"You take twenty-five grams of extract a half hour before eating, with a glass of tea," Babin said. "You have to do it regularly. If you take it just once, even a liter won't help you. A young man must be careful not to overdo it. He can overstimulate himself." Laughter again.

I asked Babin if he spoke from experience. He said he had done a little experimenting, but that was all. "In the north, we freeze and it preserves us, and then we are passionate when we thaw out," he said. "My girlfriend is still happy, so I don't need the concentrate."

What made his girlfriend happiest, however, were the rich profits in the aphrodisiac business. The antlers, he said, were separated into quality groups. The most valuable was sold for $550 per kilo, the second group sold for $260 a kilo, and the third group was $60 a kilo. In 1990 his revenue from the antlers and their concentrate was $600,000, and the laboratory equipment and tools he had bought for the process cost only $380,000. The antlers were earning more money for his state farm than the reindeer meat and the boots and clothing made from the skins.

At about eleven P.M. we gave up hope that the helicopter would return that evening. The fog still hadn't cleared. Aleksei, the women, and the children moved into the other two tepees and into pup tents that the women put up around the camp, which were normally used by herders in the field. They donated their own more comfortable tepee to their foreign visitors and pulled out the curtains to create several private compartments. They suggested we sleep closely together for warmth. No one kept fires going overnight—it was a waste of scarce scrub brush.

Fate put me between Viktor Pelz, the Gulag survivor, and Yuri Kaznin, whose incessant snoring was an alarm clock I couldn't shut off. I drew near Viktor's body for warmth, remembering only then how he had done the same for survival in the Gulag.

After more than four hours of trying to sleep, I gave up. I slipped on a pair of long rubber boots and went for a walk through the tundra. The sky was pale blue and the ground was all green and wet. I forded the cold, shallow stream, beside which was a patch of snow. I took a cup of its clear water in my hands to quench my thirst, then I put my hands immediately back into my coat, to coax some warmth back into frozen fingers.

I noticed that one of the herdsmen's dogs was at my heels. I thought it might have been a kind gesture, a concerned animal not wanting to leave his visitor along in the wilds, but I later learned that the dog was merely following his master's coat, which had been loaned to me for the day.

The dog was small and scruffy, a black-and-white mutt with tangled wet hair. We made our way across the tundra, an expanse of moss, grass, stone, and low shrubbery where all vegetation grows in miniature. The wildflowers' blooms were yellows, whites, reds, and blues, none larger than my fingertip. My favorite was an almost microscopic magenta, which if magnified more than a hundred times would have looked like a poinsettia. There were small cotton plants no larger than a Q-tip. And mushrooms, with tiny red dots on top, were the size of the ballpoint on a pen.

Although from above the tundra looked like a flat, uniform expanse, close up the changes were remarkable over even the short territory that I explored. A slight rise in the earth of just five to ten feet was enough to change moist, spongy earth with high grass into a rocky plateau. Most of the land, however, was moss-and-lichen-covered grasslands with occasional patches of scrub brush.

The silence of the frigid morning was interrupted only by sounds from what seemed to be different birds. A small black one, called a *kulik,* chirped happily as it skipped along the stream's pebbles and over the grass. I saw a couple of snipes racing past without paying any attention. Then a large gray rook flew overhead, following me for about half an hour before losing interest. There was also a mysterious sonar sound coming from the earth, but I couldn't spot its source.

The dog pursued the sound, which then turned into a muffled and threatened squeak. The squeak become more frenzied as the dog dug furiously with its paws. Suddenly I saw a tiny brown-and-white furry creature race through the dog's paws and then disappear into another hole. Aleksei later told me this was a polar lemming, which he referred to as a sort of filet mignon for the deer. He said they were reappearing after a three-year absence, a good sign because the lemmings' return meant that the overhunted polar fox, which also fed off the lemming, would again begin to appear. He couldn't explain the connection—it was simply that way.

The dog continued to dig at the lemming's new hiding place. But I sat down on a rock, atop a small rise opposite the stream and the tepees. I remained there until I saw smoke issue from our tepee, a sign that tea was on.

When I returned, Sasha was also warming up the leftover venison for breakfast. As usual, she looked after her cousin Aleksei first, again exchanging a warm glance and a casual touch.

Greenpeace's interpreter, the likable Russian-German Ella Rikert, had spent most of the previous day and morning with the women. Their main item of gossip was the two cousins, who loved each other so much that they couldn't love anyone else. Their families would never condone such a union, yet neither found it possible to fall in love with another partner. It was the scandal of the settlement, a soap opera on the tundra. The two were desperately unhappy and desperately in love—and they had no solution to their pain.

Ella had also learned something of the sex habits of the reindeer nomads, a subject I hadn't explored. She said that lovemaking took place in the tepees behind the cloth curtains only after the children were deeply asleep. One of the women explained that this was easy without the squeaky beds of the village.

The women, Ella had learned, were almost all using spiral IUDs, given to them at no cost by the collective's hospital in the village. Birth control wasn't forced upon them, however. One of the women had had six children by age thirty-three before she went to the hospital. None of them knew how the IUDs worked, nor were they familiar with the possible dangers.

Ella was surprised at how content the women seemed and at how little they complained. "I have never met Russian women who are so happy," she said.

The men also seemed content, which surprised me some because they were so under the thumb of their Russian boss. I asked Aleksei if that didn't bother him. Didn't he think that the natives should lead themselves?

His boss chose to answer the question. "They aren't capable of being the leaders," Babin said. "They can't be stern enough with their own. They don't stand up for their opinions."

"I suppose that explains why you feel you always have to answer for them," I said, irritated that he often didn't allow the natives to answer for themselves.

"The simple people can't explain their own feelings," Babin said. "They can't answer the questions you ask. Someone has to organize things for them."

I mentioned that I had met an impressive Nentsy woman who was the head of the Salekhard city council. She had seemed extraordinarily competent and articulate.

"You aren't responsible for anything when you are doing politics," Babin replied. "They do well in politics because they are better at persuading their people. But in production and organization, they fall down. They are too kind in their souls."

I asked Aleksei again if he thought his people were capable of leading themselves.

"We don't know," he replied. "The Russians have always been in charge."

The director praised Aleksei for having been instrumental in convincing his brigade that cutting antlers wouldn't harm or cause pain to the reindeer. "I need Aleksei to implement my decisions," he said. "But these people can't make decisions themselves. They need me to do that."

"What you are telling me," I said, "is that the natives need a slave master."

The chief nodded his head affirmatively.

"And you are that slave master," I said.

He nodded again.

I asked Aleksei if it disturbed him that the director said that his people needed a slave master.

"No, it doesn't really bother me," he said. "It's true. I wouldn't want to boss my own people around. I would feel uncomfortable. I don't want such responsibility. I don't want to break friendships with the people with whom I live."

For him, a child of nature, being the boss wasn't a privilege to be desired but rather a burden to avoid.

I heard the helicopter approaching. Everyone started packing to leave. Two of the women at the camp were hitching a ride with us to the village, where we would refuel—it was a rare chance for them to visit relatives without having a trek of several days. One of them was the oldest woman of the settlement, Anya Alekseyevna Satyriyova. Before we got on the helicopter, I asked her whether she thought her people were capable of taking care of themselves, without the Russians.

"Ask the Russians," she said without irony. "They are civilized and literate. They should know the answer."

I wondered whether, during her lifetime, her people had ever taken more responsibility over their own lives than now. How had life changed for her and her people? "When the Reds came, food was rationed," she said, "Then life got better. Now we have rations again. So life is the same as when the Reds first came. God knows what will happen now."

Which God was she talking about? Was it the Russian God or the Nentsy God? "Maybe God is closer to the Russians because they fly in helicopters," she said. And then we both boarded the chopper and flew away from the nomads' camp.

Chapter 20:

RAILWAY TO NOWHERE

The people have long wished to have a reliable
entrance into the Arctic Ocean from the Ob River.

—JOSEF STALIN, *circa 1946*

Our helicopter's shadow traced the winding course of ghostly railway tracks: two thin, rusty lines through uninhabited taiga and tundra. Where the tracks crossed small streams, the bridges underneath had often collapsed, leaving rails stubbornly suspended over the water. Long grass and young trees were growing between the decaying wooden ties, but the railway's path was still a surprisingly clear one, an almost unbroken line stretching for more than 850 miles across some of the world's most forbidding territory.

Stalin had had few schemes as ambitious or bloody as that of building an eastward railway from Salekhard to Igarka, on the Yenisei River. The railway was to be built primarily by prisoners, and after the war he had plenty of them—German prisoners, his own POWs whom he had branded as traitors, unreliable Baltic and Ukrainian citizens, and, of course, tens of thousands of murderers and common criminals.

They all were drafted into a project to provide rail access to a year-round harbor for new factories in the Siberian Northwest. The railway was broken into two parts. One construction group was to build from Salekhard eastward and another from Igarka westward, the two stretches then to be joined in a dramatic event not unlike the linking of the transcontinental railroad in the United States.

From the beginning, however, the project was based on the mistaken notion that a deep harbor could be built on the bay, which was too sandy and shallow for it. Planners also overlooked the fact that the Yenisei was frozen in for nearly half the year. But no one dared argue with Stalin. As a result, the unlikely project began in 1947 and continued until the summer of 1953, when it was abandoned after Stalin had died and many of his prisoners—the railway's workers—had been given amnesty. Perhaps if Khrushchev had known then that rich reserves of gas and oil would be found in the region only seven years later, he might have finished the railway, which was only sixty kilometers short of completion. But he did not, so as we flew southeast toward Igarka from Salekhard, we saw only the ruins of some of the forty-seven prison camps built along the tracks. They looked like tumbledown ghost towns of collapsed roofs, rotting barracks, and precariously leaning guard towers. The camps had a sad sameness, a new one appearing every twenty miles or so. Each had a barbed-wire perimeter, usually two layers deep, a small railway station, housing for guards and administrators near the periphery, and then six to twelve buildings within—barracks, a prison, dugouts for the earliest prisoners, a bathhouse, and a dining hall. Each could hold up to 1,500 prisoners. Some twenty to thirty workers died each day along the tracks—which added up to more than 60,000 of the total 300,000 who were "employed" during the life of the project.

And that is why the labor-camp survivors, and the reindeer nomads who often camp in the area, call the tracks *Myortvaya Doroga*—Death's Road.

As I looked at this scene from above, I began to fear that my interest had strayed too often to Stalin's excesses during the expedition. I had found a sandy bank that had regurgitated the contents of a mass grave into the river, an island of Stalin's exiles with a history of cannibalism, and the place where Stalin had been deported, only to gain his revenge two decades later by sending Kulaks there. And I was about to head north to one of the worst of all camp complexes in the Gulag Archipelago at Vorkuta. Yet these horrors were part of the landscape, like the railway, cutting a permanent gash through the Russian soul.

While Hitler's crimes were dramatic, his rule lasted only twelve years. Stalin had more time to put his mark on his people. He left permanent scars of fear, mistrust, and resignation. His mark had been impossible for me to escape.

Prisoners weren't a small fringe group during Stalin's years. The scholar Robert Conquest writes that in 1939, some 9 percent of the Soviet population was in prisons and concentration camps. He estimated that 20 million died or were executed as a result of Stalin's terror. Solzhenitsyn wrote that 40 to 50 million persons served sentences from 1928 to 1953. In comparison, the maximum number of prisoners and exiles during Tsarist times was 32,000, in 1912.

* * *

Two days before our flight, I began my study of Death's Road at Salekhard's main historical museum. A plump, matronly woman named Lyudmila Lipatova had opened an exhibit on the railway there in 1988. Across the floor, she displayed a stretch of original ties and tracks, rails made of iron imported from America. She had even re-created part of a barrack, and displayed signs and tools that she had gathered on trips to the camps. A portrait of Stalin was on the wall, seeming to supervise card files underneath him that were filled with the names of railway "laborers."

The curator's first instinct was to recite the official story: how the railway had been constructed by a mixture of Communist volunteers and convicts, and how the workers had been well paid, well clothed, and well fed at a time of extreme hardship elsewhere in the Soviet Union. Having been informed by someone (again) that we were an ecological expedition, she even told us how "environmentally sound" the project had been. "All the work was carried out by hand and not machines," she boasted.

On display were photographs of the laborers carrying banners on the Communist holidays, May 1 and November 7. Ludmilla said her one big regret was that the project had never been completed. "It can still be done," she said. "I am sorry for those who worked on the railway that they haven't seen the fruits of their labors."

Gerard had grown irritated with the woman. I had warmed to this Dutch journalist's rapier style of questioning. He got away with it by punctuating the most insulting and challenging questions with an innocent smile, which provoked even the most reticent of Siberians into talking. He asked Lyudmila how many "volunteers" had died while building the railway. He suggested that her "ecological" labor had really been forced labor that had polluted the region with their blood.

Lyudmila stepped back. She agreed that some of the workers had been prisoners and some were free. She said, however, that after prisoners had been released, many had stayed on the job anyway because of the assured rations and housing. The prisoners had even been given two pairs of underwear each, she said, a remarkable luxury when most Russians didn't have even one.

Gerard put away his notebook in disgust. He considered walking out. "How was it possible that people were happy when we have heard that so many were dying?" he demanded. "These people were brought in cattle cars. They were dehumanized." After a tense moment of silence, he asked: "Have you read Solzhenitsyn?"

The name acted like a truth serum on Lyudmila. "I have read Solzhenitsyn." She frowned. "The director of this museum at first said that I shouldn't make an exhibit on the railway—that nothing good could come of it. I didn't understand him at first because I didn't know our true history. By reading Solzhenitsyn I understood what had happened during those days."

Gerard softened his tone. Why did she find it so difficult to talk about what happened? he asked. Why had Russians quietly accepted their fate and then remained silent about Stalin's crimes for so many years?

"Why do we keep silent?" She sighed. "In those days, when I was a young girl, everything was all right. I am fifty-one years old now, and I grew up like a Communist. I thought those people behind the barbed wire were not real people. It didn't matter that they were abused. Maybe the whole country was insane, but that is how we were raised. That is how the system educated us. You can understand it only if you were born and grew up here. If a policeman asks you to go to prison, you don't ask questions. You go to prison."

Lyudmila said she found it difficult to convince former prisoners to tell her about their experiences in the camps, even though Russia had become democratic. "Everyone is still afraid it can happen again," she said. "That is the reason we keep silent. It looks to you as if everything has changed, but these people cannot trust it."

She paused. Gerard asked her what she told her children. "My children ask me now, 'Mother, why did you not resist? Why did you not speak out?' But I did nothing. That is why I put this exhibition together. To clean my soul. To show my regret to my children that I had always remained silent."

At our request Lyudmila joined our helicopter flight. Lacking the money to rent a chopper herself, joining a group like our own was her only chance to visit the camps and bring back more material for her exhibit.

After flying 100 miles southeastward from Salekhard, and past four camps, we circled a fifth near the river Yarude and then landed in a clearing. Lyudmila said she had never been to this camp before. We walked together for 100 yards along the railway's wooden ties toward the ruins we had seen from above. After passing a guard tower, tilting so precariously that it was unlikely to stand through another winter, we came to the still-intact barbed-wire fence, camouflaged with forty years of overgrowth. There was no opening.

After a little more exploration I discovered an old guardhouse behind a clump of trees through which we could gain entrance. I turned to tell Lyudmila but she had disappeared. I worried that emotion had overtaken her or that she had caught herself in the barbed wire. When I shouted for her, however, she emerged from the brush with a wide smile and an armful of jumbo-sized mushrooms, each the size of a hat. She had taken off her sweater to use as a bag to carry her haul. The history would not go away but the food shortages were so bad that no Russian would miss a chance to bring home such a rich meal.

I reminded Lyudmila that we had brought her along so that she could tell us the history of the camp.

She said that she didn't know much. She had never been to this camp before and she knew little about how such camps had organized their work. She wanted to go back to her mushrooms, but I convinced her to tour the facility with me anyway to provide whatever information she could. Historians had written precious little about Death's Road, so any knowledge she had would be a help.

In fact, the only detailed eyewitness account I had found was in Russian, in the magazine *Novy Mir,* written in 1960 from reports by the railway's prospecting engineer, Pyotr Konstantinovich Tatarinov.

Rations for prisoners, he said, consisted of 300 grams of bread daily and *balanda,* a soup consisting of water mixed with scraps of potatoes and vegetables. The prisoners would put jackets over their heads so that they could eat soup undisturbed by the mosquitos, whose bites "turned skin to blisters," he wrote. Prisoners would often sleep in trees so that their beds would be out of reach of the winged torturers.

Prisoners called *slabosilka,* or "weaklings," put up the tents, barbed-wire fences, worked in the kitchens, and built the houses. The sturdier prisoners did the heavier work of hauling logs, sand, railway ties, and tracks.

The prospecting engineer described the scene: prisoners pulling wheelbarrows slowly, their heads bent low, using all their strength to bear the load. When they emptied a load of sand, a guard gave them a chip, and each prisoner collected the chips for proof of plan fulfillment, which was necessary to receive rations. Other prisoners hardened the ground with wooden rams. Some distance away, the guards stood around the smoke of fires, more concerned with keeping the mosquitoes off than watching the prisoners, whose only escape was to a likely death in the wilderness. The sentries counted the prisoners every night merely to see how many had died or escaped.

The winter was even worse. Prisoners would often have to carry logs to their prison camps for three days across the icy landscape. The cold was so severe that thermometers refused to work. The sun appeared only for two or three hours a day. In the dugouts, where prisoners lived before barracks were completed, bunk beds were sometimes stacked three high. Prisoners would fight to avoid the bottom rung, where many froze to death. Temperatures fell as low as $-60°$ F. "Whenever you breathed, you breathed ice," the engineer wrote.

Directly to the right of us, after we entered the gate of the camp, were the guard and administration barracks. To keep the bosses warmer, the construction was better and the wood sturdier than what we would find in the prisoners' barracks. But the floorboards, which kept the men well above the cold ground, had been ripped out by reindeer nomads seeking fuel for fires. The log walls and ceilings were still intact.

Beside these barracks was a small jail with three cells. The bars on its windows were an ad hoc combination of flat and round lengths of iron, each a different gauge, soldered together in a crisscross pattern.

On the flat log walls of the cells, prisoners had left messages either in chemical pencils, which had to be licked before use, or by using a sharp object to etch a message for posterity. In one cell, ten feet long and three feet wide, a prisoner had drawn a calendar on which he had crossed out days. Beside it was a substitute for a family photograph: simple drawings of children, their ages written in figures next to their crudely drawn faces—ten, seven, and three. Three feet to the right, another prisoner had drawn a sexy silhouette of a woman, but beside it were complex mathematical equations. The prisoners had many means to preserve sanity.

In the neighboring cell, a narrow, longer version of the first, the Russian writing read: "22.10.1951 a quiet and lonely night. The windows are frozen. Volkov has not come back yet."

Beside it was another note. "Here was imprisoned Sasha Strakhansky. Three days in jail without being let out for refusing to work." There were more calendars, a signature, and two pornographic drawings.

I wandered off alone and found several dugouts half filled with water. One had a steel barrel in the middle, cut open at the top, that seemed to have served as a room heater. Barrel rings lay everywhere in the camp, left over from the barrels of frozen fish that provided a key part of the diet. The largest building was a dining hall. In the dirt nearby I discovered a six-foot-long spatula used to take bread out of its giant brick oven. The nearest and best-preserved of the buildings was the bathhouse, probably for guards; it was too small and well built to have been intended for the prisoners. The stones that had been heated to create steam still rested atop the brick oven. In the changing room, which had a plaster wall, a prisoner had written: "Kostichev Tanya cleaned the dirt in the sauna." So this had been a mixed camp.

After a couple of hours of wandering, we made our way back to the helicopter with some new exhibits for Lyudmila's museum. Dundee carried a window frame with crisscross bars that he had found on the floor of one collapsed barracks. I brought the bread spatula and old bottles. Lyudmila carried only her mushrooms.

Before boarding the helicopter, I stopped at the rusted tracks and looked down their warped path in to the distance. I knelt and pulled at one of the spikes, which slipped surprisingly easily out of a tie. I fingered it, imagining that it had been hammered into place by one of the prisoners from the camp we had just left. For a moment I worried that I should not remove it, but I could think of no reason why not. So I withdrew six more such spikes and slipped them into my pockets as souvenirs before I climbed aboard the helicopter for the ride back to Salekhard.

* * *

It was our last night on the Ob before leaving the boat and making our way by land across the Urals to Vorkuta, but no one felt much like celebrating. The conflict with Yuri had soured the mood. Vladimir nevertheless prepared a banquet, using mushrooms picked by Yuri off the grounds of Stalin's camp, atop a bed of rice. Vladimir was constantly trying to make the trip more enjoyable and comfortable—a practice for which Yuri chided him regularly. "Why do you need to serve them so?" Yuri would sneer. "You are just being a slave to the West."

The captain joined us at the table. As each ritual toast was offered, Yuri fidgeted like a chained animal at his corner of the table, his eyes shifting quickly from side to side, from one of the galley windows to the other. We had never seen him so nervous. He wouldn't look anyone in the eye, and he did not join any of the toasts.

One of my Russian friends had told me that Yuri had spent the day talking to "authorities." He had dressed in business clothes in the morning and had not reappeared until late in the afternoon, missing an appointment I had had with him for an interview. I had hoped to patch things up some, but my Russian friends still feared that Yuri was helping to lay some sort of trap for me. Vladimir again asked me if I had made copies of my notes and given them to the Dutch—I had not yet found the time.

In an effort to cut the tension, I raised a toast. I apologized that Americans were a pushy race and that journalists were the worst of the lot. I apologized for having only reinforced these stereotypes during the trip. I raised a toast to the White Bird and said I was sorry that I had driven him to bad dreams with my frequent demands for information or interviews. He had told me of a nightmare he had had that I had demanded he rent a rocket ship so that I could get a better view of the swamps. Then I apologized to Yuri. I praised him for doing his work, as a politician, and I said that our conflict came only because I was doing my work as a journalist. I spoke of the natural tension between our two professions.

I joked that the fact that people willingly talked to journalists, even when they asked unfriendly questions, was one of the great unanswered mysteries of our age. Everyone laughed except Yuri. I then proposed that we drink to a shipful of people who did their jobs as best as they could—a shipful of professionals.

Everyone smiled and raised a glass—except for Yuri. His eyes continued to dart from one window to the other as though he expected some sort of attack. His Russian friends grimaced when he rejected my gesture. In Russia, refusing to join a peacemaking toast was the deepest indignity, like spitting in someone's face.

I nevertheless retreated to my computer in a corner of the galley, not wanting to be provoked into open conflict. After I left the table, Yuri trained his sights on Greenpeace. He asked Michael Hoffmann how he would use the information he had collected during the trip. Hoffmann was noncommittal. Greenpeace was trying to decide whether it could continue working with Yuri. Hoffmann said he would study the samples they were bringing back to Western Europe, write a report, and then decide a future course.

Yuri was dissatisfied with the response and with the limited nature of the Greenpeace study. He wanted more than just the pilot project that Greenpeace envisioned.

Gerard interrupted Yuri to use this last opportunity to corner him on Tomsk 7. He probed him to discover why he had concealed information. He said the West knew what was going on in Tomsk 7, so he imagined Yuri must know as well.

Yuri fidgeted and evaded the question.

Gerard continued. He said the West knew about the extent of Stalin's crimes before the Soviets did; that it knew about the Cuban missile sites before the Soviet people knew. He said, in short, that the West had always known more about the actions of the Soviet government than the Soviets did themselves. His point was that Western revelations about what had happened in Yuri's country weren't "black information," as Yuri was arguing, but instead had given the Soviet people their only reliable source of information for years.

Gerard's questions to Yuri were getting uglier when the Greenpeace interpreter, Ella Rikert, intervened with a sugary toast. She said what a unique expedition ours had been, how much she liked everyone, and what wonderful memories she would take home with her. Then she asked me to return to the table from my corner to join her toast to all the wonderful memories.

I agreed to do so and then followed her toast with another one of my own, one more effort to repair things. I spoke of two arms controllers, a Soviet and an American. I spoke of an angry tension between them as the American provided satellite information that directly contradicted the data provided by the Soviet. The American was calling the Soviet a liar, I said, and talks broke down in an atmosphere of hatred. Then I noted how several weeks later the Soviet and American had reached agreement, bringing a historic step toward peace.

I continued. I said that George Bush and Mikhail Gorbachev, who were meeting in Washington the next week, wanted peace. I said that my travels through Siberia showed the people wanted peace. So, I said, the only problem remained in the middle, among the opinion-makers and the politicians. I raised a toast to the people at the top and on the bottom, and I expressed the hope that the people in the middle could work out their difficulties to let peace go ahead. The toast was a little corny, but the group applauded and even Yuri smiled.

But when all the others stood to toast, Yuri remained seated and didn't drink. Another gesture was rejected.

So Gerard tried, but this time not with a toast. He spoke of his three-year-old son and how nothing made more difference to him than that boy. He addressed Yuri as a fellow father and a friend. He said that he had come in friendship and he wanted to leave in friendship. "We may have scratched too deep now and then in our effort to understand the Russian soul," said Gerard, "but it was all done in the spirit of friendship." He wanted Yuri to look him in the eye (which Yuri hadn't done with anyone that evening) so that they could depart as friends.

"These are fine slogans," said Yuri, not looking anyone in the eye. "But they are inspired by drink."

Being sober, I told Yuri that he had insulted me and Gerard. We had both spoken sincerely, I said.

The conversation took a nasty turn. Gerard asked Yuri where he had been during the forty years before Perestroika—what had he done during that time to promote change? He didn't answer, but instead said that the West was responsible for those lost years. Its arms buildup put Moscow on the defensive, he said, and hence the West was the reason that Communism had lasted as long as it did. Yuri also blamed the West for the dying swamplands, caused by its hunger for Soviet oil. The West's desire for oil profits, he said, had left Moscow with nothing for itself.

"Yuri," I said, "how do you figure *we* earned from *your* oil? The West paid the Soviet Union hard currency for whatever oil or gas it purchased. And the Soviet Union then used that money to build up its military. Your country has regularly spent a quarter of its Gross National Product for defense."

I asked him how an ecologist could justify having a defense plant, an arms manufacturer, as his political sponsor. Throughout the trip, Yuri had refused to talk about what the Yurga plant produced, although his political reputation depended on this sponsor. He still wouldn't say.

Yuri argued that the people of the plant thought he was the best man for the parliament job, that the plant was the most important employer in Yurga, and, what's more, that the factory also had begun to make many consumer goods, such as washing machines.

Yuri reminded us that ours was an ecological mission and that we weren't paying enough attention to the environment. Gerard, who had organized the expedition with Vladimir, always turned angry at this. "This was a private reporting expedition that I and my friend Vladimir arranged, and we invited you along," he said.

Yuri smiled. He asked if Gerard knew that he, Yuri, was the president of the company that had organized the mission. Gerard looked at Vladimir with surprise. Vladimir, looking somewhat embarrassed, said it was true that Yuri was the company president. It was a natural choice, appointing as president an influential man who could cut the red tape and throw some political weight around. But the rest of us hadn't known about Yuri's role—and neither had his voters. He had asked his partners to keep his business interests in the expedition confidential for fear of political backlash.

I asked Yuri why he had withheld information from us about Tomsk 7. I said that public officials had a right to refuse to give journalists information—I didn't dispute that. But I wanted to know his rationale.

Instead of answering, however, Yuri said that much of the information was mere rumors passed on by former Tomsk 7 employees whose reliability was uncertain.

He started another long discourse about the nature of Western journalism. He spoke of meetings with another American journalist, from *U.S. News & World Report,* whom he had considered to be far more polite than I was. He then denied having withheld any information, contradicting his previous insistence that it was his patriotic duty to keep us from some truths.

"Have you or have you not withheld information from us regarding Tomsk 7?" I said. "And if so, why?"

Dundee translated every word simultaneously, his voice carrying the same emotion as mine, for he too had grown impatient with Yuri. However, we both made the mistake of raising our voices.

The rest of us remained awake most of the night. While the others celebrated the last night on the boat and tried to drink away the tension, I retreated to my cabin. The Russians had convinced me the dangers hadn't passed yet, and I feared the KGB would confiscate my notes and disks, perhaps even that night. So I stayed up to make copies of everything.

On the last morning aboard ship, no one was happy. The tension was exacerbated by a collective hangover. In the galley, bottles were scattered on all three tables and along the bar. They were all empty. No one touched the usual breakfast of dry bread, sour cheese, fatty wurst, and boiled eggs. The vegetables were all gone by Salekhard. The samovar, however, provided a steady stream of hot water for coffee.

Yuri Kaznin had left the boat without saying good-bye to anyone. He was leaving the expedition prematurely for Moscow, and one of the Russians feared that he might try to arrange for an unfriendly reception for me there. I assured them that those days were over—and certainly nothing would happen just before a Gorbachev-Bush summit. But they were still concerned.

The fact that Russians in our expedition had privately taken sides against a People's Deputy was, for me, hard proof that democracy was taking hold in Siberia.

* * *

The last stop on our expedition would be Vorkuta, a coal-mining city of 200,000 built by and for prisoners of the Gulag. I chose to take a twelve-hour train ride north, drawn to the journey by its history and the railway's reputation for crowded, smoky compartments and for an unruly, drunken, and often criminal clientele. At this late stage of the trip, most of my colleagues decided to avoid discomfort and fly to Vorkuta by helicopter.

But Dundee, who never wanted to miss one of the trip's adventures, gladly joined me. He was looking hung over and unshaven, clearly showing aftereffects of the traumatic previous evening. When I saw him in the breakfast room, stooped over a cup of coffee, I joked that he'd fit right in with the sorts of passengers we expected to meet. He smiled crookedly and mischievously at me, clearly still a little tipsy.

Chapter 21:

SLOW TRAIN TO VORKUTA

> Who are you, Martin Eden? he demanded of himself in the looking glass. . . . You belong with the legions of toil, with all that is low, and vulgar and unbeautiful. You belong with the oxen and the drudges, in dirty surroundings among smells and stenches . . . what are you, damn you! And are you going to make good?
>
> —JACK LONDON, *Martin Eden*

Vladimir Antonovich Rodin's thick woolen pants and brown sweater were soiled and worn. His gray beard was wild and uncombed. He smelled of fish and sweat. From my seat across the aisle of the commuter boat, he looked like another of Russia's lost souls. I was certain he had an interesting story, but I had no desire to hear it.

At the beginning of the expedition I would have walked up to him and struck up a conversation. But I was tired. I shut my eyes to catch up on lost sleep—and to regain my strength for an all-day train journey ahead to Vorkuta, our final destination and the former site of one of cruelest collection of Stalin's prison camps.

Dundee had slept only an hour that night. It was the first time during five weeks on the road that the pressure of the trip had gotten under the skin of the highly professional and educated school director. But he was a jovial drunk and he wasn't about to let me nap.

"What are we doing on this boat?" he asked in an accent even more Australian than usual. "We shouldn't need a boat to go to the airport."

"We are taking it to the train station," I said.

"What train?" he asked. "Is there a train? Oh, I can't believe that a boat will take us to a train. What kind of train? Are you *sure* we are going in the right direction?"

"A train to Vorkuta," I said. The station, which had been built fifty years earlier to accommodate prisoners en route to the prison camps, was upriver from Salekhard, in the town of Labytnangi, so we needed to take a small commuter boat to reach it.

The real draw of Vorkuta was its history. The 150 miles of track between Salekhard and Vorkuta had been laid by prisoners. So many had died from the hard labor that guards had tossed their dead bodies—the refuse from each day—into the swampy earth in front of the advancing tracks. They had then been buried under the railway bed of gravel, rails, and wooden ties that they had themselves cut from the pine forests of the nearby Ural Mountains. Dundee acted as if he hadn't any idea that he had agreed to such a trip.

"What? Vorkuta?!" he said with a bit too-exaggerated shock. "But that's the *Gulag!* I don't want to go to the *Gulag!* No, let's do an interview. I want to talk to that man over there who smells like fish."

By this point in our trip, Dundee had taken to mocking my work. Late at night on the boat, to show how simple my profession could be, he would pepper me with questions that mimicked my voice and manner: "How did your family come to America? How old are you? What do you think of Bush? Why are you a capitalist? What is unique about the American soul?"

I grimaced as Dundee walked uncertainly across the width of the boat to sit beside the fellow in the gray beard whom I had earlier decided to ignore. After a few minutes he shouted in a voice that had all heads turning our way. "Come over here—this guy has a story for you. And bring your goddamned notebook." So I decided to delay my sleep, and I joined him quickly in hopes that he wouldn't draw attention to us by shouting again.

Vladimir Antonovich Rodin's perfume of stale sweat came from two days of travel, and the scent of fish wafted from his small, brown vinyl bag. It contained Siberian white salmon that he was taking inland to Vorkuta, where he could sell it for twice the price he would get in Salekhard.

He said he was a carpenter who specialized in restoring wooden churches from the eighteenth century. He had reconditioned several of the most famous chapels in the Komi province during the 1960s and 1970s, he said. But no one cared about restoration or antiquities anymore. He couldn't even find the tools to do the job properly.

"I want to do a job with my whole soul in it," he said. "To make a beautiful house of wood—well, that is part of the Russian soul. Or I'd like to lay bricks to build a home as if I were writing a story about my history.

A few years ago I restored a church that had been built in 1714 under the order of Peter the First. It is beautiful. But people don't want quality anymore. I am tired of being just a nuisance. I want to live in a society where I am valued as an individual—as a craftsman. Your society doesn't need fools, but it is fools that are the primary ingredient in Russian society."

Dundee winked at me. His joke had turned into a chat with another one of the Soviet Union's philosopher victims.

Rodin reached into his jacket pocket and pulled out a worn advertisement from the magazine *Ogonyok*. Canadian women were seeking husbands, and he had applied. He wanted to know my opinion. Could he make it in America at age fifty-six?

"Look at me," said Rodin, giving me some time to look into his eyes, which were clear and intelligent, searching and pathetic. "Do I look like someone who could make it in the West?"

In a Russia at sea, a visiting Westerner is often asked by individuals like Rodin to help provide navigation. But I was rarely confident of the answers I should provide. Did one encourage the craftsman, saying that even a fifty-six-year-old man could make it in the West if he had drive and talent? Or did I tactfully discourage him and remark on his potential in a democratic Russia?

Luckily, Rodin changed the subject himself as the boat reached the harbor where we would board a bus bound for the Labytnangi train station. "You see that bridge?" said Rodin, pointing to a rickety steel-and-wood structure that crossed one of the Ob's many tributaries. "It was built in 1941. Before that, the prisoners simply laid the tracks over the frozen river so that prisoners could be more quickly transported north to the camps. Just before the thaw, they would remove the tracks and the prisoners would continue to come in barges. Have you read Jack London?"

Rodin offered the abrupt change of subject as we boarded the bus. He raised his voice so that everyone around could see that he was instructing a foreigner. He reveled in the legitimacy and importance bestowed upon him by my attention.

"Jack London's works were published in fourteen volumes here, and I have read them all three times," he said. "You can read his books in a breath. The powers-that-be allowed Jack London to be published because he seemed socialist to them—but I liked his stories because they were well-constructed adventure tales."

I later learned that Jack London was one of the most published authors during the Soviet Union's seventy-four-year life. Some 17 million copies of his books had appeared. Russians, and particularly Siberians, loved him because of the way he described man's struggle with nature.

Lenin's wife, Nadezhda Krupskaya, even chose to read to her husband from Jack London's *Love of Life* as he lay on his deathbed. It was an odd choice, the tale of a dying man wandering through the desolate Arctic wastes after being deserted by a comrade. The man had seen little to bring him comfort—wolves, caribou, a bear; and then the bones of his companion, picked clean by the wolves. But Krupskaya wrote in her memoirs that Lenin was "extraordinarily pleased" with the story. She read more to him the following day—and London's work would be Lenin's last memory.

I asked Rodin what his favorite London story had been.

"It wasn't the one Krupskaya read," he said. "No, I liked *Martin Eden* far better—it reminded me of myself."

Martin Eden was autobiographical London. Both Eden and London had been simple men who had grown frustrated in their self-guided search for knowledge. London had been a common laborer and Eden a sailor, but both had early experiences with the sea. Eden, like London, liked to write, although he had less success at it. And both committed suicide. The socialist view of Eden and London was simple—they were alienated individualists destroyed by their bourgeois societies.

"Right now you can grow tired of life the way that Martin Eden did," said Rodin. "In the last pages of the book, he went diving, diving, diving as deep as he could, until he couldn't breathe anymore. Soviet scholars wrote entire works about him. They made his suicide ideological—a natural death in a capitalist society. They said that's what happens to a good working-class man who tries to get up the ladder. But Jack London wasn't so silly. I think he wrote a story about us all."

By the time we left the bus, our Martin Eden had adopted us as his own. He insisted on buying our train tickets to Vorkuta—twelve rubles each (about thirty cents at the black-market rate of the time). He then guided us to the stationmaster's room for a cup of tea. He gained entrance by explaining our importance, thus underlining his own. We sat at the large wooden desk of the stationmaster and sipped tea while waiting two hours for the train's departure.

"I am like Martin Eden," he said, "but I am twice as old as he was. Martin Eden liked to study, and I also want to learn. I once dreamed of putting on a sailor's uniform and going to a merchant marine college, and Martin Eden dreamed of the same thing. I grew up without a mother and father and was a barefoot child on the shores of the water. Just like Martin Eden."

"But surely you don't want to kill yourself," I said.

"In 1938," he said, "my grandfather killed himself with a shotgun. So it is in my family. They say he got too drunk. But I think he killed himself because they had taken his son, who was my father, away to the camps."

Rodin's father had been the chief judge in the city of Kirov, during a time when all such intellectuals were held in suspicion. "Mother had a lover who was responsible for sending people to the camps," Rodin said.

"Maybe he wanted to get rid of my father. That's the way things happened then. So I grew up in a boarding school in Novosibirsk, and I begged on the streets for my food."

The conversation almost caused us to miss the train, and we ran down the tracks and jumped onto the already moving carriage. As soon as we sat down on the hard wooden seats, our Martin Eden continued to hold court. But now he had chosen fellow Russians as his students. He read to them from a book he had brought along, having gained stature in their eyes from his Western pupils. We excused ourselves and sat elsewhere.

At the next stop the train picked up a couple of backpackers carrying birch boughs for their saunas back home. A fisherman boarded with his catch in a basket, and a woman climbed on with a plastic bag full of mushrooms on one arm and a child on the other. I used the chance to run to the front of the train and convince the engineer to take us aboard with him. Dundee puffed and swore at me as we climbed up the steel ladder into the engine room of the already-moving train. By now he was hung over.

"Get away to the devil's grandmother!" crackled a voice over the loud-speaker in the engineer's cabin. That was the order for Nikolai Choyvyba, the fifty-two-year-old engineer, to give his 2,000-horsepower diesel engine gas and roll out of the station.

But after chugging along for just a couple of miles, Choyvyba cursed, as he had to apply the brakes and slow down to less than ten miles per hour. The tracks were too old and uneven in many spots to allow him to travel any faster through the Urals from Asia to Europe. His engines were powerful enough to make the 150-mile trip in two hours, but it would take twelve.

"They should dig up all the tracks and start all over again," complained Choyvyba, sticking his blackened fingers into a jar of pickled mushrooms and plopping a particularly large one into his mouth. "But I wonder what they would find. They say there is a body buried underneath every tie. Sometimes you can almost feel them under the wheels."

"Whom can you feel?" I asked mischievously.

"Komsomol members, of course," he said. Communist literature for years had it that volunteers from the Communist Youth League, Komsomol, had done the primary work in building the railway. One stop, just before we pulled into the station at Kharp, even had the original black locomotive in which the Komsomol volunteers were said to have made the first trip.

"Look over there," said Choyvyba. "There's even a Komsomol camp." He pointed in back of the Kharp station, where one of the most notorious of the transit camps for Gulag prisoners had been. Its inmates had cut the timber for the railway ties. In its place Kharp now had a modern maximum-security prison for the most dangerous of criminals. They were still forced labor, but now they produced prefabricated concrete slabs for construction—some of the slabs rested beside our train on flatbed railway cars.

As we pulled away, we gradually came nearer to the Ural Mountains, the natural dividing line between Europe and Asia. The landscape around us was fresh and green. Cold, clean creeks ran through the permafrost and tundra, with lush shrubbery everywhere. But the only trees were telephone and power poles, many of them toppled or lying at a precarious diagonal slant, holding unsteadily to ground where they could be sunk only a couple of feet into the permanently frozen earth.

It was the end of July, but the crisp air suggested that winter wasn't far off. The first snows often came in August. Choyvyba could hardly wait. He had come to Siberia as a romantic adventurer twenty years ago, drawn partly by the money but also by his belief that Siberia's riches would make it a sort of Russian Switzerland. That was before he knew much about Switzerland, he said.

The chief and his assistant, their elbows resting out opposite windows high above the tracks, looked like two good ol' boys riding down Highway 80 in their eighteen-wheelers. The older Nikolai looked worn and wise. He confidently carried out his tasks with the second nature of the veteran. His face was clean-shaven, and his blue shirt bulged with a small potbelly. His assistant was gaunt. His reddish-brown two-day growth of beard could not hide the gray pallor of his skin. He was meticulous and nervous about each of his small tasks.

"The snow reaches up to here during the winter," said Choyvyba, sticking his hand out the window more than ten feet above the ground. "You have absolutely no wind most of the time, and it hits twenty-five or thirty degrees below zero on a warm day. Your spit freezes before it can hit the ground. Sometimes the snow is higher than this engine—it's like driving in a tunnel. The window can be so packed with snow that you just go forward and hope for the best. But it's still easier than in the spring, when the land turns soft and the tracks sink and need repairs. That's when you really have to watch out."

Pay differentials that made his income more than double that of railroad engineers outside Siberia drew Choyvyba to the region, but the lost worth of the ruble had made them inconsequential. What difference did it make if a Siberian had a hundred or a hundred thousand units of a worthless currency? They both agreed that without the economic incentive there wasn't much reason to stay in Siberia anymore. All their friends were talking about leaving, but so far few had gone.

And what about Choyvyba? Why did he stay?

"It's my fate," he said.

And there it was again. Fate. It seemed to creep into the best households, take hold of the most optimistic minds, and hang like a noose around the necks of those who might otherwise have shown initiative. Few in Siberia seemed to have a destiny, but everyone had a fate.

The train stopped at the most unpredictable places, unmarked stops that only the practiced engineer would know. Old men boarded with fishing poles, and more women with buckets of mushrooms. In a region with so little summer, the locals didn't miss a minute of it.

When I returned to my carriage, it had grown crowded and pungent. The carriage smelled of campfire, fish, birch boughs, dirty socks, raw fish, vodka, mushrooms, and cigarette smoke. The atmosphere was that of a bustling café. Each carriage was subdivided into several compartments that consisted of facing benches on the lowest level, and then two additional levels of hard wooden bunks. The noise from all of them melded in a surprisingly pleasant concert—men snoring, women scolding their children, poker players laughing, mountain climbers playing the guitar and singing, and lovers engrossed in private conversations.

I was most drawn to the singing climbers, whose mood and songs were oddly somber. They had just returned from a short climb to a spot in the Urals where eight of their friends had died in an avalanche in 1988. They had placed a plaque near the spot of the deaths, and now they were returning to their homes in Syktyvkar, the capital of the nearby Komi province.

Two guitarists sat at the center of a circle of friends. One, Aleksandr Mostrov, was twenty-one and had been on the climb when his friends died. Their names were engraved on his beat-up Bulgarian guitar. (He wanted a new one, but there was a shortage.) He had dark hair, wire-rimmed glasses, and the beginnings of a mustache. He was wearing black. The other, Aleksei Deyukov, was a year younger. He was blond and nervous—he knew of the disaster only from the stories of those who had been there. Their voices harmonized in a tune dedicated to their fallen comrades:

> Good-bye to you all, good-bye, don't promise to write,
> Just promise to remember, and to keep the fire aflame
> See you after you have made the ascent,
> See you on the next mountain
>
> And there is nothing, neither gold nor ore,
> Just a road that's far too steep,
> And your heart is pounding and the snowstorm is
>   frightening
> And your friend is too dear and hell's too close . . .

When I asked Aleksandr Mostrov to recount the disaster, the members of the climbing party gathered around and leaned over from bunks where they had been sleeping. No one had dared retell the story while they were on the mountain. For most, it was the first time they had heard the details.

The October day had been particularly cold, he said, but the sun was shining, so they had decided to make a climb of the highest level of difficulty. One of Siberia's sudden storms had struck in the late afternoon. Aleksandr's group had dug in where they were, pitching tents in a spot unguarded from the wind. A second group had chosen a ravine that was warmer but ultimately far more dangerous.

"It was seven P.M., but it was very cold, so we were already in our sleeping bags," said Aleksandr. "The entrance to our tent opened in a whoosh of wind. It opened four times, although we had tied it in knots. Something supernatural was happening and we couldn't sleep."

"We heard the roar of the snow and the cries," said Aleksandr. "They shouted, 'Avalanche!' We thought they were joking. Then their voices were cut off—as if someone had suddenly gagged them. We ran to the place where they were camped, and it had been flattened."

They searched for an hour before finding three dead bodies. Their leader called off the search, assuming all had died. He feared that the buildup of more snow on the ridge could result in another avalanche. So the search party didn't return until morning for the others. "We began to pull out the bodies one by one," said Aleksandr. "But as soon as we got the first two out, we heard a voice groaning under the snow. So we worked faster. Someone was alive! He was curled up with his knees to his face— what we are taught to do to create a space of oxygen in which to breathe. He was crazy when we got to him—and his hands were stiff as ice."

A rescue helicopter took the boy to Vorkuta. He survived, but the disaster had killed eight others—and the club. This trip had been their first outing since then. "Perhaps we could start again now," said Aleksandr. "But now we can't find the food we would need—the canned meat, the dried soup in packets, the chocolate, and the powdered milk. None of it is available."

Aleksandr toyed with a crucifix that hung around his neck. It looked new. I asked him whether he had been a member of the Young Pioneers, the Communist youth group. "From age six to age ten I was an Octobrist; from age eleven to age fourteen I was a Young Pioneer; and at age fourteen I became a member of the Komsomol. I quit believing because of the Afghanistan War. When I was fourteen I was sure we had been told the truth, that the Americans would set up bases in Afghanistan and aim missiles at us from there if we didn't put our troops there. But thanks to Glasnost we saw none of that was true. Afghanistan was the breaking point for most young people.

"They said they wanted to make Afghanistan Communist—from feudalism straight to Communism." He laughed. "I wonder what Marx would have said about that? Now we don't want to poke our noses into politics any longer. Politics is only cheating. They promise one thing and do another. Who knows when democracy will disappear? If our country goes another step down, the normal person won't be able to live. Then there will be a revolution. Maybe a civil war. The Russians will then find another dictator."

The climbers seemed embarrassed when they talked about what they had once believed so strongly. They sought confirmation for each small piece of knowledge they had about America. Seventy-four years of lies had left them no longer able confidently to separate falsehood from truth.

"Do whites kill blacks in America?"

"Are blacks kept poor on purpose by the ruling class?"

"Is there a drug problem everywhere in America?"

"Do Jews control all the newspapers and banks?"

Aleksei didn't want me to think his life had been bad. "We had a happy childhood—each of us," he said. "That was when we still believed our country was the mightiest and richest. I was sure that I would be unemployed in America. I would be living in the dumpyard with nothing to eat but what I could dig up. We felt lucky to be Russian. We knew your Ku Klux Klan was everywhere, killing blacks. I remember in our school class— we gathered our pocket money to send to poor American children."

They all laughed at this memory. They had all contributed. They weren't surprised that I hadn't heard about the fund-raising or that I didn't know what had become of their money.

"What could they have done with our rubles?" said one of the boys from the top bunk, laughing. "They could only continue to starve with them."

They all laughed again.

Aleksandr began to play with his crucifix again. "I believe in God now," he said. "That's not because I'm sure of this belief, but because there is nothing else to believe in. Lenin and Marx said there wasn't a God—so there was no God. I thought, that can't be. It is too primitive to look at man as pieces of fat molecules. A man can't live if he doesn't have a soul. And that soul doesn't come from Marx and Engels, but from God. Don't you agree?"

Again they looked to me for confirmation. Aleksandr seemed more relieved than pleased when I told him that I shared his belief. He wouldn't have to question his new faith in God—at least not yet.

"I was baptized six months ago," he said. "Many young people are being baptized now. There were about thirty on the Sunday I was baptized. One man was fifty years old—but it's mostly young people."

Aleksei, his arm around his new wife, looked at her as he talked to me. "We believe in God, too. But it's too fashionable now to be baptized. I don't want to ride another wave. Everyone begins to believe in God without seeing what is really behind their beliefs. Some just want a cross on their chest—it makes them feel more secure."

One of the members of the group, who I was told only then was an Afghan war veteran, announced that he wanted to sing a song for me before I left their compartment. He had remained silent until that moment. He wouldn't talk about the war, but the tune he chose was from the front, and it was of the *blatnoi* style—the blackest backstreet jargon about the bloodiest times in a young Russian life.

> *The leaves are falling off the trees,*
> *Dancing this way and that way and back,*
> *Autumn has come, the month of October,*
> *Slushy weather . . .*
>
> *There are airplanes flying overhead,*
> *Bombers, honey barrels, trying to cover us*
> *with earth or shit,*
> *Ukrainian shit, best kind there is . . .*
>
> *And myself, a young lad aged, say, seventeen,*
> *eighteen, maybe twenty, maybe thirty,*
> *don't know myself*
> *Lie there with my leg torn off, all the way,*
> *Up to my neck*
> *My eye in my pocket, just pretending . . .*

The song drifted into the weird hallucinations of a boy dying on the front, sung in a devil-may-care tone. There was a woman in a blue dress, running across the field with a speedometer in her teeth, and a six-foot-nine-inch soldier with two left boots. And a nurse, Marka, who came to bandage the injured boy. And then the song ended abruptly:

> *And here I am in the sick bay,*
> *Twisting a hair on my gut,*
> *The longest one, the blackest one,*
> *The dirtiest one.*

The train stopped at a whistle-stop called Yeletsky, a station about eighty kilometers from Vorkuta. That strangely excited all on board. When I looked out my window, dozens of passengers dashed across five sets of tracks, with empty baskets and bags in their hands, toward a small village of flat, wooden, barrack-like houses.

I followed them into the Siberian frontier town. It had been created as a state dairy farm about twenty years earlier. I imagined an anonymous central planner armed with a map that showed him that this was a good spot from which to supply Vorkuta and other nearby villages. He must have had little knowledge of climate.

The weather-beaten wooden homes had decayed; some had large pieces of wall missing where their residents had patched them with whatever material they had found—thick sheets of plastic, pieces of tar board and cardboard nailed to the siding. As everywhere in the far north, the buildings' ground floors were built three to four feet off the ground to keep them warmer and off the permafrost. But unlike those in Salekhard, there was no cosmetic paneling here to hide the dead space underneath. Instead it was filled with garbage—discarded furniture and scrap metal.

There were two new cinderblock buildings. No one troubled to apply a final coat of plaster or paint, so they looked unfinished—blocks haphazardly placed in a lopsided construction. The wiring was external, and it ran in a wild black spaghetti out of windows and along the building's outer walls, stretching to the power poles standing beside the tracks.

Children played in the garbage that lay everywhere. Two young boys climbed into an abandoned railway car that was toppled, rusted and corroding. Two girls used a stray cement slab as a slide to amuse their dolls. They gathered water from a stagnant pool in their plastic buckets, then poured it over the slab's surface to clean off the mud so they could give their dolls a ride. "Wheee . . ."

As I was watching the girls, our Martin Eden walked up to me. He was back from the village, carrying a huge jar of blackberry juice, a bagful of canned meat, and two sorts of bread! He revealed the reason for the general excitement over this godforsaken town: its store was one of the best-stocked in the region. Some odd quirk of central planning, perhaps intended to look after weary northern travelers, had ensured that the shop was filled with goods that were rationed elsewhere. Passengers weren't even required to show ration cards for most products. The train passengers flocked to it like a suburban crowd to a close-out sale.

So who lived in the village?

"Drifters," said Martin Eden. "People who run away from sad lives, broken marriages, fugitives from the law and fugitives from family responsibility. What they have here is the chance to earn lots of money and escape responsibility. Then they move on to another such place. Everything is temporary in this part of the world. People live in a place until it is ruined and then they move on. You fill up one toilet with your shit and then you move on to the next one."

The train sat for another two hours while everyone shopped then returned to their seats in the train and ate. In a region of so many inconveniences, the delay didn't bother anyone. Everyone seemed to be having a good time—a grandmother cut off pieces of freshly caught raw fish for her three granddaughters (making the fish more palatable with a thick coat of salt), two women walked into the nearby tundra looking for berries, and the men played cards. The background music was the low roar of snoring from the upper bunks.

After we began to roll again, I accepted an invitation from a group of miners to join their card game, called "Fool." They had only met each other on the train, but after ten hours they acted like old friends. They all seemed to take turns losing to a handsome, swarthy miner named Vasily, whose knowing eyes shifted slowly to each of his opponents as he quickly proved himself their superior.

"He's been riding this train so long that his fingers are worn out from those bloody cards," said one of the perpetual losers. "And if he's not playing cards, he's playing chess. He doesn't lose at that, either."

Vasily smiled. "It all depends on your memory. I can mechanically remember the cards that have been drawn."

Vasily had landed in Vorkuta, like so many of its residents, by chance. In 1976 his construction team had been shipped off from the Ukraine for two years of work in Iraq. It had been an attractive job, where they could earn some hard currency. The KGB had banned Vasily from joining them, however, because his grandfather-in-law lived in America. So he had taken odd jobs—one being the repair of an electrical station in nearby Narilsk.

"I joined the chess club, I met a girl and I never left," said Vasily. He had grown accustomed to the high salaries and the vacation bonuses. At that time, a man could earn two or three times more in Vorkuta than anywhere else in the Soviet Union.

Another miner, Mikhail Grupina, was slim and fidgety. He never won against Vasily's cool hand. He said he had stayed in Vorkuta after he had finished his military service there. He wasn't about to return to the small farming village near Kiev where he had been raised. "Let all those fucking cows die," he said. "I would have had to work for fifteen years to buy a house in the village, where all the roads were dirt and mud and the cows weren't giving milk."

But he said Vorkuta wasn't much of a place to live unless you needed to escape an unwanted wife or bill collectors. "No one will follow you to Vorkuta," he said. "We don't have enough sun or enough vitamins. Vorkutans are all white in the face. Often we have no apples or other fruit—just lots of cabbage and potatoes."

A young man sitting across the aisle objected in an excited stammer. "Muh–muh–my father was a prisoner in Vorkuta—he had a fuh–fight with his keh–keh–commander during the war. So he was sent to the camps. I was beh–born in Vorkuta, and I like the climate. I'm a reh–reh–romantic by nature."

His young and pretty girlfriend tried to shut him up. He always stammered when he was nervous, she said. But the stammerer wouldn't stop.

"I like the neh–north of Siberia because it is teh–teh–troublesome and deh–deh–dangerous to live there. The meh–more deh–deh–difficult life is, the meh–more I like it."

He relished how the sun didn't go down in Vorkuta at all in July and how it stayed dark all day for two months during the winter. Then he spoke of the lore of Vorkuta. His father, who had helped build the Vorkuta electrical station when he was a prisoner, said that 150 men had been buried alive when a trench they were working in caved in on them. Prisoners had been prevented by armed guards from climbing in to save them. "Meh–my father could hear them under the soil, alive and keh–crying for help."

The stammerer's Western jeans and expensive boots suggested he was well-off. He would only say that he had once worked in the mines, but now he wasn't working anywhere.

The cardplayers understood the code, and they whispered to me with derision that he was a *spekulant*—a speculator trading goods on the black market.

"Anything that is meh–missing in the shops, I can get it for you," he said quite proudly. The more he spoke, the less he stammered. "I *am* a speculator. I handle any product, earning more on some, less on others. You would call me a beh–businessman, but we have not come that far yet."

The card players grew angry. Grupina said that the speculator caused shortages by bribing the managers of state shops so they would sell him fish, for instance, which he would then resell to the private market.

"I deh–don't deh–deal in fish," the speculator countered.

But did he bribe shopkeepers?

"Yes—of course," he said. "I beh–buy things that way every day. I have my people at the shops. That's how they make their living. They earn more, I earn more and the vendors at the private market earn more and the peh–people have their products. It may be illegal, but my job wouldn't exist if the economy were normal. I want the situation to be normalized so that I can weh–work normally and honestly—as a beh–beh–businessman."

He smiled.

"But there's not much danger of that happening for a while yet."

The train approached Vorkuta, which had been closed to Westerners until 1990. It rose like a mirage out of the permafrost. The hour was past midnight, but the sun still cast a haze through a layer of silver clouds that formed a high ceiling over the city. As I began to climb off the train, a man limped quickly behind me and shouted, "American! American!" He was a Gypsy, the son of a Gulag survivor. He had worked in the coal mines from the time he was eighteen until 1988, when a collapsing shaft had taken his leg and nearly his life.

He pulled up his pants to show me his artificial leg. It belonged in an antiques shop—an unvarnished piece of dark pine held together by heavy metal hinges and reinforced by thick leather straps. He pulled tools out of his pocket; he carried them everywhere to perform the frequent repairs needed to keep the leg going. He had some replacement screws for the hinges, a small hammer, and a screwdriver.

He wanted to put an advertisement in my newspaper so that an American might buy him a better leg. He had received a more modern, plastic device from a hospital in the Komi province, but it had never fit right and the doctors refused to give him another one. "That's our system," he said. "It cares so little about safety that it can take your leg, and it cares so little about quality that it can't make you a new one."

When I arrived at my Vorkuta hotel, our Russian organizers warned me that the reception desk had already been told to inform the KGB upon my arrival. "They are expecting you," said one of our organizers. "You are the only member of the expedition whom they asked about by name."

The Russians on our expedition seemed a little troubled, but mostly amused—and a little curious. They told me these stories in tones of voice that suggested that they were beginning to wonder themselves if I was a CIA plant. Why else would the KGB be so interested in me?

I was flattered and a little baffled by all the attention.

Chapter 22:

STALIN'S ASSASSIN

I am opening my soul for the first and last time. I might not have long to live.

—OLGA PETROVNA, *Gulag survivor*

Olga Petrovna Vereiskaya limped into the living room, carrying a kitchen chair with one of her thick, strong arms. She placed it in front of the wall, which was decorated with a grandson's Arnold Schwarzenegger poster. On the opposite wall, beside an oak veneer cabinet, hung a younger grandson's picture of Donald Duck.

Olga's decade of forced labor had left her with a bad leg, but she moved with energy and purpose despite her eighty-one years, twelve of which she had spent in Vorkuta's camps. Her gray hair was uncombed, and curled wildly in random wisps, but her eyes were clear and young. Olga limped back to bring another chair for Dundee, and then she sat in front of us on an armchair that had molded itself over the years to her frame.

Her smile was flirtatious even though several teeth were missing on both sides of her mouth. The curious result was a perfectly balanced smile set under high cheekbones.

Olga Petrovna's name was one of several on a list that had been given me of Gulag survivors who were still living in Vorkuta. I asked what crime she had been charged with at the time of her arrest.

"Most people will tell you that they were sent to Vorkuta for no good reason," said Olga Petrovna. "But I was sent here for a reason. I was involved in an attempt to assassinate Stalin."

The old woman smiled. I was dumbfounded. None of the hundreds of historians who had studied the Stalin period had ever come up with convincing evidence of an assassination attempt. Most concluded none had ever taken place. Olga looked at me with the self-satisfaction of a seductress who knew that she had won a new devotee. She proceeded to lay out her story in rich detail.

"The plan was that I would plant a bomb in a tribune at the House of the Soviets [on the territory of the Kremlin], where Stalin was to speak before a special Congress mostly of Central Committee members, secretaries and ministers," she said. Olga described it as a preparatory meeting in early 1936 for a future Party Congress.

She took a piece of paper out of my notebook and made a drawing of the bomb—a device she said was the size of my mini-recorder, with a linear timing apparatus that she was to set on thirty minutes. Stalin was expected to speak, as usual, for about forty minutes. The chief plotter was a KGB man responsible for Kremlin security, whose first name she didn't remember. His nickname was Akopshik, she said, and his patronymic and family names were Ovetisyanovich Avanesov. He had arranged for the bomb to be smuggled to her, and he would also be the one to activate the device shortly before the speech was to begin.

Olga described in meticulous detail how she had slipped the small bomb, with its slightly rounded back and flat face, into a secret compartment that had been built into the tribune. The compartment panel would then slide closed. "It was designed so that there would be nothing visible even if you looked straight at it," she said. The device, which would be at Stalin's chest level, was engineered so that its explosive force would hit and kill just one man—Stalin.

Olga looked directly into my eyes as she described the evening of Stalin's speech. She sat with the Ukrainian delegation, she said, where most of Stalin's enemies were concentrated. But instead of hearing Stalin's words, she was slowly counting off the seconds before the bomb was to go off. "But I felt totally calm," she said. "I didn't think I was nervous at all, but then I looked down at the palms of my hands and they were bleeding. I had clenched them so hard that my nails had pierced the skin."

I asked if the bomb went off, but Olga wasn't listening to my questions. She would usually begin talking before Dundee had a chance to translate whatever I was asking. She had her own script, and she stuck to it no matter what I asked. Her sentences were fired in bursts. She rattled off detailed descriptions of places and persons—knowledge available only to someone close to Bolshevik movers and shakers. I couldn't believe that I had opened an unwritten chapter of Soviet history.

I finally squeezed in a question that she heard. Why did she want to kill Stalin? How did this twenty-six-year-old woman find herself in the middle of such a conspiracy?

She took me back to her childhood as the daughter of a family so Bolshevist that her grandfather voluntarily turned over his factory to the workers immediately after the Revolution. Her father had been a chemist and director of a leading institute. Yet she also had noble blood. She had lived in Romania as a teenager, with an aunt named Ripnina, a name from the old Russian nobility. Her uncle was a diplomat in Bucharest, she said. (I later confirmed that a diplomat, actually a prince, named Ripnin had served in the Foreign Office during that time in the division that was responsible for Romania, one of the many small facts in Olga's story that I was able to check out later.) Her husband, who had been nearly twenty years older than she was, had friends in Stalin's inner circle and was a military officer.

Olga Petrovna figured it was a combination of these family contacts, Bolshevik breeding, and her own good looks that made her a favorite among Communist officials. When she returned as a young woman to Moscow, with the added sophistication of having lived in a diplomatic community abroad, many Communist officials—including Stalin himself—had flirted with her. She attended their parties, visited their dachas, and eventually landed a job with the Foreign Ministry, a natural move for a woman of her background.

Olga's background also brought her into close and friendly contact with another woman of solid Bolshevik upbringing, Nadezhda Alliluyeva, who became Stalin's second wife, in 1919, at the age of eighteen. Stalin was twenty-two years older than she was. Olga said she actively turned against Stalin after he murdered Nadezhda, on November 9, 1932.

I sat forward on the kitchen chair, under the Donald Duck poster, as she hit me with that additional surprise. Most historians have attributed Nadezhda's death to suicide, but rumors have persisted that Stalin murdered a wife who on several occasions tried to save her young friends from his increasing repressions.

What is known is that on November 8, 1932, a drunken and angry Stalin insulted and cursed his wife during a dinner celebrating the fifteenth anniversary of the Revolution. One report says he threw the ashes of his cigarette down her dress. Nadezhda, who had already grown distant from Stalin, left the dinner after this dispute for their small home in the Kremlin. By four in the morning she was dead. There are a number of versions about what happened during the hours between the time she left the party and when she was found dead. One is that Nadezhda killed herself with her brother's gun, driven to desperation by her despotic husband. The most dramatic version came indirectly from Nadezhda's maid, that Stalin shot his own wife after a fight during which he labeled her as bourgeois and she suggested he was a revolutionary fraud. What is certain is that for years thereafter Stalin blamed those close to Nadezhda for turning his wife against him.

I wondered why Olga was so certain that Stalin had either killed his wife or had her killed. "She wasn't the sort of woman who could have gone and killed herself. She wasn't the sort of women who kills herself. I met her on the day she was said to have committed suicide and asked if she had spoken to him [Stalin]. We had asked her to intervene with him to stop his political excesses. She said she had written him a letter. We knew he visited her that evening. They were already living separate lives at that time."

Nadezhda's death was the event that had moved Olga, but she said most of the others involved in the assassination attempt had begun plotting two years later, following the death in December 1934 of Sergei Kirov, Stalin's rival for power and a favorite of the Old Bolsheviks. They had been together for years, and they saw that Stalin was taking their Revolution in the wrong direction. After hearing Olga complain privately for a long time about Stalin, Stanislav Kosior, a Communist leader in the Ukraine, spoke to her privately during a visit she made to Kiev in 1935. "Do you want to help us get rid of *him?*" Kosior asked.

"Kosior never said Stalin's name," said Olga. "But I knew what he was talking about. In those days, after Kirov's death, everyone knew there was a struggle going on." She then rattled off a list of names of co-conspirators that I scribbled down and would discuss with her in some detail later. "There were not many of us who participated in the actual assassination attempt. And only one person—security chief Avanesov—knew what each person was doing," she said. "But many would have been happy if it had worked. Those who took part were all arrested later on other charges—nothing to do with the bombing."

I wondered what had gone wrong. Had the bomb failed?

The bomb exploded, she said, but too late. It went off more than ten minutes after the speech was over. Stalin had just left the stage and was behind the curtains, and most of the crowd was gone as well. She said a handful of stragglers were hit by splinters. She suspected that Avanesov had reset the timer before he activated it. "Perhaps he got cold feet, but I really don't know," she said. "I only know it didn't explode when it should have. But Avanesov was held responsible for the explosion. They arrested him immediately afterward."

Shortly after the assassination attempt, Olga Petrovna returned to Budapest, where she worked as a secretary in the Soviet Embassy. "We had only seven people in the embassy at the time, so it was an important job—more than just a secretary," she said.

In November 1937 she returned to visit her husband, who had remained behind in Moscow. Olga was pregnant and due to deliver their child the following February. She remembered the specific date of her arrest, November 18, because it was the birthday of a friend. Her husband sent the bags ahead in a car and the couple walked across a bridge from the Kiev train station toward home. That was when three men in a black sedan stopped and arrested her. She was convinced her husband had set her up—driven by jealousy. Olga said with a flirtatious blush that she was quite pretty and had any number of admirers.

The key evidence against her was her husband's report that she hadn't come home on the evening before the assassination attempt. He had long believed she had spent the evening with another man, which was part of the reason he remembered the day so clearly. But Olga had instead spent the night at the House of the Soviets after it had been locked up so she could quietly place the bomb in the tribune that had been specially constructed by another of the conspirators.

Olga said she hadn't dared to tell her husband the truth at the time, and he didn't believe her girlfriend's story that they had spent the evening together. Olga had had easy access to the House of the Soviets through this friend, Avanesov's daughter, who worked there. They both had also danced in a folkloric group that practiced there often. "My face was known," she said.

What had finally done her in, she learned later, were Avanesov's ramblings after interrogators broke him. "They tortured him, but he didn't confess for a long time. After a year, he went crazy and he started to cry out names. Mine was one of them. . . . After my arrest I was sentenced very quickly, on three different charges," she said. "One charge I would accept—that was the assassination charge, that I participated in planning his [Stalin's] removal. But the other two, espionage and subversive activities against the State, those I didn't accept."

Olga talked for two and a half hours, until I had to leave for another appointment. I asked her if I could return. She agreed, but she whispered that I shouldn't tell anyone what I had heard that day. She was afraid that remaining Stalinists might seek revenge. "This is the very first time in my life I've ever spoken about this," she said. "I don't talk, because I find it impossible to prove anything. Do you understand? For this reason I never gave interviews. I have no documents. There is absolutely nothing I can do to prove what happened."

When I reviewed my notes and tapes that evening, I had my first doubts about Olga's story, which had been so convincing while we sat before her. She had confused dates on a couple of occasions, and she refused to give names of those she said were still living who she said could confirm what she had done. Dundee, however, was convinced after this first session that Olga was the real thing. "You can tell that she knew these people, that she was inside this group," he said. "You can't make things up in that detail." Dundee was smitten by the story—and by Olga.

I took a break then from Olga to meet Vitaly Troshin, Vorkuta's chief architect. He would never have volunteered to live in Vorkuta if it hadn't been for the chance to have a senior administration position at a remarkably early age. Yet now he had become the central figure in efforts by the Memorial Society, for which he was the Vorkuta director, to turn the dismal city into an open-air memorial of statues and museums to the victims of Soviet repression.

Troshin was a Leningrad intellectual. His sparkling eyes, artistic energy, and impish smile all seemed out of place in a city of pale faces and dark demeanors. Yet he had become one of the city's most powerful figures— the man who refused to let Russians forget what had taken place there.

He had used his clout as Vorkuta's chief architect to lay out an ambitious plan to commemorate a city that was central planning gone mad. From 1928 to 1930, geologists discovered rich coal layers in and around Vorkuta. Stalin needed the coal, but no one would voluntarily live in a desolate place in the middle of the tundra, 80 miles above the Arctic Circle. So, beginning in 1934, he sent tens of thousands of political enemies, real and imagined, to Vorkuta to mine the coal in its sixty-three forced-labor camps that were—by chance—arranged in the shape of a human skull.

Starting in the 1950s, central planners began to replace the forced laborers with civilian coal miners drawn to Vorkuta by generous vacation benefits and rich bonuses that added up to nearly triple the average Soviet salary. The city had expanded by then to 200,000. Some, like Troshin, were attracted less by the money than by the chance to have jobs of significant authority at an early age. There just wasn't much contest for such positions in Vorkuta.

"In Leningrad I would have been competing with more than 300 people for my position," said Troshin. "Here there was no one. Who wanted to come here?" He had planned to put in a few years in Vorkuta and then move to a better job in a more civilized place, having management experience under his belt. But then he discovered Vorkuta's history.

Troshin was the deputy city architect when he arrived in 1986. At first he campaigned for the construction of more cheerful structures than the gray cement prefabs and cinderblock smaller buildings that made up the city. He also tried to sell the city on a garden-planting and building-painting project to make the place a little more friendly.

But no one would back Troshin's projects. In the view of most Vorkutans the ugly city was not worth the energy. And no one planned to stay there very long. Built atop the skulls and bones of its founding fathers, Vorkuta had remained the sort of cold and inhospitable place that neither paint nor gardens were likely to change. Winter meant two months a year of total darkness and temperatures that dropped as low as $-70°$ F.

Sudden blizzards blotted out all signs of life. Vorkuta was also a place of decaying former prison barracks, in which people still lived because of housing shortages. The alternative was the soulless, cement low-rises— ashen buildings against an ashen sky. Even what one didn't see in Vorkuta was disturbing—underneath its huge sewage plant, underneath a local hospital and several apartment buildings on the town's outskirts, were the unmarked graves and cemeteries of the prison camps.

One day, while looking through archives for ideas that he could draw from history, Troshin discovered a treasure trove that Vorkuta's prisoners had left behind: a wealth of architectural drawings and paintings that were creative and visionary. "They were brilliant, works of genius," Troshin said. "I hadn't known such talent was in the camps."

He investigated further and discovered that some of the Soviet Union's leading lights had lived and died in Vorkuta's labor camps. "The cultural level here was much higher then than now," he said. The local theater offered performances by prisoners who were well-known actors and actresses, in plays written and directed by other prisoners. The audiences were mostly guards and administrators. Senior administrators were said to have picked out favorite performers, particularly beautiful women, and protected them, perhaps for the price of an affair.

Troshin slowly drew up plans to ensure that Vorkuta's roots weren't forgotten. He raised money from local companies, many of which had once exploited the forced labor. He held artistic competitions to create schemes for a number of different sites. One hill would be cut open in the shape of a broad cross. Its white marble walls would be engraved with the names of Vorkuta's victims—a grander and more ghostly version of Washington's Vietnam memorial. On another hill, white stone would be carved to give the impression of endless numbers of bodies trying to escape from their graves.

And on the outside of town, near mass graves for coal miners massacred during the Vorkuta uprising of 1953, a well-known Russian artist would sculpt a giant granite statue called "Raped Russia," a fractured woman with chunks missing from her face, torso, and breasts. A row of sixteen small bronze statues of prisoners with their hands tied behind their backs would line the promenade that led up to her from the existing cemetery of wooden crosses, marked only with the prisoners' numbers.

Troshin spoke about his work as a mission, one that he would continue within the Memorial Society even if one day he quit as Vorkuta's chief architect. Until Russians came to terms with their past, he said, they had no hope of tackling the future. Drawing on the mistaken impression that I was in Vorkuta on an ecological expedition, he said, "You can't clean up the environment until you look after the ecology of the soul." What had happened in Vorkuta, he said, was more than imprisonment. The whole city symbolized something dark that had touched almost every Russian family.

I was eager to return to Olga Petrovna the next day, and she seemed pleased to see me, Dundee, and my friend James, a quiet reporter who drew out those he met with his calm intelligence. She had prepared cakes and tea for us. "The big one is with nuts," she said. "Please take a big piece. I made it for you." I took a big bite and smiled at its sweet, creamy taste.

Again, Olga set the agenda. She wasn't yet ready to be cross-examined. She knew where she had left off the previous day—with her arrest—and that's where she would pick up. James and I virtually disappeared for Olga, and she focused her attention on Dundee, who was mesmerized by her story.

Olga said her interrogations hadn't begun until February, three months after her arrest, because she had been pregnant. "My daughter was born in the prison," she said. "Until that happened, they did not touch me at all." Even Stalin had rules. One was that pregnant women weren't tortured until after they had delivered their children. Another was that confessions could not be falsified, so the accused needed to be tortured until they would "confess."

"At first I refused to talk to the interrogator and they didn't have any direct evidence on me," Olga said. Avanesov had cried out her name, but apparently he hadn't provided much detail on what she had done. When Olga refused to talk or give names of others involved, she said they put her into a torture chamber known as the *banya*—the bathhouse.

"It's a small room and you cannot sit down or turn around in there," she said. "It's a special kind of torture. They start to put drops of water on you. Very slowly. One after another. I had a very strong character, and I managed to bear 124 drops. Well, at least I managed to count to 124 and then I lost consciousness. I don't know how long they did this to me. You can never feel the time."

Solzhenitsyn also wrote about this "classic torture." The method was to lock up the prisoner naked in a concrete alcove configured so that he could neither bend his knees, nor straighten up and change the position of his arms, nor turn his body. Then came the cold water dripping onto the scalp "which then ran down the body in rivulets." After that, wrote Solzhenitsyn, came unconsciousness and then often madness as well.

Olga said her interrogator was surprisingly friendly at their next meeting. He acted as if he were her friend, and he offered to help her get a lighter sentence and avoid further torture. "The interrogator said that I should put all the blame on myself, as if nobody else participated in this plot," Olga said. "In that case, he said, my sentence wouldn't be so long." It was one of the many ways an interrogator would get an initial confession, by convincing the prisoner that he was on his side.

"My interrogator acted like he really wanted to help me," Olga said. "He even helped arrange a meeting with my husband so I could find out what he had told them. That's when I found out that he had told them about the night I didn't come home. At that moment I understood that my husband had denounced me. He told me that it was easier for him that I ended up in jail—in that case nobody else would be able to make love to me. He was jealous. He was much older than I, and I had been living quite an independent life."

So she gave the interrogator the confession he had sought, hoping that would get her off easy. During their next session, however, the interrogator said his superiors wanted more names. "The more people they destroyed, the better," Olga said. The old woman frowned when I asked if she had named others—she wasn't certain anymore. She had been imprisoned with four doctors with whom she was tried. She had never seen any of them before, but they were all accused of belonging to a common criminal group.

The doctors were being connected to espionage charges against her, Olga said. The charges alleged that she had passed on information to the BBC that doctors were putting sane people into mental hospitals for political reasons—information that had been allegedly given by these doctors. She thought it probably wasn't coincidental that one of the doctors jailed with her had attended to Avanesov at the time he had broken down and spat out her name. That had made the doctor too dangerous to remain free, Olga concluded.

Olga turned to Dundee, whom she had warmed to as he translated our conversation. "Has anybody ever put needles up your fingernails? They did that to me. After that, I had a sort of breakdown. This happened to me after I had relieved myself of the child and suffered the 124 drops. They put me in a separate room where you could not harm yourself. Everything was padded. That was in Butirkakh prison. The door to the room was open slightly—just a bit—and it was stuffy, so I tried to open it a little more. But there was no door handle. So I used my fingers and put them in the small opening to pull the door towards me, and then it was slammed shut on my fingers." She lost the fingernails under which the interrogators had been putting needles, Olga said.

"When my interrogator met with me for the last time, he said my sentence had already been decided," said Olga. "He said my case was closely watched from high levels. He said I was to be shot, but eighty-four days later they changed the sentence to ten years of hard labor. To this day I don't know why. Maybe my father's friends helped."

Olga was transferred to Vorkuta in July with a group of 500 other prisoners. Despite the widespread starvation, Olga said she wasn't ever desperate for food. "You know, I never did eat much, so whatever they gave us was enough for me. Sometimes I gave part of my food to the men. The men needed food the worst."

The work she was given would be the toughest in Vorkuta. "It was written into my file: to be abolished—*Na Unichtozhenie*. That meant I should die in the camp, that I should be destroyed."

Her first job in the summer of 1938 was the building of new mines. "Mine Number 8, where I was sent, was the first and the worst of all because it passed under the Vorkuta River. So you had to work standing knee-deep in water, and the water dripped down on you from the ceiling." It reminded her of her 124-drops torture.

In 1939 Olga Petrovna was transferred to work on the new railway. She worked from six A.M. to six P.M. every day. Her job was to pour gravel into the marshy tundra to create a railway bed for the tracks. The gravel was brought on a flatbed railway car on narrow tracks built up to the point of construction. Then two prisoners would shovel the gravel off.

"It was so frustrating," Olga said. "The gravel would just disappear in the swamp. Even when you thought you had done well, you would come the next morning and nothing was left. When it was cold, we had to use a pick to break loose the frozen pieces of gravel from the platform. We never knew how many carriages would come from the gravel pit on any day. We just worked as fast as we could, because if you didn't, there was a man there with a whip.

"The soldiers were there to guard us. But they didn't pay much attention. There was nowhere for us to run to. They just stood there burning fires in barrels and keeping themselves warm. They just watched us die; about thirty prisoners died every day." She said a special team at the end of a shift would collect the bodies and throw them down there in the swamp ahead of the tracks. Then they would be buried under gravel that was shoveled off by the next shift.

"By the way, my number was L-742. For twelve years, that was my only name," said Olga.

The key to staying alive in the winter, she said, was to keep working. "If someone sat down for only a little while, he was finished," she said. "Frozen dead. You would keep working because it kept you warm. Even in the middle of a strong windstorm, you were not taken back to the barracks. In the morning they took you to work, frost or no frost."

She said that during the *purga,* the blizzards, visibility was so bad that prisoners would hold on to steel cables that were strung from their barracks to the canteen to help guide them. "If you lost hold of the cable you were as good as gone," she said. "I once lost my mitten and grabbed at the cable with my warm hand. It froze to the cable and parts of my skin stuck, glued to the steel by the frost. But bosses wouldn't relieve you from the job for that; you bandaged your hand because you had to go back to work."

After a year of working on the railway, she returned to the mines in 1940. She recalled the fire that year in Mine Number 11; 1,500 people were drowned when the bosses pumped in water to put out the flames. "None of them escaped," she said. Her other memory was of all the graves—they seemed to be everywhere. "You couldn't dig them in winter, so they would prepare them there in summertime for all the dead they expected during the winter. If they hadn't dug enough, they would burn wood on top of the soil in the winter to make the ground soft enough to dig a grave."

By 1948, when her term was over, Olga still hadn't been "abolished," but she had seen hundreds of others die. "I am a very strong person, and I can switch myself off even for two hours. I remain alive, but I don't feel any of the pain or anything around me. Very often I had to do this. I still get up at six every morning, have a cold shower, and do exercises. I can press my body off the floor twelve times even now."

Her additional sentence of five years in exile should have begun then, she said, but orders arrived that she should be held in the camps for two additional years. She didn't know from whom the orders came or why they were issued. During this time she worked primarily in a nursery that was taking care of the children born into the camps to the new wave of women from the Baltics and the West Ukraine, rounded up after World War II.

"We began to have many more babies then. There was a women's team that worked at the brick plant and men who worked there with them. The women of my age thought a lot about children. The men thought about what men thought about. That's how it happened. For example, down in the mines it was warm enough to undress. There was a part of the mine where men and women would meet. And at the brick factory, the same thing was happening."

Pregnancy also meant a year out of the mine for the mother. "It was permitted because these were healthy women and they fed the babies with their breasts," said Olga. "After one year, however, the children were taken from their mothers, who went back to work. The children were never given back—their mothers were enemies of the people. So we looked after the children. Later on, they sent some of these women away from Vorkuta, but the children didn't go with them. The women tried to jump over the barbed wire to get to their children. But the women were beaten, put in trucks, and taken away."

The children would stay in the prison nursery until they were three years old, and then they were turned over to a State orphanage, she said. Olga remarked that she never understood why women, sometimes sentenced to fifteen years, would fight for control of their children. "It was hard, but I told them that the children would have a better life without them," she said.

The evening grew late and Olga was tired. I hadn't had a chance to investigate her assassination story any more closely—she wouldn't allow it. Olga wasn't a woman who could be guided into any unwanted conversation. I asked if I could come back the next day to talk about the assassination plot. For the first time, Olga was uneasy. What I considered journalistic caution, she regarded as my suspicion of her story. She consented reluctantly to another meeting. Olga was unhappy with me for another reason, too. "You haven't finished your cake," she said. "Is something wrong with it?"

When we returned to Olga the next day, we again sat at the kitchen table. But this time there were no cakes and no linen tablecloth. Olga looked tired. Since last we had talked, I had spoken with Olga's lawyer. The lawyer insisted Olga was sane, energetic, and clearheaded. However, she had never heard Olga tell any story regarding Stalin (in deference to Olga, I didn't provide her lawyer any details).

We also met with a psychiatrist in town, who explained to us that those sent to the camps without justification often invented elaborate crimes they had committed, in order to come to terms with their punishment. After years, the crimes became real to those who had invented them. This doctor also suggested that a woman like Olga might be telling an essentially true story, but much of it could have been forgotten. Some of the story, he said, could also have been embellished or misshappen through the years or through new information drummed into her during torture. And there was always another possibility, one that Dundee still hung to at this point: that Olga's story was true.

I asked Olga about her life after leaving the camps. Did she ever meet with those who knew about her role in the assassination attempt? She spoke of a visit to Moscow in 1957, after her release and five years of additional exile in Vorkuta. Stalin was dead, and she was traveling there to apply for rehabilitation for her new husband, whom she had met in the camps. She said she had needed witnesses to confirm who she was, so she had visited two acquaintances.

Her first stop, she said, was at the home of Aleksandra Kollontai, one of the few original Bolsheviks who had survived Stalin's purges and gone on to have an illustrious diplomatic career as ambassador to Sweden and, briefly, as foreign minister. Kollontai, said Olga, had provided the testimony for the espionage charges against her, although they had hardly known each other. If it was true that Kollontai had served as an informer, it would be one explanation why she had survived while her Bolshevist colleagues were all killed or sent to camps, I thought.

Her second stop, she said, was Andrei Vyshinsky, the prosecutor general during the worst of Stalin's purges, who had convicted her and sentenced her to death.

"I visited both of them," she said. "I needed them to confirm who I was—and I wanted to show them I was still alive and not destroyed." Olga said she visited Kollontai at her home. The ambassador had been the one who had provided the evidence—false, according to Olga—that she had passed on information from Soviet doctors to the British about political prisoners being put in mental hospitals. "She even said that she had seen me in the clinic, talking to the doctors," said Olga. "But she was in Sweden the whole time. How could she have known where and what I was doing?"

Olga said this earnestly and angrily. She hated Kollontai above all others. "How could she say things like that about me? When I was working at the ministry, we never saw each other. When I went to see her at her home—she was retired by that time—we got into a big quarrel. Then her granddaughter ran into the room. She [Kollontai] said, 'Well, here is my granddaughter.' And I said to Kollontai, 'Well, it is pleasant to see her. But you put a woman into prison—and that woman had two children.' "

Olga looked at me and shook her head about Kollontai. "People like that could work in any government. They have no principles."

The granddaughter ran away crying and brought back her mother, Kollontai's daughter. "The daughter said to me, 'How dare you speak to my mother like that? My mother is a very ill woman. You shouldn't say things like that.' "

Kollontai died ten days after their argument, Olga said. She was sure that the upset from their discussion played a role.

Her visit to Vyshinsky, she said, caused even more problems. "He received me because the appointment wasn't made under my name, but under the name of my husband," she said. "But he immediately recognized me and he felt very bad. He was looking at me with wide eyes, not believing that this was me. Even in those days nobody thought I was older than thirty years of age [she was already forty-six at the time]. But Vyshinsky already knew I was in Moscow because my first visit was to Kollontai and she had told him. He didn't look very good. I said, 'Which of us has turned out better? Look at yourself and look at me. We are the same age.' "

"He said, 'Yes, five years' age difference isn't much.' He was about to be retired, but still had a government office at the *Prokuratura*. But Redenko by that time was the prosecutor general of the USSR."

She said that Vyshinsky was friendly enough and promised to help with her husband's rehabilitation. But when Olga left and walked down the stairs, she said, she was seized by men in white jackets who put her in a straitjacket and led her away to a psychiatric hospital.

After six months in the mental hospital, during which she said she avoided the worst of the drug treatments, her first husband returned to the scene to buy his former wife's freedom. She said, smiling, that he had never fully fallen out of love with her. He bribed hospital authorities to give her the papers of a woman with a name similar to her own who had died, so she was released under that woman's name.

Her first husband, a doctor, was Aleksandr Sergeyevich Osipov. He had also been a military officer. I asked if we could confirm this story with him or his relatives. Olga frowned—he had died in 1980. She didn't know where we could find any relatives.

Again, after several hours, I had to excuse myself for another appointment. She hugged me and held me for a long time. She apologized that she couldn't tell me more—she insisted I already knew more than she had ever told to anyone before.

The Vyshinsky and Kollontai visits raised the most serious elements of doubt to me thus far. The stories seemed so crazy and improbably coincidental that either Olga was relating a most amazing truth or spinning a fantastic fantasy. I discovered after leaving Vorkuta that Kollontai and Vyshinsky had both died long before 1957, when Olga said she had visited them. Kollontai had died in 1952 and Vyshinsky in 1954. When I phoned Olga from Berlin to ask about this, through Dundee, she said that it was in 1952 that she had flown to Moscow—she was mistaken during our meeting in Vorkuta. But both Kollontai and Vyshinsky were rarely in Moscow at that time—Vyshinsky worked as the United Nations ambassador and Kollontai as ambassador to Sweden.

During many weeks of investigation after I left Vorkuta, I never did track down a historical reference to Olga's central figure, the KGB security officer Avenesov. However, my research did turn up many of the names she had cited as co-conspirators. Three in particular caught my attention:

POSTYCHEV: Pavel Petrovich Postychev, an early Bolshevik and revolutionary hero, was a leading Ukrainian Party official and for a time head of agitation and propaganda. He was stripped of his posts at the February–March 1937 Central Committee Plenum. The cause of his death, in 1939 or 1940, isn't clear. Postychev, who was associated with Kirov, was known as a moderate who questioned Stalin's draconian agricultural collectivization, and he and others were known to have tried to put Stalin's purges to an end.

PETROVSKY: Pytor Grigoryevich Petrovsky, the son of a prominent Bolshevik, Grigory Petrovsky, was also among the early Party purists who was thought to have opposed Stalin. Inspired by his father, he had taken part in the storming of the Winter Palace and was director of agitation and propaganda in Leningrad. All that is known is that he was arrested in the late 1930s and died, probably in a prison camp, on September 11, 1941.

KOSIOR: Stanislav Vikentevich Kosior, who Olga said first approached her in Kiev about joining a conspiracy, was one of the highest-ranking Party officials purged during the late 1930s. He was a firmly Stalinist leader in the Ukrainian Party and was charged in 1938 with having had communications with "foreign counterrevolutionary organizations." Petrovsky later wrote that he had been present when Stalin personally interrogated Kosior, and in his "secret speech" at the 20th Party Congress, Nikita Khrushchev said Kosior had undergone "long tortures." Some say Kosior was executed on February 26, 1939, the day of his sentencing, while others say that he died in prison in 1941.

*   *   *

One of the best leads came from reading Robert Conquest's *The Great Terror.* He wrote of a rumored assassination attempt by a young noblewoman. Olga had said she was from a noble background.

I also found some evidence that an officer of the Kremlin Guard (perhaps Olga's Avanesov?) had been arrested and shot for being involved in an assassination plot. Anton Ciliga, in a 1940 book of memoirs, *The Russian Enigma,* said this in his account of a trial that took place in the summer of 1935 at which one of the most influential Party leaders, Lev Kamenev, was accused of hatching a plot against Stalin. Ciliga said thirty prisoners appeared, including "Kremlin servants and women of the former aristocracy, now wives or mistresses of the accused."

Ciliga's memoirs said the main character in bringing Kamenev to trial was the young Countess Orlova-Davydova, who had allegedly prepared the attempt on Stalin's life. However, she is said not to have lived to be tried; she was shot immediately after her arrest, ostensibly on Stalin's order. So either this attempt was totally unrelated or Olga Pavlovna is Countess Orlova. But Olga said her attempt took place in 1936, and she knew nothing of the Countess's case.

Dundee, who had been the most convinced by Olga's story, also slowly came to doubt her, as more elements couldn't be confirmed or were contradicted. "My problem was that I so much wanted to believe her," he said. "I wanted to believe that someone had tried to get away with it all. I *needed* to believe in this old woman."

I returned for one more evening's chat with Olga while I was in Vorkuta. She wore an old housedress—and her gray hair was even more tousled than usual. She said that she hadn't slept the previous night. I hoped that I hadn't been the reason. She said that her insomnia had predated my arrival by several months.

"Lately, I can't sleep in the evening," she said. "It seems the dead are coming from the ground and asking me to do something for them. The best people of our country—the colors of Russia—were liquidated, and they need something great from me. So many great people were killed." I again asked if anyone was still alive who could tell me about the bomb explosion at the 1936 meeting. Could anyone confirm that any such plot had taken place?

"My direct superior in that operation is still alive, but I will never say a word about him. Never. It was like this. We had one Georgian, one fellow from Latvia. Avanesov was Armenian and most of the rest were Ukrainians. We paid no attention to nationalities. There are ten of us who are still alive who could tell you something. But I won't talk about them. Stalin still has many supporters who might take revenge."

She said that preparation had been made for such an assassination for more than four months, including the building of the special tribune in

SIBERIAN ODYSSEY   289

which the bomb would be put. "Everyone involved had his own secret,"
she said. "Everyone had his own instructions. And no one knew what the
others were doing, except maybe Avanesov. We were all afraid of each
other, especially once they started to arrest people.

"Nothing was ever published about it. It was all hushed up. This was
an extraordinary meeting, not the normal congresses with all the advertising and publicity. This had been an unscheduled one. Just the ministers,
their secretaries, and Central Committee members, but not a General
Congress. This is why everything could be kept so quiet, as if nothing had
happened."

Olga's story remained an enigma. I doubted that she could have invented it all, but I was certain that a large part of it was either fabrication
or had been lost or fogged by the memory of an old woman who had
suffered much.

When I bade Olga farewell, she hugged me tightly. "I've opened my soul
to you for the first time and for the last time," she said. "I may not have
long to live. But I feel that a burden has been lifted from me. From having
talked to you, my soul feels young tonight."

Chapter 23:

SURVIVOR

A woman and a wife you see,
No slave as you portray,
However hard my fate may be
My heart will not give away.

—NIKOLAI NEKRASOV, *"Russian Women,"* 1826

The old woman hid her hands underneath the table. She saw that I had noticed the tattoos. What appeared to be a man's name was etched on each hand, on the skin between the thumb and the forefinger. Her left forearm had a larger tattoo that stretched from the wrist to the elbow. It showed hissing serpents wrapped around a saber. She held that arm flat so that the tattoo could rarely be seen.

I wanted to ask her about the tattoos—perhaps they were souvenirs from her years of hard labor in Vorkuta's mines. But her body language suggested that this was a subject that should wait. She smiled at me gently.

Julia had been born in 1918, only a few months after the October Revolution. She was roughly the same age as the Soviet Union, although she looked more resilient than the system under which she had been raised.

Julia began the conversation with the sort of small talk one makes only in a place like Vorkuta, politely asking what prison-camp sites I had seen in town so far. I gave her a brief review of the grave sites and Gulag locations that we had visited. "Have you been to Rudnik?" Julia asked. She said Rudnik had been the site of Vorkuta's cruelest forced-labor mine. It had been Julia's home for five years.

"I'd like to take you there," she said. "It was an unfairly beautiful place. You would come out of your barrack in the morning and see the soft slope that led down to the river. I'd like to show you the spot where the headquarters of the military guards were. The chief of Rudnik was an evil man named Kastikhin. One morning during roll call he made us count off by threes. He then shot every third person. I was lucky. I had drawn the number two. There was a trench on that spot that was dug by the convicts themselves. The bodies fell into the trench. We tried not to watch too closely. If you screamed or if your knees buckled, you could be his next victim."

"Why did Kastikhin do it?"

Julia hadn't heard my question. She asked Dundee, who was interpreting, to shout it a little bit louder in her other ear. She was embarrassed by her partial deafness, the result of her days in the mine. "I once had a hearing aid," she said, "but it caused my blood pressure to go up. So I don't use it now. My children, when they speak to me, they must talk loudly. I don't hear a normal conversation. But if you call me on the telephone and I hold it against my ear, well, I can hear that. Do you understand?"

So Dundee and I picked up the vinyl-covered chairs that Julia had brought from the kitchen into the living room. We shifted them around several times until we had it right. Against the wall was a sofa with sheets and a pillow on it. Julia said her heart was weak and she had been lying there for the previous three weeks. She had made herself up to look good for our visit. Her eyes sparkled above high cheekbones, and her charcoal hair, with strands of gray, was neatly combed.

I sat in front of her so I could look into her dark-brown eyes and at her natural, soft smile, with which she punctuated her conversation. Dundee sat by her right ear.

"What was I saying?" she asked.

"Kastikhin's killings!" shouted Dundee.

"Yes," she said. "Kastikhin. He would get dark and swollen eyes, and then he did whatever he wanted to. It was said he had been sent to Vorkuta himself because he had told a joke about Stalin. They said he was trying to prove himself. But I think he did it because he wanted to. Sometimes I saw the killings and other times I only heard the shots. Then we would watch to see who didn't return to the barracks in the evening."

Kastikhin's shootings were frequent, but Julia said more people died of malnutrition. Kastikhin withheld rations to sell for his own profit. When State orders said the prisoners should have 200 grams of bread, Kastikhin gave them only fifty grams—a small slice.

"It wasn't really bread," said Julia. "It was *konoplya* [hemp]. They squeezed all the seeds and oil out of it and afterward it became a sort of bread. Do you understand me?"

I asked how Julia had survived.

She smiled proudly. Survival was her achievement in life. "The women did better in the camps than the men," she said. "And the Russian women did best of all. There's something hidden somewhere in our nature."

The history of Russian women in Siberia was one in which she found great pride. Because the Tsars had treated Siberia primarily as a penal colony, the first women sent there had been a particular lot. The historian George St. George wrote that some 80 percent of them had been exiled for the murder of husbands or lovers. However, part of the reason they had been sent there was to relieve the chronic shortage of men in the area. Attractive women were looked upon with suspicion in the early days of Siberia. St. George wrote that "strong legs were more important than shapely ones" in a world in which partners had to help each other to survive.

Women became more available after World War II, when the Soviet Union was left with 25 million more women than men. The proportion was even more lopsided in Siberia. After the amnesty following Stalin's death, former prisoners were often given money to travel to their native homes to find a wife and then to return to their place of exile. With the pickings slim for the women, it usually didn't take the men long to accomplish their task.

Of the strong women who came to Siberia, only the strongest stayed, and only the very strongest survived the camps. "Perhaps I survived because I cut my fifty grams of bread into three parts and ate it at different times during the day," said Julia. "A man would eat the bread all at once, and then he would starve. In 1937 and 1938 we didn't have any strong men, really. They were the intellectual people. They weren't built for such harsh conditions. We had great scientists among us, great writers, artists, and mathematicians, but they weren't great survivors. Do you understand me?

"I remember a great professor whom I saw on the prisoner transport train. He was a very important mathematician—the head of a big institute. When I first saw him, he didn't look bad at all. But in a half year's time, I met him in the camp. He had gone so far down the drain. There was nothing human about him any longer. I remember he waited outdoors near the kitchen to eat the rotten turnips they threw into the garbage. He didn't live long. There were so many of these stories. The people who worked with their minds—that's how they all died. It was common to them all.

"*Kak mukhi umirali,*" she said—they died like flies.

She thought women survived because something inside made them live so that they could bear children. By protecting themselves, they were protecting something sacred.

She looked at me the way my grandmother had when recalling the difficult first days of German immigrants in America during the Great Depression. Julia put her cold, wrinkled hand on my knee, just as my grandmother had done. "I survived because I had a real belief that I should pull through and live. I had so much life ahead of me. I wasn't thirty or forty years old, but only twenty."

She giggled and tossed her head back. "It's very pleasant for me to talk to you," she said. "You are such a nice young man."

She picked up a book from the couch. "Do you see what I'm reading," she said. "A terrible thing I'm reading. I'm reading the memories of Yevgenia Ginzburg. She was also in the camps."

She opened the book carefully and put on her reading glasses. She was reading each word as if it were her own autobiography. "Her life is a kind of repetition of what I went through. Our hopes, our dreams, seem to be the same. She passed through the same phases of hope and desperation. She was in Kolyma, in the northeast. Maybe it was in some ways even a little worse. Yet it was all so common." Then Julia took off her glasses without reading from the book.

"The women *were* stronger," she said. "It's true even now. If my daughter gets ill, if she has a bad headache, she takes a couple of aspirin and continues to look after her family. But as soon as her husband has a slight temperature, he's dying. I think I'm telling the truth. It's always been that way."

She cited the epic verse of the celebrated nineteenth-century poet Nikolai Nekrasov, called "Russian Women." The poem glorified the wives of the Decembrists, the rebels who fought Tsarist rule in 1825. The women of these condemned men voluntarily followed their husbands into Siberian exile. Julia got through the hard times by quoting by heart the most famous passage, about one of the women, Princess Trubetskaya:

> *A life of deep and boundless woe*
> *My husband's fate will be,*
> *And I do not desire to know*
> *More happiness than he . . .*
>
> *Come death. I do not mind.*
> *No weak regrets have I.*
> *My husband only let me find*
> *That near him I may die!*

She recited methodically like a school girl, proud that she had remembered her lessons, and looked directly into my eyes. The hands gesticulated for a moment, but then she folded them neatly in her lap, again so that the tattoos couldn't be seen.

"Would you like to see a photograph of me taken in 1937?" she asked. From an album she pulled out a small photograph. It showed a dark woman with alluring eyes and long raven hair. I sighed in obvious approval, and she smiled proudly. "That was taken just before we were arrested. It was only a photograph for a passport, but it isn't bad."

I still wanted to know about the tattoos. But I was still reluctant to ask about them. I had read that the women in mixed camps—particularly the political prisoners—had been frequently mass-raped by *urkas,* the criminal prisoners. Women prisoners of all sorts had traded sex for protection and even bread from guards and camp officials. The scholar Robert Conquest wrote that those who didn't submit "were given the heaviest possible tasks until they gave in."

The women were all the more in demand because they made up only 10 percent of the prisoners—and most of them were hardened criminals, not the soft and vulnerable kind of young woman that I had imagined Julia to be. The women criminals, who called themselves "little violets," also brutalized their sisters who were political prisoners. They disparaged them as "little roses."

"I was a copy of my father," Julia said, looking at the photograph again. "He was slightly shorter than I, but otherwise we are much the same."

And what of her mother?

"She abandoned me at the maternity house," she said, turning angry for the first time. "She found another man—another husband and another life. Maybe my life would have turned out quite differently if she hadn't abandoned me."

When Julia was born, the year after the Revolution, her father had been busy fighting the *Basmachi*—the central Asians resisting Soviet expansion into Islamic areas. "So my relatives brought me up until my father returned," she said.

When he did come home, he brought Julia a charmed life. He was a head-turning handsome officer who coddled his daughter, and she had a child's crush on him. She still remembered the night they were arrested together on March 12, 1937. "I remember the date because it was my father's birthday. I was quite a big girl at that time—nineteen years old. We had celebrated together. It was a special celebration just with me—we didn't invite any friends. We went to the Prague Restaurant. It was a fine restaurant in Moscow. When we came home, my father sat down to do his writing. He was preparing for a lecture. It wasn't unusual that he was still awake—he was often up in the evening working like that. I was lying down and resting, not really sleeping. Then, at two A.M., there was a knock at the door . . ."

Julia stopped. She had forgotten an important piece of her story. "I should say one more thing to you. It was his birthday, but he wasn't happy. Inside, he felt something was wrong. In the restaurant he wasn't his usual self."

She said the men from Stalin's secret police arrived in an ordinary car, showed their identification, and came into the flat. "I realized that I was being taken to prison when they said take all the things that you find necessary. But they didn't say that to my father. Just to me." A man who was to be executed, she sighed with a pitiful frown, didn't need much luggage.

"They accused my father of terrible things," she said. "They threw everything at him. So many military men got it all in a heap. Do you understand me?"

She said his biggest crime was the one they didn't mention: he was a senior aide to Marshal Mikhail Tukhachevsky, a Red Army hero against whom Stalin was gathering "evidence" sufficient to have him convicted and executed a few weeks later. Her father's alliance with Tukhachevsky would be his death sentence.

Julia stifled a sob. I told her that she didn't need to talk about it anymore. Or rather, Dundee shouted that in her half-good ear. But she wanted to go on. She said her father's execution had come within days of his arrest—as it had for all of Stalin's most important enemies. But as they had been riding in the car toward prison, her father had given her advice that kept her alive when others died all around her.

He had spoken with the tone of an officer talking to a young and unprepared soldier whom he was reluctantly sending into battle. "He told me that no matter what happens in life, I should never lose my spirit. He also told me to keep control of myself. He said if I would keep my spirit and control, then I would survive.

"But I thought my life was ended," she said. "I knew from that point forward that I couldn't count on anything good anymore in my life. Tukhachevsky was arrested, all the others were arrested, and it was clear that it wouldn't stop. As we say in Russian, when wood is cut, the splinters fly."

Julia was kept in Lefortovo Prison in Moscow from March to July for "interrogations." Julia insisted to her interrogators that she didn't know any of her father's business, but that didn't stop them from torturing her. The worst of the interrogators, she recalled, was a man named Domansky.

She said he wrapped her with a straitjacket with long straps coming off the sleeves that he tied behind her back. He jerked her feet backwards and tied them together with her hands. "Then he picked me up and flung my body against the wall. He hit me across the face when I was speaking. He put strong lights on me. Your mind goes crazy—it doesn't understand what is going on. After each interrogation, I couldn't walk away. I was always carried away. It depended on his mood how bad it would be. He did terrible things to me."

She was sentenced to ten years in forced-labor camps and five years of exile thereafter. She traveled east in a long train of cattle wagons, each of which was filled with seventy prisoners. "We were packed so tightly together that when we were sleeping, if one person wanted to turn over, then everyone would have to turn over," she said.

The first stop for the group of 1,500 prisoners in Julia's group was Naryan-Mar, near where the Petchora River flows into the Barents Sea. Naryan-Mar was a fishing village, and the prisoners' job was to fix nets and wash barrels for three months until the river thawed and allowed further passage in barges. They lived in crowded tents on the bank of the river.

Julia again picked up the tiny photograph. "I had very beautiful long hair. When I would sleep, it would freeze to the tent floor. Sometimes I had to tear part of my hair off to get up in the morning." She said that during the coldest days, women's clothes would freeze to the ground while they were sleeping, and when they got up they would have to crawl out of them in the freezing cold and then rip them from the ground.

"The only warmth came from a steel barrel that we made into a stove in the middle of the tent," she said.

The intermediate stops were cruel enough to kill off the weakest, weeding them out before they reached Vorkuta's mines. "It would happen that a man would turn ill and he would fall when we walked in our convoy to work," said Julia. "The guards wouldn't lift him up. They'd stab him with a bayonet. And they would just walk on. He might even still be breathing as they left him behind. There were thirty to thirty-five deaths every day. My lungs were ill as well; I was coughing all the time. I remember that."

"How many died?"

She hadn't heard the question.

"How many died?" Dundee continued to shout my translated questions into her ear—questions that should have been delivered in a whisper.

Her eyes closed; the memory was painful. "Quite a lot died along the way. We began with 800, and when we got to Vorkuta we had left about 100 behind on the road. Others were left behind in barracks. They were very tired and very ill. I never saw them again."

She was haunted most of all by the memories of the common criminals, rough and unprincipled men appointed as team leaders over the political prisoners. "They were the small bosses in the camp. When you got up in the morning, they were the ones who marched you to work and told you what to do. They had big power. Whatever they had in mind, they could do."

Julia folded her hands again to hide her tattoos.

She calmly recalled her work when she arrived at Vorkuta's Rudnik camp—near Mine #1. "I pushed loaded coal carriages. They would then turn over the wagons and empty out the coal and then push the empty wagons back into the mine." She worked from seven A.M. to seven P.M.—twelve-hour days pushing the wagons. "I was just a young girl then, and ill, and I had to push it with my shoulder. My skin was always raw there. To fulfill my plan, I had to empty sixty wagons per shift. I had to push it fifty meters."

For those who didn't fulfill the plan, rations were cut. At the best of times, rations were raised from fifty to 300 grams of bread a day and soup. "At least they called it soup, but it was just make-believe soup. You know how children warm up water and then call it soup?" she said. "If you got a job, you had to stick to that job because you got a piece of bread."

Happy times were few. Julia remembered one coming after she began spitting up blood—the first sign of tuberculosis. After months of suffering, the illness finally allowed her to escape the cruelty of the mine for the civility of the camp hospital.

"We had big specialists among us who worked there," she said. "There were doctors, professors, and scientific workers—all prisoners themselves. These people, regardless of their condition, tried to help people of their own kind. In the cruelest of situations, the political criminals maintained a level of kindness that was astonishing. The brutality only came from others—never from the politicals. Do you understand me?"

Her worst memory was the isolation cells, where she was sent often. "My tongue was my enemy," she said. "I wouldn't swear hard at the guards. The worst word I would use was 'rascal,' but that was enough to be punished."

She recalled "isolation" as a small room with cement walls and an earthen floor. The cell wasn't large enough to lie down in. It had no heating. She remembered the cold and damp spring there as being far worse than the even colder but dry winter. In the spring, water would come up through the ground and turn the cell into a torture chamber.

"I sat in water that was up to my neck," she said. The guards wouldn't bail her out. Weary and emaciated, Julia would struggle to stay awake for fear she'd drowse and then drown.

"At that point I was comparing myself to Princess Tarakanova," she said. Something in Julia's romantic Russian soul transformed hunger and starvation into a poetic experience. The self-professed daughter of the Tsarina Elizabeth I, Princess Tarakanova (a name she never used, but was given by nineteenth-century writers) had been arrested as a pretender to the throne of Catherine the Great. Her interrogator described her in 1775 as sensitive and temperamental, knowledgeable and perceptive, slender and beautiful—like Julia. The princess even had a consumptive cough that brought up blood, like Julia. And there was the legend of the princess's martyrdom. Julia knew it from the K. D. Flavitskii painting depicting "Princess Tarakanova" in her death throes, in a flooded, rat-infested casement—a hell like Julia's.

"It stank," Julia said at the thought of her isolation room, and the old woman crinkled her nose. "I was cold and hungry. But why should they care for the prisoners? The more of us who died, the better. There were always more coming. And I wasn't always such a good worker, so they didn't have too much interest in keeping me alive."

When she was not in isolation, it was the older women prisoners—"wives of the big Party leaders and officers and such"—who kept Julia's spirits up. They did everything possible to make life more tolerable for the young women.

"We were isolated, we were depressed, but as people we weren't lost," she said. "We remained human beings. Sometimes it came in the form of a kind word, other times in a gesture. Someone would say to me, 'Take my jacket, you are cold.' There were very many such kindnesses. They meant very much to us."

Julia began to feel safer at the end of 1939, when they finally divided the political inmates from the common criminals. The murderous camp official Kastikhin had also gone too far in exacting his own justice; he was taken away and prisoners were told he had been executed. Julia had another stroke of "luck"; her consumptive cough turned into a diagnosable case of TB. The authorities released her from the camps in 1942, after she had served only five of her ten-year sentence. But she would have to spend ten more years of exile in Vorkuta. Once she recuperated, she went back into the mines. She had married a former fellow prisoner and had a new family to support.

I asked how she had met her husband.

"I'm shy about telling you this story," she said. "He was a common criminal and I was a political criminal. But his crime wasn't so bad. He had caught his wife in bed with a police officer in Leningrad. He was so angry that he took the police officer, who was wearing only his underwear, at gunpoint to the station to say what had happened. But instead the police arrested him for threatening to use arms against a policeman. Things happened like that then."

Her husband was one of the team leaders who had supervised Julia's brigade. But he protected her. He wasn't like the other "criminals," she said.

"They abused us, they took away our food, our things. They were terrible people—animals. That's what they were. They were wild animals."

She finally drew her hands from under the table, to show them to me as evidence. The name "Vova" was written on the left hand and the initials "MV" on the right. She said the two men who oversaw her group had held her hands down and forced her to accept the tattoos. That was before she had met her husband.

I thought about the prisoner numbers that the Germans had branded into Jewish skin. I looked again at "Vova" and "MV." I silently wondered if these men had raped her. Without my asking, she gave her reply.

"I know what you are thinking," she said. "But I was coughing up blood. I didn't look much like a woman. Most of the time I looked more like someone about to die. That wasn't the kind of woman they wanted.

"My granddaughters are growing up and asking about what happened to my hands. I don't know what to tell them. How do I explain it to them? They ask me if the Germans did that to me. They know the Germans were our enemies. How should I tell them that Russians did this to their own?

"When they get older, I'll try to explain it to them," she said. "I always tell the truth to them—I call things their proper names, so I must tell them everything one day."

In a country where most people hide their scars, I found the tattoos a welcome candor. No rewriting of history nor coarse bar of soap could remove them.

Dundee told me later that he doubted the tattoo portion of Julia's story. He thought the brands were too neat, too precise, to have been applied to someone putting up much resistance. I only hoped the tattoos had somehow made her life easier, if only for a while.

In our long conversation, it was the only time that Julia said anything that gave reason for doubt. Her quiet honesty was calming after the crazed hours with Olga.

In the years after Stalin's death in 1953, a large number of prisoners were released from the Gulags, but few left Vorkuta. Some had no choice: they were sentenced to continued internal exile, and many cities wouldn't issue them residence permits. For most, however, like Julia, there simply was little reason to go elsewhere.

"I got used to Vorkuta," said Julia. "I like the cold. And part of my heart was left in Rudnik. Next year will be the fifty-fifth anniversary of my being here. This isn't the motherland where I was born, but that motherland was left behind long ago. Vorkuta is where I left my labor behind, and whatever else that was inside of me."

And her husband? The prisoner who protected her, was he still alive? "I don't want to talk about it," she said angrily. Her soft, grandmotherly eyes turned hard. The kindness disappeared from her face. "He doesn't bear my respect." It was the only subject she refused to address.

I mentioned Solzhenitsyn's comments in *The Gulag Archipelago* about how the Germans had prosecuted 34,000 of their own after World War II, while the Russians hadn't punished more than a handful for Stalin's crimes. Did Julia want judicial revenge?

"Bring them to trial?" she said, shocked by the concept. "I think they are already condemned. They ended up the same way we did. They were also destroyed. I met my interrogator here in Vorkuta. Domansky." She was referring to the man who had tortured her after her arrest and then provided the evidence to condemn her.

Julia said that she had felt a pair of eyes watching her when she was working at the mine as a free woman. She had turned around and came eye-to-eye with Domansky. She could never forget his face. And he hadn't forgotten hers.

A prison guard walked up to Julia the next day and said, "Listen here. What did you do with that man? He's offering to pull out all his golden teeth to pay someone to come and kill you."

Three or four days after the first meeting, the guard walked up to Julia and said that Domansky had hanged himself. She figured he had gone crazy with savage fright. He understood that this free woman could easily bribe any prisoner to cut his throat while he slept for a fee of nothing more than some sugar or tea. Julia wasn't surprised when she was told he had hanged himself. "I think he was like a dog," she sneered. "The dog knows whose meat he's eaten. I was free and he wasn't. All he had done might have come out if I had wanted it to."

This was a side of Julia I hadn't yet seen. It was unforgiving, vengeful, relishing God's justice in the absence of any appropriate national one. Yet it also revealed some of the inner strength that had allowed her to survive.

It was this Julia who had sneered when the soul-cleansing Communist leadership rehabilitated her politically in 1957. A faceless bureaucrat merely took her papers, signed them, handed them over, and then told her to go away, like a pharmacist who had just filled a prescription. "It was as if something casual was happening. He was a general, but he was sitting there like a dumb turkey. So I thanked him for my crucified life."

I asked if her life had grown better under Glasnost. Now she could speak freely of what had happened to her. And the local council, like government bodies all over the country, had given her special privileges in 1990 that were comparable to those given World War II veterans, survivors of the Leningrad siege, and pregnant mothers. They were allowed larger rations and given the right to shop in better-stocked special stores.

"Those flowers are too late," Julia said. "I have no fire left inside me, no health, no future. I am smoldering only like the embers of my former self."

One day in 1964 the mother who had abandoned Julia at the maternity house appeared on her doorstep and asked her daughter to take her in.

Julia had never stopped wondering if she might have avoided the camps if her mother hadn't left her. She always wondered why her mother never did anything to gain her freedom. "She came to me because no one needed her any longer," said Julia. "Everything was squeezed out of her that could be squeezed out.

"To this day I can't forgive her. Do you understand me? I gave her conditions where she could live, and she got along fine with my children. Up to this very day they remember her well. But I couldn't warm my soul to her. Yet I opened my door to her. A person who has never gone through the hardships I endured, who has never been abused, might not have done this. Do you think I did the right thing?"

I told her she had been angelic.

"But I couldn't ever forgive her, not even now," she said. "Do you understand me?"

I did.

Julia looked weary. We had come in the early afternoon and it was approaching midnight. As I started to thank her, she asked me for a favor. She went to the cabinet and carefully removed two large candles and five smaller ones. There was no particular reason for the numbers—but they were all the candles she had. She wanted me to light them at the site of the trench in which her fellow prisoners had been buried after they were shot by Kastikhin.

"Orient yourself by the old school," she said, drawing a map on a piece of paper. "It is still there. In front of the school, there is a road passing by. It is of asphalt, but under it are bones. Human bones. To stand on that road is like standing on a graveyard.

"I'd ask my daughter to light the candles. But she doesn't really understand. And she's very busy. She works near there, just opposite the school, in the city offices. That was the headquarters building of the guards, right beside where the school is now."

The description was vivid and detailed. "What happened yesterday, I can't remember." She laughed. "But what happened fifty years ago, I don't forget. It is like a photo. I am a lady who is very attentive and sees small things."

So it was that I ended my trip early the next morning on a patch of ground in front of the asphalt road that ran past the school. It was raining. The architect Vitaly Troshin, who had introduced me to Vorkuta, held an umbrella over my head while we looked around for a dry spot for the candles; we found a place under an overhanging rock. The flames would not be doused there.

Julia had wanted me to light the candles for the dead—for those fellow prisoners who were resting under my feet. But I was thinking about the survivors. About Julia. She had survived the mother who had abandoned her, the interrogator who had tortured her, and the camp official who had killed so many others. She would also outlive the Soviet system, in whose infancy she had been born. The system had destroyed the country and itself, but not Julia. In her, I found a glimmer of hope for Russia's future.

Epilogue:

THE RUSSIAN SOUL

And oh, you well-fed, devil-may-care, nearsighted, irresponsible foreigners, with your notebooks and your ballpoint pens . . . how much you have harmed us in your vain passion to shine with understanding in areas where you did not grasp a lousy thing.

—ALEKSANDR SOLZHENITSYN, *The Gulag Archipelago*

Although Vorkuta's concentration camps and cemeteries were hidden now—buried under the ugly cement low-rises, the sewage plant, and the general hospital—I was relieved when Aeroflot Flight 2036, bound for Moscow, didn't pass over the city. Instead, it banked hard to the west and took a path along the railway that had brought tens of thousands of prisoners to its camps.

The plane followed the tracks toward Moscow. Valentine Akishkin, the forty-five-year-old school director who had become my friend and ally, sat beside me. He liked the nickname I had given him; even his Russian friends were calling him "Dundee." His Australian accent had become more pronounced and his English more perfect with each day that we traveled farther north. He'd never seen the movies about the Australian crocodile wrestler who had been pulled from his natural habitat and brought to New York, but he was just as uncomfortable as the movie character might have been about the prospect of visiting Moscow.

"I feel myself better in my Siberian swamps," he said. "That's where this crocodile belongs."

For the first time Dundee asked me for a favor. He wanted to buy his wife a gift with the money he had earned as my guide and interpreter. She had put up with a long absence, and he thought the present should be something especially fashionable, bought at one of Moscow's hard-currency stores—perhaps an Italian leather coat, a jeans outfit, or some shoes. He asked with embarrassment if I would come with him. "I don't know how to handle myself in those shops," he said. "I wouldn't know where to begin. You don't have to hold my hand or anything—but would you mind coming along?"

I struck a deal with him. I'd go with him to the shops if he would accompany me to the Kremlin Wall. I wanted to visit the grave of Big Bill Haywood, my fellow Utahan, who had tried to create a workers' paradise in Siberia.

Dundee was all for it. He suggested that we take him some flowers so that "he doesn't feel so lonely."

"Have you found the Russian soul yet?" Dundee asked in a mocking voice. We had both agreed by then that my search was somewhat preposterous.

"Afraid not," I replied. "Got any clues?"

Dundee said he had given the matter some thought. He had decided that the Russian soul and the Soviet soul were really quite different—although they were often locked up in the same bodies. He figured that he could explain both through our visit in Narym, the place of Stalin's exile. "You remember that old woman who invited us into her home near the timber yard where Stalin had exiled her and her husband?" asked Dundee.

He said it was the old woman's Russian side that had prompted her to open her door and welcome strangers warmly. She had done this even though she was convinced an American's visit could only cause her further problems with the authorities after an already nightmarish life. The problem, Dundee said, was the Soviet part of her soul, which had prompted her to shake each time I wrote anything she said in my notebook. In the world according to Dundee, hospitality and warmth were Russian. Fear and suspicion were Soviet.

I told Dundee that I wasn't convinced. Even Peter the Great, the legendary Westernizer, had ruled through fear and terror. Dundee's conclusions illustrated another Russian characteristic instead—a boundless romanticism that made it possible for people to see the Soviet years as an aberration that hadn't anything to do with their true Russian selves. I told him that I thought Russians were hospitable, warm, fearful, and suspicious.

Whatever the Russian soul was, I said, it seemed terribly beat up and in need of some healing. I asked Dundee if he considered himself to be as Russian as his neighbors.

"I haven't told you the whole story about how I got to Russia," he said. His father had been a prisoner of war in Germany during World War II. Dundee's mother, whose family had fled from Odessa at the beginning of the war, was working at the POW hospital in Germany where Dundee's father, Anatoly, was dying. When they had met, Anatoly Akishkin was just nineteen, and blind from starvation. The young nurse had seen him chewing the leather strap of his belt. She saved his life and then they fell in love.

Anatoly feared a return to the Soviet Union. Stalin had told soldiers to shoot themselves rather than surrender, and now his courts were condemning POWs for treason. So the Akishkins moved to Australia when Dundee was just three years old. At first they lived in tents in Albury with other immigrants along a new railway line. Dundee's father cleaned the coal ashes out of the engines, and his mother worked as a maid at the local hotel.

However, it was the Australian bullies that Dundee remembered best. One day a group of them waited for him as he walked home through "Basher's Lane," where the after-school fights were staged. Dundee recalled how the toughest of them announced: "You bloody Russian, you fought with the Germans in the war and you are going to pay for it."

Dundee didn't know enough to correct their history. But physically, at least, he held his own. He decked the Australian boy, and the bullies left him alone after that. But Dundee had trouble feeling at home in Australia; the children mocked him for being Russian and his father clung to the old country. Dundee remembered the smell of fresh printer's ink on copies of *Pravda* that arrived by post at their home. His father subscribed through the Soviet Embassy, which was in New Zealand at the time. The front page of *Pravda* Dundee remembered best was from the day that Stalin died.

"His body was under some sort of glass case," Dundee said. "My father kept that copy around for weeks."

That was when his father began to plan his family's return home. In 1956 the Soviet government said that all former POWs could return without fear of punishment. That began a fight between Dundee's parents. His mother wanted to join her mother, father, and an uncle, who by that time had made good in Chicago. She considered her homeland to be "any place that can feed and pay me well." She applied for and had received visas for the whole family to emigrate to the United States. But Dundee's father had been homesick for Moscow ever since he had left it for the Western Front at the age of sixteen as a volunteer soldier. He obtained visas for the Soviet Union.

At the end of 1958 the Akiskhins set off with two sets of visas. As they sailed from Melbourne, the twelve-year-old Valentine was crying. He didn't want to leave. He'd finally reached his peace with the bullies, and he was one of the best students in the class. He tied a fishing line to the dock when he boarded, with a child's hope that it would prevent departure. While others threw streamers toward friends waving on the beach, he clung to his fishing line. After about 200 yards he gave up and let it fall.

His parents fought all the way to England about which visas they should use. In Perth, Singapore, Bombay, Egypt, and Lisbon, they continued to argue. As the ship approached the English coast, Dundee's father took both sets of visas to the deck. "My father got his guts together and tore up the visas for the United States and threw them in the water," Dundee said. His mother cried as the fragments fluttered into the English Channel.

When they arrived in Moscow, young Valentine's Russian aunt went through her nephew's clothes and tore off the Western labels. Such labels would make the family ideologically suspect. Dundee only knew that he couldn't figure out which was the front and the back of his sweaters. "I was upset and annoyed about that," he said.

His mother, who had grown resigned to the prospect of living in Russia, was devastated when told that the authorities wouldn't give the family residency permits for Moscow or Leningrad, where they had relatives. They would issue papers only for Siberia. So the Akishkins took the next train to Belovo, an ugly coal-miners' town near Kemerovo.

When they arrived, Dundee remembered the locals looking suspiciously at their luggage, piled up on the dirt road and plastered with shipping labels from all over the world. The only taxi in town picked them up and took them to a coal miner's cottage—the housing they had been promised hadn't yet been built.

"I felt even less at home there than I had in Australia," said Dundee. Children made fun of the stitching that ran down the outside of his jeans, saying he was wearing his pants inside out. They pestered him to give them chewing gum; he'd brought a large supply along. Young Valentine was an outsider, but he was also a prankster.

"I remember that I had a white eraser I had brought with me," he said. "It disappeared from my desk one day—one of the boys put it in his mouth, thinking it was chewing gum. I got angry when I saw him spit out the useless remainders of my last eraser. I promised to bring him Australian chocolates the next day. Instead, I brought him Australian chocolate-flavored laxatives that I took from my parents. He made a dash for the door of the classroom fifteen minutes after he devoured a handful of them.

"I always considered myself unique," he said. "My life was disconnected from those Russian children. I thought better of myself than I did of them. I felt more Russian in Australia, when the people from the homeland got together to sing their songs, than I ever did in the Soviet Union. That was the last time I felt at home—among Russians in Australia. All that Communist blah-blah never seemed Russian to me. I guess I chose to believe some of it in the mind, but never in the soul."

Dundee figured it was his unusual background that helped carry him to the center of a political hurricane, as a school director pushing for an overhaul of the Soviet educational system. He seemed to be enjoying the storm. Dundee had pioneered a new system that separated each age group into four levels, according to capabilities. He had sold the plan to parents, who approved it by a vote of 290 to 2.

"Stalin said it was only a question of breeding and you could make out of a man whatever you wanted," said Dundee. "But people are starting to realize there are talents given as gifts to a man when he is born. We are taking the approach that we must now find those talents and develop them." He wanted to transform the "nuts and bolts" of Communism into the "combustion chamber" of the free market.

After a year of operation, all the students were performing better except those at the bottom level. "I've never seen such wonderful children and such excellent oral examinations," he said. "The students are becoming more individual. The only problem is that class four is filled with failures, and it is becoming something of a humiliation for the parents." Dundee said it was an admission that capitalism had it right—one group will remain behind no matter what you do.

My Dundee wasn't an outback crocodile-wrestler, but an educated school director who viewed himself as one of the social engineers who would try to drag Russians away from the bad habits of seven decades.

When we landed in Moscow, Yuri Kaznin greeted us with a sheepish smile and an armful of data. If he had been hatching a plot against us, it had failed, and now he wanted to rejoin our party for its final hours in Moscow. I liked him less with his sickly smile than I had with his threatening scowl.

Dundee and I grabbed our bags, bade farewell to the others, including Kaznin, then jumped into a taxi and headed for the hard-currency stores of the Mezhdunarodnaya, the luxury hotel built by American businessman Armand Hammer for Leonid Brezhnev. Soviet citizens were forbidden from entering the hotel unless accompanied by a foreigner. Dundee began to sweat as we walked by the guards, who checked my passport before allowing us through the revolving doors. We were transported to the sterile world of a Western hotel—the atrium, the fountains, the glass elevators, and the hotel's famous, ludicrous, giant mechanical clock that crowed like a metallic rooster every hour.

"What kind of country is it that builds a fantasy world like this that its own citizens can't enter?" he said. "I don't feel myself well here."

The prices in the shops were higher than I had remembered—these were boutiques for the expense-account business traveler. Dundee looked ill. I told him just to talk in Australian. He said his beat-up old shoes would give him away as Russian. But I said that only very rich people in America dressed so casually when they came to such shops—a sign of their confidence. That made him feel better, but he still edged up close to the clothing racks and counters to hide the shoes underneath them.

Dundee in the end settled for some red shoes of sleek Italian design, with black bows on the toes. He couldn't remember his wife's size, but he said he could fit her just by looking at the shoe. "I've known her foot for years," he said, holding one of the shoes lovingly in his large palm.

Having completed his agenda, we turned to mine. Rather than wrestle with the hard-currency taxi drivers who lurked like vultures in front of the hotel, we took the Metro, starting at the stop called simply "1905." It was the year the Tsar had first confronted a Communist uprising, and when Haywood had helped found the Industrial Workers of the World, the closest America ever came to a significant socialist workers' movement.

After one transfer, we rode up the escalator at Red Square. Moscow was different from when I had visited two years earlier. Young women were dressed more fashionably and colorfully, many in Western styles. On a stretch of pavement that I remembered as cold and deserted, a woman was making embroideries with a pedal-operated sewing machine and selling them. A teenager was selling Superman comics, and a vendor offered popsicles and darning needles for torn nylon hose. Without new nylons for sale in any shops, they were selling fast.

I stopped at a sidewalk florist and asked for some pink roses. Dundee protested and said carnations would be cheaper and more proletarian. When I started choosing carnations of various colors, he told me that only red was acceptable. So I started to purchase a half-dozen red carnations, and Dundee insisted upon seven—even numbers were considered bad luck.

We walked across the black stones of Red Square, laid securely enough to bear the weight of tanks during military parades. Dundee kept pace beside me, loaded with a shoulder bag and wearing a black mohair sweater and khaki military overcoat. He had been dressed warm for Vorkuta, but he was sweating in sunny Moscow on a steamy August day. He mentioned to me that his shoes still carried the dried mud from the unmarked graves of Vorkuta, where we had walked that morning.

"Dirt from a less conspicuous grave," he said, looking at Lenin's Mausoleum.

We arrived at five P.M., during a changing of the guard. Lenin was being put to bed for the night, and those who looked over him were goose-stepping around the place with vestigial reverence. But we hadn't come to see Lenin. Dundee walked up to a guard patrolling behind the flat chain barrier and requested that I be allowed to visit Haywood's spot in the red brick wall. Dundee told him Haywood and I had been born in the same town. The guard looked bored. "If you can find him, be my guest," he said.

We walked down the stone path to the left of Lenin's rose marble Mausoleum. The guard walked behind us. Behind Lenin stood other tombs resting underneath busts of the big shots—the acceptable Party leaders (not Khrushchev) and fathers of the Soviet Union.

Dundee told me he had never been to the Kremlin Wall. "But I've got some accounts to settle here," he said. "If you give me a sledgehammer, I'll fix up some historical details obviously mixed up here. Sverdlov, Dzerzhinsky, Kalinin, Zhdanov, Stalin, Voroshilov, Brezhnev, Andropov, Chernenko. You have to wash your mouth out after you say the names. I'd break the busts up slowly and thoroughly without any fuss or emotions. I'd put a grain of the dust on the grave of every man, woman, and child who was killed, tortured, or humiliated. We have suffocated in this Communist illusion. I'd like to put a big neon sign over the Mausoleum and lock up all the corpses inside there. The sign would read: HERE LIES THE BIGGEST GROUP OF RASCALS THAT THE WORLD EVER KNEW."

I hadn't seen Dundee that worked up before. I had been moved by what I had seen on my trip—the pollution, Stalin's graves, the natives dying of drink, and the survivors of Vorkuta—but every experience had cut deeper into him. I was happy the guard couldn't understand Dundee's English. He only tried to rush us along.

I noticed that only under Stalin's bust, the biggest rascal of them all, were there bunches of fresh flowers. I asked the guard why that was so. "It's always like that," he said. "He's the most popular. It's mostly old people who bring the flowers, though. The young people don't care enough to put flowers anywhere."

I asked the guard if he considered Stalin and the others he watched over to be heroes. He shrugged. "We shouldn't judge those who served us in the past by the standards of today," he said. But he was certain every grave had a right to remain.

We walked up a short set of stairs to the wall and then turned to the left, where most of the plaques were located. Dundee got angrier. He pointed with disgust at Vyshinsky, the prosecutor general who had given the judicial stamp of approval to Stalin's purges and executions in 1937–1938. Then he pointed at Kalinin, who Dundee said had allowed his wife to be sent to jail as one of Stalin's enemies without doing anything to protect her. Dundee cited the sins of each honored man, one after another. Then he pointed to the plastic red carnations that rested in every grate beneath each of the 114 plaques. "Only the most decent people should be here," said Dundee. "They should take away those who have blood on their hands. Maybe they can't chisel them out of the wall right away, but they could at least take away the flowers from those bastards who don't belong."

We made our way to the far right, where five plaques were on their own—set off from the others. They were the earliest to have been buried in the wall. First was Miron Konstantinovich Vladimirov, a Bolshevik underground hero; then Charles Emil Ruthenberg, an American Communist; Arthur McManus, the founder of the British Communist Party; and Jeno Landler, a Hungarian Communist leader. The very last name was William D. Haywood. His name stood out in Latin lettering, and, underneath, in Cyrillic: born November 11, 1869, died May 18, 1928. I knew that only half his ashes were in the wall. At his request the other half had been buried in a common grave in Chicago for workers killed in the 1886 Haymarket workers riot.

I asked Dundee what he would want to say to Haywood if he could bring him back from the grave. Dundee wasn't about to continue playing my game here. "I wouldn't like him to come back here at all," Dundee said. "He's the type of person we don't need. I'm frightened of such people who believe their ideologies so strongly. They are too willing to impose their beliefs on others and ignore individual needs. So tell your Haywood to stay away."

"Okay," I said. "But if you couldn't keep him away, what would you tell him?"

"I'd tell him that you can't make a whole people happy. The reason people are dissatisfied with their lives in Russia now isn't because they are worse off than five years ago. It's because they are now comparing themselves to others in the world. Happiness isn't for a mob. Happiness comes in small pieces that belong to every person. We've learned to be careful of people like Bill Haywood who come and say, 'I know what we have to do to make everyone happy.' "

The head of one of my red carnations had fallen off, so I left only six. Dundee didn't mind anymore about the even number—how much more bad luck could Russia have?

Now we were thirsty. We searched without luck for somewhere to buy a soft drink for rubles, finally giving up and heading to the Intourist Hotel's dollar bar. The place had been spruced up since I was last there. The bar area was now part of an atrium.

I carried two shots of vodka and two glasses of orange juice back to our table, but Dundee had disappeared. He returned minutes later with a plastic bag from one of the hotel shops. He had bought his wife a leather jacket and boasted that he had convinced the shopgirls that he was on business from Australia. "It worked like a charm," he said. And he had negotiated a good price.

Dundee insisted on buying the last round, and we walked together to the bar. He looked me in the eye, but offered no toast. We'd both tired of the interminable toasts delivered along the way. I wanted to thank him, but it seemed like anything I could say would be ludicrous. He winked at me just the way his namesake might have done at the end of a film. "Just shut up and drink your bloody vodka," he said.

I asked Dundee if he ever regretted that his father hadn't chosen Chicago.

"Not for a minute," he said. "And not now, either. I thank my father for it. I never would have felt myself comfortable in America. I'm a Russian. That is what is inside of me. This place may look like shit to you. But it is my shit. Anyway, my life is much more interesting than your life. You never know what is going to happen next here."

Shortly before this book went to press, Dundee phoned me from Siberia. So much had happened since we had parted ways in Moscow. Gorbachev had survived a coup and then not survived it—forced to resign as a sort of Commonwealth was formed. Communism had been banned after it had already died anyway. Boris Yeltsin was leading Russia into the future, but who knew for how long or what kind of future.

And Western Siberia was at the forefront of change—and of resistance to change. The Kuzbass province in the south was falling all over itself to attract Western capital with investment incentives. But the price rises and inflation had given birth to a neo-Communist movement that was striking to reverse the free-market reforms that the Kuzbass's historic coal miners' strikes had helped introduce.

The lines were clearly drawn in a battle of the new, riskier world of the free market against the old, ossified remains of Soviet power. The West was helping, but not so much as to ensure that progressive forces, who were still very much a minority, would triumph at perhaps the most historic moment of change in Europe since World War II. A war was on in Russia, a war whose outcome would have great ramifications for the West, and it wasn't at all certain who would win it.

What was clear was that Dundee and Vladimir Sukhatsky—the White Bird—had cast their lot with the reformers. They formed a new company to help Westerners make contacts in Siberia—and to arrange adventures for a hardy class of tourist. On a visit to Berlin, they found a German partner. Once I learned that Yuri would not be part of the firm, I happily invested, using part of the advance from this book.

However, I had some doubts about purchases they made while in the West. The fax made sense, and I couldn't quarrel with the floor tiling for their new office, but I thought the microwave was a bit of an extravagance at a time when many Russians were worried about starvation. I teased Vladimir about his desire to be the first in his neighborhood with a microwave.

Now, on the phone, in the dead of the Siberian winter, Dundee's voice was curiously light and cheerful. "You know how you were making fun of the White Bird's microwave?" he said. "Well, he's putting it to good use. He's got twenty-five loaves of bread out on the balcony and they are frozen solid. It's thirty below here this week. Every time he needs one, he just brings it inside and pops it into the microwave."

Vladimir got onto the phone and laughed. "It is the answer to our future." He laughed. "Western know-how. Russian wit."

READING LIST

This is by no means a comprehensive list of the books available on Western Siberia or Siberian history; it is merely a collection of titles used at one point or another in my research. There are asterisks beside those works which I considered particularly valuable—or just plain good reading.

GENERAL ON SIBERIA

Fisher, Raymond H. *The Russian Fur Trade, 1500–1700.* Berkeley and Los Angeles: University of California Press, 1943.

Leptin, Gerd. *Siberien: Ein Russisches and Sowjetisches Entwicklungsprogramm.* Berlin: Berlin Verlag, 1986.

Maddox, Robert J. *The Unknown War with Russia: Wilson's Siberian Intervention.* San Rafael, Cal.: Presidio Press, 1977.

Middendorf, A. Th. von. *Auf Schlitten, Boot, und Renntierrücken.* Leipzig: Brockhaus Verlag, 1956.

Mowat, Farley. *Sibir: My Discovery of Siberia.* Toronto: McClelland and Stewart, 1970.

Portisch, Hugo. *So Sah Ich Sibirien.* Vienna: Verlag Kremayr & Scheriau, 1967.

*Rasputin, Valentine. *Siberia on Fire* (stories and essays). De Kalb: Northern Illinois University Press, 1989.

———. *In den Wäldern die Zuflucht.* Munich: Goldmann Verlag, 1976.

Roos, Johanna. *Siberien zwischen Ökonomie und Politik (Zur Erschliessung der Energieträger Öl und Erdgas)*. Cologne: Verlag Wissenschaft und Politik Berend von Nottbeck, 1984.

Semyanov, Yuri N. *Siberia: Its Conquest and Development.* Baltimore: Helican Press, 1963.

St. George, George. *Siberia, the New Frontier.* New York: David McKay, 1969.

Swearingen, Rodger. *Siberia and the Soviet Far East: Strategic Dimensions in Multinational Perspective.* Stanford, Cal.: Hoover Institution Press, 1987.

Taylor, Robert H. *Asia and the Pacific,* chapter entitled "Siberia and the Far East." New York, Oxford: Facts on File, 1991.

Treadgold, Donald W. *The Great Siberian Migration.* Princeton: Princeton University Press, 1957.

Unterberger, Betty Miller. *America's Siberian Expedition, 1918–1920.* New York: Greenwood Press, 1969.

Sibirskaia Sovetskaia Entsiklopedia, published in Novosibirsk, 1929–1931, contains an extensive bibliography covering all aspects of Siberian history.

ON "BIG BILL" HAYWOOD

*Carlson, Peter. *Roughneck: The Life and Times of Bill Haywood.* New York, London: W. W. Norton, 1983.

Dubofsky, Melvyn. *Big Bill Haywood.* New York: St. Martin's Press, 1987.

Grover, David. H. *Debaters and Dynamiters.* Corvallis, Oregon: Oregon State University Press, 1964.

*Haywood, William D. *The Autobiography of Big Bill Haywood.* New York: International Publishers (copyright 1929), 1974.

Morray, J. P. *Project Kuzbas: American Workers in Siberia, 1921–1926.* New York: International Publishers, 1983.

ARTICLES ON HAYWOOD AND THE COLONY

Harn, Harrm. "An American Trade Unionist in Ruined Russia." *American Federationist* (May 1923), 369–379.

Kennel, Ruth, several articles on the Kuzbass Colony and Big Bill Haywood. See *The Nation,* "Kuzbas: A New Pennsylvania," May 2, 1923, 511–512; "A Kuzbas Chronicle," January 3, 1923, 7–10; "Kuzbas in 1924," November 26, 1924, 566–568; "The End of Kuzbas," February 6, 1928, 171–172. See also "The New Innocents Abroad," *American Mercury* XVII, May 1929, 10–18.

ON STALIN AND THE GULAG

Barron, John. *KGB Today: The Hidden Hand.* London: Coronet Books, 1985.

Brändström, Elsa. *Among Prisoners of War in Russia and Siberia.* London: Hutchinson & Co., 1929.

Buca, Edward. *Vorkuta.* London: Constable, 1976.
Bullock, Alan. *Hitler and Stalin.* New York: Alfred A. Knopf, 1992.
Ciliga, Anton. *The Russian Enigma.* London: G. Routledge & Sons, 1940.
*Conquest, Robert. *The Great Terror: Stalin's Purges of the Thirties.* London: Oxford University Press, 1991.
Ginsberg, Jewgenia. *Gratwanderung.* Munich, Zurich: Piper Verlag, 1989.
———. *Marschroute Eines Lebens.* Munich, Zurich, Piper Verlag, 1989.
Nikolaevsky, Boris I. *Power and the Soviet Elite: "The Letters of an Old Bolshevik" and Other Essays.* New York: Hoover Institution, Frederick A. Praeger, 1965.
Scholmer, Joseph. *Vorkuta.* London, 1954.
Shifrin, Avraham. *UdSSR Reiseführer durch Gefängnisse und KZ's in der SU.* Seewis, Switzerland: Stephanus Verlag, 1980.
*Solzhenitsyn, Aleksandr. *The Gulag Archipelago, 1918–1956* (abridged, one volume). London: Collins Harvill, 1988.
Ulam, Adam. *Stalin: The Man and His Era.* Boston: Beacon Press, 1989.

ON THE NATIVE PEOPLES OF SIBERIA

Dioszegi, V. *Glaubenswelt und Folklore der Sibirischen Völker.* Budapest: Akademiai Kiado, Verlag der Ungarischen Akademie der Wissenschaften, 1963.
Dyrenkova, P. *Shorskiy Folklore.* Moscow-Leningrad, 1940.
Kozlov, Viktor. *The Peoples of the Soviet Union,* Second World Series. London: I. B. Taurus & Co., 1990.
*Levin, M. B., and Potapov, L. P., eds. *The Peoples of Siberia* (translated). Moscow: Russian Academy of Science, 1956; Chicago: University of Chicago Press, 1964.

NATURAL RESOURCES IN SIBERIA

De Souza, Peter. *Territorial Production Complexes in the Soviet Union—with Special Focus on Siberia.* Gothenburg: Department of Human and Economic Geography, University of Gothenburg, 1989.
Shabad, Theodore. *Basic Industrial Resources of the U.S.S.R..* New York and London: Columbia University Press, 1969.
Wood, Alan. *The Development of Siberia.* London: Macmillan, 1989.

ARTICLES

Report of Greenpeace from the Expedition: "Der Naturraum Westsibirien und Seine Drohende Vernichtung durch die Menschen," by Michael Hoffmann, October 19, 1991. Available through Greenpeace.
Wolfson, Zeev (Boris Komarov). "The Environmental Risk of the Developing Oil & Gas Industry in Western Siberia." Hebrew University of Jerusalem, October 1983. Paper No. 52.

ON THE VOLGA GERMANS

Bartlett, Roger P. *Human Capital: The Settlement of Foreigners in Russia, 1762–1804.* Cambridge: Harvard University Press, 1979.

*Conquest, Robert. *The Nation Killers: The Soviet Deportation of Nationalities.* New York: St. Martin's Press, 1970.

Giesinger, Adam. *From Catherine to Khrushchev: The Story of Russia's Germans.* Battleford, Saskatchewan, 1974.

Koch, F. C. *The Volga Germans in Russia and the Americas From 1763 to the Present.* University Park, Pa., 1977.

Stumpp, Karl. *Die Russlanddeutschen. Zweihundert Jahre Unterwegs,* Stuttgart: Landsmannschaft der Deutschen in Russland, 1966.

ON TOMSK 7

Cochran, Thomas, and Norris, Robert. Natural Resources Defense Council paper, Russian/Soviet Nuclear Warhead Production, April 2, 1992 (updated regularly).

Articles in the German newsmagazine *Der Spiegel* on Tomsk 7 and other ecological issues:

"Wir Haben alles Verloren," *Spiegel*-series über die Umweltzerstörung im Sozialismus, numbers 48 and 49, 1990.

LETTERS GIVEN TO THE AUTHOR

Guriyev, Nikolai Nikolayevich. "An explanation of my leaving the Party . . . ," sent to the Party organzation of the administration of the Siberian Chemical *Kombinat.* 7 pages, author's copy.

Straishyt, A. V. Letter concerning disappearance of plutonium and other problems of Tomsk 7, 1990. 8 pages, author's copy.

ON THE KULAKS

Belov, Fedor. *The History of a Soviet Collective Farm.* New York: Praeger Publishing Co., 1955.

Nove, Alec. *An Economic History of the USSR.* London: John Lane, 1969.

Volin, Lazar. *A Century of Russian Agriculture: From Alexander II to Khrushchev.* Cambridge: Harvard University Press, 1970.

(These books also contain information on Stalin.)

OTHER BOOKS USED FOR RESEARCH

*Chekhov, Anton. *Unknown Chekhov,* Avrahm Yarmolinsky, trans. New York: Ecco Press, 1987.

Cooper, James Fenimore. *The Last of the Mohicans.* New York: Viking/ Penguin, 1986.

Gilbert, Martin. *Russian History Atlas.* London: Weidenfeld and Nicolson, 1972.

Krupskaya, N. *Lenin o Literature.* Moscow, 1941.

———. *Lenin o Kulture i Iskustve.* Moscow, 1956.

London, Jack. *Martin Eden.* New York: Airmont Books, 1970.

*Nekrasov, Nikolai. *Poems.* Westport, Conn.: Hyperion Press.

———. *Who Can Be Happy and Free in Russia?* Westport, Conn.: Hyperion Press.

*Pasternak, Boris. *Doctor Zhivago.* New York: Ballantine Books, 1990.

*Solzhenitsyn, Aleksandr. *One Day in the Life of Ivan Denisovich.* New York: Praeger, 1963.

———. *The First Circle.* New York: Harper & Row, 1968.

Wieczynski, Joseph L., ed. *The Modern Encyclopedia of Russian and Soviet History.* New York: Academic International Press, 1984.

Siberische Märchen. Hanau: Verlag Werner Dausien, 1980.